WALKING
on the EDGE
of the WORLD

WALKING
on the EDGE
of the WORLD

George Leonard

A Marc Jaffe Book

HOUGHTON MIFFLIN COMPANY

BOSTON 1988

For information about permission to reproduce selections from this
book, write to Permissions, Houghton Mifflin Company,
2 Park Street, Boston, Massachusetts 02108.

Library of Congress Cataloging-in-Publication Data

Leonard, George Burr, date.
Walking on the edge of the world / George Leonard.
p.   cm.
"A Marc Jaffe Book."
ISBN 0-395-48311-5
1. Leonard, George Burr, date.   2. Journalists — United
States — Biography.   3. Look (Des Moines, Iowa)   4. United
States — History — 1961–1969.   5. United States — Social condi-
tions — 1960–1980.   I. Title.
PN4874.L37A3 1988
070'.92'4 — dc19   88-12837
[B]   CIP

Printed in the United States of America

Q 10 9 8 7 6 5 4 3 2 1

Portions of Chapter 18 first appeared in *The Nation* and are reprinted
by permission of the Sterling Lord Agency. Portions of Chapter 20
first appeared in *The End of Sex,* copyright © 1983 by George Leonard, reprinted by permission of Jeremy P. Tarcher, Inc., Los Angeles.
Several passages, notably portions of Chapter 27, first appeared in
Education and Ecstasy, copyright © 1968 and 1987. The author would
like to thank Oxford University Press for permission to reprint a portion of Christopher Fry's poem "Dark and cold we may be . . . ,"
from *A Sleep of Prisoners,* and Leo Litwak for permission to reprint
portions of "A Trip to Esalen Institute: Joy Is the Prize," copyright ©
1967 by Leo E. Litwak and reprinted from *The New York Times Magazine,* December 31, 1967.

For
MICHAEL MURPHY,
fellow explorer

The real voyage of discovery consists not in seeking new landscapes but in having new eyes.
MARCEL PROUST

ACKNOWLEDGMENTS

From the very beginning, my wife, Annie Styron Leonard, has not only given me the kind of personal support any author would dream of, but has also contributed superb editorial advice.

I'm fortunate to have a group of friends and colleagues who have offered generous counsel on other books I have written as well as on this one. What is different here is that each of them has an important role in the pages that follow. They are Price Cobbs, Paul Fusco, T George Harris, Leo Litwak, and John and Julia Poppy. The journey that we began in the 1960s is still under way.

Esquire's editor emeritus, Phillip Moffitt, deserves a special note of gratitude. Both professionally and as a friend, he has done much to further this work. I also appreciate the support of *Esquire*'s current editor-in-chief, Lee Eisenberg.

My literary agent, Sterling Lord, first suggested I write this book and has continued to gladden my spirits with his enthusiasm and encouragement.

It's rare that an editor can offer strong guidance while remaining true to the spirit of the manuscript and sensitive to the author's deepest aims. Marc Jaffe of Houghton Mifflin has done just that, and the guidance has been precisely on the mark. It has been a joy and a privilege to work with him.

Of the many books and documents I consulted in preparing this work, two were particularly useful: *The Upstart Spring: Esalen and the American Awakening,* by Walter Truett Anderson, and *The Sixties Papers,* edited by Judith Clavir Albert and Stewart Edward Albert. Daniel Free did invaluable service in organizing my own notes and documents of the period. My thanks go as well to Liz Duvall at Houghton Mifflin and to the Mill Valley (California) Public Library, especially to reference librarian Joyce Crews.

If this book is a story of a decade and a movement, it is also a story of a magazine. *Look* magazine is now only a memory, but for me that memory is a vivid one. I have used notes for my *Look* stories and the stories themselves as guidance in creating scenes and dialogue; in several cases, including the opening chapter, I have taken passages directly from those stories. I am grateful for all those who made that vivid magazine possible. I especially give my thanks to William B. Arthur, Patricia Carbine, Martin Goldman, Will Hopkins, Marilyn Kelso, and James Martay.

Finally, I can't start to express my gratitude to the extraordinary individual who has enriched my life in ways that perhaps even he doesn't realize, and to whom this book is dedicated.

CONTENTS

PART ONE

DISCOVERING THE SIXTIES

1

What Did They Do
at Night?

1936

DURING MY EARLY TEENS, I stayed three summers in Monroe, a town of some five thousand people. While my father commuted by car to Atlanta, my mother, sister, baby brothers, and I shared the life of a typical mid-Georgia country town in the late 1930s. Our summers revolved around my grandparents' spacious white house on Walton Street. I had every reason to feel peaceful, protected, and serene. My grandfather was one of Walton County's best-loved citizens. From 1931 until 1946 he served either in the Georgia House or in the Senate. As the county's only undertaker, he had prospered and won the respect of whites and blacks for miles around. He was a farmer, too, operating several nearby farms with black tenant families.

Sometimes my grandfather would let me ride with him in his Chevy to one of the farms. (He didn't like voters to see his big black Buick, so he saved it for special occasions.) We would start in the morning, before the heat of the day had had a chance to weigh down on the earth. We would drive past the icehouse and the silvery water tank at the edge of town and out into the country. After we turned off onto a dirt road, about three miles remained to go, and my grandfather traversed this distance at a majestic pace, hailing every soul we passed: "Howdy, Mose. . . . Howdy, Luke. . . ." They smiled. My grandfather smiled. The car smoothed out the bumps in the road. Field and forest rolled unevenly beneath an endless sky. The world seemed good.

I remember those rides for the odors of the southern earth: dew drying on dusty weeds; fresh manure; tasseled corn; and, most pungent and immediate of all, arsenic dust on a field of cotton. Years later, even a hint of that smell would transport me back to the Walton County countryside, and I would feel again the goodness of the earth and see the sympathetic, creased face of my grandfather next to me in the car, as relaxed and happy as he could be.

When we reached the mystic place on the road "where our land comes to," his eyes would grow narrow with pleasurable concern, and he would judge the progress of Marcus's plowing or dusting, or the growth of the crop. Then he would turn off to the right and mount the bumpy road that led up to Marcus's house.

Whatever was going on ceased. The smaller children stopped their play and stood where they were, hands clasped behind them. The larger children stopped their chores in the barnyard, edged close; then they too stood still and mute. More small children slid from the house, followed by Roberta, belly swollen in her shapeless dress, and they too stood still. Marcus smiled broadly, stocky and competent in overalls and crumpled hat. John, sleek and a head taller than his father, was expressionless. My grandfather got out and stood easy, hands on hips.

"Morning, Marcus."

"Morning, suh," Marcus answered, hat in hand.

Both smiles were broad; the distance between the two men was appropriate and fixed.

"See you got the cotton weeded."

"Yessuh. Yessuh. Sho'ly did."

I always stayed in the car for a while. My eyes sought out the boy nearest my age, who was wearing my last year's shirt, and the little girl who was wearing my sister's dress of two years ago. The clothes were faded, and it made me somewhat uneasy to look at them.

"Sho' need some new plow harness."

"What you talking about, Marcus?" my grandfather said good-naturedly. "Your old lady keeps it patched up, doesn't she?"

Marcus paused. Though his face was fixed in an ingratiating smile, his eyes were cool and shrewd. He seemed never to look directly into my grandfather's eyes, and yet, like a gambler watching for a fifth ace, he managed to keep a constant check on his expression. "Yessuh," he answered. "But she can't patch no more when ain't nothing there to patch on."

My grandfather laughed richly. He walked casually away from the house. Marcus and John followed. The dark figures in the yard began moving again, as they trudged away to hoe cotton.

I got out of the car and walked over to the barnyard. I looked into the chicken house and the barn, then climbed the barnyard fence to survey the surrounding fields. Somehow, I had always sensed that it would be wrong of me to go into the house itself; but since no one was near, I drifted over in that direction, leaned into the front door, and quickly looked around.

Later, back in the car, I could visualize only fragments of what I had seen: pictures of Jesus nailed onto a warped, unfinished wall; a kerosene lantern; iron-framed double beds with mattresses that sagged almost to the floor; a rocking chair. But I had a powerful memory of the acrid, earthy odor that permeated the place.

"Their house is so little, and there are so many of them," I remarked about halfway back to town. "There isn't room for them."

"They've got the whole farm to stretch out in."

"But in the winter . . ."

"They keep each other warm." A knowledgeable smile moved over my grandfather's face. "Why, you get all those pickaninnies in there, it's steaming warm."

"I know, but — "

"Listen, son, they don't know any other way of life. Why, they wouldn't *want* it any other way. They have plenty of food, and we certainly keep them in clothes. Don't you ever worry about those folks. They're a lot happier than any of us."

He drove on, occupied with his own thoughts.

"But what do they do at *night*?" I asked.

"At night? Why, they just sleep. When the sun goes down, they go to sleep, just like the birds. They sleep peaceful. None of us is ever going to be as happy as they are, I can tell you that. Life is simple for them. They know their place in the world, and they know their work. They're good, God-fearing people. Now, when a colored person goes to the city or gets out of his place or starts trying to be smarter than he is, then he'll be just as unhappy as . . . then he won't be happy anymore. But Marcus knows his place, and he knows his work. He's a good man, and I want you to know that I hold him in very high regard."

Again my grandfather withdrew into his thoughts. I started to ask another question, but something held me back. I had wanted to ask what they did *before* they went to sleep. There must, I thought, be a time like that. I had a vague yet powerful vision of all of them there in that small house, the sun down, the darkness gathering about them. Were they really so easily asleep? Didn't any of them lie awake for a while daydreaming or talking? The car glided on toward town; fields and woods and farmhouses swept past me. I could smell the arsenic on the cotton fields, sharp and dizzying. I tried to imagine the black family lying in the darkened house, sleeping, breathing. But my thoughts blurred, and a feeling of strangeness came over me. There was something big and unexplained in my world, something I couldn't understand.

What did they do at night? During the daylight hours, our docile darkies appeared at their appointed places, performed the tasks decreed by the white world; then, when darkness fell, they went away, leaving white Monroe with hardly a trace of their passage. Were they sleeping? The moon that shone into my sleepless room also shone in their windows. Did the moon make them restless too? What happened when they got sick? Did they have doctors? Did their children have homework? Did they read the newspapers? There was no way for me to know.

A half mile away, past trees and unplowed fields, most of the town's blacks lived. I never had to be told that this was forbidden territory. Late one moonlit night, when we were bursting with excess energy, my sister, two friends of my own age, and I ran for our bicycles, and before we knew just what we were doing, all four of us were racing out of town on the dark blacktop road that ran past the black section. We kept going for three or four miles, pumping as hard as we could. Physically spent, we turned and started slowly back to town. We were aware now of our aloneness, and we became silent as we neared the houses clustered off to the right of the road. As we passed the houses, we could hear laughter, a baby wailing, dogs barking, radio music, someone — was it a man or a woman? — singing. I strained to hear words and see people. But the houses were too far away, and there were no streetlights. Still, the windows glowed with the warm yellow of kerosene lamps, and the houses were unmistakably filled with wakeful life. Again a feeling of strangeness rose up inside me.

My sister gasped. I turned to see her bike swerve from a dark figure standing almost directly in our path. I swerved too, gripped by terror. No word was spoken, and I could not make out the man's features, but he was looking at me very directly. He made no move toward any of us, and it was all over in a moment. But the inexplicable terror remained as we pumped quickly and quietly home; and I, never daring to look around, felt a tingling on the back of my neck until we were safe on Walton Street again.

Later that summer, I woke up one hot morning with the immediate knowledge that something awesome was happening. The phone had been ringing several times into my morning drowse, and when at last I came fully awake, I heard my mother ending a conversation: ". . . my feeling is, the less said about it, the better." I tried to get her to tell me what was going on. She answered in the generalities that are part of every southerner's repertory. Her vague words were meant to reassure, but actually made me extremely uneasy. As soon as I could dress, I started downtown on my bicycle. On the way I met my best friend, who was riding to get me. "That big buck nigger that raped a white women," he said with relish. "They're taking him into the courthouse today, and there's a crowd says they're gonna take him out of there. Let's go down to the square."

I felt a sudden stab of deep depression and then a strong desire to turn and go back to Walton Street. But I found myself pedaling alongside my friend past the Methodist church, toward the courthouse. For a moment I thought of praying. I tried to think of God or the merciful Jesus of the Methodist Sunday school. What could Jesus do for the man they were after? For some reason this seemed an improper question, and I was left with a sense of utter helplessness and futility.

The tree-shaded lawn before the old red-brick courthouse was filled with "country people." A few were carrying slabs of wood. Farm children were there too, the smaller ones in their mothers' arms. The air was still beneath the trees, and everything was locked in a peculiar silence, broken only by commands from a state trooper.

My friend led the way, and as I followed him into the crowd, I had the feeling I could hardly breathe. I really did not want to go forward, but seemed to have no control over my motions. We worked our way almost up to the walk that led from the street to the courthouse steps.

All at once a dull, inhuman sound rose all around me. Peering out between two farmers, I could see a state patrol car approaching: I glimpsed a dark head in the back seat. The strange sound, neither a roar nor a hiss, faded away in the hot, still air, and I felt heavy bodies pressing forward against me. As the car pulled to the curb, I could get only intermittent glimpses of what was happening. The front doors were open. Two troopers got out and stood looking at the crowd. The back door opened. The crowd swayed forward. Troopers, arms outspread, pressed against the crowd, and I heard the trooper nearest me cursing under his breath. The press of bodies against me did not matter now; I was possessed with a compulsion to see the black man, to look into his eyes.

My memory has him in chains, shackled to the two troopers in the back seat. Another dead sound rose from the crowd as the troopers dragged him from the car, and he struggled to find his feet. The crowd swayed forward again, and again a grotesque silence gripped the courtyard. In this silence the troopers walked the man to the courthouse. As he passed only a few feet from me, he turned quickly one way, then the other, and it seemed his eyes met mine. But I knew he saw nothing. Fear had blinded him.

The crowd did not press forward again, and after a while some of the farmers started drifting away. My friend and I rode back to Walton Street without speaking. I went inside and lay on my bed, sick in body and spirit.

Something had happened to me when my eyes had met those of the black man. *I had felt what he felt.*

The sickness left me, but it was days before my spirits rose. And there was another thing: Never again could I believe what my elders said about the blacks. They did not sleep like babies. They never really slept. They spent their nights in passion and waiting and terror, their eyes white in the darkness. In the moonlight or during the blackest night, I felt their presence. They were not asleep.

2

It Might Have Been a Scene
from Another Planet

1960

I ALWAYS WONDERED why people couldn't see it coming — I mean that awakening, that upheaval, that ripping away of constraints that we know as "the sixties." The decade began with almost all the pundits still commenting on the dullness of the times. It was the age of apathy and conformism. It was "the Silent Generation." There was hardly a hint of the coming storm. Even after a special issue of *Look,* one of the nation's most widely read magazines, came out at the end of 1960 predicting the upheavals to come, under the title "Youth of the Sixties: The Explosive Generation," the assumptions stayed put. A year *later,* in fact, Dr. George Gallup did a major poll showing that the young person of the sixties "is most unlikely to rebel or involve himself in crusades of any kind. The United States has bred a generation of nice little boys and girls who are just what we have asked them to be."

Time plays one very cunning and deceptive trick. As soon as the unthinkable achieves reality, it tends to become unremarkable. Much of what would have been considered revolutionary in 1960 is commonplace today. As we near the end of the twentieth century, it's hard for us to remember just how different things were at the end of the fifties.

In 1960, Eisenhower was finishing his second term in valedictory triumph after eight years of relative peace and prosperity. It was supposedly an uncomplicated and carefree period, a favorite setting for nostalgic movies of later decades. But the innocence of that period was the innocence of unawareness, of injustice unredressed, of inequities barely imagined.

Take the matter of race. In 1960, despite the Supreme Court's desegregation decision of 1954, a fourth of the nation still lived under an American apartheid. Blacks ate, slept, went to school, even drank water in facilities entirely separate from those of whites. Poll taxes and rigged literacy tests denied almost all of them the right to vote. Not only that, they had to walk a certain humble way. Looking into a white person's eyes could result in a lynching. The Deep South had said "Never!" to desegregation, and experts on the subject predicted that simply getting eating facilities opened to blacks would mean a bloody struggle lasting into the 1990s. My father could more easily imagine little green men from Mars walking through town than blacks and whites in the same swimming pool — to say nothing of a black mayor of Atlanta.

Most American women in 1960, as Betty Friedan was to point out three years later in *The Feminine Mystique,* were led to believe that the only really desirable role they could play was that of wife, mother, and housekeeper. According to a national 1957 survey, 80 percent of Americans (and that figure included women) believed that women who preferred to stay unmarried were "sick," "neurotic," or "immoral." Abortion was illegal. There were no rape crisis centers, no battered wives centers, no affirmative action, and no equal opportunity employment. Women were "girls," and job discrimination against them was not even an issue.

Men as well as women were locked in standardized roles. There were bohemian enclaves in some large cities, but most of the men you saw going to work wore either suit and tie, often with hat, or blue work clothes. Men were supposed to be strong and reliable, and not to express feelings of vulnerability. Some alternative lifestyles did exist, but the alternatives remained largely in the shadows. Homosexuality was spoken of only in whispers, and rarely if ever mentioned on radio, television, or in mass magazines.

Much of the stuff of life, in fact, was hidden away in dark and dusty closets. Polite conversation allowed only the briefest, most guarded mention of such things as cancer, alcoholism, child sexual abuse, and death and dying. Spousal rape would have been considered a contradiction in terms, if it had been considered at all. Sexual feelings other than those of the most standard, stereotyped sort were rarely acknowledged, much less discussed. Unmarried couples sometimes did share apartments or hotel rooms, but not openly. As for couples in bed together on television or in the movies — unthinkable.

War in that strangely innocent time was still a regrettable but honorable enterprise. It was something America always won. It was John Wayne with his troops in Normandy: "We didn't come here to stand around shooting the bull, men. We're movin' up."

Ecology? The environment? Blank stares. In 1960 these words were simply not used in the sense we use them today. As late as 1967, in his book *The Year 2000,* futurist Herman Kahn entirely failed to mention anything in the nature of environmental problems.

It was, in short, a different world, a different life. It was in that world that my adventures of the sixties began. It was, in fact, at around nine P.M. on Thursday, March 30, 1960, in the Sheraton-Park Hotel in Washington, D.C., that I realized the sixties, in spite of everything the experts might have been saying, were going to be different, explosive, something new in the American experience.

I had come out of Georgia via two tours in the air force to what any romantic young southerner of the time might have dreamed of: a job as a senior editor on a major magazine in New York City. I had lived in New Canaan, Connecticut, commuted to the city on the New Haven line, worn a gray flannel suit. I had traveled around the country and around the world, done scores of stories, won six national awards for education reporting, and even found time to publish a first novel, which had quickly become a rare book. But no matter; I was young and there were other novels to be written. I had been married and had had two daughters and had been divorced and had remarried. In 1956, after three years at *Look,* I had been transferred, with sinking heart, to faraway San Francisco. But no matter; I still spent up to a third of my time on the East coast, where the real action was.

And now I was at the Sheraton-Park in Washington on a most unusual assignment. Dan Mich, *Look*'s editorial director, had told me to attend the White House Conference on Children and Youth, not to do any particular story, just to be there. In six and a half years at *Look,* this was the first time I had had five days with no responsibilities. It would be fun, I thought, to wander from one meeting room to another, to buttonhole delegates in the lobby and ask significant questions, to play the role of the noted journalist in search of background material. It often seemed to me that life was a game, and that I was only playing at being an adult. I was thirty-six, and most of the delegates were older than I, but even those younger seemed somehow more grown-up. But I could wear a suit and tie as well as they could, and I could pretend to be what I actually was.

For a while it was fun. But by the second day it was all I could do to hide my boredom. The conference was enormous, with 7570 voting delegates, 550 sponsoring organizations, 18 daily forums, 210 workshops, and more than 300 speeches. I had spent a lot of time with children on my education assignments, and what I was hearing here bore little resemblance to the poignant *presentness,* the awesome shadows and shifting colors of any classroom. The panels were inconclusive, the workshops tedious, the speeches prime examples of Eisenhower era mush. More and more, I found myself visiting the lobby newsstand or going up to my room to check on the latest radio and television news.

For in spite of all the bland reassurances, in spite of the massive dullness of this conference on youth, something terribly exciting was going on among young people in my native South. At that moment, in fact, hundreds of young blacks — maybe more than a thousand — were in southern jails for having attempted to eat at "whites only" counters.

I had not yet developed a coherent organizing principle for my life or a clear vision of the world. But there was one thing about which I had no doubt: I was absolutely, unequivocally, passionately committed to the fight against segregation in America. I came to this commitment with the conviction of an apostate southerner, turned from the segregationist faith at an early age. Every report of a new "racial incident" lifted my spirits. I hoped with all my heart that the demonstrators would succeed in filling the jails to overflowing, in paralyzing the southern communities that continued to resist desegregation. What I wanted, without reservation, was an overthrow of my own ancestral way of life. What I dreamed of was almost unthinkable to most southerners at that time: not only a reform in the administration of justice, but also a revolution of hearts and minds. As far as I was concerned, it couldn't happen too soon.

By late Tuesday I was beginning to feel an almost painful restlessness, and by midday on Wednesday I could hardly bear to stay indoors. I walked around outside the hotel. It was a balmy day and a few blossoms were out. Strangely, there was an odor of warm gasoline in the air, and also the smell of freshly mown hay. I thought of my childhood in the South, and of all that was happening there right now. What would it take to convince white southerners that their darkies were not sleeping like babies? How many demonstrations, how many arrests, how many deaths? Even now, most of the whites, my people, wouldn't let themselves admit the truth. They blamed the sit-ins on "outside agitation," on a Communist plot. They would blame moon rays if they thought that story would stick. But at last the truth was coming out. Nothing could stop it now, not police dogs, fire hoses, tear gas, or guns. The lies of many generations would be brought to the light, and not just the South but the whole nation would be changed.

And it was clear to me that the young were leading the way. Most of the demonstrators in the South were of college age. The *New York Times* had reported the previous week that demonstrations in sympathy with the sit-ins had been held at more than twenty northern colleges. I felt I knew young people. I had covered education for *Look*, had visited hundreds of classrooms all over the country, had stayed at some schools for weeks, really getting to know the students. My eleven- and twelve-year-old daughters were bursting with new ideas. I couldn't see America's young people as being apathetic or dull. The youth delegates I had talked with at the White House conference were as frustrated by the proceedings as I was. It was the conference that was dull. Ruled by its own inertia, it droned on and on. Papers were read, constituency needs addressed, organizational priorities fulfilled — as if the nation were not in the throes of a major social and moral crisis.

Then everything changed. It was Thursday night, the last night of the conference, the youth delegates' turn to run the general session. Things started out badly. The young man chosen to chair the meeting seemed totally lost. At one point he admitted sheepishly that he really didn't know Robert's rules of order. On several occasions it appeared the meeting would dissolve in total confusion. But that didn't matter. The youth delegates were brimming with a sense of purpose, a desire to do something about the state of the nation and the world. The sit-in movement was a clear case in point: a critical moral imperative being hammered out by direct action. Again and again, through the babel and disorder, the delegates returned to this point. Their faces were flushed; their eyes were alight with commitment and belief. The enormous room, the speakers' platform, the impressive podium were just as they had been when the adult delegates had held forth on the previous nights. But everything was different. It might have been a scene from another planet.

I was sitting two thirds of the way back among the delegates rather than in the section reserved for the press. I looked around for some point of reference, some other grownup who by means of a slight smile or a knowing nod of the head might validate my perception that something extraordinary was going on. But all around me were only the young people with their new and radiant faces, gathered here in Washington from all over the country. Ever since my childhood summers in Monroe, I had been vaguely searching for some high edge to walk, some path that would lead out of the society in which I had been born and into another life that I couldn't begin to define. Now, in the midst of this delicious confusion, I sensed something momentous, an opening, a message that was still to be deciphered.

The resolutions the youth delegates passed (or didn't pass, because of procedural mistakes) might have been poorly formulated or ill-advised, but they were neither dull nor apathetic. There was a resolution fully supporting the southern sit-ins, and a plan for their own direct action: a protest march in downtown Washington the next morning. And I was leaning forward in my seat, feeling — for the first time in five days — wide awake and fully alive.

Was this the Silent Generation? Or was it a startling new generation waiting to be born?

The jet age was young. The airlines vied with one another to make flying swift and luxurious. I took a Viscount turboprop from Washington to Chicago, then a Boeing 707 jet from Chicago to San Francisco. It was sweet to be flying home after a two-week absence. I pressed my head against the window, watching the badlands of Nebraska giving way to the western desert. The warmth from my drink spread through my body, but it was the view of America from 38,000 feet that intoxicated me. There it was, stretching out to the horizon, incredibly spacious, a nation of surpassing energy and potential, the one place, as Thomas Wolfe said, "where miracles not only happen, but where they happen all the time." The western horizon was turning golden, the sky more opulent and strangely luminous as it deepened from cobalt to midnight blue. Seven miles down, the earth was dark; not a void but a mysterious presence imbued with massive and imponderable powers.

I turned from the window, reclined my seat, lay back, and closed my eyes. The Silent Generation? It just wasn't right, no matter what the experts said, or what their studies showed. Something was happening in the country. The struggle against segregation was the start of it, but it was more than just that. The smell of change was in the air. God knew where it would lead, but the new generation would be at the forefront of it. The sixties would be not at all like the fifties, but something new, a climactic decade.

The air was smooth and there was no sensation of motion or place. With my eyes closed, I could have been anywhere in the universe: unbounded, disembodied consciousness. Then one thought caught my attention, brought me back to place and time. It was simple: *Look* should do a special issue on the youth of the sixties, how different it was going to be. A whole issue. Dan Mich was coming out the following Sunday for one of his twice-a-year staff visits. I would ask him to let me plan and edit it.

3

Looking for Unexpected Angles

IN 1960 the general circulation magazines — *Life, Look,* and to a lesser degree *The Saturday Evening Post* — wielded considerable power over public opinion in America. Television had grown explosively during the past decade. Whereas in 1950 there were TV sets in only 9 percent of U.S. households, that figure had increased to 87 percent by 1960. But television's function was mainly to entertain. All twenty top-rated programs for the 1959–60 season, from *Gunsmoke* to *Maverick,* fell in the entertainment category. With a few notable exceptions, television was yet to demonstrate its full potential in news, news analysis, and documentaries.

Then too, fewer than one percent of American homes had color sets. An advertiser wanting to show a new product to the whole nation in all its color and gleam had to use the seventeen-inch, high-resolution page or the twenty-four-inch double-page spread (both measured diagonally) of *Life, Look,* or the *Post.* And those slick and shiny pages reached a huge audience. Whereas the average network news show in 1960 was viewed by only some 14 million people, *Look* alone reached an average of 27.5 million people eighteen or older from a circulation of around 6.3 million copies every issue. That was a significant proportion of people who read magazines and kept up with things. When I did a major story, I assumed that anyone I met anywhere in America as likely as not would have read it.

The influence of the mass magazines was pervasive and strangely anonymous. New ideas appearing in *Look* or *Life* were rarely credited by subsequent writers of scholarly articles or opinion pieces. It was as if the information in the magazines was a part of the air the nation breathed, thus free for everyone to use without giving it a second thought. By failing to analyze or even acknowledge what the mass magazines were saying, scholars and opinion makers gave them an even greater power over public opinion than if they had criticized or objected to them.

Journals of record those magazines were not. That function was held by the *New York Times* and the *Washington Post,* along with some other large metropolitan dailies, as well as by *Time* and *Newsweek.* The *New York Times* was the unquestioned arbiter of information. It piped in material provided by the most reputable spokespersons from government, business, arts, science, and the academy, then piped it out on a daily basis, thus defining not only what was worthwhile but sometimes, it seemed, what was real. The official story, as told by the *Times,* then influenced law makers and opinion makers, who in turn channeled new information back to the *Times.*

The mass magazines had their own channels to the Establishment, but their greater power lay in blanketing the whole country with new information, in talking directly to a broad and diverse cross section of Americans. I was especially pleased whenever I saw a copy of *Look* (address label in place) on an enamel kitchen table in an Iowa farmhouse, or on an overstuffed couch in a little town on the sun-baked plains of Alabama. I knew there were young people in such places whose view of the world was being shaped by what they saw on our pages.

Wouldn't I really rather work on a magazine such as *The New Yorker?* a friend asked me. Only if I wanted to talk to people who already agreed with me. Working for *Look,* I said, was more challenging and more fun. When, in 1955, I did a nine-page, word-and-picture feature on a black air force major who commanded a fighter squadron made up mostly of white southerners, I knew it would shock and outrage millions of my readers. But having seen it once, I thought, they wouldn't be nearly so shocked and outraged the next time.

Life had started publishing in 1937, and *Look* had followed six months later. At that time, *The Saturday Evening Post* and *Collier's* were the unquestioned leaders in their field. But the new picture magazines quickly closed the gap, and by the end of World War II *Life* led the field with a circulation of 4.5 million, followed by the *Post* with 3.5 million, *Collier's* with 2.5 million, and *Look* with 2 million. At that point, *Look* began a steady rise in circulation, passing *Collier's* in 1948. When *Collier's* folded in 1956, *Look* bought its subscription lists, thus increasing in circulation to 5.2 million and passing the *Post.*

By 1960 the *Post* was in financial trouble, and *Look* was close on the heels of *Life* in circulation. While *Life* had increased its circulation by 2.5 million during the postwar years, *Look* had shown an increase of 4.5 million. By the second half of the 1950s, *Look* was beginning to dominate not only the general magazines but all magazines in national awards for excellence. We sometimes wondered what the people at *Life* — that haughty, magisterial dreadnaught of the Luce empire — thought about these developments.

To my continuing amazement, many people saw a great similarity between *Life* and *Look.* The truth was that, except for having large pages and a common interest in picture journalism, the two magazines could hardly have been less similar. *Life* was published weekly and had a very short production time. Words and pictures sent to press on Friday could appear on the newsstands on Monday. *Life* was proud of this capability and made a great point of exploiting it to the full. *Look,* on the other hand, was published every two weeks, and had a long lead time. Six weeks or even more might elapse between preparing a story and seeing it on the newsstand. And there were at least two weeks of dead time before publication, during which no changes at all could be made.

This seeming disadvantage turned out to be our greatest strength. It forced us to dig deeper, to approach stories from unexpected angles, to bring additional insights to bear on what other media covered simply as news. We dealt with significant events by printing predictive stories just before they happened, or — more likely — by coming up several weeks later with something that was still fresh and new.

These contrasting schedules were reflected in contrasting ways of producing stories. *Life* tended toward the production-line method, with many people, each a specialist, involved in a story. Photographers and reporters from around the world would be sent out on assignment, with memos from the editors in Rockefeller Plaza explaining what was expected of the reportage and the photography. The reporters' notes and the photographers' exposed film were sent back to Rockefeller Plaza. Assistant picture editors there picked out what they considered the best photographs, which they gave to assistant art directors for layout. Meanwhile, the research department did its bit, providing relevant data on the subject. Finally, all of this — reporters' notes, research report, and layout — was given to a writer, who furnished the text and captions. Both the text and the layouts were subject to revision by editors all the way to the top. The people who selected the pictures, made the layouts, and wrote the story generally had never met the people in the story.

Sometimes, in fact, those pictured in *Life* could barely recognize themselves. It is not true that pictures don't lie. Since it stops time, a still picture is a form of magic, an illusion. You can take a thousand photographs of someone over a period of two or three days, and pick out five that show him as a sage, then another five that show him as the village idiot. If you've never met the person involved, never had any personal dealings with him, you are quite free to select those that match your preconceived story line or ideology. The final judgment at *Life* came not from life but from Rockefeller Plaza.

Look, with its longer lead time, employed what might be called the craft system, with one person, the senior editor, responsible for the story from beginning to end. As a senior editor, I would either be given an assignment initiated by the editorial board or think up my own assignment and have it approved by the board. From that point on, in either case, the story would be mine. I would go to the research department and request any data I might need. The photographer assigned to the story and I would set up appointments and travel arrangements. If the subject of our story was a second-grade teacher in a small town in Illinois, we would stay in her classroom every day for several weeks, and frequently accompany her home. In this way we would not only get thousands of pictures and thousands of words of notes, but also come to know her, her students, her family, and her colleagues in a close and personal way.

Back in the Look Building in New York, the photographer and I would spend many hours going over contact prints of the thousands of photographs, selecting about a hundred to be made into larger prints. After culling these prints further, we would devise a general layout scheme, including tentative title and subtitles. Then the two of us would sit down with one of the three art directors for a layout session. When the completed layout was approved for publication, I would write both the picture captions and the text. The senior copy editor would work with me to improve the writing, but I had the privilege of approving all changes. I was required, in fact, to initial the final photostats for accuracy and completeness, thus signifying that I, like all *Look* senior editors, assumed full accountability. That, along with our high degree of authority over story production, was rare indeed in the communications field.

These strikingly different modes of operations made for strikingly different magazines. *Life* displayed a sleek professionalism *Look* sometimes lacked. It could marshal formidable journalistic forces almost anywhere in the world at a moment's notice. It could bring complex events to a clear (if often oversimplified) focus. It could give even the most transient news event its place in destiny, its role in what founder Henry Luce in 1941 called "the American century." And its coverage of men at war had a sweep and immediacy that was unmatched in *Look* or in any other magazine.

But *Life* often seemed cold and distant, with a deeply ingrained tendency toward depersonalization. This tendency was revealed in a type of picture that kept coming up in the magazine: An entire organization with all its equipment — say an army tank battalion — would be spread out on a concrete tarmac and photographed from a high angle. In these pictures, the human individual was shown as I suspected *Life* really saw him — as a chess piece that had its proper and clearly delineated role to play in an organizational or ideological scheme.

Look, on the other hand, was personal to a fault. Even if I had wanted to, I would have found it very hard to depersonalize someone I had known intimately. Where *Life* was cool, *Look* was warm. Where *Life* passed judgments generally aligned with those of the power elite, *Look* raised questions the power elite had never thought of. Where *Life* was consistent and predictable, *Look* was inconsistent and surprising. *Life*'s production line yielded a reliable level of professionalism, issue after issue. *Look*'s craft system depended on the abilities of individual senior editors, and those abilities varied considerably.

And what about the people on the two magazines? *Life*'s editorial staff remained a mystery to us. Though our buildings were only two blocks apart, we hardly ever saw each other. We ate in different restaurants, went at stories in different ways, and ran in different circles. Supposedly, all Luce staffers were tall, square-jawed, racket-toting Ivy Leaguers, and the two I knew lived up fully to the stereotype. We at *Look* assumed that despite our rapidly growing power and prestige, the people at Rockefeller Plaza looked down their noses at us — if indeed they looked at us at all.

Our staff was a mixed lot, tinged more with cornstalk and Spanish moss than with ivy. The magazine had spent its first two years in Des Moines before moving to New York in 1940, and some of the original Iowans were still on board. There were few Ivy Leaguers. Some of the old-time *Look* photographers hadn't gone to college at all, and the senior editors rarely discussed their educational backgrounds. On one occasion, seven of us were gathered at the Berkshire Hotel's Barberry Room, our after-work hangout. I asked if anyone in the group knew where anyone else had gone to college. We all looked around blankly. For the twenty or so *Look* senior editors, only one thing mattered, and that was how well we could do our jobs. And since we worked as individuals rather than as members of a production line, our work was clearly on display.

Though each of us had a great deal of control and authority in the production of his or her stories, we were by no means citizens of a democracy. *Look* could best be described as a monarchy that operated by the grace of a benevolent and permissive deity (founder Gardner Cowles). It consisted of a group of dukedoms of varying power (the senior editors) under the rule of a small but effective court (the editorial board) and an absolute monarch. This extraordinary potentate was editorial director Daniel D. Mich, and it was to him that the magazine's remarkable postwar success generally was credited.

Dan Mich! An austere, awesome individual whose presence could make even the most seasoned journalist weak in the knees. He was just under six feet tall, but looked much taller. He had broad shoulders, an upright stance, strong jaw, strong nose, and a full head of white hair. His skin was almost as white as his hair, and so transparent that it revealed every flush of emotion. When a free-lance photographer named Andrew St. George wrote an article for a photography magazine about doing a *Look* story on Fidel Castro in the early days, he described his meeting with *Look*'s editorial director. Mich, he wrote, "had the appearance of a Renaissance archbishop and wielded approximately the same power."

Dan Mich was midwestern to the core, having come to *Look* at the very beginning from the *Wisconsin State Journal*. He was never completely at home in New York City. He disliked large groups, and was ill at ease during public appearances. Mich was generally to be found either at his comfortable apartment on East 38th Street with his wife, Isabella Taves, and his beloved Dalmatian, or at the *Look* office. He worked from ten in the morning until four-thirty or five in the afternoon, and he left with a clean desk. He might have been ill at ease everywhere else, but on the eleventh floor of the Look Building at 488 Madison, he was king of all he surveyed.

Art director Allen Hurlburt once said that Mich had a very rare faculty: the pure rather than the conditioned reaction. He was able to leave his office with a clean desk because he knew exactly what he wanted. A senior editor and photographer could work on a story for six months and lay it out for fourteen dazzling pages, only to have Dan Mich say, "No, we're not going to run this," primarily because he didn't like the looks of the man or woman in the story.

Look staffers spent hours trying to figure out Mich's pet likes and dislikes. Everybody knew, for example, that he liked the Dodgers but not the Yankees, that he liked polka dots and hated eagles. Actually, he despised predators of any stripe, and couldn't bear to see any animal hurt or killed. Once I was in the process of showing him a series of pictures about a young couple who, rather foolishly, had set up a cattle ranch in Alaska's frigid interior. When I told him that I had a very dramatic picture of the wife coming to the door with a kerosene lamp at midnight to see a dead calf held in the husband's arms, Mich leaped to his feet in horror, shouting, "Don't show it to me!"

More than anything else, Mich favored the underdog. He was fiercely partial to the poor, the weak, the downtrodden, the dispossessed, the victim of prejudice or injustice of any kind. This partiality was not in the least intellectual or philosophical. It came from the heart, his viscera, every cell of his being. Maybe his feeling for the victims of injustice had something to do, as it did in the case of Franklin Roosevelt, with a physical disability. Nobody ever mentioned it, but there was something wrong with one of Mich's feet. Even though he wore a special, built-up shoe, he walked with a noticeable limp.

*

I knew he liked me and liked my work. In 1954, only a year after my arrival, he had given me what I considered the best office among those of all the senior editors in New York, and in 1956 he had picked me to go out and open a San Francisco office. Still, I was cautious when I talked to him. I didn't want to do anything that would set off his hair-trigger temper. I couldn't bear the thought of his yelling at me, as I had seen him do to other *Look* staffers. I was not withdrawn or unenthusiastic in selling my story ideas, but I chose my words with care.

When I moved to San Francisco, my relationship with Mich took a new turn. Once or twice a year he flew out for what was officially termed a "staff visit." Actually, the trips were lavish, expense-account retreats for him and often for his wife, Isabella, as well, with me and my wife, Lillie, as attendants. Sensitive to the letter of the law, I would bring a file folder of *Look* work to at least one of our meetings during his visits. He would look at it suspiciously, then give me a reluctant ear for ten or fifteen minutes before saying, "That's enough work." There was really no need for us to discuss business in San Francisco, since I was in New York on an average of more than once a month.

Instead of working on *Look* business, I had the much more difficult job of figuring out a schedule of amusements fit not only for a king, but for a king who was totally unphysical and rather easily tired, a king who didn't care for amusements that put him in contact with other people. I would try to find out what he wanted to do. I would try to elicit some hint of his preferences. But his response was always the same: "It's up to you, George."

"Well, would you rather go to Ernie's or the Blue Fox?"

"It's up to you, George."

There was a slightly ominous tone to this phrase. I learned to quit asking. Lillie and I would go ahead and plan drives to San Francisco's most spectacular vistas (bearing in mind his fear of heights), lunches at the best restaurants, afternoon jaunts to the wine country, overnight trips to the Pine Inn in Carmel. We started out by inviting local celebrities to dine with us, but discovered that Mich took little pleasure in their company.

What he really enjoyed became clear after a few visits: We would pick up Dan and Isabella at the hotel, do some sightseeing, go to lunch at a carefully selected place, and return them to the hotel. Then at five o'clock we would show up at their suite — generally a balcony suite at the Fairmont — dressed as if were going to a cocktail party. Five was the mystic hour before which Mich never took a drink and after which he drank slowly and steadily until going to bed.

Our party was held right there in the suite, a party for four, with cocktails and dinner by room service. Mich's drink was Grant's Eight-Year-Old Scotch with water, and we tended to follow suit. For dinner he ordered filet mignon and potatoes and salad. After dinner we all had grasshoppers — creamy, sickeningly sweet potions made of crème de menthe and brandy. Before ordering dinner, we would go to the balcony and watch the red and gold of the setting sun reflecting off distant windows in the Oakland hills over across the bay. We would clink glasses, and I would watch the twinkle come to Mich's eyes, the broad grin light up his usually austere countenance. We were just the right group. We were in our own world. Everything was taken care of. For a while there were no problems for us to solve.

Mich liked Lillie. He admired her quick mind and independence of spirit. He appreciated the fact that she was unawed and willing to state her views candidly. Lillie was ravenously interested in almost everything that came within her view, especially anything out of the ordinary. She had been working as an editorial assistant for *Look* when we met in New York. She moved to San Francisco shortly after I separated from my first wife, and got a job as a reporter for UPI. From the beginning our relationship was a vivid mosaic of light and shadow, highs and lows. We were never bored.

Mich also was pleased by the fact that Lillie looked a little like Isabella. Both had gamine quality. Isabella — also a former *Look* staffer and now a free-lance writer — was a pleasingly curvy pixie in her forties with a penchant for wearing polka dots. Lillie was slim and in her twenties, and if she wore polka dots for Mich it was as a joke.

The Grant's Eight-Year-Old did its mysterious work during our private parties at the Fairmont, melting Mich's stiffness and reserve, dissolving his inhibitions. We talked about almost everything. Though he never showed it in the office, he was tremendously interested in my personal life, as well as that of each member of the staff. His Irish intuition was always turned on, and he knew far more about us than I had at first realized. Lillie and I were having alimony problems with my ex-wife. Dan and Isabella had had similar problems, and that created a special bond between us. The one thing he didn't talk about was his childhood. But as the evening wore on and we circled around to his past, there was sometimes a shift in the rhythm of our conversation, and his every pause seemed filled with an odd, unexpressed anguish that refused to be entirely denied.

Still, Mich was a master of control. However much of himself he might reveal under the spell of Grant's Eight-Year-Old, he never appeared to be drunk. And after we left, as he told us, he always took a pill to put him to sleep. "Sleeping pills are not addictive," he said. "I've taken them for twenty years, and I'm not addicted."

Through all of this, I came to like Mich more and more. You could look all the way down inside him and see that everything was real: his support for the underdog, his unwavering journalistic integrity, his amazingly accurate intuition, his uncompromising loyalty to his staff. Some *Look* staffers were bothered — some even quit — because of what they considered his lack of sophistication. But for me he had something better than sophistication, or maybe a deeper and truer form of it, and that was the pure reaction, the unconditioned response. I realized that in spite of our rather formal relationship, I had a special affection for this difficult man.

April 10, 1960, less than two weeks after my trip to Washington. I'm driving Dan Mich through Golden Gate Park, moving slowly and aimlessly along its gently curving roads. There is a low, soft gray overcast that makes it seem as if we are at the floor of a tropical rain forest in a world of almost supernatural green. I start talking rather casually about the White House Conference on Children and Youth. I tell him about the deadness and predictability of the adult delegates and the aliveness, commitment and passion of the young people. I connect this with the sit-ins in the South and the demonstrations on northern and western campuses.

Mich is listening, but he seems somewhat distracted. Maybe it's too early in the day for me to have brought this up. I'm surprised at how excited I am; I can feel my heart beating. I go on, making a conscious effort to talk calmly. Something's up in the new generation, I tell Mich, and I have a hunch there's going to be an explosion in the sixties. He remains silent, his eyes tracking a field ablaze with flowers.

I know how important it is to be absolutely straight with Mich, so I take special pains to explain that my ideas go directly against conventional wisdom on the subject. We would have to do some kind of opinion poll or survey to back up what's now just a hunch. Still no response. I plunge on, proposing that I do a special issue on youth of the sixties. I've never before planned, supervised, and edited a whole issue, but I'm sure I can do it.

My words trail off at the end, and I sit in silence, concentrating on my driving. Mich grunts and looks out at another field of flowers. Finally he speaks:

"I'd be interested to see any ideas you might have, George."

I know exactly what he means. If I'm serious, I should turn in fifteen or so well-thought-out story proposals — enough to fill fifty to sixty editorial pages. The ball is in my court.

Normally I would have started working on a plan for the youth issue as soon as Mich flew back to New York. But I had a series of short assignments to get done right away so that I could be in town in June for the birth of Lillie's first baby, my third. Then too, I had just come up with a new plan for my second novel, and I was spending all my spare time thinking about it and making notes in my journal. My first novel, based loosely on my experiences at an air force training base in World War II, had been too youthful, too optimistic for the critics. My new novel, with its theme of a suicide planned far into the future, was dark enough to satisfy what I sensed was the current fashion for the pessimistic, even the grotesque. I let myself be swept up by delicious imaginings. Sometimes it seemed right, just the work I had always wanted to be possessed by. Sometimes it seemed hopelessly melodramatic, gothic.

Though I was deeply committed to journalism, fiction still seemed the highest calling in the climate of those times, and I persisted in seeing myself as a fledgling novelist who happened to work for *Look*. Many of my San Francisco friends — Herbert Gold, William Kelley, Barnaby Conrad — were novelists. Chandler Brossard, a most improbable *Look* senior editor with whom I hung out in New York, had written what was called the first hipster novel, *Who Walk in Darkness,* as well as many other books. I kept making notes, and finally, early in May, I started writing, sometimes staying up until three A.M., making progress in fits and starts, but making progress.

The birth was a difficult one. Lillie's labor pains started rather tentatively in the midst of an impromptu party at our flat, with San Francisco friends and visiting *Look* staffers streaming in and out of the bedroom. When the pains become stronger around ten, the party atmosphere suddenly changed, and we rushed off to the hospital. For hours I sat with Lillie as she practiced her natural childbirth breathing and relaxation techniques. Now and then a nurse came in, and I occasionally wrote a few lines in my journal, but mostly we were alone and silent and still. Time shifted into another dimension, passing mysteriously, disappearing without a trace. At eight-fifteen the next morning the doctor told me he would have to do a caesarean. He tried to be reassuring. But was there a somber undertone to his voice?

The operation seemed to take an eternity, yet it was over before I knew it, and there I was pressed up close to the window of the nursery. I saw her only moments after her birth, and she was still splattered with blood. The nurse brought her close to the window. She peered out of one eye skeptically, then opened both eyes wide and looked around with great interest. I had read that newborn babies could see only blurs of light and dark, but that was incorrect. Her eyes clearly met mine, and in that instant it was as if we had always known each other. A charge of energy rushed through my body. I had had this experience before, but I had been very, very young; the intervening years had sharpened my sense of vulnerability. Now it was not happiness I felt, but something different and very large, a feeling for which I had no name.

Later, when Lillie was back in her room and resting easy, I went out to eat. Everything seemed fresh and brand new: the dazzling blue of the sky, the luminescent fogbank pressing in from the sea, the blustery breeze fresh on my cheeks. A page from a newspaper sailed on the wind down the middle of the street; I followed its flight with total fascination. A bulky city bus blared its horn; the sound of it was unexpectedly delightful. I was suddenly very hungry and, though I hadn't slept all night, wide awake. I went into a little place on a side street called the Café Renaissance. I sat in a chrome and plastic booth, and before I knew it, tears of thanksgiving were running down my cheeks. I thanked God for Lillie's safety and for the amazing gift of that new being, that one-of-a-kind, unique-in-all-the-universe arrangement of energy and intelligence with whom I already had shared unfathomable knowledge. Compared to such a miracle, the idea of a book about a young man setting a date for his suicide seemed not only melodramatic but absurd.

A few days later, I got a phone call from Mich's loyal lieutenant and managing editor, Bill Arthur. He asked that I send all ideas I had on youth to New York as soon as possible. If they liked the ideas, I could go ahead and do the issue.

4

"Youth Everywhere
Is Exploding into Action"

WHAT MIGHT HAVE BEEN a hunch in early April seemed a sure thing by mid-June. Civil rights demonstrations spearheaded by young people had continued throughout the spring. In California there was a furor among college students concerning the execution of Caryl Chessman, which took place, in spite of huge demonstrations, on May 2 at San Quentin prison. Then, on May 13, the news media were taken by surprise when hundreds of people protesting the House Un-American Activities Committee hearings, most of them students from nearby colleges and universities, were washed down the steps of San Francisco's City Hall by fire hoses.

Nor was this wave of student activism limited to the United States. In South Korea, hundreds of thousands of students, many of them high school girls and boys, rose up in riotous demonstrations against the rigged election of Syngman Rhee, and in mid-April the world witnessed the unusual spectacle of a strongman and his government toppled by teenagers. In Turkey, students defied troops and tanks to march for freedom. Soon that government too was overthrown. In Japan, over a million students surged through the streets to show their opposition to Premier Nobusuke Kishi's support of a U.S.-Japanese defense treaty. Their power was enough to force President Eisenhower to cancel a trip to Tokyo.

It didn't take any special expertise to see what was going on; the story was right there in the daily papers and the evening news. In Haiti and Cuba, in Poland and Hungary, in the Congo and in South Africa, in India and Indonesia, throughout South America, in London, Berlin, Paris, and Algeria, on all sides of every question (but rarely on the side of the status quo), youth was exploding into action.

And what about the Kennedy phenomenon? The junior senator from Massachusetts was winning one Democratic primary after another. If this Roman Catholic dark horse should be nominated, then elected, he would be (after Teddy Roosevelt) the youngest, and certainly the most youthful, president in our history.

My main worry about the *Look* issue was not that I was wrong about the new mood of youth but that some other magazine would beat us to the punch. There were, however, no signs of that. Magazine articles about youth continued to repeat the familiar words: "apathetic," "silent," "materialistic." In its June 13 issue, *Newsweek* reported on yet one more "symptom of apathy." To find out how "beat" college students really were, the Johns Hopkins alumni magazine invited 291 graduating seniors to submit essays defending their own generation. Only one responded, and his was an essay of despair: "We are resigned to a position of grayness and indecision. If my generation seems inert, it is not because we do not care; it is because we feel helpless. . . . Left without roots, without inspiration, without direction, what can we do but adjust?"

A few days after Lillie came home from the hospital with Lillie II, I returned to my office in downtown San Francisco and started planning the youth issue. I had a tentative title, "Youth of the Sixties: The Explosive Generation," and planned to use the logo "Explosive Youth" at the beginning of every article. I would open the issue with an essay illustrated by a strip of black-and-white photographs showing youth activism all around the world. The essay would be followed by a portfolio of color photos designed to capture the new mood of youth. There would be stories on youth and science, youth and sex, early marriages, and juvenile delinquency. I was especially eager to show the idealism and activism I had seen at the White House conference. There was an organization named Operation Crossroads Africa that charged American college students $875 for a nine-week trip to Africa, during which they were expected to pitch in and help build such things as water systems, bridges, and rest houses in backward villages. I thought it would be wonderful if we could do a picture story on this organization (which turned out to be a precursor of the Peace Corps), focusing our coverage on a white female college student from the Deep South. I also wanted to include an article of some sort on the sit-in movement. But this subject had already been fully covered in other magazines and on television. I would have to come up with something new, and I couldn't imagine what it would be.

Except for the sit-in story, the proposals came rather easily. My main concern was the survey of American youth that would prove or disprove my thesis. The obvious solution would be to hire the Gallup organization for a scientifically weighted opinion poll of American youth. But I seriously doubted the ability of conventional polling to pick up changes in the human climate. Gallup and other such groups did a reasonably good job of predicting the outcome of elections a few days before the elections were held. But in matters of values, feeling, and behavior they were not very helpful, tending to err on the conservative side of every subject. Their stodgy questions produced stodgy answers. And anyway, it wasn't necessarily the masses that initiated change in a nation. If George Gallup had done a poll of the thirteen colonies early in 1776, it's rather doubtful he would have predicted an American revolution.

What we needed was not a static picture of where youth was standing but a dynamic picture of which way it was facing. We needed some sort of survey that would indicate *direction*. I considered calling on the National Opinion Research Corporation in Chicago, an organization I knew to be innovative in the polling field. But then I got an idea. The way *Look* worked, *we* could be our own best pollsters. We would send as many *Look* editors and researchers as possible out to communities in every geographical region of the country. At each locale we would interview young men and women of two age levels, fifteen and nineteen or twenty. At both age levels, the first group would be top scholars and student leaders. The second group would be students rated by school tests as average in intelligence and achievement. We would also interview some typical noncollege nineteen- and twenty-year-olds to include in the second group. Each young person would be asked a set of standard questions, but the interviews would be open-ended and personal.

Such a survey would be quite unorthodox, and we would make no claims that it was statistically representative. But it would provide just what was needed. When all the results were in, we could compare the answers of the two groups, then draw an arrow, a vector, from the "typical" answers to the "top" answers. This arrow, I figured, would indicate the probable direction that youth would take in the sixties.

I mailed my story proposals to New York, along with a complete description of the survey method, which I rather grandly named "vector analysis." Within a few days, the editorial board gave a full go-ahead.

Sunday, September 4, 1960. I'm on a plane to Atlanta. I won't arrive until two A.M. It's the earliest plane I could get. My father died this morning of a massive heart attack.

My forehead is pressed to the window of the 707. I'm in a country for which there are no maps. A huge gray whale is swimming past the window. Other phantasmagoric forms inhabit all the space within my view. There's a floor of boiling white below, a diaphanous veil above. I'm at home in this world of silent motion and ambiguous shapes, cut off from anything that might circumscribe my thoughts.

I tell myself that it was good my father died suddenly, with no lingering illness. He had served in two world wars. He was proud he had missed only one day of work in all of his life. He wouldn't have liked old age. He would have hated being sick and feeble. I couldn't even *imagine* him sick and feeble. His was a vivid presence. When he walked into a room, everybody noticed him; he made sure of that. I saw his face: the sparkling dark brown eyes, the rather prominent nose, the debonair moustache, the youthful smile that flickered around the edges of his mouth and hinted that one was about to be let in on something marvelous. He was born of the old, impoverished southern aristocracy, and he thought he had come into the world to fulfill some historic destiny.

But what was the destiny? Surely not to become an insurance executive, even if finally he had achieved a certain prominence in his field. My father was a sucker for the *Who's Who*-type directories that list your name and your *vita*, then try to sell you the oversized, overpriced volumes in which you're listed. He had a whole shelf of those books. But he wanted more than that: something mythic, worldwide fame, a hero's apotheosis.

I search my mind for some mention of my father, even a footnote, in the history books of the future. Actually, there had been one moment in his life that would go down in the records of his times. And like the best material in all histories, it was a moment tinged with irony. My father had always favored racial segregation. Race, in fact, was the only subject that had created angry words between us. Whenever the subject came up during my teenage years, he had resorted to the same argument: "It's nature's way. There are blackbirds and bluebirds and redbirds. The blackbirds don't mingle with the bluebirds, and the bluebirds don't mingle with the redbirds, and the redbirds don't mingle with the blackbirds." At last, when I had heard that argument one time too many, I said, "Yes, that's why they call them birdbrain." I was immediately sorry that I had hurt my father, who, whatever his views, loved me totally and unconditionally, and never complained, in spite of considerable scandal in the neighborhood, when I had black musicians over to the house for jam sessions.

Even after the 1954 Supreme Court desegregation decision, he clung to the conventional wisdom of his native land that the races should be and must be separated. Then, just a year ago, he had been called to serve on a Fulton County grand jury that would take testimony and make recommendations on possibly the most important legal and moral question since the Civil War. A federal court had ruled that the Atlanta public schools must be desegregated as of the opening of the school year in September 1960. This decision went directly against a recently passed Georgia state law prohibiting integration of the schools. Caught between two powerful legal forces, the public schools were considering not opening at all.

It was a precarious situation. Ninety-four percent of the South's blacks still attended segregated schools, and there was as yet no desegregation at all in Alabama, Louisiana, South Carolina, Mississippi, and Georgia. Another civil war? Not likely, but in some way possible. In the struggle against American apartheid, Atlanta was the linchpin. The upcoming Battle of Atlanta would be the Gettysburg of the fight for civil rights in the South. If Atlanta held out against desegregation, the entire Deep South, as the pundits predicted, would face a long and bloody struggle. If Atlanta fell, and fell gracefully, without bloodshed, the rest of the South would probably follow, and desegregation would be in place long before the year 2000. It was up to the grand jury, in effect, to advise the Atlanta school board as to what action it should take.

I had been in Atlanta a few months earlier, just after the grand jury released its report. When my father met me at the door, his eyes were shining. He had something to show me. It was a front-page newspaper story on the grand jury report. I sat down to read it before unpacking. He was eager for me to turn to an inside page where the entire text of the report was printed. He told me he had drafted it, and I could recognize his rather florid style. I could hardly believe what I was reading. The grand jury had recommended that the Atlanta schools be kept open at all costs, *even if that meant they had to be desegregated*. That was by no means the end of the struggle. The Battle of Atlanta was still ahead of us. But the grand jury statement would go a long way toward setting the conditions of battle.

I looked in my father's eyes. His mother had died when he was two, and he had been reared by his grandmother, a woman who, at sixteen, had refugeed by train from Atlanta southward just ahead of advancing northern troops; she had stepped over dying Confederate soldiers at the train station, just as Scarlett O'Hara did in the famous scene from *Gone With the Wind*. My family still had a marble-top bureau with a hole in it from a Yankee bullet. All my father's background, conditioning, and life experiences had pointed him in one direction — and he had come out on the other side. If this was possible, then what was not possible? He was looking at me rather shyly. He wanted me to be proud of him, and what I wanted to do was to put my arms around him and hug him. But we were southern men, and southern men didn't hug. I reached out my hand to shake his hand, and to offer all the praise that I could offer without becoming unseemly in the emotion that I felt.

Somewhere between Missouri and Georgia, I awaken not with a start but with a frightening clarity of perception. I don't have a father. I'm the oldest son. There's no longer anybody between me and death. I'm *next*. It's all up to me.

One forty-five A.M. Sweeping down to Atlanta in the pale moonlight, I recall those phone calls of the morning as if they were memories from long ago, another era. The anguished words, the fragmentary descriptions, are running together, coalescing to become a family myth that will be passed down to children who never knew him:

He was standing with a group of friends at the edge of the lake at his small country place, discussing the party they had had the night before. A large snake came out from under an overturned rowboat. He ran to his cabin to get a gun. It was a short distance up a slight incline, but my mother, at the cabin, said "George, you shouldn't run like that." He said, "It's *good* for me." He ran back down to the lake, shot the snake's head off, held it up by its tail, then fell dead.

*

I'm flying over Atlanta and all the lights are twinkling. "Pray to God," my mother had said this morning on the phone. But what if there isn't a God? Then isn't it scary and wonderful that we've done all this?

From a plane, all night cities twinkle. But those with many trees twinkle the most. Atlanta has many trees.

The youth issue went smoothly. I flew to New York in early September to make assignments and whip up enthusiasm for the issue. *Look* teams fanned out around the United States, to Europe, to Africa. Each team, in addition to doing its primary story, conducted a survey of young people at the locale of their assignment. Researchers visited areas not covered by editor-photographer teams. I picked Atlanta and environs as the locale for my own survey, not just to bring my familiarity with the territory to bear on it but also to spend time with my grieving mother and my brothers and sister. Altogether, 14 *Look* people interviewed 369 young people.

Early in October I returned to New York with Lillie and the new baby. We sublet an apartment, and I spent every day at the *Look* office putting the issue together. As the final deadline approached, there was still one gaping hole. No matter how much I tried, I couldn't think of a way to cover the sit-ins. Then came one of those breaks you come to expect when your luck is already running. A free-lance photographer named V. Thoma Kersh phoned collect from New Orleans. I had never heard of him, but I accepted the call. He said he had some very good candid shots of a southern white girl participating in a sit-in, being arrested and taken to jail. The southern white girl was Margaret (Sissy) Leonard, a sophomore at Sophie Newcomb College — my nineteen-year-old cousin.

I asked Kersh to send the photos to New York by the fastest possible means. They arrived the next day, and there was blond, fine-featured Cousin Sissy with two well-dressed, good-looking black students at a planning meeting for the Congress on Racial Equality (CORE). And there were the pictures of the sit-in and the arrest and the jailing, marvelous for my purposes in that they had an obviously stolen quality.

Sissy was the daughter of my aunt, Margaret Long Leonard, a novelist and newspaper columnist and one of the main influences in my youthful conversion to all-out support for racial equality. Aunt Maggie's regular column in the *Atlanta Journal* was chatty, highly personal, and to many readers shockingly nigger-loving. She received letters written on toilet paper, and a cross was once burned on her lawn. I knew that Sissy was a fine writer, as existential and understated as her mother was colorful and verbose. I phoned Sissy and asked her to write the story of the sit-in for *Look*. She said she had already written a report for CORE. Well, would she send that to go with the photos?

As soon as I read Sissy's first paragraph, I knew we had just what we wanted:

> About halfway to the door, a woman took my arm and asked me to go with her. She told me she was a policewoman. Several policemen then talked to me. One asked me if I was a Southern girl. I said yes, I was raised in Macon, Ga., and Atlanta. He asked why, as a Southern girl, I was doing this, and I said something about wanting to demonstrate how I felt about discrimination. He said he knew that, but why did I feel that way? I just said I always had.

By early November the results of the survey were in. To check the common assumption that young people were highly materialistic, we had presented those we interviewed with a list of "possessions" ranging from a new car to a Ph.D. degree, and asked which one would make them most look up to a person. A conclusive 62 percent answered "a Ph.D." The other percentages rounded out a picture startlingly different from the stereotype: the ability to play a musical instrument, 16 percent; a large book collection, 12 percent; none of the things listed, 6 percent; a beautiful home, 4 percent; expensive furniture and appliances, 1 percent; expensive clothes, less than 1 percent; a new car, less than 1 percent. On this question, the typical teenagers differed little from the top scholars and student leaders.

Asked "Would you like to be a pioneer?" 54 percent of typical and 65 percent of top teenagers answered yes. The question "Do you think someone who does not believe in our present form of government should be allowed to make a speech in your town?" drew a yes from 77 percent of the typical and 90 percent of the top teenagers. Only 13 percent of the typical and 8 percent of the top teenagers admitted having "any bad feelings" about members of other races.

One after another, the *Look* teams came back with their photographs and notes. The stories were laid out and put up on the wall in our main conference room. Dan Mich and the editorial board gave the issue their approval. The wheels of production began to turn. At *Look,* most of the writing was done last. I had some trouble getting started on the lead essay, but by then it was too late for any doubts.

The issue hit the stands on December 20. An ebullient young woman with a fresh face and hair blowing in her eyes is smiling straight at the camera. She is holding a book, which a young man in the shadows close behind her is reading over her shoulder. And there are the words in big block type: "A surprising new look at THE EXPLOSIVE GENERATION."

The opening paragraph set the tone for the entire issue:

> Youth everywhere is exploding into action. Members of the new generation have looked at the world their elders made. They do not like what

they see. They are moving fast and hard to change it. Better educated and less tradition-bound than previous generations, they often feel separated from their parents by centuries. And in a very real sense they are; for the tempo of history has been doubled and redoubled, and social changes that once took decades are now happening overnight. But even this headlong pace is not fast enough for youth of the sixties, the war babies who at last have grown up to give voice and vehemence to a generation that has been called "silent" and "cautious."

"Obviously, many young Americans are still uncommitted," I wrote near the end of the essay. "But a strong new desire for goals and causes is rising among them. This urge is a powerful — and largely unrecognized — source of energy in an explosive age. The realities of 1960 demand that adult Americans take a fresh look at the new generation. . . . They have felt the current of discontent that is running through the world. They fear, not change, but stagnation."

"What I worry about most," said a New England college senior, "is the most terrible of all curses, found in the Book of Isaiah: 'Make the heart of this people fat, make their ears heavy, and shut their eyes.' I would like to see the opposite of this." A surprising new generation is eager to do battle against the prophet's curse. "In one way or the other," said a college-senior coed from Utah, "everyone can make his voice heard, if he cares to try hard enough. And I care."

So there it was. *Look* had raised a weathervane into the winds of the future, and it was clear which way it was pointing. It was also clear that every other weathervane that I could spot in the entire culture was pointing in just the opposite direction.

One year later, *The Saturday Evening Post* came out with its own analysis of youth. It was based on a survey of three thousand young people between the ages of fourteen and twenty-three, conducted by "the Gallup Poll's scientific facilities," and it was coauthored by Dr. George Gallup himself. Like ours, this report on youth appeared in a year-end issue (December 23–30, 1961), and it seemed to be designed as a rebuttal to the *Look* youth issue. The *Post*'s report, entitled "Youth — The Cool Generation," included the following key findings:

Our typical youth will settle for low success rather than risk high failure. He has little spirit of adventure. He wants to marry early — at twenty-three or twenty-four — after a college education. He wants two or three children and a spouse who is "affectionate, sympathetic, considerate and moral"; rarely does he want a mate with intelligence, curiosity or ambition. He wants a little ranch house, an inexpensive new car, a job with a large company, and a chance to watch TV each evening after the smiling children are asleep in bed. . . .

He wants very little because he has so much and is unwilling to risk what he has. Essentially he is quite conservative and cautious. He is old before his time; almost middle-aged in his teens. . . .

In general, the typical American youth shows few symptoms of frustration, and is most unlikely to rebel or involve himself in crusades of any kind. He likes himself the way he is, and he likes things as they are.

The United States has bred a generation of nice little boys and girls who are just what we have asked them to be. . . .

The publication of the *Post*/Gallup report gave the reader a clear-cut choice. How would the sixties turn out? Would the new generation be cool, or would it be explosive?

5

The Dragon and the Prophet

1 9 6 1

Cal Bernstein and I are sitting near the front of the balcony in the Tower Theater. It's hard not to look around at other members of the audience, but we keep our eyes straight ahead. The stage is aglow with the medieval robes of the Ku Klux Klan — gold and blue, vivid green, scarlet, black and gold, shining white. A grave-looking man in a business suit is speaking:

"If the Nigras get in our schools, here's what you'll be seeing."

A small boy and girl emerge from the wings at the left and walk hand in hand across the stage. The girl is white. The boy is white, but is in blackface. The speaker goes on. "That's not the end of it. Oh, no. Those two will grow up, and then here's what you'll be seeing in the schools of this great state." At his words, a couple in their late teens starts across the stage. The young man is in blackface and is wearing black gloves. His arm is wrapped tightly around the white girl's waist. As the two disappear in the right wings, the speaker goes on in grave, hypnotic tones: "And then there be some minister somewhere, some misguided minister. . . ." The couple comes onstage with a man dressed as a minister. The three pantomine a brief wedding ceremony before walking off.

"But that's not all. Oh, no, my friends, that's not the end of this terrible story. Because if we don't do something, here's the kind of thing you're going to be looking at."

The blackfaced young man reappears. Following several steps behind, head bowed, is the girl. She is leading three children — two white, one in blackface. The young man gestures roughly, and as the group moves across the stage, the voice of the speaker drones on: "Oh, yes, folks, he'll be traveling around with her, ruining her morals every day. . . ." The audience seems to be hardly breathing.

The theater is not hot, but I feel myself sweating. I would very much like to be somewhere else. The speaker is continuing: "The good, God-fearing people don't want integration. I'll tell you who wants integration — the Communists and the Jews." A strange sound, a sort of low-pitched mutter, rises throughout the theater. "But all Jews aren't bad," the speaker says. "It was a Jew that rented us this theater."

The low-pitched mutter becomes an invocation: "Kill the Jews. Kill the Jews." It seems to start behind us, then quickly spreads — left, right, all around — taking on the deep, sonorous quality of a Buddhist chant. I feel a hundred eyes focused on the two of us. Cal Bernstein wouldn't easily be mistaken for an Aryan.

"Kill the Jews. Kill the Jews."

From the corner of my eyes, I see that Cal is moving his lips in the rhythm of the chant. At this moment, maintaining whatever tatters of protective coloration we have left to us seems the better part of valor. I too begin moving my lips.

So here I was in my hometown again, assigned with photographer Cal Bernstein to do a major story during the demonstrations marking the first anniversary of the lunch counter sit-ins. The prewar Atlanta of my childhood no longer existed. Things were moving faster than expected in the South. The world was pressing in, and all that had been concealed behind soft words and a harsh racial code was being forced out into the open. The electricity in the air had nothing to do with the idylls of my youth. The past was secure and forever unchanging; I didn't even look up my old friends. It was January 1961, and what would have been utterly unthinkable before the war, or maybe even last year, was now taking place.

The second Battle of Atlanta was under way. The first one, in July 1864, had ended with a Confederate defeat and a city burned to the ground by hostile forces — the only American city ever to meet that fate. The current battle would not decide whether the Old South would rise again; there was no chance of that. But it would go a long way toward deciding how violent and prolonged the struggle for school desegregation would be, not only in Atlanta but in many other southern communities as well.

On the side of nonviolent change in Atlanta were a mayor and police chief who intended to carry out federal court orders, the city's two major newspapers, the Chamber of Commerce, and most of the faculty and administration of Atlanta's ten colleges and universities, five of them black. Atlanta's leaders were not enthusiastic about integration, but they had made the painful decision that violent resistance was bad for business. Chamber of Commerce president Ivan Allen, Jr., showed me a study of economic stagnation in Little Rock since its anti-integration riots of 1957. "We won't let that happen here."

Atlanta also had a large black population — more than a third of the city's half-million people — led by well-to-do, fairly conservative adults who were having trouble keeping up with the fiery young people of the student movement. And there was Dr. Martin Luther King, Jr., who had moved to Atlanta from Montgomery, Alabama, to make this key city the headquarters for his new organization, the Southern Christian Leadership Conference.

The forces of resistance were also strong. As the state capital, Atlanta was the bastion of old-fashioned southern racism. Georgia's anachronistic county-unit system gave the reins of the state's political power to the rural counties. On several occasions during my childhood, my grandfather from Monroe had taken me to sit with him at his desk, first in the legislature, then in the senate, and I remembered feeling bewildered and queasy as one speaker after another rose to the defense of "the flower of southern womanhood" against what veiled evil I couldn't at first imagine. Years later, while covering the 1957 Little Rock riots, I discovered that Georgia's political leaders were encouraging Arkansas governor Orval Faubus in his defiance of federal court orders. My father helped me get the story. He arranged a Trojan Horse meeting between me and then Georgia governor Marvin Griffin. We went to a Georgia Tech football game together, and in the course of our conservation I got all the facts I needed to pin down the connection. When the *Look* story created newspaper headlines, my father seemed pleased, though it had cost him the governor's friendship.

The Georgia Klan was not large, but it was powerful. And Atlanta held a special significance for Klansmen everywhere. Stone Mountain, a stark monolith seventeen miles to the east, had been a traditional site for cross-burning ceremonies and initiations since the Civil War. Another racist organization, Georgians Unwilling to Surrender (GUTS), had enlisted more than a thousand "respectable" Atlanta segregationists under the leadership of cafeteria owner Lester Maddox. The Black Muslims were segregationists of a different complexion, with fifty hard-core members and an unknown number of supporters in Atlanta. And the picture was further complicated by the presence of crackpots of various persuasions who had smelled the battle from afar. "They're descending on us from every side," reporter Douglas Kiker of the *Atlanta Journal* told me, "crazy evangelists, witch-hunters, and especially anti-Semites. By September this place may look like a convention of nuts." Still, the shock troops, the most committed and disciplined warriors in this strange new battle of nonviolence against violence, were the young, incredibly courageous members of the black student movement.

The lights are out above the lunch counter. The place has been in semidarkness for an hour, ever since four black Atlanta college students entered and took seats. All the white patrons have gone. From the corner of his eye, one of the students, a tall eighteen-year-old freshman named Leon Green, sees the lunch counter manager coming out of the kitchen. Uh-oh! Leon thinks. He's got his meat cleaver again.

The white man moves toward Leon, who keeps his eyes focused on the menu he is gripping with both hands. "Get your hands off that counter," the man says, raising the meat cleaver, "or I'll cut one of them off."

Leon does not move. He keeps his eyes on the menu. The manager jerks it from his hand, but Leon manages to hold onto the inside flyleaf. Infuriated, the manager rips the flyleaf from Leon's hand and tears it up. He lifts the cleaver again. "All right. I mean it this time. Get your hand off the counter, or I'll cut it off."

Leon does not move his hands or his eyes. The manager draws back to strike. Leon does not flinch. The manager walks away.

Later, Leon says, "I really thought he was going to do it today."

The Pickrick Cafeteria sold miniature ax handles as well as southern fried chicken. According to Lester Maddox, the owner of the cafeteria, these undersized weapons were "just souveniers." Still, they rather neatly summarized one method of dealing with integrationists.

"Now you boys just go on through the line and get y'self some fried chicken," Maddox told us. "Then we can set for a spell and talk about *Look* magazine."

He was a slim man of medium height wearing rimless glasses. His face, with its high, rounded forehead and balding dome, had the bland quality of a face drawn by a child: a simple oval with eyes, nose, mouth, and ears penciled in. He sat with both elbows on the table and legs turned sideways, as if he might leave at any moment. I gnawed on a fried drumstick as I attempted to explain our mission. We were going to show the forces on both sides of the current struggle. We wanted to interview him and take a picture. I pulled my notebook out as he began to talk. He saw his cause as a noble one. It involved not only fighting desegregation but also restricting the power of the Supreme Court, removing federal influence over education in the states, opposing foreign aid, and supporting the House Committee on Un-American Activities. He believed that the people who were fighting for integration were doing so for political or economic gain. Wherever those motivations didn't apply, he saw a Communist conspiracy. I wrote furiously, getting my notebook slightly greasy from the fried chicken.

"What about this picture you boys want to take?" Maddox suddenly asked.

Here comes the hard part, I thought. "Well, we'd like to get you in front of a Georgians Unwilling to Surrender sign." That was, after all, the name of his organization.

He looked from one of us to the other. "Well, Br'er Leonard, I'm gonna have to think on that. You boys come on in here anytime you want to have y'self some good fried chicken." He got up and walked off.

We spent a few more minutes working on our chicken, which I could barely taste at this point. The other patrons were eyeing us, and I was aware of the hollow ache in my solar plexus that was always with me in such circumstances. Trying to look as nonchalant as possible, we got up to leave. Maddox spotted us. He accompanied us to the door and bid us goodbye with the cheery phrase he used with all his patrons:

"You stay segregated, y'hear?"

A long-distance call to the *Atlanta Journal:* "I want the number of Martin Luther King."

The caller is connected to reporter Doug Kiker.

"Do you know this nigger, Martin Luther King?"

"Yes."

"What's his number?"

"I don't know."

"Well, call him and tell him he'll be dead before sunrise. We've drawn straws to see who'll kill him, and I've won."

Kiker tries to reason with the caller. "Don't you know murder will get you nowhere?" The caller hangs up. Kiker phones the police. They tell him they already have a squad car circling Dr. King's house.

They were a jaunty and irreverent bunch. They referred to Martin Luther King, Jr., as "M. L., Jr." They believed they had a piece of history in their hands, and they came to each moment as if it were alive with delicious possibilities. They drove around town with us in our overpowered rented Ford, telling us their war stories, pointing out the targets of future operations. They invited us to clandestine, all-night planning meetings, and greeted us with big smiles when we walked into their public rallies.

"On February first, we plan some dynamic action to mark the first anniversary of the sit-ins," the speaker was saying. "The movement is not asking you to go to jail at this time. We're hoping to arouse the conscience of the white merchants of Atlanta."

I sat with an audience of students from the five campuses of Atlanta University Center while Cal moved around taking pictures. The speaker was twenty-one-year-old Benjamin Brown, president of the Clark College students and a picket-team captain for the Committee on Appeal for Human Rights. He was dressed in a three-button suit, a white shirt, and a striped bow tie. He had already been in the Atlanta jail three times. "I consider each time a badge of honor," he had told us earlier, "a moral protest against an unconstitutional antitrespass law designed to support the un-Christian institution of segregation." Now he went on speaking to the students, who listened in absolute silence and stillness.

"You're gonna grow up and read about this in the history books — the greatest student movement in the history of the United States. Your children are going to ask if you were there. . . . You'll all be thoroughly orientated. I know it's the first day of school, but you'll always be glad to say you missed a class for the cause of human freedom."

Ben Brown was the focal subject for our picture story on the student movement. Cal had already shot hundreds of pictures of him with other members of the movement, but we wanted to photograph him sitting in at a lunch counter. That, as it turned out, was far from easy. The Atlanta merchants had adopted the tactic of closing down at the first hint of an impending sit-in. After giving some thought to this matter, Cal and I came up with our own tactics. At the least, we figured, we could shoot the confrontation that was bound to occur when the students entered and the merchant closed down.

A drugstore on downtown Peachtree was the target. For two days prior to the sit-in, Cal and I visited the store to get the employees accustomed to our presence and the rather peculiar behavior we had devised to cover up the actions we planned during the sit-in attempt. I would wander around looking at the merchandise, then would buy a newspaper or magazine and some mints. Cal would go to the cigarette display, a good spot for photographing the lunch counter, where he would pick up different brands of cigarettes and examine each pack up close, sometimes taking his glasses off and rubbing his eyes as if he had very bad eyesight.

On the day of the sit-in, Cal brought his Minox spy camera, about the size of a cigarette pack. We had everything timed to the second. Just a few seconds before Ben Brown and three other students were to enter, I engaged the manager in a conversation about a watch he had for sale. Cal then palmed his Minox and brought it up to his eye. At the instant he made that move, our plan fell apart.

"We're closed," the manager yelled. "We're closed!"

He ran to the door before the students could get in. Other employees rushed around pulling down the shades. All the lights went out.

"This store is closed. Everybody out. Out! Out!"

He was standing holding the door, a tall thin man with a potbelly and a prominent Adam's apple. "You should know you can't take pictures in here. Why don't you Yankee newspapermen go on back where you came from?"

I started to tell him that my southern ancestry on both sides went all the way back to the earliest settlers in Virginia, and that he was obviously nothing but a cheap carpetbagger and scalawag. But I knew from past experience covering civil rights in the south that he would never believe I was a real southerner. Anyway, we should have realized from the beginning that our plan wouldn't work. Cal was a large man with a shambling walk, an upright carriage, and a head mounted on his body like a lookout on a fortress. Everything about him said New York. At six-four and 185 pounds, I was a skinny WASP, as southern-looking as anybody. But no matter. My southern credentials were long gone. There was no way we could disguise ourselves. In the South in 1961, Cal was a New York Jew and I was a Yankee newspaperman. And southern racists had antennas a mile long. They could sense that we were coming, it seemed, before we even got close.

On January 20 we interrupted our work to race back to the hotel and see the inauguration ceremony on television. It was a cold day in Atlanta, and it was obviously frigid in Washington. Robert Frost's breath came out in clouds as he read the poem he had composed for the occasion. And when the young president came to the podium, I found myself hardly daring to breathe, I was so anxious for him to speak strongly and truly, to open our eyes and ears, to give us a vision. He paused for a moment (that faint, knowing smile on his lips), then started saying just the words I might have dreamed he would say, the cloud of his breath streaming in the cold, clear air. "The torch has been passed to a new generation of Americans," the president said, and I thought, yes, he's only seven years older than I am; it's my generation he's talking about. And my God, yes, we can do it. Look what's already happening just in the matter of race. Nothing could be more deeply ingrained, more crucial to the way we live. If we turn that around, then what can't we do?

Time for some more southern fried chicken. We sat at a table in the Pickrick Cafeteria, waiting for Lester Maddox to come talk with us. As far as southern cooking went, our dinner of chicken, butter beans, collard greens, rice, and cornbread, with cole slaw on the side, wasn't bad. But again I could hardly taste it.

We saw Maddox approaching from across the room. He didn't sit down, nor did he offer any verbal niceties. "Well, Br'er Leonard and Br'er Bernstein," he said cheerfully but not without a touch of malice, "I'm not gonna let you take that picture of me in front of the sign you're talking about."

I took a sip of iced tea to help me swallow, took a hurried breath, and started trying to persuade Maddox to change his mind. He should be proud to stand in front of a sign of the organization that he had created, I said. But his mind was made up. We tried to finish our dinner but left quite a bit of fried chicken and vegetables on our plates. As we walked out, there he was at the door again.

"Y'all stay segregated, y'hear?"

We met Martin Luther King, Jr., in his office at the Ebenezer Baptist Church. The room was rather dark and unusually hushed, considering the traffic on Auburn Avenue out front. King was extremely courteous but somewhat distant. I told him what our story was about, and we discussed the situation in Atlanta.

"I am optimistic," he said, "and I base it on Atlanta itself. The pre-

dominant sentiment is, 'We must keep our schools open at all costs.'
Here we have all the forces on both sides, but the forces of defiance are
not as strong as those who realize it's futile to stand on the beaches of
history and try to hold back the tide."

He spoke softly and chose his words carefully, as if he were speaking
for the record, for the history books. I sensed a majestic sadness about
him. His eyes, it seemed, were already focused on another world.

We went into the sanctuary of the church for Cal to shoot the portrait.
There was a small, illuminated cross behind the altar, and above that a
small, round stained glass window showing Jesus kneeling in prayer. Cal
shot from a low angle, so that the cross and window were positioned just
above Dr. King's right shoulder. King's face, the folds of his robe, the
cross, and the window would be glowing with natural light; the rest of
the picture would be somber, almost totally dark. During my years at
Look, I had developed the capacity to hear an imaginary bell ring with
each click of the camera when the picture promised to be extraordinary.
Now I was hearing one bell after another.

"If this picture's half as good as I think . . ." I said as we got in the
car.

"Well, I don't know," Cal said. He was a great worrier.

Doug Kiker set up an appointment for us with Calvin L. Craig, the Grand
Dragon of the Georgia Ku Klux Klan. We drove to his house on the south
side of Atlanta at eight in the evening. He met us at the door of a rather
modest dwelling, but didn't invite us in. Instead, he guided us around to
the back yard, where there was a one-room building: his headquarters.
He got us inside and started showing us a variety of KKK literature.
Craig was a large man with a round face and sensitive, rather hurt-looking
brown eyes. He told us that several other Klansmen would soon be coming over to be in the picture, as we had requested. I asked him if they
would all have their robes, and he assured me they would. I got my notebook out and started asking questions. I learned that he ran Craig's Dry
Cleaning and that he was disturbed by the current public image of the
Klan.

"We are for the Christian Protestant religion, the U.S. government and
Constitution thereof, and, of course, white supremacy."

Craig spoke in a deep voice, as formal in its way as Dr. King's. The
Klan, he said, opposed violence. I had learned from my newspaper sources
that eight of the nine men arrested in a recent anti-integration riot at the
University of Georgia were Klansmen, but I let that go. Craig said that it
was the Communists who were really behind integration. He probably
would have said the Jews as well as the Communists, except for wanting
to be polite in Cal's presence.

In his cramped headquarters, Craig seemed ill at ease, and so did we. The interview was proceeding, but there were uncomfortable silences on both sides. Suddenly Craig brightened.

"We made a record," he said. He reached over to a shelf and handed me a 45 rpm disk. The label was printed — rather cheaply, it appeared — in red ink: "The Klansman."

"Would you like to hear it?"

"By all means," I said.

He put it on a portable record player and stood back with a pleased look on his face. Chords on a church organ introduced a baritone voice singing of our country's dire peril and calling on members of the Klan to protect the honor of our women and children. The effect was so sentimental and lugubrious — it sounded as if the turntable had been slowed down — that I had to struggle to keep from laughing. It ended with a long, almost entirely unmusical phrase about the pledge of the knights of the Ku Klux Klan to keep our nation free and to fight for truth and liberty.

By then I had controlled my desire to laugh (a good thing, since Craig kept looking into my eyes to check my reaction), and I asked if I could buy one of the records. He said they cost a dollar but he would be pleased to give me one free. I took the record, thinking of how much fun it was going to be to play it for my *Look* colleagues in New York and my friends back in San Francisco. I found myself almost liking Craig. Up close, he was not a terrifying racist avenger but just another guy eager to please, to be understood, to be liked.

But when he put on his Grand Dragon's uniform — vivid green robe, green and blue hood, tall pointed green headpiece with gold dragon insignia — he was fearsome and demonic. No wonder. He was wearing an outfit designed to terrify blacks and any white person who might dare support their cause.

Cal shot his portrait out in the yard. He had Craig up close, lit from the left so that his face appeared as a lurid half-moon. In the background, lit from the front against the black night, were three Klansmen wearing white robes trimmed in red. One of them had a red headpiece and hood, and a red mask covering his face. Once again I could hear bells ringing every time Cal tripped his shutter.

We arrived at the photo store as soon as the film was ready. The pictures of Martin Luther King happened to be in the same batch as those of Calvin Craig. I stood watching as Cal opened one little yellow box after another, glancing at three or four slides in each box to make sure that there was at least an image on the film. In the car he looked at the slides through a portable magnifying viewing box. Now and then he silently passed the viewer to me. There was King in his robe, and there was Craig in his robe. The juxtaposition of the two images was overwhelming.

Cal looked both pleased and worried. "They're not bad. It would still be nice if we could get Lester Maddox."

"We'll get Maddox," I said.

If we couldn't get pictures of Ben Brown sitting in at a lunch counter, we could at least get him in the forbidden act of sitting in the front of an Atlanta bus. Cal and Ben waited at a northbound Peachtree bus stop. I sat in our car half a block back, motor running. A bus pulled up, Cal and Ben got on, the bus started off, and I pulled up close behind.

People were waiting at the next bus stop, but oddly enough, the bus passed them by and in fact increased its speed. It also sped past the following bus stop, despite a group of frantically waving people, and went through a traffic signal on the yellow. I followed on the red. Now the bus was going between 45 and 50 in a 25 mph zone, weaving crazily through the rather light late-morning traffic, passing every bus stop, running traffic lights. I couldn't see what was going on inside the bus. What if Cal and Ben were being beaten by a bunch of bus-riding racists? I stood on my horn. For racists, the only thing worse than a black riding in the front of a bus was a black being photographed riding in the front of a bus.

Now what the hell was I going to do? I remembered that yesterday we had had a candid and genial interview with Atlanta police chief Herbert Jenkins. I pulled into a filling station, tires squealing, ran to a pay phone, and demanded to speak to Chief Jenkins. He was on the phone almost immediately. I told him that my photographer and a black student leader were being held captive on an Atlanta city bus. He said he would have it intercepted. I jumped into the car and spun my tires getting back on the street. I drove out Peachtree, horn blaring. Several miles north, I spotted the bus pulled into the parking lot of the Pig 'n' Whistle drive-in, one of the haunts of my teenage years. A bus company supervisor's sedan was nose to nose with the bus, and shortly after I arrived a squad car pulled in. The passengers stood around looking bewildered. Cal and Ben stood off to one side.

"What happened?" I asked Cal.

"The driver just wouldn't stop. I took my pictures. I told him I wanted to get off. Wouldn't let anybody on, wouldn't let anybody off."

I was furious. I strode around to the driver's window.

"You did the wrong thing," I shouted up to him. He was leaning on the steering wheel, looking down at me as if I were a rather loathsome but not very interesting insect. "What you did was *kidnapping*. You held two people against their will."

"You can't take pictures on this bus."

"Are you crazy? A bus is a public place. We're free to take pictures in any public place anytime we want. That's the difference between this country and the Soviet Union." I was about to accuse him of communism, but thought better of it. "Don't you know anything about our Constitution? Freedom of the press is the basis of our democracy. You did the *wrong thing.*"

Cal was standing next to me. "Let's get out of here," he said, tugging my sleeve.

Before leaving, I said it one more time, noticing that my southern accent was getting thicker with each repetition.

"You did the *wrong thang!*"

The preacher kept coming back to the same phrase, not so much spoken as intoned. Again and again he would lead his congregation to the depths of despair with stories of tyranny and injustice throughout human history. Then once more he would sing it out: *"But life cannot be fooled."* And he would tell us of the tyrant overthrown, injustice overwhelmed by the intrinsically redeeming forces of existence. His voice was like music *("Life cannot be fooled"),* bringing forth soulful cries from the congregation: *"Yes Lord!" "Praise Jesus! "Say it clear!"*

Cal and I had come early to the Ebenezer Baptist Church to get good seats for the regular Sunday service. We were near the front of a sea of black and brown faces, standing to sing the hymns with the rest, closing our eyes for the prayer by Martin Luther King, Sr., a patriarchal presence with a voice that could still a cathedral. "If we thought Martin Junior was good," Cal whispered, "his father is even better." But then Martin Junior, the assistant pastor, began the sermon, and within minutes we, with all the congregation, were transfixed.

The message was simple. Creation, justice, harmony — these are the ultimate laws of the universe. Sometimes injustice arises to challenge heaven, grows strong and seemingly irresistible. But every Napoleon has his Waterloo, every Hitler his fiery bunker in Berlin. *"Life cannot be fooled."* King approached his subject philosophically, historically, religiously, and emotionally, switching from one mode to another with an inexorable rhythm. He quoted Nietzsche, Kierkegaard, Schopenhauer, and Gandhi. He sketched the story of Israel's flight from Egypt in a dazzling two-minute vignette. He drew a picture of the African slave ships so compelling that had he continued another minute, he would have had the congregation crying aloud. Then, unwilling to let us lose ourselves in emotion, he brought us back with a telling point from the *Nicomachean Ethics,* and reminded us of our duty to live according to universal law, even if it meant suffering and death.

During this incredible performance, Martin Luther King, Sr., would sometimes hit the arm of the great oak chair in which he sat and laugh aloud with wonder. At one point a voice from the back of the church rang out: "Preach! Preach! That man can preach!" Cal and I, like all the others there, were swaying in rhythm with King's words, and though the church was cool, our faces were wet with perspiration and tears. Now and then I could hear Cal saying "Yes, Lord!" along with the rest of the congregation, and I heard myself doing the same. Once Cal leaned over to me and whispered, "Too bad this isn't being recorded. Everyone in the country should hear it." "Maybe we're not ready for it," I whispered back. "It's too beautiful."

That's how it was for me: nearly too beautiful to bear. The church became a mythic place. The passing moment seemed balanced on the knife edge of history and timelessness. Colors were more vivid than usual. In his dark robe, King stood before us like a prophet. His faintly oriental eyes glistened with ancient knowledge, and he spoke of human destiny with the vehemence and majesty of music.

Ralph McGill, publisher of the *Atlanta Constitution,* had been one of my heroes as far back as I could remember. His daily front-page column was a beacon of light for Atlanta and the whole South. He had fought the good fight against bigotry, and had paid the price. We sat in his office, and he told us about obscene letters, threats on his life, a bullet fired through his front door. He talked in the casual, offhand way that people regularly under fire have of dismissing personal danger. He told of how his young teenage son had recently picked up the phone to be greeted with a stream of obscenity; he had simply held the phone away from his ear and said, "It's for you, Dad."

After we had talked for a half hour or so and Cal had taken close-ups for our gallery of portraits, McGill leaned forward and said, "I have some stuff you might be interested in."

All at once the atmosphere in the room was somehow different. I found myself glancing at the closed door.

"It seems," he continued, "that Martin Luther King has a rather color-ful sex life."

"What do you mean?" I asked.

"Well, the FBI has been on his tail, and they've got some interesting stuff. Orgies. That kind of thing."

My mind was spinning. A series of priorities flashed before my mind's eye, then a quick, firm decision. "You know, I'm really not interested in Martin Luther King's sex life. That's his private life. That's his business."

McGill was a bit taken aback. "I thought it might be pertinent to what you're doing."

"I don't think so," I said.

We left a few minutes later. I thought, McGill's a hero, but he's still part of my father's generation. I thought, What if it's true about King? I thought, Nothing's as simple and clear as it seems.

It was after midnight, and the steering committee of the Committee on Appeal for Human Rights still hadn't decided on a strategy for the big demonstration to be held on February 1, 1961, the first anniversary of the sit-ins. Everyone agreed that Rich's, Atlanta's largest department store, would be a major target. But should the students sit and run, or sit and stay? Should they march through Rich's, or just march around it? Should they take jail with bail, jail with no bail, or should they avoid going to jail? The small classroom was crowded, and everybody was so tired that it was easy to get a laugh.

"We are now entering the period of the year when our Lord was crucified," Lonnie King said, and there was a good chuckle all around. King (not related to Martin Luther King) had been a Morehouse College fullback, and now, at twenty-four, was chairman of the committee. "We should, as far as possible, initiate action in the basic areas of our present concerns: the segregation of eating and drinking facilities, job discrimination in the stores, and the segregation of theaters. Let's keep talking, and I'm sure we'll arrive at a synthesis on this thing soon."

Someone came up with a new tactic. A group of very light-skinned students would buy theater tickets. They would keep the stubs and show them to the manager later, thus proving that the theater had already been desegregated.

"And we can send Middlebrooks in his turban," Leon Green said. There was an explosion of laughter. Middlebrooks, the group's jokester, was known to appear at times as an Indian guru.

All the lights went out. When they came back on a few seconds later, a questioning look passed around the room. Was it a signal? A student quickly and silently got up and left the room.

Later, when every option had been considered and still no decision had been made, Ben Brown suddenly jumped to his feet.

"I've got it," he said. "First we'll write the press release, then we'll know what to do."

There was a moment of silence, then a hubbub of approval. It was a brilliant clarification. At the dawn of the media age, Ben Brown had pared the situation down to its essence. The appeal for human rights was first of all an appeal to the media of communication. The Atlanta students, along with other members of the movement, were putting their bodies, maybe their lives, on the line to force the white community to show its true face, to reveal the bigotry and injustice that had been hidden for generations behind lies and rationalizations and chivalrous circumlocutions. But without the media to show that face abroad, their actions would be like a tree falling in the deep woods, heard by no one.

Still later, the press release had been outlined, and the basic plan had come clear. Up to a thousand students would meet on the campus on the morning of Wednesday, February 1. After singing and praying, they would march to downtown Atlanta. Then separate teams would peel off the main group. Each team would circle one block, carrying signs directed at stores on that block. On that day and the days and weeks to follow, they would continue sitting in. A car equipped by students with a two-way radio would cruise the town. When an open lunch counter was spotted, the radio car would call headquarters, and a "guerrilla team" of sit-inners would be dispatched to the counter.

The press release would stress goodwill and a desire to work harmoniously with the merchants. The demonstration of February 1 would be nonconfrontational. But if lunch counter segregation wasn't ended, the students would begin a "jail-in" campaign, refusing to post bail when arrested. They would, if necessary, fill the jails. They would not rest until Atlanta was fully desegregated.

We stopped in at the Pickrick in midafternoon. At that time of day, no matter what happened, we wouldn't have to eat any more fried chicken.

"Tell me, Mr. Maddox," I said, "what sign *would* you stand in front of?"

"You'd have to let me think on that, Br'er Leonard."

"Let me put it this way: What *do* you stand for? Exactly what *are* you proud of?"

He thought for what seemed a long time. "Well, I might stand in front of a sign that said 'Americans Unwilling to Surrender Constitutional Government and States' Rights.' "

"Let me write that down." I printed his words in capital letters and showed them to him. "Let's shake on it." He took my hand with not much enthusiasm. "We'll be back in about an hour."

We stopped the car at the first phone booth we could find, and I looked up a sign shop in the yellow pages. I explained what I wanted and said price was no object. "If you can have it ready in a half hour, I'll pay double, triple your regular price." The man at the sign shop said no, that wouldn't be necessary. The regular price was $8.75, and he would have it ready in about thirty minutes.

The sign was exactly what we wanted: Maddox's words in big block letters of red, painted on a three-by-five-foot poster board. We put it in the car very carefully, since the paint was still wet. We drove back to the

Pickrick and balanced the sign on a wall outside the restaurant. Then we asked Maddox to stand in front of it. Cal shot his picture so that the sign entirely filled the vertical frame, with the oval of Maddox's head appearing in the lower right corner. When Cal had finished, I got Maddox to sign a photo release, and we bid him goodbye. As we left, he said, "Y'all come on up anytime you want some good fried chicken."

We noticed that he didn't ask us to stay segregated.

The gym floor was covered with an aqua-green plastic cloth, and everybody was dancing to the soulful beat of the student band. It was Monday night, just two days before the big demonstration, and the Committee on Appeal for Human Rights was holding what was billed as the Flunkers' Ball. "If we're all gonna flunk from missing so many classes," Ben Brown explained, "we figured we might just as well celebrate it." The dance was actually a pep rally for the coming demonstration.

Cal and I sat on the second row of bleacher seats and let the music and rhythm and color wash over us. I felt more relaxed than I had for two weeks. We had all our portraits and interviews, and we had our picture story on Ben Brown and our notes on the student movement and on Atlanta in general. We would shoot the demonstration Wednesday, and then I would go home to San Francisco for a few days before flying to New York for layout.

For now, I could simply surrender to the music echoing all around me and the motion swirling before my eyes. The dancers were beautiful. The color of their skin ranged from a shining ebony to a light tan, and they dressed with a cool collegiate chic: sweaters, jackets with natural shoulders. Most of the young women wore Capezios, and some wore white leather coats. Cal and I smiled as one male student swept by in an Inverness cape. They danced their own version of the continental and then the Indiana stomp, both to a medium bounce tempo. I began to experience a sensation of déjà vu. Everything was strangely familiar. I felt that somehow I had come home, not to the Atlanta of my childhood but to something else.

The music stopped and the Spellman College girls were summoned to the front. They poured through the crowd like water through a sieve. They took their places in front of the bandstand, linked hands, and began singing, really singing out, their voices clear and reedy and rich in overtones, and sometimes clapping their hands high above their heads like the flutter and rush of a flock of birds taking off. After a few Spellman songs, they crossed their arms in front of their bodies and clasped hands, and everyone in the auditorium joined them, and they all began singing solemnly, reverently:

We shall overcome,
We shall overcome,
We shall overcome some day.

The anthem was one I had never heard before, its words a simple affirmation, its melody so haunting that I took a piece of folded paper from my jacket pocket and wrote down the notes to remind me in case I didn't hear it again.

The music and the dancing resumed, and again I was struck by the sense of déjà vu. There was something almost painfully familiar about the young men and women dancing so gracefully in front of my eyes — the lift of a chin, the set of eyebrows, the glint of eyes. Then the realization hit me. The reason the dancers seemed so familiar was that some of them could have been my cousins. There was almost as much Anglo-Saxon as African blood in the young blacks on this dance floor. *I was surrounded by my kinfolk.*

The enormity of our southern history stunned me. It was hard to face the horror that had created all of this: the routine rape of female slaves by their white owners. I had always known, just as every southerner had always known, for our deepest, most shameful secret was plainly written on the faces around us. But we had managed to pretend — what insanity! — that neither the horror nor the beauty existed. And now, thanks to the courage of people such as those dancing here in this gym, everything that had been hidden away was to be examined and acknowledged. Nothing was to be left undisturbed. The music and rhythm and color dissolved, and I was enveloped in a magical silence, knowing that the suffering of the past could be redeemed only by more suffering, and by love.

Victory in the second Battle of Atlanta was nearly certain. The voices of commerce, of enlightened self-interest, had spoken clearly: We must avoid what happened at New Orleans and Little Rock. "We're a city too busy to hate," Mayor William B. Hartsfield had told me. "When racists come to *this* town, they know they're going to get their heads knocked together." The battle was not over. There would be more confrontation, and many students would probably still have to go to jail to demonstrate that they were not bluffing. But I now felt sure that by September the lunch counters and the schools would be desegregated. And Atlanta's example, despite the pain and tragedy still to come in other parts of the South, would prove decisive in the long run. The second battle of Atlanta would go down in history not because it was a violent battle but because it wasn't one.

*

The sermon neared its end. The words that had held us in a spell became more stately in cadence and tone. In spite of all the tortured years of slavery and suffering, Dr. King told us, "the wonderful Negro people" had prevailed over injustice, transmuting bitterness to compassion in a crucible of love that might now constitute a great redeeming force in the world. The civil rights movement, he said, was offering us a chance to join our lives with the flow of the universe. The mighty would fall. The songs of slaves and sharecroppers would rise to the heights of earth and heaven. Even the most glittering tyrant eventually would learn how futile it is to stand on the beaches of history and try to hold back the tide.

The sermon ended, the prayer, the benediction. Unrecorded, the precise words slipped away, but I knew the experience would stay with me long after I left Atlanta. *"Life cannot be fooled."*

6

The Border Held the Fascination
of a Nightmare

"I THINK it's a tougher assignment than you realize," Ed Korry told me. "The East-West border has always been a sensitive area. But now . . ."

Korry shook his head and smiled at me — rather pityingly, I thought — from across the table at Sardi's East in New York City. It was September 19, 1961. Construction of the Berlin Wall had begun a month ago, and the work was still going on. Just the previous weekend, in fact, there had been reports of new efforts by the East Germans to reinforce and enlarge the wall against the continuing trickle of refugees attempting to run, swim, or batter their way into West Berlin.

"It's an extremely tense time in Europe," Korry continued. "You'll need contacts in every host country."

"We're contacting everybody we can here in New York," I said. "Consulate people, official tourist representatives."

"I mean contacts on the scene," Korry said patiently. "*Local* contacts."

Korry, a tall, balding man with heavy glasses and a smile that was both genial and domineering, was *Look*'s European editor, based in Paris. His predecessor, Bill Attwood, had taken a leave of absence from *Look* to work on the Kennedy campaign, and had been rewarded with an appointment as ambassador to Guinea. Korry made little effort to hide his ambitions along the same lines, and he used his job to make as many Foreign Service contacts as he could. He happened to be in New York the same time I was, and I was pleased to get as much of his advice as I could.

I had first heard of the assignment less than a week ago in San Francisco. The idea had originated with Fletcher Knebel of *Look*'s Washington bureau. Knebel had sent a brief memo to Dan Mich. The Berlin Wall, he wrote, reminded him of something that most Americans didn't even realize: The Iron Curtain wasn't a mere figure of speech. It was a physical barrier of barbed wire, minefields, watchtowers, and armed patrols stretching from Finland to Iran, a distance of more than six thousand miles, three times the length of the Great Wall of China. Knebel proposed that *Look* trace the entire barrier, photographing it at key spots all along its length.

I wondered if Korry thought it strange that I rather than he got the assignment. Actually, it might have seemed strange to almost anyone that I would be plucked up from the western edge of the United States and sent all the way to Europe and the Middle East. But *Look*'s journalistic beats were by no means geographical. Dan Mich simply sent whomever he wanted to do a story, regardless of location. And though I dreaded the travel and the possible dangers, I was eager to go. Momentous things were happening all around the world. In the American South, the walls between people were beginning to crumble and a spirit of hope was in the air, while in Berlin a new wall was going up. I wanted to know why. I wanted to look beyond the conventional sociological and geopolitical explanations. I wanted to understand why there were walls in the first place. Was there some essential combativeness, some xenophobia, in human nature? Or was society flawed in some fundamental way? I wasn't particularly drawn to physical adventure; it was something else, an undefined desire for a new understanding of the human puzzle, that fascinated me.

Waiting for lunch to be served; I sipped a Lowenbrau and explained my basic plan to Korry. Photographer Paul Fusco and I would start at the Finnish-Soviet border in Lapland, nearly two hundred miles above the Arctic Circle. Then we would go to the border between East and West Germany, east of Hamburg. From there we would visit the Bavarian-Czech border in the Bohemian Forest. Next we would go to the Austrian-Hungarian border not far from Vienna. After that we would make our way to the Greek-Bulgarian border north of Salonika. Our last border segment would be the one between Iran and the Soviet Union, north of Tabriz. To cap it off, we'd fly back to Berlin to photograph the wall itself. But we'd do more than just photograph the physical Iron Curtain. All along, we'd show the day-by-day existence of the people on the western side who lived near it. And I would write an essay to wrap up the package.

When I finished talking, Korry just shook his head.

"How long do you think it'll take us?" I asked.

He paused for a moment. "I'd say that with good local contacts, you could do it in six weeks. Without contacts, three months."

I felt a slight jolt in my solar plexus. "I couldn't stand to be away from home three months," I said. "We'll make it, without contacts, in less than six weeks."

"Would you care to lay a bet on that?" Korry asked.

"Sure, any amount," I said. But I managed very quickly to change the subject.

Nine P.M., Friday, September 22. Pan Am's nonstop 707 from New York to Helsinki was taking off on time, with very few people on board. Paul Fusco and I, in fact, were the only passengers in the first-class cabin. Light on passengers but heavy on fuel, the 707 took a long time getting off the ground, and I found myself leaning forward as if to help it gain speed. Once in the air, the plane angled sharply upward. I breathed deeply, loosened my seat belt, and reclined the back of my seat. Paul and I exchanged grins, then I pressed by forehead against the window to gaze at the lights of Long Island as we climbed northeastward. It was an unusually clear night, full of stars, with a nearly full moon riding along above us. After a while I turned from the window and leaned my head back against the seat.

Now it was beginning, and who knew how it would turn out. I let myself enjoy a luxurious sense of possibilities: vague presentiments of success and fulfillment, without shape or form. Maybe, though, we couldn't pull it off. Ed Korry had said that we might not be allowed anywhere near the border at certain places we had chosen. But I couldn't believe we would fail.

I glanced at Paul. He was reading the *New York Times* very carefully, every word of it. I was glad to have him along. He was one of the newer photographers on the staff — we had done only one previous story together — but he had already proved himself to be one of the best. Some of the old-time *Look* photographers were monuments to the human ability to resist sophistication. But Paul was constantly studying, practicing, learning — seeking not only to improve his craft but also to understand the world. He had been a decorated combat photographer in Korea, and had graduated magna cum laude in fine arts from Ohio University. Owing to the fact that he was extremely taciturn (he rarely initiated a conversation), most *Look* staffers were unaware of his intellect. But no one who had worked with him could be unaware of his integrity and courage. He would never, in any way or under any circumstances, falsify a picture. And at age thirty-one, five-eleven, and 145 pounds, he was the most physically gifted photographer on the staff. He moved like a cat, and would go anywhere for a picture. Paul had a wonderful smile, broad and luminous, made all the more interesting as a contrast to the habitual brooding quality of his countenance. With slim hips, broad shoulders, large blue eyes, and a craggy jaw, he might easily be mistaken, I thought, for an Italian movie star.

Time passed. The coast of Newfoundland was behind us, and we were out over the open ocean. Paul was dozing and I, who could rarely sleep on a plane, was sitting in one of the front seats, chatting with the purser and one of the flight-attendants, telling them about my experiences as a pilot in World War II. The door to the flight deck opened and the captain went into a lavatory. When he came out, he walked back and joined us.

"Say, Captain," the purser said. "This guy was a World War II pilot too."

"What did you fly?" the captain asked me.

"I instructed in B-25s, then I did my missions in A-20s. Southwest Pacific."

"I was in C-54s. Flew the Pacific run for a while."

"I got a ride over in a C-54. Maybe you flew me."

"When was that?" the captain asked.

"March forty-five. Very late in the war."

"No, I was stateside then." He looked around the first-class cabin. No one was to be seen except Paul, and he was sleeping. "Would you like to come up front for a while?"

"Love to," I said casually, trying to mask my enthusiasm.

I followed the captain onto the flight deck. He introduced me to the flight engineer and the first officer, and pulled down the jump seat so that I could sit between him and the first officer. I had flown jet fighters on *Look* assignments, but had never before been up front in a commercial jet in flight. I sat there and let my eyes absorb the marvels all around me, as happy as any five-year-old on Christmas morning. I concentrated on the flight instruments and the major engine instruments, quickly translating mathematical abstractions to less abstract matters of speed, altitude, position, temperature. Only then did I open my eyes to the magnificent view of the night (so different from what can be seen from a passenger's window): the vast, silvery sky, the faintly gleaming metallic surface seven miles below. Unexpectedly, a voice came from the loudspeaker above my head, startlingly clear and intimate, a voice from a plane a hundred miles or so ahead, telling us that there was absolutely no turbulence, that the night was clear, that the air was as smooth as silk. How magical it seemed: a voice filling our cockpit and our consciousness, emanating from another spark of consciousness suspended somewhere high above the ocean among the stars, just as we were. I felt as wide awake as I had ever felt, and totally relaxed, my every sense in harmony with all that was in me and around me.

Suddenly a red warning light on the instrument panel went on. Just that. It had not been on and now it was on.

"Check the fluid levels," the captain said.

"No problem there," the flight engineer said. "Open the system interconnect?"

"Not yet."

Something was wrong with the hydraulic system. It was not a trivial system. If it failed completely, the pilot would be unable to control the plane.

"Pressure's below normal but stable," the first officer said.

"Keep watching it," the captain said calmly.

As the crew members went on talking, I found myself not at all frightened or even anxious. What I felt was a deep, almost hypnotic fascination with the dangerous puzzle unfolding before me. The captain didn't ask me to return to the cabin, and I was glad of that; I would have been terrified, not knowing what was going on. Nobody spoke to me, but I was there, a silent witness to the slightest waver in the magical dials and needles glowing on the instrument panel, the slightest nuance in the voices of the crew. By now the moon was low in the west behind us, and the stars were gaining a new dominance over the night. How lively, how friendly, how close they seemed. Whatever happened would be all right. The stars were where they should be, and the calm, laconic conversation in the cockpit was like music.

Up ahead and to the left, a huge flat cloud gathered shape, low on the horizon, floating just above the surface of the ocean. I kept glancing at it as we came closer. What a strange cloud — so shiny, so fixed in its position. Then I realized it was Greenland.

So here we were in midpassage, at the point of no return, nothing but water and ice all around, and there was that red light glowing steadily on the instrument panel. We passed Greenland with its ghostly, gleaming falls of ice. Near the coast, a single light shined up at us. What could it be? I didn't ask, not only out of consideration for the crew's task but to avoid breaking the spell. My silence was a part of that spell.

Later: a floor of clouds far below, pale light in the east, and the flight engineer's voice: "We've got a high temperature reading on number three engine."

I had been getting slightly drowsy, but now I was wide awake again. Should we shut down number three engine? Not yet, the crew decided. But if the temperature rose any higher . . . we sailed along at 38,000 feet. The sun burned its way up out of the bank of low clouds. The radio crackled with technical and logistical talk, a discourse on matters of life and death that was electric in its very calmness. We would land in Stockholm rather than Helsinki; better maintenance facilities. I said nothing. I was deeply involved.

At last they shut down the number three engine, the crew members like priests, consulting the operating manual as if it were a holy book, reading each item on the checklist aloud, passing their hands across instruments and switches, moving levers and knobs in a sequence as inexorable and charged with taboo as any holy rite, the least deviation from which might bring disaster.

An hour out of Stockholm, doing just fine on three engines and a faulty hydraulic system, we were flying into the sun over a floor of blindingly white clouds that stretched as far as we could see in every direction. Time for me to go back to the cabin.

"Interesting flight," the captain said as I took my leave.

"Very. I really appreciate your letting me stay."

"Nice having you."

"We want to cooperate with you every way we can," a Finnish colonel in Helsinki told us. "But you see, we have a treaty of peace and friendship with Russia, signed in 1948. It's not that we particularly wanted this treaty. But we are realists. Russia is a large, powerful country. And we —" He raised his hands in a gesture of resignation. "According to the treaty, we must not let anyone take pictures within three kilometers of the border. We are allowed no information about the territory on the other side. I hope you understand."

We agreed to abide with the restriction on photography. Still, we wanted to go to the border and see it for ourselves. We wanted to photograph the native Lapps who lived near the border. More than anything, we wanted to get pictures of Arctic reindeer to show how far north this end of the Iron Curtain extended. The colonel said he would put us in touch with the border police and would help us get an interpreter.

Our emergency landing in Stockholm had made us twelve hours late getting to Helsinki. We had missed our Saturday appointment with the colonel, which had made us miss our Monday flight to Ivalo, a small town in Lapland near the Soviet-Finnish border 175 miles north of the Arctic Circle. If we waited for the next scheduled flight on Thursday, our whole schedule for the next several weeks would be thrown out of kilter. I phoned Finnair. Could they charter us a small plane to Ivalo for this afternoon? They had no small planes, but they did have a DC-3 available after ten P.M. The charter fee would be sixty-eight thousand finnmarks, about three hundred U.S. dollars. That much for just flying me, Paul Fusco, and our interpreter? Yes, there would still have to be a crew of three — pilot, copilot, and flight attendant — even if there were only three passengers. Regulations.

I thought for a moment, then said we would take it. I went down to the Finnair office to sign a five-page aircraft charter agreement, which specified, among other things, that the "service en route" would be "coffee/tea with bread."

It was a miserable flight. We were in the thick fog the whole way, and the DC-3 bounced around like a cork in boiling water. The cabin was too cold, and the fact that there were only three passengers aboard made it seem even colder. I had no desire for the tea and sweet bread our flight attendant offered us halfway through the flight, but took it anyway. After all, it was part of our contract.

Our interpreter, it turned out, was something of a prig. He was a rather handsome twenty-five-year-old, with a fair complexion and blond hair combed straight back and plastered to his scalp. He questioned us about the racial uprisings in America. He claimed that he wasn't hostile toward the Negroes; he simply couldn't believe that there could ever be any kind of equality between the races. Paul tried to explain, at first patiently, then with increasing exasperation. Our interpreter wouldn't let it go. The argument went on and on as we jolted and wallowed northward.

Officers of the Finnish border police received us the next morning with the somber hospitality of a people who have always confronted a chilling world. The major in command showed us a map of his territory, served coffee and cake, and sent us off with a young first lieutenant. We drove in our rented car toward the border, across flat, rock-strewn country not yet covered with snow. It was only about forty degrees, not nearly as cold as I had expected. Three kilometers from the frontier, Paul photographed a sign marking the frontier zone. Then he put his cameras away, and we drove on to the Finnish border post, in clear view of the two Russian watchtowers.

The lieutenant in charge was a rough-hewn man who had risen through the ranks. His twenty-five years of service were almost over, and he was in an expansive mood as he insisted that we join him for coffee and cake.

"The only problem up here," he told us, "is reindeer. We have a fence to keep them from going over to Russia. When they go, the Russians don't return them. . . . We have no way of knowing what's on the other side. The only thing I know is that two weeks ago a two-hundred-and-fifty-pound bear from Russia broke through the fence, tore the barbed wire clean."

Human beings, he said, don't often do that well. "It really *is* an Iron Curtain," said the first lieutenant, our escort. "We only know that no Russian civilians live anywhere near the border."

When we stepped outside, Paul started to wave at the Russian watchtower. "Do you wave at them?" he asked the Finns.

The lieutenant looked at us with an ironic smile. "We have generally," he said, "not waved at them."

After returning the lieutenant to his post, we started driving aimlessly around the tundra, asking anyone we might meet for the whereabouts of a reindeer roundup. We drove all day as the sun worked its way around the horizon. We found no signs of reindeer.

"It's too early in the year," our interpreter said. "Too bad you didn't come later. You'll never find a roundup."

The next day we started again. I drove, and we took every side road we came to, traversing great areas of flat land and bare hills, not knowing exactly where we were or how we would get back. The sky turned gray; a misty rain was falling. Then, far ahead and to the right of the road, I noticed a perturbation of the earth, a sort of elongated movement in the distance.

"I wonder what that is," I said.

We came closer, as close as we could along the little dirt road.

"It's a goddam reindeer roundup," Paul said.

I stopped the car and he was out in a flash, two cameras around his neck, a camera bag slung on his shoulder, walking as fast as he could straight toward the distant movement. I jumped out and caught up with him. The interpreter followed several steps behind.

"You can't just walk out there," he said. "These people are Lapps. I can't interpret for you."

We came to a low fence and Paul went over it as if it weren't there. I followed, as did the interpreter. Now I was two steps behind Paul and the interpreter was falling farther back, stumbling on loose rocks like a young dog being pulled along on a long leash.

"A roundup is a ceremonial event," he called to us. "Outsiders aren't allowed. I can't interpret for you."

"Just keep smiling," Paul said. He had a big grin on his face.

There were hundreds of reindeer, a sea of antlers. They were in a large corral, running full speed, eight to ten abreast, in a great circle. Their mouths were open, breath steaming. In the open area in the middle of the circle were Lapps in their ceremonial costumes: oversized four-pointed hats of red and midnight blue, suits of the same dark blue with red and yellow trim. They carried lassos, and somehow they were picking their own deer out of the swirling herd. As we came closer, we could feel the earth vibrating.

"You must *not* go into the corral," our interpreter called as we approached the corral fence. "It's *not allowed*."

Without a moment's hesitation, Paul started climbing the fence. Several of the Lapps were staring at us. Paul answered their dark looks with a broad smile. I reluctantly followed him over the fence, forcing a big smile. Our interpreter stayed outside. Paul kept walking. I followed, two steps behind. And sooner than I thought possible, having no idea how I got there, I found myself not in the clear center of the circle, but precisely in the middle of the stream of onrushing reindeer. Paul was a few yards downstream, taking pictures as fast as he could.

Before I had a chance to worry about being trampled to death, I saw that the reindeer were veering off to either side of us at the last moment, just as a roaring mountain stream splits around a rock, passing by close on either side, then rejoining. I faced the reindeer, and in a needless but somehow satisfying gesture directed them right and left, as a police officer directs traffic.

"This is *great*, George!" Paul shouted above the thundering sound.

I trusted the reindeer's intention to avoid hitting us, but couldn't help noticing that one would occasionally slip while trying to veer around us. I kept directing traffic, using body English to help keep them from slipping and being slammed into us by the momentum of the charge. I turned to glance at Paul. He was using his 180 mm lens. He was shooting the head herdsman, who appeared to be up to his chest in a turbulent sea of reindeer bodies and antlers.

We were standing at the middle of a river on the end of a bridge. The East Germans had torn down their half of it, leaving the western half jutting out over the water. From our vantage point, we could see a two-man East German patrol approaching from the left and another from the right. Both were quite distant. We watched them with binoculars as they followed the twists and turns of the freshly plowed death strip between two barbed wire fences.

Suddenly one of the guards approaching from the right jumped as if a bullet had whizzed past his ear. He had spotted Paul's cameras. The two guards darted behind a bush. They remained there warily peering out now and then, but always drawing their heads back when Paul so much as feinted in their direction. Now the guards coming from the left were hiding too.

For three days we visited the border between the two Germanys. The West German government had furnished a Mercedes, a driver who (judging from the way he drove) was sorry he was too young to have been in the Luftwaffe, and a charming female interpreter. We could go up to the border wherever we wished. On a North Sea beach on the Priwall Peninsula, we saw West German children playing almost in the shadow of East German watchtowers. The beach on the other side of the fence was completely deserted. It was clear that the Iron Curtain was designed not to keep westerners out but to keep eastern bloc citizens in.

Near the border city of Lübeck, we ran into a well-dressed young man standing in the rain at a barrier.

"Why do you come here?" I asked.

"It's interesting."

"What's interesting about it?"

He shrugged his shoulders.

"Do you come often?"

"Yes. I'm a student. I come here almost every day after class."

"What do you see here?"

"The guards pass near here — maybe something will happen."

We stood watching. The rain was falling steadily, and everything was quiet. A crow was cawing in the distance, and a large dog barked near the East German guard post, about a hundred yards away. Since Paul had his cameras with him, a guard was hiding behind a tree, peering out only now and then.

Some five miles south, at the village of Rothenhausen, we talked with a well-to-do man from Hamburg who had a vacation cottage within sight of East Germany.

"For you to understand our feelings about this border, you must imagine an uncrossable barrier down the middle of the United States. One gets used to it. What can you do? Still, it is very strange."

The border held the fascination of an anachronism or a nightmare. At every accessible point, the West Germans came to look. They drove up in gleaming Mercedes-Benzes or neat little Volkswagens. They strolled to the border in the manner of sightseers approaching some Point of Interest. They took out binoculars. They leaned down to their children and tried to explain the watchtowers, the barbed wire, the plowed death strip, the armed guards. It was hard to read their faces.

"It's a routine operation," the young U.S. army captain said with a knowing smile. "You just happen to be going along."

The helicopter was beating its way toward the West German – Czech border in the Bohemian Forest on a beautiful early October morning. The eight soldiers the captain had brought with him were dressed in combat gear and fully armed. They sat motionless in bucket seats, their faces fixed in the still, sober expressions of men going into battle. As we approached the border, the captain pointed out a line of watchtowers, and the fence itself.

"It's eight feet high and electrified. It can kill a large animal. Or a man, of course."

As we descended, the soldiers rose and stood at the door. We touched down, the door opened, and the men hit the ground running. They fanned out to form a squad front, facing the fence. Paul and I and the captain jumped out and walked forward until we were in front of the line of soldiers.

We had landed in a broad meadow, which descended gently some 150 yards to the fence, partially hidden in bushes and undergrowth at this point. Three Czech watchtowers were in plain view. About 150 yards to the right of us, on a slight rise, was an American Jeep on which a machine gun was mounted. A soldier was manning the gun. The soldiers who had been in the helicopter took their positions in a line between the helicopter and the fence. They were kneeling on one knee, guns at the ready. Paul and I and the captain started walking toward the fence.

"Right now," the captain said, "we're being watched by twenty-five or thirty people with binoculars, and you won't see them. It's a sneaky thing. You can't explain it."

When we got about fifty yards from the fence, the captain spoke to me in a low voice: "Look closely. There're troops right ahead of us, hiding in the bushes. They're armed." He reached down, unsnapped the holster of his .45 automatic, and snapped off the safety.

My God, I thought, we're about to start World War III just so Paul can get some pictures. We were being covered by a machine gun and eight carbines, and God knows how many Communist guns were lined up on us.

"This is far enough," the captain said. Paul came to a reluctant stop about fifteen yards from the fence. There was an unearthly silence. I was filled with a sense of desolation.

"It's awfully quiet," I said.

"I know," the captain said. "It's hard to believe, but even the night creatures don't sing over there."

Paul was pacing back and forth ("like a cat," the captain said), trying to get a clear view of the Czech soldiers in the bushes. But they ducked whenever he raised his camera.

"No photography!" one of the Czechs snapped in English.

"This is free country where I'm standing," Paul barked back.

"Really read him off," the captain said to me with a smile.

I sat on the ground to get a steadier view with my binoculars. There was a Czech officer just across the border in dense undergrowth. When Paul moved away from me, the Czech let me see his face, but always kept it hidden from Paul.

Now Paul's frustrated pacing was bringing him within a couple of feet of the border. I mentioned this to him, and the captain reminded us of the Czech penalty for border violations: three years in the beet fields. We forced a laugh. A few moments later, the Czech officer said something to his men, and they laughed in an equally forced way.

The U.S. soldiers were calling. They motioned urgently for us to return. When we reached them, a sergeant said, "There, where the border bends around, almost behind the point where you were standing, a couple of Czechs popped up. They were sort of between you and us. We thought you should come back."

We wheeled around to look for the two Czechs who had been behind us, but now they were hiding. Back at the point we had just left, the officer stepped out from behind the bushes. Paul lifted his camera. The officer retreated. The game continued. Paul was getting an occasional partially obscured picture of a Czech soldier, but it was tough going.

Late afternoon. The sun is low and red. Our day at the border is over and we are ready to fly back to the army base near Straubing. We walk to the helicopter. It is perched on a grassy landing pad built up as high as the tops of the surrounding trees. There are children all around the helicopter, truly German children with golden hair and spots of color on their cheeks, children as young as three and as old as twelve, leaping and whirling, their faces transfigured by excitement and anticipation. We get in the helicopter and I keep looking out the window at the children. I've slept little over the past few days, and this day has been a particularly tense one. But now I feel the tension dissolving, and it seems to me that I am seeing everything around me with unusual clarity.

The engines start and the children quickly form a circle just beyond the periphery of the slowly turning rotor blades. They look at each other and laugh. The sun is about to set. It makes a flame in their hair, and their shadows are infinitely long, extending over the horizon to the ends of the universe. But what are the children doing? Why are they so happy?

The blades turn faster and the children spread their arms. Our pilot adds more power and they lean forward, their hair streaming in the wind. Some of them are leaning at forty-five-degree angles. And now, as the helicopter begins to leave the ground, they lean even farther, so that they are stretched out on the wind as if in flight, their mouths open, their cheeks round, their arms like the wings of angels. We swiftly rise and they look up at us with their faces angled charmingly one way or another, as angels might look up at God. I am transfixed, knowing that for as long as this moment lasts they really are angels, every one of them, more beautiful than any angel Michelangelo could paint.

Paul has been taking pictures of the children, and for a moment I hope for a miracle. But that's foolish. No film, no image on canvas, could ever capture a moment so everlasting yet so quickly gone. Paul and I smile at each other. We gain altitude. The sun drops down in the west.

Not for years had there been such a fine season; the vines were heavy with bunches of tiny, glowing grapes that turned to liquid at the touch. It was a warm, hazy October day in Austria. Peasant families were moving along the vines, and a young boy was sleeping on the ground between two of the rows. The vineyards stretched for as far as the eye could see to the west across plains and gently rolling land. Overhead, a flock of starlings wheeled.

A few feet to the east was a high fence topped with several strands of barbed wire. Beyond that fence lay a weed-covered minefield, a strip of plowed earth, and then another fence. A couple of hundred yards or so down the fence stood a watchtower. It appeared to be empty, although we had seen two armed men climb into it a few minutes earlier. We knew they were now hiding inside. To the east of the fence, the land lay fallow and desolate. No human life was visible, except for two Hungarian guards directly opposite us about thirty-five yards away.

The guards were hardly more than boys. They were very nervous. Both of them kept shifting their submachine guns about; one was moving his hand up and down the stock. We had heard reports of border guards firing over the heads of tourists who photographed them. Two West German journalists had recently been shot and their bodies dragged under the fence by East German guards. Paul had caught these two guards in the open and was steadily clicking away. I wondered aloud to our Austrian interpreter how they would react. He shrugged.

"If they started to shoot," said the police official accompanying us, "I wouldn't even try to shoot back. I have only a revolver."

By day we ranged along the Austrian-Hungarian border. At night we lived in luxury at the Hotel Imperial in Vienna. One evening we attended a performance of *Tosca* at the State Opera House. We had orchestra seats near the front. In the last act, Puccini pulls out all the stops. But what might normally have seemed shamelessly melodramatic now penetrated my heart. As Tosca stood on the parapet ready to leap, the whole orchestra sounded a huge, tragic chord. The bass trombones, aimed precisely in our direction, shook me to the roots. Paul began shaking with laughter, not out of humor but from an emotional overload. Our feelings were very close to the surface.

"The situation is tense," an information officer in Athens told us. "The Bulgarians are moving Greek Communists up to the border. These are men who went over to Bulgaria after they were defeated in the civil war in 1948. We fear they will infiltrate our borders. We have tightened security measures. The entire border area is restricted."

Permission for us to photograph the border had to come from the general staff of the Royal Greek Army. For two days we waited. We had left New York eighteen days ago. We visited the Acropolis on a day of pale but luminous blue, with soft white clouds sailing from north to south, filling the sky from rim to rim. We hung around the Hotel Grande Bretagne. No decision.

"Let's force the issue," I said to Paul.

We took a plane to Salonika, a lovely Aegean seaport town less than a hundred miles from the border. The next morning we had breakfast near the quay, at a spot where it was impossible to tell where the sky ended and the sea began. Everything was lucid, liquid. After breakfast we phoned Athens for permission. No decision.

"We're not getting a yes," I said, "but we're also not getting a no. Let's just start driving and keep phoning."

We drove north in a rental car so flimsy that the gearshift lever waved erratically every time we hit a bump. We stopped every half-hour or so to phone Athens. No decision. At the army base at Serrai, only twenty-five miles from the border, we picked up an army lieutenant who said he would go with us as far as we were allowed. Continuing north, we saw more and more groups of Greek soldiers in trucks or on foot. Every bridge was guarded by armed men.

"Between us and Bulgaria," our lieutenant told us, "is truly a war of nerves."

We phoned again about ten miles from the border. No decision. We kept driving, and soon found ourselves standing on a bridge only a foot from the line that marks the edge of Bulgaria. Had permission been granted? We didn't ask. A few moments later we were in a watchtower overlooking the Bulgarian village of Kulata. It was the first western watchtower we had seen.

"The Bulgarians have a barbed wire fence strung with tin noise boxes," a Greek lieutenant in the watchtower told us. We could see three Bulgarian watchtowers. "Also they have a plowed strip fifteen meters wide. This is mined. People should come here and see the misery of the Bulgarians. They live a collective life, go to work together, and go to amusement together, always under guard."

The lieutenant was young and cocky. "The Communists are afraid to be in their watchtowers. Their morale is low. We Greeks laugh at them."

The Beirut airport was a madhouse. We had two hours between planes, and we wandered in a daze, trying to make sense of the kaleidoscopic images swirling around us. There were people of various nationalities dressed in western clothes, and men and women in the flowing white and black robes of the Middle East, and men in the military uniforms of many nations. I could discern no pattern in the movement of all these people, no order, no connectedness. I sensed myself as a particle caught up in the random motion of a subatomic world, somehow comfortable and safe because of its very randomness.

In a trance I headed toward a men's room, and there, coming out of the door and walking straight toward me, was Lowell Thomas, one of the most famous American radio and television commentators, the voice of countless newsreels of the war years. He was smiling and he looked completely at home in this deranged place. Our eyes met, we exchanged greetings as if we had always known each other, and he walked on.

I was washing my hands in the men's room when the door burst open and a sheik walked in, followed by his three wives. He was dressed in a white burnoose, and his wives were all in black, with only their eyes showing. Looking neither left nor right, he led them to the toilets. They went in and closed the doors. He stood guard. Though he was less than six feet tall, the sheik, with his powerful nose and fierce, wild eyes, looked much taller. I got the feeling that if anyone made the slightest move to question what he was doing, a razor-sharp blade might appear from beneath the folds of his robe.

We took off at dusk in a Lockheed Electra prop-jet. The moon came out over the Iraqi desert, and for a while our flight path paralleled an immense wall of thunderclouds over a hundred miles long. We were at 20,000 feet, but the wall of clouds, not far to the left of us, towered much higher. We flew in moonlight, in air as smooth and still as ice, and I pressed by head against the window and watched a fireworks display greater than any that man could produce. Jagged tongues of lightning ricocheted from cloud to cloud, probed to the desert floor, illuminated the massive, billowing thunderheads from within. Our plane seemed small and frail and incredibly brave to dare so close to such deadly grandeur. I felt myself shudder, not with terror but with awe. Perhaps, as it was sometimes said, all the great journeys had been taken and this planet had been shrunk to manageable proportions. But at this moment I felt myself a voyager, and I knew that the world was immense and mysterious and forever beyond my grasp.

Tehran: Friday, October 13. Since it was the Islamic sabbath, we couldn't see the Iranian military officials who could give us permission to visit the border, so we drove around the city, stopping to wander through bazaars. There was a high-pitched, almost hysterical quality in the people who crowded the markets and the streets. On three separate occasions that afternoon we chanced upon approximately the same scene: Two Iranian drivers had collided and were fighting, swinging wildly and ineffectively but occasionally drawing blood. Onlookers surrounded the combatants, and there was also a policeman on hand. The policeman was leaning on one of the damaged cars, casually watching the fight.

Harrison Salisbury, the *New York Times*'s Moscow correspondent, was also staying at the Park Hotel. We had dinner together, fellow Americans in a faraway city. Paul and I commented on the rise and fall in the quality of the beer as we journeyed south and east from Finland to Iran. Then we got onto the subject of the quality of life in the Soviet Union. Salisbury told us that he often went in and out of Russia by way of Helsinki. Going over from New York, he found Helsinki to be a somber, colorless place. When he came out, after six months or so in Moscow, Helsinki seemed full of color and gaiety, a carnival.

We made the necessary contacts with the Iranian military command in Tehran, then flew 350 miles north to Tabriz, where we were taken in hand by U.S. military advisers. We drove out into the desert in a Jeep and a weapons carrier. Paul spotted a camel caravan in the distance, moving parallel to the road. It shimmered in the waves of heat rising from the desert, seeming to change its size and shape, occasionally vanishing entirely. He ordered the sergeant driving the Jeep to stop, jumped out, and ran full speed straight into the desert. I followed, but after about a hundred yards gave up. Let him go, I thought. I walked back to the vehicles and stood silently with the sergeant and the major, watching Paul's figure getting smaller and smaller until it too became a mirage. He returned forty minutes later, dust-streaked and angry.

"They got away," he said. He sat brooding as we drove on.

We found camels in a tiny village stuck up against the valley walls of a mountain. A camel driver made us pay him to bring the camels into the shadow of a hill. There were sheep and goats, and cattle flowing down the curves of the land. Paul photographed a girl of six or seven herding cattle, a boy of the same age washing water buffalo.

Farther north, near the town of Dzhulfa, we came upon a sight that by now was so familiar it was almost comforting: watchtowers along a fence of barbed wire.

"Our two thousand and forty-eight kilometers of border are all the same," an Iranian colonel at the border told us. "The Russians have watchtowers and seven rows of barbed wire, plus a plowed strip. We have no watchtowers, nothing. If communism is so good, why do they build this Iron Curtain?"

We drove into the desert along the Soviet border. The fence and the line of watchtowers stretched away out of sight across glaring wasteland. Barren, magnificent mountains rose in the distance. No human being was in sight.

Back to Tehran, to Paris, to Berlin. We arrived after dark on Thursday, October 19, to discover that no hotel rooms were available in the entire city. It took us two hours on a pay phone to find a spare bedroom in an elderly woman's apartment.

The wall had an ugly, unfinished look. West Berliners stood in groups staring at it. It held the eye with the power of a horror, a monstrosity. We saw a beautiful young mother on the roof of a Volkswagen bus holding up her baby for her mother on the other side to see, smiling at first, then dissolving before our eyes; in the haze-softened sunlight, her tears were like crystals of ice on her cheeks. A man waved to his wife, who was standing in a window on the other side, afraid to wave back. A handsome, well-dressed woman in her early thirties and her husband leaned on the cold, concrete wall and waved across a canal to a sister in a factory window. They took turns with ineffectual dime-store binoculars. Paul attached a telescopic lens to a reflex camera so that they could see better. On the Saturday evening before the wall went up, the woman told us, she and her husband had been dancing in West Berlin. They had intuitively stayed overnight because of all the military activity in East Berlin. They were now free because they liked to dance. Farther along the wall, a boy stood silently looking at us through several strands of barbed wire. His hand was resting on one of the strands. His eyes were infinitely sad. He would be on the cover of *Look*.

Paul photographed all this with a feeling of deep, muffled anger that was just this side of tears. Everything that had been stretched out across miles of countryside now was concentrated, brought painfully close to us: the fortifications, the watchtowers, the people separated from one another, the armed guards. The East German police who patrolled the wall, the Vopos, were as afraid of cameras as anyone along the fence, and they tried to hide whenever Paul turned toward them. But he got pictures of one Vopo throwing a rock at him, and of another threatening us with a tear-gas grenade.

We were physically and emotionally exhausted. We got hotel rooms after the first night, but we couldn't sleep. We walked silently along the Kurfüstendamm, Berlin's sadly glittering main street. We didn't say anything. We didn't have to. Each of us knew what the other was feeling. We were overwhelmed by the wall and the six-thousand-mile-long fence of which it was an extension. We were awed by the will, the enormous human effort that had brought it into existence. The sheer weight of it crushed the human spirit. The Fence (that would be a good name for our story) was a steel and concrete manifestation of a pitiless force in the world, a deadly ideological way of thinking for which the tragedy of parents split from children, wives from husbands was as nothing. What could the individual do against such a force?

I flew directly back to San Francisco. Paul stayed in Berlin for two more days. We would meet later in New York to lay out the story.

When the Lufthansa jet took off from Paris, I leaned back in my seat and let a sense of satisfaction, even triumph, wash over me. We had completed a journey that no one else had ever attempted — if only because no one else had ever thought of it. We had made our way to every border point in our original plan, and more. We were prepared to demonstrate beyond all doubt that the Iron Curtain was not a mere figure of speech. And with no prior local contacts whatever, we had completed the entire journey in four weeks rather than the six predicted by Ed Korry. During those four weeks we had flown more than twenty thousand miles, and Paul had shot approximately twenty thousand pictures.

I twisted around in the seat, hoping that this time I could get the sleep my body demanded. As I began to doze off, however, images from the past four weeks rose in my consciousness: the glowering watchtowers; the young border guards skulking like hunted animals at the sight of a camera; the rows of barbed wire stretching endlessly through forests, meadows, vineyards, and deserts; the tragedy in Berlin. The Fence spoke for itself. There was no question but that the Communists had created an enormous prison for millions of people. They had built a deadly barrier between "their side" and "our side." They had split families. They had split the world.

But there were other splits, other barriers. I recalled the South of my childhood, the South of today: the tenant shacks, the "white" and "colored" drinking fountains, the averted eyes, the recurrent rumors of lynchings. And it was not just a question of black and white. Six months ago I had spent two weeks on assignment in a Kansas City slum school. Vivid images flashed to my mind of visits to tenements where the students lived — falling plaster, beds with no mattresses, leaking pipes, rats — and a slender, dreamy-eyed, malnourished, sleep-starved white girl of eleven named Beverly standing at an ironing board reading Walter de la Mare's poetry: "Poor tired Tim! It's sad for him. . . ./Up to bed with a candle to creep,/Too tired to yawn, too tired to sleep." In the wealthiest country in the world, what barriers would Beverly face?

There were barriers everywhere, not just between nations and races but also between husbands and wives, children and parents, between parts of our own selves. (I had loved and admired my father, but I had never seen into his heart. I had let him take his secrets down into the grave.) Everywhere I looked, I saw the human world as split, divided against itself. The Fence spoke for itself, but it also spoke to a universal human situation. There have always been fences, and maybe there always will be.

But maybe not. Maybe someday, somehow, the Fence will come down — and maybe other fences too. I was wide awake now. What could one person do (even in the smallest, most modest way) to help reconcile the world, to repair splits, to bring down fences? The question had a strange, dizzying pull on me. At the same time, a red warning light flashed in my consciousness. Even to consider reform on such a grand scale was definitely not the thing to do. The journalist's proper stance was one of cynicism, of ironic distance; wisdom lay in the recognition of limits. The "serious" novelist wrote of suicide, death, despair, the Human Condition. Utopias had given way in this age to dystopias: *Brave New World, 1984.* We had learned how easily radical reform can go sour. The very phrase "to make a better world" had a somewhat ridiculous ring to it.

And yet there was Martin Luther King. There was the black student who would let a hand be cut off to break down a barrier, to bring down a fence. There was the new generation of young people I had spotted at the White House conference, now demonstrating against racial discrimination with increasing fervor, now clamoring for places in the newly formed Peace Corps. And there was Jack Kennedy, already making mistakes, but also making life exciting and vivid, bringing us hope.

Yes, there could be no greater work than helping break down the fences we have erected against ourselves. Anyone who had any idea of what to do would be irresponsible not to try, even against long odds. But what could I do? I tried to think, but spectral images of the Fence swam again into my consciousness. I had done my story. Why was it so hard for me to sleep on a plane?

7

A New Game, New Rules

WE LIVED in a third-floor flat on Russian Hill just two doors away from the Lombard curlicue, the steep, one-block-long stretch of zigzagging red brick road that shows up in San Francisco tourist guides as "the Crookedest Street in the World." All day tourists wound their way down the precipitous grade past copious beds of flowers, then stopped in the intersection at the bottom to take pictures. Groups of Japanese men dressed in identical dark suits sometimes took identical pictures of us as we parked our car and walked to our door. We imagined ourselves in countless Tokyo scrapbooks: "Native San Franciscans carry groceries and baby to residence near Crookedest Street." From our bay window we could see Telegraph Hill and Alcatraz Island, freighters and passenger liners and navy ships moving in and out of the bay. With binoculars we could read the ships' names and home ports, and at night we could see Hawaii-bound liners ablaze with lights as they headed out to the dark Pacific.

San Francisco was a jewel of a city. Or perhaps, as some critics claimed, it was only a glittering bauble, without much substance or value. In either case it was easy to enjoy; you could reach out and grasp its pleasures without much effort. In 1961 the city had not fallen prey to the plague of high-rise development that already was spreading across the nation. There were few traffic or parking problems, and you could get from one spot to another in a matter of minutes. Climate as well as geography invited nights on the town. The bracing sea breeze, the cool, moist fog on your face, could reawaken your sense of adventure, even after the darkest, smokiest nightclub or bar.

Except on assignment or when escorting visitors, however, Lillie and I hardly ever did the town. Actually, we led a double life. On *Look* business, while entertaining editors and story sources, we ate at the best and most expensive restaurants in town. On our own, we frequented a small group of eating places, the existence of which we shared with only our closest friends. There were three or four Italian family restaurants in North

Beach where you could get a five-course meal plus a small bottle of red wine for around two dollars. There were Basque dining rooms such as the one in the Hotel du Midi where for even less you could sit at long common tables and eat spicy bouillabaisse and thick chunks of braised lamb. And there were two incredibly inexpensive restaurants on Buchanan Street, barely visible from the outside, where we first learned the joys of Japanese cuisine.

We lived modestly in a city that made it possible to do so with style. I had given up a new Ford convertible as well as furniture, books, and records — practically everything I owned — in my 1958 divorce. Now Lillie and I drove a blue 1957 Chevy standard sedan given to her by her brother. The right door had been bashed in while the car was parked (probably by one of the tourists coming down the Lombard curlicue), and we had left it unrepaired for months, not just because we didn't want to spend the money, but also because we really didn't care about appearances.

Our circle of friends was made up of men and women in their twenties and thirties. We came from different parts of the country and from varying social backgrounds, neither of which was considered important in the least. Most of us had achieved a certain degree of success in what might be considered interesting fields, which probably brought us together at the beginning. But what bonded us into an enduring social group, with friendships that would last a lifetime, was a common playfulness. Some of the men in the group had left college or even high school to serve in the war and then had come back to the rather dreary postwar educational milieu of the GI Bill, with wives and babies, and diapers to change while studying for exams. So it could be said that we were simply trying to enact the carefree campus life we had previously missed. For whatever underlying reason, we all dearly loved to play. We entered into our games with an air of self-deprecation, but also with the earnestness of children. We played various forms of charades and word games. We used a high-quality reel-to-reel tape recorder to make farcical taped plays on such themes as life in California tract houses, the freedom rides, and Nabokov's novel *Lolita*.

Every Sunday at eleven A.M., whatever the weather, our group met at Golden Gate Park, not to play touch football in the style of the Kennedys but to engage in a particularly strenuous form of Frisbee based on a principle called Maximum Performance that a fellow pilot named Hugh Knowlton and I had developed during World War II. What it meant was simply that even if the runway was ten thousand feet long, we would try to land on the first ten feet. The rules of our new game defined the play: You stood between fifteen and twenty yards from your opponent in a large open area. When your opponent threw the Frisbee, you had to make an all-out effort to reach it and catch it, using only one hand. This entailed hurling yourself through the air in a horizontal dive if necessary. If your opponent threw the Frisbee in such a way that you couldn't possibly reach it, you took one point. But if you could have reached it but didn't — if, in other words, it was within your range and you misjudged it or failed to make an all-out effort to reach it — you were required to give one point to your opponent. If you touched the Frisbee but failed to hold on, you had to give your opponent two points. If you made a successful catch, no points changed hands; Maximum Performance was expected.

There were no boundaries and no officials. The presence of either would have spoiled the game. Every time you failed to catch the Frisbee, you had to define your own "strike zone" and manifest your own sense of morality. Players of widely varying foot speeds could compete on an equal basis; you only had to run as far and as fast as you could run, and be honest about it. And since the Frisbee was constantly being thrown at or near your limit, you were pressed again and again to go all-out, and then, if you failed to catch the flying disk, to exercise your moral sense in calling the point. And the measure was not some arbitrary boundary, net, or goal, nor was it the judgment of some official, but rather your own potential.

To me, this form of Frisbee seemed a clear departure from sports as we had known them, truly a new game with new rules. It was, I told newcomers, "the first breakthrough in game theory since the ancient Greeks."

Those of us who played the game had come from the east, from New York, Atlanta, Detroit, Cleveland, St. Louis, to a place of strange skies and uncertain seasons, of chill August winds and flowers that bloom in January. It was farther from home than we had expected; Europe seemed in many ways more familiar. We had come to a city that was as entrancing as a dream and sometimes just as lonely. It was easy to go adrift in San Francisco. We discovered it was up to us to put down new roots, to create our own social groups and rituals, our own games.

When it rained — the soft, steady winter rain of the northern California coast — only six or seven of the most dedicated players showed up. Some of the finest games took place on those days: tense, silent, tightly focused, the bright yellow Frisbee luminous in the grainy, gray-green air. We dove and rolled on the waterlogged sod. We slid fifteen feet on our bellies through standing water in a low-lying area of our field. We left the park soaked to the skin, coated with mud, and thoroughly exhilarated, every bruise and abrasion an emblem of our exuberant physicality and good health. And there were sparkling, chilly midsummer mornings with a fresh breeze from the sea (only three miles away down at the other end of the park) bringing news of salt spray, waves breaking, whales spouting.

But best of all were the lingering Indian summer days when the sunlight was tangled like antique gold filigree in the thick foliage that bounded our playing area, our "Frisbee green," and the air was absolutely still, as if waiting for something, some momentous change, that might never come. In that golden late October stillness, the sun was warm enough to bring a fine sheen of sweat to the faces of those who sat waiting for their turns to play, but there was also a faint autumnal chill in the air, especially poignant because it was so subtle, evoking other times, other weathers.

I returned from the Iron Curtain trip during a period of just such days, and my first Sunday morning of Frisbee seemed nothing less than heaven. Everybody was there. Herb Gold arrived with his girlfriend, Margaret Rose Freedman, both of them walking with a jaunty, upright stride, as if they owned everything in the world that was worth owning. Herb had come to San Francisco after living in Paris and New York, and after some celebrated feuds with East Coast writers. He was generally considered one of the more promising writers of the postwar generation, having already published five novels, a book of stories, and an anthology, *Fiction of the Fifties*. Herb wanted his prose to be as bright as his name, so he got the plain stuff (basic narrative and dialogue) down first, then added the glitter. His mind was never still. He had a sharp eye for pretense and sentimentality, which he rarely failed to shoot down with a quick turn of phrase. For all his abrasive wit and often brutal candor, Herb was a loyal, caring friend, the first and favorite grown-up boyfriend of my sixteen-month-old daughter.

One of the writers in Herb's anthology, a man named Leo Litwak, was another regular member of our group. Leo moved through life on a fine line between skepticism and surrender, finding no comfortable home in either. I had read his story "The Solitary Life of Man" before meeting him, and had been captured — there's no other way of putting it — by the powerful beat of his prose. I went over his words again and again, trying to understand how a series of quite short sentences could produce sonority rather than choppiness, and evoke tragedy without naming it. Leo had taught philosophy at Washington University for nine years, then, during an unhappy love affair, had taken a summer to write a series of short stories based mostly on his experiences as a medic with General Patton's forces in Europe.

Bill Kelley, who years later would win an Oscar for his screenplay of *Witness*, was one of our most ferocious players. His first novel, *Gemini*, had spent several weeks on the *New York Times'* best-seller list. It was based on his Catholic upbringing and his three years in a seminary. When Bill's faith collided with reason and lost, he left the seminary with Ivan Karamazov's nihilistic outcry, *Everything is permitted*. "My wife has given me mistress privileges," he told me five minutes after we met in my office, showing me his most charming and ingenuous Irish grin. Bill modeled himself after Hemingway. He liked to walk into a saloon, slam his hand down on the bar, and shout, "Set 'em up." If anyone there disapproved, they were invited to meet him for further arbitration either outside or in any appropriately enclosed space.

Then there was Merla Zellerbach, the beautiful wife of paper manufacturing heir Steve Zellerbach. Merla's first novel, *Love in a Dark House,* had just been published and was creating a minor stir in San Francisco. (One of the characters was clearly modeled after columnist Herb Caen). And there was KCBS talk-show host Scott Beach and his wife, Neva; and Gerald Mason Feigen, a distinguished surgeon who used an obnoxious ventriloquist's dummy named Becky in counseling his patients; and philosopher and race-car driver Michael Scriven from Australia, currently at U.C., Berkeley; and lobbyist Hunt Conrad and his publicist wife Marion, who ran the best salon in town, recklessly mixing writers, journalists, socialites, left-wing radicals, and visiting CIA officials. Other players came and went. Paul Fusco pursued the flying Frisbee with the same intensity he gave to his photography. Novelist Chandler Brossard, after playing his first full game, said, "This is a veritable morality metaphor." But some out-of-town visitors simply shook their heads and smiled, faces frozen between politeness and derision, as one might smile if unexpectedly caught in the company of lunatics.

We took possession of a sizable plot of land: three level rectangular lawns bounded by shrubbery, walkways, and towering eucalyptus trees. We set up a spectators' area with blankets, spreads, and towels at the edge of the largest lawn, which we called the Main Green. It was there that our full-scale tournament games of twenty-one points were played. The Side Green and the Back Green were used mostly for warm-up games. We had no doubt that all this land was ours and were outraged when nonplayers, people out for a pleasant stroll in the park, happened to walk across one of our greens. Their passage was marked by cries of "Obstacle! Obstacle!" If they didn't get this message, one of the players would aim a Frisbee in the intruders' direction. The other player would go for it and execute a spectacular dive a few feet, or inches, in front of the intruders. This approach generally got the message across, and seemed far more politic than Bill Kelley's. He was given to advancing on any intruder and saying "Veer off" in an ominous voice.

The first tournament game of that fine October day after my Iron Curtain trip was between Lillie Leonard and Herb Gold. The score was even at the halfway point. Scott Beach was describing the game in his best media voice, using a silver-plated antique fireman's megaphone that had been passed down to me from George W. Burr, the great-grandfather for whom my father and I were named, and inscribed to him from the Defiance Fire Company No. 5, Macon, Georgia, May 2, 1870.

Herb had developed a trick throw; it started out to the left, fluttered, then turned sharply right, a puzzle to inexperienced players. But Lillie had seen it too often to be fooled. Hers was a power game. She took a long backswing and put her whole body into the throw. The Frisbee whistled across the green inches from the ground. Herb dived forward, the Frisbee bounced off his hand, and he gave Lillie two points. The spectators cheered Lillie's throw, Herb's wholehearted attempt, and his call of the points.

I glanced over at the Side Green where Bill Kelley and a German emigré named Peter were playing. Peter was a problem. Our game and all that went with it would fall apart if players called points in a way that favored either themselves or their opponents, and it had been noted that Peter's calls were less than impeccable. Peter agreed. "It's not that I'm immoral," he told us. "I'm amoral." I wondered if his game with Kelley would end in fisticuffs. On the Back Green — I could barely see it from where I was sitting — Gerry Feigen was playing a warm-up game, gingerly, with Neva Beach. His play was inhibited by a fear of damaging his sensitive surgeon's hands. He had once accused Bill Kelley, quite seriously, of "trying to Frisbee me to death."

For me, it was all wonderful. I loved the tentative warmth of the sun on my skin, the autumnal coolness of the air. I loved the Frisbee's spinning up into the sunlight, hovering there for a moment like a falcon above its prey, then sweeping down to draw a perfect curve in space and time. I loved the fresh, tingling smell of eucalyptus, the shining silver megaphone, good friends, cold beer, laughter, cheers.

How can I say it? We were there. There was nothing else. Barbed wire and watchtowers, racist chants and Klansmen's masks might just as well have been a dream. But this too was like a dream: the play of childlike adults in some distant, unanticipated paradise where hatred and injustice didn't exist and the fitful march of life toward death could be forgotten. But only for as long as the games went on.

It was my turn to play Bill Kelley. I took my place on the Main Green and let my eyes sweep all around me, seeing every irregularity in the grassy field, laying the magical web of my consciousness over my opponent, the spectators, the asphalt walkway fifteen years behind me, the glistening shrubbery on one side of the green, the giant eucalyptus trees on the other — drawing all this inside me, incorporating it, until there was no clear distinction between inside and outside, between me and my surroundings.

Bill and I were evenly matched, but we had different styles. He was aggressive, a slugger, while I played in a sort of trancelike calmness. The harder he threw, the calmer I became, the more completely I incorporated my surroundings, the more easily I understood the Frisbee's secret intentions. Bill reared back and let the Frisbee fly. The instant it left his hand I turned directly away and started running as fast as I could. The Frisbee passed over my head, outdistancing me, then slowing as it settled gradually toward the earth. I pursued it at full speed, coming closer, seeing it spin; then, at the last instant, diving, catching the Frisbee, and rolling head over heels some thirty or forty yards from where I had started.

I jogged back to my place on the green, as happy as I could be. During most of my waking hours, it seemed, I managed to play it safe. Telling myself that I wanted to be committed to some great work, I worked out ingenious ways to stay just this side of commitment. Telling myself that I wanted to be possessed by the moment, I regularly managed to observe the moment from a slight remove. But now I held nothing back. I wanted to win, but I wanted even more to be taken to my limit, knowing (if only until the end of the game) that paradise isn't a place where you are the passive recipient of eternal bliss but rather a state of being in which you are offered the incomparable privilege of abandoning caution, of giving your all, of realizing every last shred of your potential.

After thirty minutes of play the score was twenty to twenty. On more than one previous occasion, Bill Kelley and I had reached that same penultimate point where any error, any break in concentration, would mean the end of the game. Everything became unusually quiet. The spectators stopped cheering. Scott Beach stopped describing the game on the silver megaphone. The players' concentration became even more intense. On just about every other throw, one of us had to dive.

Then Bill made a throw that, one way or the other, would probably end the game. The Frisbee left his hand and whistled across the green, shoulder high, far to my right and curving sharply away from me. It appeared to be out of my range, but the only way I could prove that and take the point was by doing my very best to catch it. I sprinted hard to the right and launched myself into space.

Everything went into slow motion. It was not so much that time slowed down as that it expanded. I was aware of my body floating pleasantly in a vast expanse of time, my joints lengthening, my hand reaching out, out, and the very tips of my thumb and middle finger hooking the edge of the Frisbee and holding on. If the Frisbee had been a millimeter farther away or a split second earlier, the connection couldn't have been made, even with my very best effort. At that moment there was a powerful, silent click in my consciousness, and I had the strange sensation that in the act of connecting myself with the Frisbee I had also connected myself to everything else; that, in fact, everything in the universe — all the stars and planets, all the elementary particles, all the components of life — was already connected in just such a precise and critical way. I had the feeling (the words came later) that at some level of understanding, maybe at the most significant level, the universe was always stretched to its limit; the play was always maximal.

Time contracted as I came to earth, holding tightly to the Frisbee, not in the least worried about my safety as I hit hard and rolled. Bill's throw and my catch had done nothing to change the score. I got up and moved into position to make the next throw. The Frisbee green shimmered in the late October sunlight. I wished the day would never end.

8

"We're All Going to Be Californians"

1962

MOST OF MY COLLEAGUES lusted after foreign travel. They considered a year wasted that failed to include a trip to Ireland, Spain, Japan, Bali, or more exotic lands. I was different; enjoyed no port so much as my home port. Travel for its own sake had long since lost its charm for me, and when I told Dan Mich that I had been out of town 134 days in 1961, it was more of a complaint than a boast.

If I had to travel, I preferred the United States to overseas. My assignments in the areas of education, race relations, politics, popular culture, and what was to be called lifestyle had afforded me an insider's view of America's social dynamics, and I was increasingly fascinated by what I saw. To follow a school board election from the point of view of one of the candidates, for example, was to come very close indeed to the heart of local politics.

And there were the All-America City Awards. Every year *Look,* in cooperation with the National Municipal League, picked eleven cities to be honored for civic achievement. After the winners were selected, it fell to *Look* editor-photographer teams to visit each of the communities, check out the claims made to the *Look*–National Municipal League jury, then do a short text-and-picture story on the reforms that had led to the awards. Most *Look* staffers hated these assignments, but I found myself rather pleased to take them on. Sometimes I would visit one or two of the eleven chosen communities, sometimes three or four; and more often than not I would come across a peculiarly American phenomenon. A small group of private citizens had seen something wrong or something lacking in their community. They had banded together, and working on a purely voluntary basis had produced real change: reforming the governing structure, creating cultural centers, forcing the construction of low-cost housing.

I couldn't imagine this kind of volunteerism in Europe. Even political revolution had failed to erase the sense of tradition and hierarchy that shaped European communal life. The informed European saw the most enduring wisdom in cynicism: The officials are corrupt, the aristocracy is selfish and dissolute, the common people are stupid and cunning. That's the way it always has been and always will be. *Plus ça change, plus c'est la même chose.* By comparison, American communal life seemed remarkably fluid. And the informed American citizen was still naive enough to think that positive change was not only possible but, given the right push, probable.

I had a large map of the United States on the wall of my office, and I would sometimes look at it as if the country were an enormous laboratory of social change. There was the South, where a tradition so deep that only a native southerner could fully understand it was being overturned before our very eyes. There was Washington, D.C., where the Kennedys were creating the climate and style if not the substance of a shining new era. There was the Midwest, the heartland, good *Look* country. I got many favorable letters from the Midwest on my reform-minded *Look* stories, and I had learned never to sell that region short when it came to openheartedness and willingness to entertain sensible change. There, on the upper right side of the map, was the Atlantic seaboard and New England, still reluctant to upset the status quo but happy to serve as an information and financial marketplace, providing prodigious energy for experimentation elsewhere in the country. And there, dotted all over the map, were the college and university campuses where thousands, tens of thousands, of students were awakening to injustice and the stultification of their own best impulses. It wouldn't be long, despite the contrary opinions of pundits and pollsters and *The Saturday Evening Post,* before the campuses would explode.

When my eyes drifted over to the left side of the map, I smiled and shook my head. There it was: land of Hearst and Disney, of beatniks and religious freaks, of astrologers and food faddists. I remembered how my heart had sunk when Dan Mich had called me into his office and asked me to go out and open an office in San Francisco. From the perspective of the Look Building in New York City and my home in New Canaan, Connecticut, everything about California seemed insufferably tawdry and shallow. But now, five years later, I was beginning to understand California's significance to the rest of the country. If the United States was a laboratory of social and cultural change, California was the part of the lab where the most advanced experimentation was taking place. By early 1962, more than a thousand new inhabitants were entering this state every day. In the very act of leaving their homes in the generally more stable communities to the east, they were demonstrating their willingness to try something new.

What they discovered was a place where everything was up for grabs. California was the world center of scientific research and technological innovation; twenty-six Nobel Prize winners in the sciences had lived within its borders, compared with nineteen in New York and only five in all of the Soviet Union. Its electronic and aerospace industries were not only doing a new business but also doing business in a new way. Its sprawling suburban communities, built mostly since the automotive explosion, had no stable structure, no tradition except the tradition of the new. Even the climate was liberating.

Here in this sweeping landscape, far from kinfolk, old friends, village elders, ward bosses, and the certainties taught at prep schools and on ivied campuses, the new Californians were free to create ad hoc communities, experimental social forms, new ways of viewing reality. They were doing human research and development for the rest of the nation. Willy-nilly, for good or for ill, they were creating the future. If the sixties were to be an era of explosive social and cultural change, California would surely play a major role.

I tried to share these ideas with my San Francisco friends, but they were more interested in the latest novel than demographics and social experimentation. *Look* colleagues in New York liked to visit California but generally refused to take it seriously. Lillie was interested in almost any new idea, and we often discussed the exotic new land in which we felt alternately exhilarated and lonely. But my impassioned ally and eventual co-conspirator in these matters turned up, ironically, in the Luce organization. His name was T George Harris (no period after the *T*), and as soon as he came out from New York to take over *Time* magazine's San Francisco bureau early in 1960, he called up. "I learn more from competitors than editors," he said in a casual yet purposive southern drawl. "Let's have lunch."

At age thirty-six, T George Harris was already a legend in his field. Getting the news was for him not just a job but a holy crusade, as was almost everything else in his life. On the day of his birth, I later learned, his mother had had a vision of some great work that would be his and his alone to accomplish. There was an older sister, but the light of God had fallen on T George's head. All through his boyhood on a Kentucky farm, his mother had never let him forget her vision, or the compact she had made with God to further his work. His mission would be of transcendent importance to humankind. But there was a problem: She never told him what it was.

T George was seventeen when the war began in 1941. The religious beliefs instilled by his mother prohibited the taking of life, and for a while he thought he would have to become a conscientious objector. But everything turned around when he saw a movie about the World War I exploits of Sergeant York, a religious man who captured a whole company of Germans while quoting the Epistle to the Romans on the necessity of combating the agents of the devil. T George joined the army with the avowed purpose of ending the war and stopping the killing as quickly as possible. The man who had almost been a C.O. became a relentless warrior. As a forward observer for artillery in the European theater, he flew 116 missions over enemy lines. On the ground, he set up his observation posts as far forward as possible, pushing the term "calculated risk" to the limit. His commanders recognized his contribution to finishing off the war. They honored him with a battlefield commission during the battle of Bastogne.

The war ended and T George, still driven by his mother's vision, majored in social psychology at Yale, regularly tangled with his classmate William F. Buckley, Jr., in the Yale Political Union, graduated Phi Beta Kappa in three years, and was snapped up by Time, Inc. T George didn't precisely match the Ivy League image, but he rather quickly became a favorite of Henry Luce himself. In 1952, at the age of twenty-eight, he was appointed Chicago bureau chief to *Time, Life,* and *Fortune* — certainly one of the youngest men in the history of the organization to head such a large operation. When I first met him in Little Rock in 1957, the Chicago bureau had twenty-four editorial staffers. Some entire national magazines were not that large.

This vivid, larger-than-life combination of journalistic visionary and commando was hard for a large organization to take. In 1958, before the Chicago office could overshadow all the rest of the Luce empire, T George, while on vacation in Palm Springs, received an emissary from Henry Luce. "The boss says you don't get to play anymore," this top executive told him. "You've got to go to work." What this meant was that he would be pulled back into the New York office as a staff writer. T George did the best he could, but he was a man of action, a line officer, not a staff officer. After two frustrating years in New York, he managed a transfer to San Francisco as bureau chief. The city by the Golden Gate was not as big as Chicago, but it was, he thought, on the edge of something new and strange and perhaps significant.

We met for lunch at the Garden Court of the Sheraton Palace Hotel, a restaurant from another era, with marble columns, a high dome of frosted glass, and a string trio behind the potted palms. My office was nearby, and the maitre d' always saved me one of the best tables up on the front row. A part of me wanted to impress the legendary T George Harris with this Victorian grandeur, but he was uninterested in the usual ways people have of establishing status; nor was he one for indulging in small talk. Within minutes we were into the heart of things. What really needed to be said about the West Coast that wasn't being said? Whom should he talk to? How did I get my stories? He had already seen some of my stuff, and wanted to see more.

After lunch I collected tear sheets of my best pieces from the past several years and mailed them to T George. He phoned two days later, and with no preliminaries said, "What you're doing is exactly what I want to do, and can't get in the magazine."

We started meeting regularly for lunch, then getting together socially. I invited him to join our Frisbee group. He came occasionally, but generally was too deeply involved in his work to do something as frivolous as throw a plastic disk around for two hours on Sunday morning. Once he and his wife, Sheila, and Lillie and I rented two canoes and paddled fifteen miles down the Russian River, seventy-five miles north of San Francisco. When I told this to our friend Marion Conrad, she said dryly, "Who won?"

Our meetings almost immediately turned into orgies of agreement. We agreed that the United States was by far the most interesting country in the world; that it, and especially California, was a vast laboratory of social and cultural change; that the decade of the sixties was going to be a momentous one. We also agreed that by and large, the media were failing to get the real story about what was going on in America. T George had a theory that events could be divided into two categories: "the news" and "the News." The news included most of what appeared in the media: wars, fires, plane crashes, crimes, political campaigns and elections, power struggles between individuals, states, and nations. The news was essentially repetitive and interchangeable; except for the names, dates, locales, and other particulars, one year's newspaper was pretty much the same as another's. The News was something else again. It involved the basic structural changes in technology, demographics, and human relations that would have long-term effects on how people lived.

"The transistor and the birth control pill," I said, "are going to change the life of the average American much more than who's elected president."

"The automobile has already done it," T George said.

"And the freeway," I added.

"And the tract development."

T George felt that a picture-and-word essay that Paul Fusco and I had done, "The Changing American Family," was an example of the News, as was the special issue on youth of the sixties. We groped for a term that would subsume this type of story — "way of living," "living style," "life-style." Meanwhile, T George was becoming increasingly frustrated. In addition to covering the news in a heroic fashion, he kept on turning in story ideas on the News, only to have them turned down flat by *Time* managing editor Otto Fuerbringer, a strong, stubborn, opinionated individual who was less than charmed by T George and his mission. On one occasion, however, seven of the eight ideas T George turned in were accepted. Was it a miracle, a sign from God? No. It was only that Fuerbringer was on vacation, and Hedley Donovan, chairman of the editorial board of Time, Inc., had stepped down to edit *Time* for a week. Then Otto came back, and T George was again stymied.

In combat, T George had had the opportunity to be totally committed, to operate at the peak of his powers. He was in the habit of encouraging the people who worked for him to play over their heads, to stop collecting souvenirs, to rise to their own dreams. How could he bear to do less?

I shouldn't have been surprised, but I was, when T George asked if he could come to work for *Look*. My mind went into overdrive. This wouldn't be a routine shift of allegiance. To my knowledge, no one had ever come over to *Look* from the Luce organization, certainly no one of T George's status. I told him it could easily be arranged, and as soon as possible got on the phone to Dan Mich. Mich was even more surprised than I. He was due out soon for one of his West Coast visits, and could negotiate with T George then.

It all happened very fast. A couple of weeks earlier, Mich had asked me to take over management of the entire West Coast editorial operation, which meant moving its headquarters from Los Angeles to San Francisco. My administrative duties, he said, would be minimal; I could keep on doing stories and special issues. I flew south to check out office space in one of the new high-rise buildings on Wilshire Boulevard. In San Francisco, we moved into larger quarters in a small building across the street from the Palace Hotel in March 1962, just before T George Harris came aboard.

When T George let Time, Inc., know of his decision, Henry Luce's personal deputy, Bill Furth, came out to try to change his mind. T George, as unpredictable as ever, invited me to join the two of them for lunch at the Palace. Furth was an elegant man, graying at the temples and wearing a beautifully tailored suit. He rose to greet me with a charming if rueful smile. "Mr. Leonard," he said, "your name is a hissing in the ears of the Luce organization."

T George Harris joined *Look* with an exuberant shout. He was like a captive lion suddenly released onto a vast plain dotted with game. On the Sunday afternoon before his release from *Time* became official, he picked me up in the black Chevy convertible with tail fins he had bought from his predecessor. We drove to Golden Gate Park and started brainstorming ideas for a special California issue, to come out in October, just as the state was due to pass New York as America's most populous. We talked calmly enough at the beginning. But as George guided the car around and around the park's wide, gently curving drives, our excitement escalated, and we soon found ourselves shouting ideas at each other at the top of our lungs. We'd been thinking and talking about this subject for months and now we didn't need notes. We bellowed with laughter. We cheered. We beat on the dashboard and steering wheel. The car swerved from side to side. We drove straight from the park to the office, and by midnight had sketched out twenty-six story proposals. To T George's amazement and delight, Dan Mich accepted twenty-four of them. We were on our way.

The winter rains had passed, and all the hills around San Francisco had turned from bronze to a rich and vibrant green. There were flowers everywhere, even along the sides of the freeways, where dense beds of ice plant were sprinkled with blossoms of lavender and rose and yellow and white. On snow-covered slopes in the sierras, it was sometimes warm enough in the midday sun to ski bare-chested. And sunbathers along hundreds of miles of beaches in this place of unexpected weather sometimes scurried for sweaters and blankets when the wind shifted and a wisp of fog came ashore.

California in the spring of 1962 was bursting with energy. Forty-one percent of all the U.S. government funds for research and development were being spent in this one state. (New York State was next, with 12 percent.) More than half of all the canned vegetables in the world were being produced here. But the state's major crop was people, and they were pouring across the borders by the thousands. No wonder California's imminent ascendency to the status of most populous state was big news all across the nation.

T George and I had our theme: *California is a window into the future. To see the future now, both the good and the bad of it, look carefully at this state.* There was no question about the bad of it. With so much human energy let loose in a place of such unusual beauty, there was ample opportunity for the demonic to assert itself. With so many individuals in mad pursuit of their individual dreams, the future might turn out to be a nightmare. Our proposal acknowledged the dark side:

> With the fastest growing numerical population in the U.S., California already aches with the growing pains that eventually will strike at almost all of America. The poisoning of the air and water, the rape of the wilderness,

the depletion of farmland for housing, traffic strangulation, urban sprawl and ugliness, political instability — how California handles these problems will point the way, right or wrong, for Americans everywhere.

Would California be a harbinger of hope or of future horrors? We would pose this question again and again throughout the issue. But it was going to be hard to be negative in such an exuberant landscape. I assigned four stories to myself, including an opening piece to set the stage and a closing essay, "California: What It Means." T George also took four assignments, including a picture story on "The Way-Out Way of Life" in Palm Springs and an essay on California politics. We called on editors, photographers, and researchers from Los Angeles and New York to do the rest. All that spring, the twenty-one of us crisscrossed California, from Death Valley to Mendocino, from Yosemite to Carmel-by-the-Sea, then back and forth between San Francisco and New York.

T George reveled in his new role. The first time he visited *Look* headquarters in New York, I saw him at the elevators with a dazed and happy look on his face.

"I've met them all," he said. "I've touched them all. In ten years at Time-Life, I never met all the people who run things. I just saw everybody who runs *Look* in one room."

His newly found freedom and authority, however, only added to the burden of T George's already burdened feeling of obligation. With such an opportunity to achieve and serve, he would have to work even harder. Back in San Francisco, he stayed at his typewriter past midnight and sometimes ended up sleeping on a couch in the office.

A clock was always ticking for T George, and for me too, I guess. We just handled it in different ways. He stayed at the office all night, dreamed of a media network that would inform and indeed join all Americans, and wore the hair shirt of duty and obligation. I played Frisbee, dreamed of writing a novel that would illuminate the seemingly impenetrable mysteries of existence, and pursued the elusive connection with the infinite that just might be possible through the joining of bodies, or maybe even through the touching of hands. Both T George and I, it seemed, had visions so large and bright that they were destined to remain always beyond our grasp. A line from Thomas Wolfe sometimes repeated itself in my mind: "There is no happy land. There is no end to hunger."

Still, it was fun welcoming visiting *Look* staffers, having coffee and lunch, exchanging gossip, then seeing them off on the quest for words and pictures that would become part of an issue devoted to saying something revealing about American culture, something never said before. The feeling of impending change that had struck me at the White House Conference on Children and Youth was even stronger now. President Kennedy had recovered from the Bay of Pigs disaster, and his popularity had risen as high as 77 percent. The civil rights movement was showing no sign of losing momentum. Peace Corps volunteers were beginning to take up their posts in distant lands. There were troubling reports of as many as five thousand American military personnel serving as advisers and even going on combat missions in one of those distant lands — this one called Vietnam — but surely Jack Kennedy wouldn't let that situation get out of hand.

The younger generation? There was plenty of ferment on the campuses, if not the explosion I had predicted a year and a half earlier. But I held to my belief that the explosion would come, and in a bigger way than anyone might imagine. I had been invited to address the National Education Association convention in Denver in July. Six thousand delegates were expected, the largest audience I had ever faced, and I had fantasies of shaking them up. "Someday not very long from now," I imagined myself saying, "blood could well be shed over the content, form, and organizational structure of education." Would I dare say that?

T George never stopped pressing. After all the pictures were in, he wanted us to get one more picture. He wanted us to get one more fact, one more interview, one more article. No matter how much he did, he reproached himself for not doing more. That reproach (though he didn't say so) seemed to apply to me and everyone else as well as to himself. I assured him we were in good shape.

A faint pall of yellowish smog hung in the sky. We sat in lawn chairs in a glade high in the Hollywood hills, protected from the sun by tropical trees. From all around there came the sound of hundreds of thousands of cars rushing along unseen freeways, roads, and streets, a sound not much louder than the whisper of distant summer wind. The tall, thin, elegant man sitting across from me spoke in a proper Oxford accent.

"Mankind should not fear a Martian invasion," he said. "We are our own Martians. With the help of science and technology, we are destroying much of what is beautiful and valuable on this planet."

I felt slightly disoriented; it was hard to take notes. For me, Aldous Huxley was a historical literary figure rather than this concerned-looking man I was interviewing about California. I had started reading Huxley's books when I was thirteen in Monroe, Georgia. During three magical summer vacations, my cousin Ed Stephenson, five years my elder, had taken me in hand and introduced me to the world of philosophy, psychology, and literature. With no formal arrangement whatever, he had become my enthusiastic tutor, I his willing and often dazzled student. Ed was a dedicated apprentice scholar, an undergraduate at the University of Georgia. I thought he was wiser than God. He read *The Canterbury Tales* aloud to me in Middle English, explicated Freud's theory of dreams, insisted that I read the novels of Ernest Hemingway, Thomas Wolfe, Somerset Maugham, John Dos Passos, Sinclair Lewis, and Aldous Huxley.

I remember lounging on a daybed in my grandparents' spacious white house when I was thirteen reading *Point Counter Point*. Huxley's brittle, talky London made its own bizarre counterpoint against the musty smell in the house, the pulsing heat outside, the mindless rise and fall of the cicada's song.

> On the grey silk of the couch, her foot was flower-like and pale, like the pale fleshy buds of lotus flowers. The feet of Indian goddesses walking among their lotuses are themselves flowers. Time flowed in silence, but not to waste, as at ordinary moments. It was as though it flowed, pumped beat after beat by Walter's anxious heart, into some enclosed reservoir of experience to mount and mount behind the dam until at last, suddenly . . . Walter suddenly reached out and took her bare foot in his hand. Under the pressure of those silently accumulated seconds, the dam had broken. It was a long foot, long and narrow. His fingers closed round it. He bent down and kissed the instep.
>
> "But my dear Walter!" She laughed. "You're becoming quite oriental."

Could such a world exist? My mouth was dry, my brain scorched. In my grandparents' house, nothing that was really important was ever mentioned, much less discussed — not the pervasive presence of death, not the dusty black people who filled the streets on Saturday afternoon then became invisible at night, certainly not the suffocated sexuality that pervaded all those stately houses with lawns and magnolia trees and lavish beds of funereal flowers. I had left the South, had gone to war, and had come back to join a magazine in New York. Huxley had left England, had shed his cynicism, and had embraced some sort of Eastern thought that admirers of his sophisticated early novels could never quite understand. And now here we were, the two of us, in California.

"When I wrote *Brave New World* in 1932, I had no idea how soon so much of it would come true. I had no *idea* — I don't think anyone did — how swiftly science would develop, how fast the population would increase, how effectively people would be organized in larger and larger groups. Already we're working out most of the techniques for controlling the mind as I saw them in my book. What's more, our power for controlling, or devastating, the outside world already has proceeded beyond what I could have foreseen."

He paused and leaned toward me. "You must tell people they don't have much time. We all must start thinking like mad. We must *do* something."

"But *what* shall we do?" I asked him. "*What* shall I tell people?"

"That's hard to say. The Founding Fathers of this country were concerned with the sources of power of that time and with humane restraint of that power. Now new sources of power have developed — enormously greater than anything previously imagined. I feel we need some kind of new constitutional convention, a new meeting of 'Founding Fathers' who will take steps to ensure that the power released by science will not limit human freedom or destroy the world."

"Yes, but how are we to organize such a convention?"

"It would be difficult, of course."

"In the meantime, what specific steps do you think we should take? What shall we do to stave off what clearly seems to be disaster?"

Huxley paused, then shook his head. "I don't know. I just don't know."

Like a plane making S-turns to lose altitude, my rented Ford convertible glided downward from Aldous Huxley's house toward the Hollywood Freeway. I let my eyes go soft, and the car seemed to drive itself as Huxley's words reverberated in my consciousness. *"You must tell people,"* he had said. But *what?* Maybe *Look* should help organize some sort of model constitutional convention outside of government to take a new look at the humane restraint of power. But maybe that kind of thing was already being done here in California — at places such as the Center for the Study of Democratic Institutions in Santa Barbara or the Center for Advanced Study of the Behavioral Sciences in Palo Alto or the Stanford Research Institute; at board meetings of private corporations or planning groups; in state and city governments; and sometimes even in the living rooms of tract houses, whose inhabitants had come not so long ago from Iowa, Maine, or Georgia. Maybe the very formlessness of life in this state would make it possible for anybody who cared enough to make some kind of impact on the future.

The car had brought me down from the large houses built precariously on the slant of the hill, with their redwood decks and screens of shrubbery, to smaller houses built on the level, with lawns and flowers. The sky was a harsh, vertical blue, faintly tinged with smog; there was not a cloud in sight. Yet the gutters were running with fresh, clean water, the overflow from scores of lawn sprinklers, water that had come two hundred miles from the Owens Valley, stolen from ranchers and nature lovers so that this once brilliant desert could be made into this hazy oasis. And there was the freeway not far ahead, a mighty river of metal and focused fire pouring down a concrete channel. What were we going to do with power of such magnitude? Even if it were humanely restrained, we might still spend our lives, all our days and nights, waiting for some illumination, some fulfillment that might never come. Is this the way it has to be? Are we doomed to live forever in Plato's cave, seeing only shadows of reality, never perceiving life in its original colors?

Huxley had written a book called *The Doors of Perception.* Though I hadn't read the book, I knew the source of the title. My cousin Ed had introduced me to William Blake during one of those magic summers in Monroe, Georgia, reading him aloud to me with delighted and outraged laughter. ("Blake really believed he went down into hell and talked with the devil. And can you guess what kind of thing he asked him? He asked the devil what kind of *ink* he used on his *printing presses!*") Much of what I had learned in school and college was long forgotten, but Ed's teaching still was sharp and clear in my memory.

"When the doors of perception are cleans'd," William Blake had written, "all things will appear as they are; that is, infinite."

A new constitutional convention might be a start, but it wouldn't be enough. As the car brought me closer to the freeway, something very bright but vague in all its particulars appeared in my inner vision. I felt my mind circling it as a fish circles a shiny multicolored lure, coming closer and closer, not knowing what it was, but filled with a sense of delicious possibilities.

But there was the freeway. I swung onto the on ramp, and then the acceleration lane. I would have to merge with all that power, that never-ceasing river of metal and fire. I shifted in my seat and took conscious control of the car. The vision vanished in the noxious fumes from thousands of exhausts.

Our California issue hit the stands on Tuesday, September 11, 1962, the leading edge of a media avalanche on the state. An enormous setting sun glowed through the Golden Gate Bridge on the cover of the magazine, and our thesis was printed there in bold letters: "Tomorrow's hopes and tomorrow's headaches are here today in our soon-to-be largest state." *Life* magazine came out with a California issue nearly a month later. It opened with a handsome color portfolio on the state, but otherwise seemed to me weary and predictable; having no compelling theme, it simply restated the current California clichés. Once again *Life*'s editors couldn't resist the group picture. Twenty-one new California arrivals were gathered at the Bel Air Hotel in Los Angeles and photographed, smiling.

As for our thesis, within weeks it began appearing simply as a given in newspaper, magazine, and television reports. I became accustomed to turning on my television, even years later, and seeing some commentator standing on a hill in Los Angeles proclaiming in portentous tones that what happens in California today will happen in the rest of the nation in the future.

T George left to join the New York staff in September. He told me later that his first *Look* experience marked a turning point in his life.

"Because our ideas got clarified in the issue, it gave me a new way of looking at things. The whole notion of inventing your own life, writing on a clean slate, is terrifying to people. This kind of freedom invites the need for community. It also can create anomie, and I began to see the rise of ultraright groups in California in that light. I realized that in the future we're going to have to create our own environments, wherever we are. We're all going to be Californians."

T George passed down to Lillie and me the house that had been passed down to Sheila and him by his predecessor at *Time*. It was a classic Victorian at 1818 California Street, with thirteen-foot ceilings, tall bay windows, and exquisite workmanship throughout, including a sculptured marble fireplace in the living room that would be difficult if not impossible to replace at any price. For all that, as well as the services of a Japanese gardener who came once a week to tend the grounds, the rent was $200 a month.

9

"We're Not Going to Just Stand Up Here and Let That Nigger In"

On the last day of September 1962, five days after *Look*'s California issue had gone off the newsstands, the Kennedy administration faced its worst domestic crisis. Less than a month later the Kennedys were confronted with their worst international crisis. The domestic crisis involved the first black student at the University of Mississippi and almost precipitated a state-sized civil war. The international crisis involved Soviet missiles in Cuba and almost brought about a large-scale conflict between the United States and the USSR. During this period I was once again to come face to face with the tragic effects of the fences that men have built to set human beings apart from one another.

The briefing map that was uncovered just before each of my combat missions in World War II always had a bold red line, a "bomb line," running across it. Bombs could be dropped only on the far side of that line. More important to us pilots, we were liable to be taken prisoner if we had to parachute or make a crash landing anywhere beyond the line. It was enemy territory. For reporters from national publications, all of the Deep South might be said to lie on the other side of a bomb line. But it was when I entered the state of Mississippi that I got the strongest feeling that I was crossing into enemy territory. There was something hard and unregenerate about white Mississippians in the early sixties, something anguished, untamed, and unpredictable. If Atlanta had arranged a reasonably graceful surrender to integration and now was reaping the rewards in terms of financial growth, most Mississippians didn't hear or didn't care.

So when a black student named James Meredith was flown by helicopter onto the campus of the University of Mississippi (Ole Miss) under federal protection on Sunday, September 30, 1962, a mob numbering in the thousands quickly formed. Members of the mob, made up not only of students but of segregationists from all over the state, attacked the

federal marshals guarding Meredith with rocks, bricks, Molotov cocktails, acid, and bullets. Two people were killed, dozens wounded. The
marshals, trapped in the Lyceum, the university's administration building, responded with barrage after barrage of tear gas, and were nearly
overwhelmed on several occasions during the long night. While the riot
was at its height, President Kennedy went on national television to explain the situation. Later, when he realized how bad things really were,
he ordered units of the Second Infantry Division to the campus.

Two days later I was at the Ole Miss campus in Oxford, Mississippi,
with a *Look* team that included T George Harris, Christopher S. Wren,
Paul Fusco, and illustrator Robert Fawcett. The gracious, tree-shaded
campus was overrun with reporters from all over the world and soldiers
with M-1 rifles, gas masks, and full battle dress. The area around the
Lyceum still reeked of enough tear gas to make the eyes water.

By all appearances, the story was a fairly straightforward one: last-
ditch southern defiance overwhelmed by determined federal force. Most
of the reporters on the scene were in the process of wrapping up their
coverage and leaving for home. But we were under instructions from Dan
Mich to stay on the story for as long as it took to get an hour-by-hour,
minute-by-minute account of the riot and the events that led up to it. We
were to personalize the story, tell it through the experiences of its key
participants. As it turned out, we were to discover that the Ole Miss
affair, far from being simple, was a web of bizarre plots, conspiracies,
and secret deals.

After three days at the scene of the riot, we decided to split up. Fusco
and Fawcett would go back to New York. Chris Wren would stay in
Oxford, where he would interview students, administrators, soldiers, and
the two Oxford ministers who had tried to stop the riot. Though he was
twenty-six and a former paratroop officer, Chris looked young enough
to pass as a student. Already he was eating his meals at Ole Miss fraternity houses. One group of students, though they knew he was a reporter,
had gone with him to buy an Ole Miss sweatshirt. T George Harris would
go to Jackson, the state capital, where he would interview the governor
and other state officials as well as members of the Citizens' Council and
the bankers and businessmen who made up the state's more moderate
permanent leadership. I would go to Washington and interview the U.S.
marshals and Justice Department officials who had been on the scene, as
well as Bobby Kennedy, who had been in charge of the whole operation
from his Washington headquarters.

I figured on taking my time, starting out by interviewing marshals,
then working my way up slowly to Bobby Kennedy. But on my second
day at the Justice Department, Kennedy's press officer, Edwin Guthman,

said, "Bob wants to see you." He escorted me into Kennedy's office.

Kennedy wanted to know what I had in mind. I launched into an enthusiastic description of our plans. As I talked, I had the impression that he was trying to size me up. He was sitting behind a large desk in a very large, rather dark office. The sleeves of his white shirt were rolled and his tie was loosened. With his tousled hair and small, compact frame, he might have seemed lost in such impressive surroundings: a teenager playing around in his big brother's office. But there was that well-known Bobby Kennedy toughness — ruthlessness is what his detractors called it — and that curious iconic glow that attaches itself to those who have appeared countless times on television; perhaps only Jack Kennedy possessed more of that glow. I was impressed, but didn't want to show it. Kennedy said little, but now and then interrupted my account with a terse, dry question. He sat facing me, leaning back in his chair, with one arm across his midriff, the other hand propping up his chin.

"I'd very much like to interview you about your role in this affair," I said, "but I'd prefer to wait until I've talked to everyone else." I hesitated. "So I'll be prepared to ask the right questions."

He paused for a moment, then said, "All right. Let's see what happens. Keep in touch with me through Ed Guthman."

There was another pause. I knew it was time for me to leave, but both of us seemed to be waiting for something. Then he looked very directly into my eyes and smiled. It was not the famous Kennedy grin, but something much more subtle and intimate. I smiled back, somewhat mystified. Was he amused at my enthusiasm, or was he simply trying to charm me, or did he know something essential about the Ole Miss story that I didn't know?

The next morning Guthman said, "It looks like you're going to be here for a while." He had found a spare office I could use for my interviews.

I settled into a routine. Every morning I arrived at the Justice Department and went to work, interviewing marshals and the high-ranking officials who had been members of the Mississippi task force. I either had lunch alone at the Justice Department cafeteria or went out with one of the officials. Every night I phoned T George and Chris Wren, checking what I had learned during the day with what they had learned. The work was tedious, but it had a detective-story quality that kept me fascinated.

T George had rather quickly gained the confidence of the Mississippians, and was putting together an explosive scenario that the rest of the news media had entirely missed. What happened had been bad enough, he told me, but it was a pep rally compared to what might have happened. A group of Mississippi leaders had been secretly planning to form a wall of unarmed bodies that would not yield until knocked down and trod upon by federals. Many segregationists were prepared to go to jail. Many were ready to fight with fists, rocks, and clubs. Some resolved to stand until shot down. Others planned to defy the orders of their leaders and conceal pistols on their persons.

"In retrospect, I'm thankful that five to ten thousand — maybe fifteen to twenty thousand — fellow Mississippians didn't go there and get killed," Dr. M. Ney Williams, a director of the Citizens' Council and adviser to Governor Ross Barnett, told T George. He might have been overstating, George said, but no one who really understood Mississippi's "wall of flesh" strategy estimated that fewer than hundreds would have been killed had the plan been carried out.

Why wasn't it? That was one of the things we had to figure out.

Our nightly phone calls also allowed us to make sense out of occurrences that those in the heat of the battle had not been able to understand. For example, at twilight on the day of the riot, three of Governor Barnett's closest advisers had landed in a blue and white Cessna 310 at the Memphis airport on their way to the Ole Miss campus, and had been terrified when Deputy Attorney General Nicholas Katzenbach and press officer Ed Guthman had run up to their plane and peered inside. The Mississippians had expected "search and seizure." But the Justice Department officials had had no idea that they had encountered the governor's closest advisers. Nor did the governor's men know that Katzenbach and Guthman were actually looking for the black student, James Meredith, who had just landed in an almost identical plane.

One seemingly trivial item proved to be a turning point in my work with Justice Department officials. Deputy Attorney General Katzenbach, a balding, big-boned law scholar who had been in charge of Kennedy's task force at Ole Miss during the riot, had been a hard man for me to interview, rather impatient and uncommunicative. One morning, on a hunch, I decided to tell him something that Mississippi state senator George Yarbrough, who had confronted Katzenbach on the campus during the riot, had told Harris.

"Senator Yarbrough made a comment about your shoes."

"What about my shoes?"

"Well, he told George Harris that he couldn't help noticing your shoes during the riot. He said they were the strangest shoes he had ever seen. Said you looked like a man from Mars."

"God damn him!" Katzenbach said, slapping his desk. His face, his whole head, turned crimson. "What the hell's wrong with my shoes? I paid a hell of a lot of money for these shoes."

He lifted a foot so I could see one of them. The shoe seemed to be made of alligator hide. It was rather large, even for Katzenbach's large frame. I didn't say anything. I wondered if I had made a mistake. But Katzenbach's anger stayed focused on Yarbrough rather than turning against me. As we went on talking, I could tell that his mind kept coming back to the subject of his shoes. "Man from Mars," he once muttered darkly. "Damn him!" I could also tell that he was more eager than before to let me know what had really happened in the Meredith affair. And what had happened, I was beginning to realize, was quite different from what had appeared in the media.

The days passed. The other reporters were long gone, their attention on other events. I began to feel at home in the Justice Department. My office was not far from Bobby Kennedy's. I talked with him whenever I could, trying to learn more about an increasingly complex story but sometimes just chatting — about American education, the civil rights movement, the media. During that same time the sensational press had reported that Kennedy had had a fistfight with novelist Gore Vidal, a cousin of Jackie Kennedy's. He said that was not true. Vidal had been dancing with Jackie in a way he didn't like, he told me, and he had simply taken his arm very firmly. "Don't ever touch my sister again," Kennedy had said. I was struck by the fact that he referred to the president's wife as "my sister" rather than as "my sister-in-law."

The day finally came when all my questions about the Ole Miss affair were being answered candidly, not so much by Kennedy himself (though he must have given the signal) as by his aides. And the story that emerged was so strange I could hardly believe it. But it fit perfectly with what T George Harris and Chris Wren were getting, and it explained things that otherwise had been inexplicable. I flew to New York to confer with Dan Mich and our legal counsel. The story was legally explosive. We needed more corroboration. I flew back to Washington early in the morning and reclaimed my office in the Justice Department. That afternoon, as I was standing chatting with Ed Guthman in his outer office, he opened a folder containing a sheaf of carbon copies.

"You might be interested in this," he said, holding the papers so that I could see them.

I read a few lines and felt my heartbeat speed up. It was a transcript of taped phone conversations between Ross Barnett and Robert Kennedy. Guthman didn't say a word, nor did I. I just took the yellow legal pad I was holding and started writing as fast as I could, using the informal shorthand I had developed as a reporter: a large scrawl of about four words across, double or triple spaced, indecipherable to anyone except me. Guthman turned the pages, always just a little too fast for me to finish copying; he never let me touch the transcript. We stood there for ten or fifteen minutes in silence as I wrote furiously, sweat covering my forehead. When Guthman turned the last page, he closed the folder and locked it in a file cabinet. Neither of us said a word about it.

Back in New York, T George, Chris Wren, and I checked all the pieces of the puzzle to make sure they fit together. By juxtaposing the transcripts with what T George had learned from the Mississippi viewpoint, we could draw a detailed picture of the four days that led up to the riot:

By noon on Thursday, September 27, a great force had gathered at Ole Miss. Barnett and Lieutenant Governor Paul Johnson were there. Near the university's east gate, some 250 state troopers and county sheriffs were lined up, surrounded and infiltrated by a restless crowd of more than two thousand students and others. All were waiting for James Meredith and whatever U.S. marshals he might have with him. Here was Mississippi's wall of flesh.

During this dangerous impasse, Robert Kennedy awaited a call from Ross Barnett, who, through a representative earlier that day, had suggested a way out. The call didn't come. Now, at 2:50 P.M. Washington time, Kennedy took the initiative and put a call through to Barnett.

"Hello," said Kennedy.

"Hello, General. How are you?" Barnett said hospitably.

Previously the governor had been intractable. Now he was worried about the contempt-of-court hearing coming up the next day. He knew that if he didn't let Meredith into Ole Miss, he might face a huge fine and possibly jail. He was also beginning to get sober counsel from the state's moderate leaders, who backed his segregationist principles but wanted to avoid a bloodbath. Barnett got right down to the business of his plan, which would allow him to be overwhelmed by the federals while crying "Never!" for the segregationists' benefit.

The plan called for Barnett and Johnson to stand at the university's gate, backed up by unarmed state patrolmen. Kennedy would have chief U.S. marshal James McShane and twenty-five to thirty other marshals bring Meredith to the gate. Barnett would refuse to let Meredith in. Then McShane would draw his gun, and the other marshals would slap their hands on their holsters. Barnett would step aside and allow Meredith to register. The Mississippi highway patrol would maintain law and order.

In his talk with Kennedy, the governor worried about how the scene would look to "a big crowd." If only one man drew his gun, Barnett felt, he couldn't back down. So Kennedy reluctantly agreed to have all the marshals draw their guns. Under federal guns, Barnett could surrender to prevent bloodshed.

Bobby Kennedy had explained to me that he knew his own duty in this situation: to uphold the courts and do everything in his power to avoid bloodshed. He didn't want to use federal troops against, as he put it, "my fellow Americans." And for the sake of a long-term solution, he wanted to leave law enforcement in state and local hands. Barnett's scheme, however bizarre, would accomplish these purposes. Kennedy set about making plans to send Meredith and twenty-five marshals down to Oxford from their base at a naval air station near Memphis.

But an hour later Barnett called and asked for a postponement until Saturday the twenty-ninth. He seemed shaky and unsure of his control over his people. He put Lieutenant Governor Johnson on the phone. Johnson spoke worriedly of "intense citizens," sheriffs and deputies not directly under state control. It might take time to "move them." Everything was held in suspense until Barnett phoned again. Be there at 5:00 P.M. Mississippi time, he told Kennedy. It was then 2:20 P.M. at Oxford. Barnett repeatedly promised there would be no violence.

A convoy of thirteen green government sedans glided south from Memphis. Meredith, cool as always, rode in the back seat of one. He knew he was making history. At 3:35 P.M. Oxford time, Kennedy phoned Barnett to check on the situation. Barnett's answers were disturbing. He spoke generally of keeping order "all over the state. . . . We always do that." Kennedy asked for more specific guarantees.

At that point, however, Kennedy couldn't possibly realize the governor's dilemma. Barnett had set in motion forces he couldn't control. The brigade at the gate didn't know that their leader was negotiating surrender with the enemy. Their job, as many saw it, was to stop the federal marshals, even at the cost of their lives. Barnett feared the "hotheads" would call the turn.

Judge Russell Moore III, a blocky ex-Marine in command at Oxford for the governor, had originally disarmed all highway patrolmen and sheriffs. But when he got word that the feds were bringing in "the goon squad," equipped with billies and gas, he broke out helmets, nightsticks, and gas masks for the highway patrol, and let his sheriffs carry blackjacks, keep their gas guns handy, and bring in police dogs. "If the marshals had come with their guns drawn," Oxford sheriff Joe Ford said later, "they might have got by the patrol, but when they got to the sheriffs, they would have had to use them." At least one deputy carried a hidden pistol. "We're not going to just stand up here," another said, "and let that nigger in." Both troopers and sheriffs had their regular weapons locked in car trunks, near at hand. No matter what Barnett said, the crowd's emotion would have set off violence. "It would have been a donnybrook," Judge Moore said later.

At 4:35 P.M. Oxford time, Barnett phoned Kennedy again. The governor said he was worried. He was nervous. He felt unable to control the crowd. The way things were going, he thought a hundred people were liable to be killed, and that would "ruin all of us." It would, he said, be embarrassing to him.

"I don't know if it would be *embarrassing*," Kennedy said. "That would not be the feeling." He ended the conversation and ordered the convoy, which was then only thirty miles from Oxford, to turn back.

The next day, Friday, September 28, a circuit court gave Barnett until 11:00 A.M. Tuesday to purge himself of contempt. That meant, among other things, allowing Meredith to register. Now the governor had his deadline. But Robert Kennedy had a worse one. Getting Meredith into Ole Miss would be difficult and dangerous. Arresting the governor of Mississippi in his own state capitol would be much worse. Kennedy imagined the mob around the capitol building — troopers, sheriffs, hot-heads, and racists from all over. Two days earlier, the radical ex-general Edwin Walker had spoken on the radio, calling for ten thousand volunteers from every state to come to the aid of Ross Barnett. Kennedy knew he would have to do everything in his power to get Meredith into Ole Miss by Tuesday morning. If the federal government backed down, the cause of integration would be set back, maybe for a long time. That Friday afternoon he began meeting with military leaders to set up the forces that would be needed if Mississippi's defiance continued.

Just before noon the next day, a lovely early autumn Saturday in Washington, Kennedy got a call from Jackson. He wasn't expecting any change, and none was forthcoming. Kennedy put down the phone and looked around grimly. "We'd better get moving," he said, "and get in there with the military." At 12:15 he reached the president at the White House. The president told him to come over. Before leaving, the attorney general shook his head and said softly to Ed Guthman, "Maybe we waited too long."

At the White House, the president, with his brother and other advisers, set to work on military planning and on a television address to the nation, tentatively set for Sunday night. Meanwhile, Governor Barnett was on the phone again with a new charade. He proposed that on Monday morning, he, Johnson, the troopers, and the sheriffs would stand defiantly at the entrance to Ole Miss. While they waited, Meredith would be sneaked into Jackson, where facilities would be set up to register him. A "surprised" Barnett would complain bitterly of federal trickery. But on Tuesday he would allow Meredith to come to Ole Miss. He promised the president that the highway patrol would maintain law and order.

All Saturday afternoon the men in Washington considered the proposal. In a 7:00 P.M. telephone call, the president himself and Governor Barnett agreed to this plan. The governor assured him that Meredith would be safely on the campus by Tuesday morning, so the president held back his proclamation and canceled the television time set aside for his speech. Robert Kennedy returned to the Justice Department, then went home around 10:00 P.M. Just after he left his office, the phone rang. It was Barnett. Well, here we go again, Ed Guthman thought, as he heard Nick Katzenbach tell the operator he could reach the attorney general at home.

Guthman was right. The governor called off the plan. It would be too politically embarrassing, he said. Bobby Kennedy's anger rose. This seemed a clear breach of an agreement between the governor and the president. But the conversation ended amiably, with the understanding that the federal marshals would arrive with Meredith at Oxford Monday morning — in force. Barnett said he would phone again Sunday at 11:00 A.M. Washington time.

That Saturday night many men were on the move. Troop transports flew through the darkness from North Carolina to Memphis. Racial agitators drove toward Oxford from as far away as Los Angeles. At the night football game between Ole Miss and Kentucky, Ross Barnett made an emotional but equivocal speech. He knew that events were closing in on him.

Sunday, September 30, was another beautiful day in Mississippi and in Washington. Robert Kennedy and his task force were at work by 9:00 A.M. Tuesday's deadline pressed them hard. Now Kennedy was considering putting Meredith on the campus that Sunday. He knew that most of those coming to fight the government didn't expect the action until Monday or Tuesday.

Then Ross Barnett was on the phone with yet another scheme. It was basically Thursday's charade, but on a grandiose scale. On Monday morning, October 1, he would wait at the university gate, backed by a phalanx of state troopers, who would be backed by sheriffs, who would be backed by citizens — all without guns. Meredith should arrive with a large army force. The governor would read a proclamation barring him from Ole Miss. Then Kennedy's men should all draw their guns. Barnett would surrender, and the troopers would clear a way for Meredith to enter.

The attorney general could hardly believe his ears. He felt his indignation rising, but he spoke to Barnett in a cold, controlled tone. Barnett was responsible, Kennedy said, for more than his own political future. He had a responsibility to his state and the nation. Kennedy then shifted to a new tack. Unless the governor cooperated, he said, and helped maintain law and order while Meredith went on campus, the president would go on television and tell the country that Barnett had broken his word. To prove it, the president would tell all about the behind-scenes dickering.

This had a devastating effect. The governor's resistance seemed to melt away. Again and again Barnett asked that the president say nothing on television that would unveil the nature of the secret phone calls.

Kennedy suggested that Meredith be flown onto the campus by helicopter on Monday while U.S. marshals and state troopers, working together, controlled the crowd. Barnett, who knew of the secret wall-of-flesh plans for that day, voiced a fear that on Monday hundreds of people would be killed. He spoke of Mississippi's mood and of the agitators on their way from other states. Because of Monday's danger, the two agreed that Meredith should be brought in before dark on Sunday afternoon, and that the state highway patrol should help get him on campus and maintain law and order.

So ended the secret negotiations between Robert Kennedy and Ross Barnett. Our story in *Look* would go on to describe the violent events of that Sunday evening in detail. But the part about the secret deals was what would make headlines all over the country. I was convinced we had it down cold. I flew back to San Francisco for a long weekend before returning to New York to write the story with Harris and Wren.

While I was in San Francisco, the world came as close as it ever has to nuclear war. On Saturday, October 20, President Kennedy cut short a two-week political campaign tour, supposedly because he had a bad cold. Actually, he went directly into day-and-night crisis meetings with his cabinet and all his chief advisers on what to do about the Soviet missiles that had been sighted in Cuba. On Monday, October 22, he went on television to inform the nation of the crisis and to announce a naval blockade of Cuba.

How would the Soviets respond? In previous times such questions of war and peace had been discussed urbanely, atlas in hand, with brandy and cigars. Now it was a matter of life and death, of strange lights in the sky, of the possible end of all things. Distance was no longer a shield. The machine guns, the deadly watchtowers, were here, now, on California Street. Some Americans panicked that night, cowering in their basements, driving aimlessly in their cars. I went to sleep, then awakened sometime after midnight, hearing the thunder of jet engines, not just one plane but three or four: enormous wings spreading over me in the darkness, coming ominously closer and closer. In the war I had been the predator, strafing and bombing people on the ground. Now I was prey. Everyone in the world was prey. It was a different world.

I flew back to New York two days after the president's speech. Chris Wren, T George Harris, and I sat down to the task of weaving the separate strands of our reportage into a single article. After a week and a half we came up with a fifteen-thousand-word version: a small book, not a magazine article. Mich told us to cut it to ten thousand words, still a gargantuan magazine piece. Working with senior copy editor Martin Goldman, we weighed every sentence, every phrase. Chris Wren, the magazine's most junior writer, was cool and effective, a wizard at saying complex things simply. T George was as impassioned as Chris was cool. He kept wanting to say more. Even as we cut, he kept trying to add. "We've got to get this in," he would argue. "We've *got* to. Can't you *see?*"

At the same time, T George was adamant in keeping us from taking the easy way and drawing the segregationists as caricatures. He helped us realize that you can't fight against the dehumanization of blacks by dehumanizing their detractors. However much we might disagree with them, the Mississippians were human beings, and we ended up showing them as such. It was one those things that nobody notices and that everybody feels.

After three days we had cut our article to eleven thousand words. Then came our greatest ordeal. Frank Dean, our legal counsel, suggested that we meet with him in one of the executive conference rooms on the floor above the editorial offices. When I saw the galley proofs of our article, my heart sank. They were covered with a rash of red pencil marks. Dean, a small man with a New York accent, a worried look, and a serious heart condition, wasted no time.

"I have two hundred and fifty-seven specific legal objections," he said, "but they're less important than my main objection, which is that the story *in toto* is libelous. I'm recommending that it not be run. Of course, Dan Mich can overrule me."

Dan Mich will overrule him, I said to myself. It was like a prayer.

"If this article runs in *Look,*" Dean continued, "it will ruin Ross Barnett. He'll *have* to sue."

"He won't sue," T George said. "I know Barnett and he won't sue. We've got him cold. He won't want to bring all this stuff out again."

"Let me remind you gentlemen," Dean went on grimly, "the trial will be held in Mississippi. Do you want to be put on the stand by one of those Mississippi lawyers, before a Mississippi judge and a Mississippi jury?"

"He won't sue, Frank," T George said like a teacher correcting an errant student.

"Let's get on to those two hundred fifty-seven objections," I said.

For three days, from ten in the morning until seven in the evening, we went over the article, word by word. Frank Dean would bring up his objection, we would present our backup evidence, and we would then argue about wording. We sometimes altered the wording, but never yielded on a major point. Sometimes Dean clutched at his chest. I winced. I suggested we take a break. But I didn't give in on the point I was making.

Dan Mich took our final version home to read. The next morning I ran into him as he got off the elevator. He looked paler than usual. His health was obviously worsening.

"I'm running it," he said gruffly, and walked on to his office, limping slightly.

T George offered to bet Frank Dean a bottle of Jack Daniels that Governor Barnett wouldn't sue. Dean took him up on it. "This is one bet," he said, smiling ruefully, "that I sure as hell hope I lose."

At lunch T George told me that in spite of his confidence, he could sometimes imagine a Mississippi courtroom scene and "that hard, flat southern drawl in my ears." I too could hear that drawl, those Mississippi voices. Like T George, however, I was convinced that Barnett wouldn't sue. I agreed that he wouldn't want to have our material come out in court. But there was something else, a theory I had been considering ever since I had started covering the civil rights movement: Maybe every racist, at some level, *wants* to be overwhelmed. Maybe deep down he knows how wrong he is, and wants someone to make him right that wrong. Maybe underneath all the rhetoric, the cries of "Never!" there is a silent, insistent voice begging the reformists to come, and to come with irresistible force. *Do not leave us with our madness. Hurry.*

I flew to Washington for one more check of the material. The missile crisis was cooling down. The Soviet bases were being dismantled, and it had just been reported that the Soviet ships bringing the missiles had turned around when confronted with the U.S. naval blockade. Word had already starting leaking out that Bobby Kennedy had been the hero of the crisis meetings at the White House, staying cool and decisive while many of the other cabinet members and advisers had become flustered and scattered, and coming up with imaginative proposals when they were most needed.

"I hear you've had an interesting time since we last met," I said as we shook hands in his office.

"Very," he said dryly. Then his face broke open in the famous Kennedy grin.

I sat in front of his desk, galleys in hand, and went over every part of the article in which he was involved. I lunched with Ed Guthman, and spent the rest of the day double-checking our account of the Ole Miss riot with Justice Department officials who had been there. Late that afternoon I went to Guthman's outer office, where there was a television set, to watch the evening news. Just as it began Kennedy walked in, and the three of us, Kennedy, Guthman, and I, stood watching the first pictures of the Soviet freighters being turned back by the blockade. They were wonderful shots, obviously taken from an American aircraft flying slowly from the freighter's stem to stern. As the commentator called our attention to the missiles on the deck, completely covered but poorly disguised, I glanced at Kennedy. He was, as usual, wearing a white shirt with his sleeves rolled up and his tie loosened. His hands were in his pockets, his shoulders slightly hunched, and his shirttail partly out in the back. Here he was, the archetypical little brother, perhaps the second most powerful man in the free world.

When the television sequence ended, Kennedy turned to me and smiled shyly. It was that same subtle, intimate expression that had charmed and mystified me at our first meeting. I was well aware of Bobby Kennedy's reputation for being manipulative, ruthless, and as hard as nails. But there was something else about him, something ineffable that quite transcended his reputation as a tough guy on the one hand and his effectiveness and charisma on the other. At that moment I found myself liking him very much.

The Ole Miss story appeared in the December 31, 1962, issue of *Look*, and made headlines all over the country; *Look*'s clipping service sent us major articles from more than fourteen hundred newspapers. And Ross Barnett? On a trip to Chicago, he advanced angrily on a reporter who had questioned him on the *Look* article, and his aide struck the reporter in the face. Barnett knew the truth: The revelation of his secret dealings with the Kennedys was devastating. His political career was finished. More than ever, I realized the power of the national media.

Shortly after the Ole Miss article appeared, a major publisher suggested that T George, Chris Wren, and I expand the article into a short book, to be published as quickly as possible. Though the book wouldn't have been hard to do, I found myself uninterested. Not only was I busy with another *Look* assignment, but it seemed to me a book wasn't needed. *Look* had been the perfect medium for the job, and the job had been done.

There was something else. By the time we were asked to do the book, I had experienced one of those unexpected moments of illumination that can permanently alter the way one views the world. It was not a blinding light — nothing like that — and it happened in the most modest of circumstances. Still, it was to be decisive. For a long time, it seemed, maybe ever since I was thirteen, I had been searching for something that would give my life purpose and meaning. After that moment on January 10, 1963, I would have no clear set of answers, no credo, but at least I would know what I was searching for.

PART TWO

THE HUMAN POTENTIAL

10

It Doesn't Have to Be This Way.
We Could Do It Better.

1963

EVEN IN THE WILD, EUPHORIC YEARS after 1965, when I was considered by some people to be a threat to an orderly society, by others an emissary of the devil, and by one respected writer an "ambulatory schizophrenic," I always thought of myself as rather conventional. I turned my assignments in on time. I paid my bills regularly. I was never late for an appointment. I did not let my hair grow long, nor succumb to the psychedelic fashions of those times. I continued to wear Brooks Brothers suits.

At the same time, I knew very well that I marched to a different drummer, that I viewed the world not from its center but from its edge, and that, as a matter of fact, I *was* somehow "different" and "special."

Most people, of course, feel the same way, and in my opinion they are absolutely right. The circumstances of my birth, childhood, and youth however, added a certain poignancy to that universally shared sense of specialness. My maternal grandfather, as I've said earlier, was a small-town undertaker, state senator, and owner of black tenant farms. My paternal grandparents were the children of southern aristocrats whose homes and wealth were destroyed by Sherman's forces as he marched from Atlanta to the sea. One branch of my father's family recovered magnificently from this disaster; a distant cousin eventually headed the Coca-Cola Company. But my father grew up in modest surroundings, filled with that aching sense of being both chosen and dispossessed.

In any case, my father let me and my younger sister know from early childhood that we were of an aristocratic line. His middle name, and mine, revealed kinship with the nation's third vice president, the brilliant and notorious man who shot Alexander Hamilton; and it was easy to imagine that if Aaron Burr had succeeded in establishing a monarchy in the Louisiana Territory, we could have turned out to be earls or dukes. My father worked hard in the insurance business, and when I was seventeen was finally able to buy a large house in one of Atlanta's better neighborhoods. Prior to this, however, I might have looked around in vain for any objective signs of my aristocratic background. But modest surroundings didn't count. Wherever we lived was special. Whatever we did was special.

"It's what you have inside that matters," my father told us again and again. "They can take away all your material goods, but they can never take what you have inside — your talents, your knowledge, what you can feel."

Though my father was not explicitly antisocial, his sense of specialness tended to keep us away from group activities. Summer camp was not for us. We had a series of country places: rustic cabins in the Georgia pines, in the mountains, on the Chattahoochee River. One of them, named Camp Leonard, had a crude swimming pool, and it was there, at age twelve, that I finally learned to swim.

Except for music, which my father rated very high among the gifts that "they" can't take away from you, I was offered nothing in the way of formal instruction. Nor did he make any attempt to push for academic achievement. On the days my sister and I didn't feel like going to school, he was happy to sign excuses. But he fully supported the numerous hobbies I pursued at home and at our country places. Wherever we lived, space was made for my "laboratory," and there was always a piano and several other musical instruments.

As for my mother, she was very pretty, she cried a lot, and she went along. She was like one of the children, sometimes more dependent than my sister or I or the two younger brothers who came along much later. Her lifelong "nervous breakdown" began when I was five, and by the time I was six I knew it was my job to cheer her up, to bolster her confidence, to reassure her when she thought she was going to faint — in short, to be the man of the house when my father was away on his numerous business trips. Because of my mother's "sickness," my father asked his older sister, my maiden aunt, to come live with us. She served as duenna for my mother and as devoted and tireless servant for me. In her eyes, I was definitely royalty. My sister, a princess in my father's eyes, she despised.

There was also the matter of physique. Fashions in body types as well as in clothes change over the years, and in the thirties, during the Great Depression, the ideal masculine body was beefy and chunky. A well-defined musculature was not required. Beef alone would do the job, and the postpubescents who developed it were the ones who got the girls, got the student offices, and walked around school with an easy confidence. Of the few diet books that were then available, just about as many were about gaining weight as losing it. To be skinny in the era of the beefy was a painful and potentially defeating experience. But I always had a few good friends to back me up, so I dealt with the challenge of looking different by being different. Rather than withdrawing, I put myself forward, not as the leader of my crowd but as someone to be contended with. I figured that I entered every male encounter at a disadvantage, but I didn't give an inch. Lacking beef, I relied on quick reflexes, intelligence, and strategy — especially strategy. Success lay in always being a few moves ahead. But being ahead had the disadvantage of somewhat distancing me from everyone except a few close friends. I tended to see things from a certain remove, from a viewpoint different from that of most of my class-mates. I prevailed, but only at the cost of a certain inner loneliness.

I was never a wild-eyed rebel. I loved and trusted my father and mother, and my aunt. I knew they loved and trusted me. My teenage persona was somewhat theatrical — by the time I was seventeen I was driving one of the town's more colorful cars and had organized a successful thirteen-piece swing band — but my behavior was essentially conventional and I was generally happy and pleased with my life. At the beginning of my teens, however, I had already developed a distrust of conventional wisdom that would last throughout my life and shape the perceptions and actions that in the late sixties would land me in the thick of controversy. The origin of this distrust lay in my culture's treatment of what the grownups called "our darkies."

Like every child, I had received a standard version of what was real and right. This version was presented not just verbally but also by action and example, by sidelong glances and unpremeditated bodily move-ments, by what was left unsaid as well as by public statement, commu-nity structure, and those physical arrangements that involve a place to live, food to eat, and even water to drink. And at the heart of conven-tional wisdom in the South of the thirties was the matter of race. Segre-gation was not only real, it was right. The separation of the races was man's way and God's way. Our darkies were happy with things just as they were.

This was not a view that was open to question. It was held by my father and all his friends and business associates. It was held by my grandparents and all their friends and acquaintances. It was held by our family doctor and the minister of our church and all my school-teachers. It was held by the police chief and the sheriff and the mayor and the governor and all the members of the state legislature and the state senate and by both our U.S. senators and all our congressmen. These were not "bad" men. Many of them tried their best to be good parents. They went to church regularly. They donated to charity. They were exceedingly hospitable. They ran a society that, though relatively poor, seemed to work. How could anyone question that what they said was real and right?

Still, somehow, perceptions change. We are probably mistaken to think that they change all at once, in a blinding flash of light. Every cataclysmic shift in perceptions and belief follows a long period of preparation, much of it subliminal. But if there was a moment of illumination for me on the matter of race, it came during the summer when I was thirteen, when I looked into the eyes of the young black man in chains in the courthouse square of Monroe, Georgia. What I experienced was a sense of utter horror, a sickness and despair that stayed with me for several days. I emerged with one unshakable certainty. They were all wrong — my father and my grandfathers and all the ministers and doctors and teachers and politicians. My whole society was terribly, tragically wrong on a matter of immense importance. Segregation was neither man's way nor God's way. The life we led was based on injustice, humiliation, the waste of lives. Our darkies were not happy. *And neither were the whites.*

Even before the episode in the courthouse square, I had felt there was something strange about the grownups I met: the forced joviality of the men, the wearying attempts to be "nice" among the women. The nicer and more jovial they had tried to be, the queasier I had felt. After the courthouse square, I realized what was making me feel that way. The niceness was all a sham. Beneath the smiles, behind the soft words was something hard and shameful, something stuck in the throat, frozen in the eyes. It was an enormous realization: My whole society was mistaken. Most of the adults were constantly fooling themselves. My father and mother were part of that wrongness, that unreality. When they were with their friends, they were as falsely jovial and "nice" as the others. But happily, when we (our own special family) were alone and apart, they were not. Somehow, I knew I would be all right. When I grew up, I would do something different. I would be something different.

And there was my cousin Ed — he was not like the others. His impassioned tutoring had prepared me for the moment in the courthouse square. The books he had given me had opened a window on a world larger than that of the South, other possibilities, another reality. Later, throughout my teens, I kept on reading. I found friends, a few of them, who shared my feelings. At sixteen, that happy offspring of jazz called swing burst upon my life like a whirlwind or an earthquake, and further corroborated my feelings about race. The brilliance and wit of the great black musicians of the time — Ellington, Basie, Lunceford, and their side-men — put forever to rest the white southerner's denigration of the black as intrinsically inferior. On the rare occasions when I was privileged to drive across the railroad tracks to jam with some of Atlanta's black musicians, I was so awed that I could hardly bear to bring my clarinet to my lips when it was my turn to solo.

Those experiences of my teenage years left me with a question that has haunted me ever since: If conventional wisdom can be wrong on something as important as race, then might not conventional wisdom be wrong about other matters as well? It became a habit of thought to look for alternative explanations for everything that was presented to me, especially if it was presented as gospel truth by the leading authorities on the subject. As I grew into adulthood, this habit deepened. By the time I became a journalist, it wasn't so much that I tried to find new angles as that I couldn't help it.

School. The familiar sweet-sour smell of unwashed hair, processed meat, mayonnaise, mustard, Oreo cookies, ripe bananas, the drying, decaying residue of milk. Chalk on the blackboard, not quite squeaking but on the verge of it. When will it squeak? Now? Not quite. Laboriously your hand reconstructs the curves and straight lines marching relentlessly across the blackboard. The teacher's voice begins to blur and fade. Up ahead across the aisle, that girl is pulling at her hair again. She won't stop. And the boy with the crazy frozen smile is squirming out of his chair and up on his desk again. The teacher will make him sit down when she turns around. Your shoulders are tight and there's a hollow feeling in the middle of your chest. Your left heel is drumming on the floor. You stop the drumming. It starts again. When did it start? Why didn't you notice it? You look out of the window. A bird flashes past. The period's not even halfway over.

I did my first education story in 1955. Dan Mich told me to produce a special feature of fifteen or twenty pages on the plight of the teacher in America. He said I should plan and supervise it and hire experts on the subject to do most of the writing. At that time it seemed that every magazine except *Look* had its own expert education writer, and all these experts were vying with one another in attacking the public schools and those who taught in them. After reading what they had to say and talking with educators in several cities, I decided I would do all the writing myself. I would be a nonexpert. I would take the viewpoint of just who I was: a parent with daughters in the second and third grades of a public school. I got photographer Charlotte Brooks to work with me. We traveled around the country, visiting schools, interviewing leading educators. We traveled light, carrying as few preconceptions as possible.

Finally, in Decatur, Illinois, we came upon the teacher who would be the focal subject of a candid picture story. In Carolyn Wilson's second-grade classroom in Garfield Elementary School, I took an even more radical viewpoint: that of the student. I crammed my six-four frame into a child's desk near the back of the room, and after a day or two the children seemed to start seeing me as one of their own. When the teacher turned away, they proceeded to do their mischief in my plain view.

We stayed there three weeks (it seemed an age), and Charlotte's camera became a clear crystal through which might be seen the shifting lights and shadows of those twenty-eight lives, the boredom and unease, the anguish, the rare and magic moments of learning. When the story came out, I was already working on something else and never dreamed of doing any more stories on the schools. But "What Is a Teacher?" wouldn't release me so easily. It struck some sort of national chord. There were showers of letters and wires, newspaper articles, requests for reprints. Practically every national and state education journal reprinted parts of the article. The National Education Association got permission to do their own full-scale reprint, which sold more than 1.5 million copies. The text was reprinted in many languages, including Russian, and the story won both major national awards for education reporting that year.

So I often found myself in the schools in the years that followed, reporting on gifted children, school boards, superintendents, slum schools, the teaching of writing. I worked hard at not becoming an expert. Each story would be best approached as the first. And these stories kept right on winning national awards, to an extent that became embarrassing to the organizations that gave the awards, and finally to me. To be so honored by the education Establishment must have meant that I was missing something.

"What Is a Teacher?" had been, all in all, an impassioned defense of teachers against the experts, whose curious remedy was to "go back" — back to the three Rs, back to phonics, back to tough, no-nonsense subject matter drills, back to *McGuffey's Readers*. But in the heyday of *McGuffey's Readers*, only about 5 percent of the sixteen-year-olds were in school. Elementary education was a cut-and-dried affair, and high school was for the elite. The situation in the late fifties and early sixties was obviously quite different. The experts by and large talked to other experts. I doubted that any of them had spent weeks on end sitting in a child's chair. Let them try that before making their simplistic recommendations. From where I sat, I saw teachers doing the best they could in a bad situation.

But it was a bad situation. The more schools I visited and the more hours I spent in classrooms, the more I realized just how torturous and ineffective the conventional classroom setup was. When you really looked at it, the whole idea of children sitting motionless at desks listening to the same material being presented at the same rate was appalling. I began to see first grade as a violent shock to the healthy human organism. The six-year-old has just completed the most awesome learning task on this planet, mastery of spoken language, with no formal instruction whatever. He is, in fact, a master learner, happy to explore, eager to try new things. Then comes school, and he gets some stunning news: He must try to learn what the teacher says when the teacher says it, whether he's ready for it or not. He must learn to stop exploring, to reject the unfamiliar, to focus on a limited number of stimuli, to make repetitive, standard responses. He must learn — and what a hard lesson this is — that learning itself is generally dull and boring.

I made it a practice in every school I visited to take a little trip. After spending some time in a kindergarten classroom, I would walk to a fourth-grade classroom, perhaps only a few doors down the hall but a distance great enough to reveal clearly the corrosive effect of schooling on the human spirit. The five-year-olds in the kindergarten room are for the most part spontaneous, unique. When you tell them to dance, they move naturally with a sort of unorganized grace. Read them a story, and their eyes give you back its suspense, fear, laughter. We like to say their faces "light up," and when we look into this illumination, we are not ashamed to let our faces glow in return. All of this, we assume, is a natural condition of the very young. Walk down the hall to a fourth-grade classroom, and right away you notice that something has been lost. Not so many eyes are alight. Not so many responses surprise and delight you. Too many bodies and minds seem locked in painful self-awareness. This too we carelessly attribute to the natural order.

But is it really? Is it really necessary for the human animal to lose in spontaneity and imagination as it gains in knowledge and technique? Or does our conventional mode of schooling have something to do with it?

If the trip down the hall from kindergarten to fourth grade was distressing, the trip across town to high school was even worse. There were exceptions, of course — individual teachers and teaching staffs who through extraordinary talent and effort managed to create oases of real learning — but by and large what I saw was a steady deterioration in learning ability from kindergarten through high school.

And college? When I broached this subject to my friend Harold Taylor, a former president of Sarah Lawrence, he told me about what he called "four of the most depressing days of my life," during which he met, on subsequent days, with students from each of the four classes of a small, elite eastern college — one day for each class, starting with freshmen. The experience had the quality of stop-action photography, in which the effects of four years of college were compressed into that many days. The freshmen, Taylor said, were still to some extent open and inquisitive, ready for new ideas. Each subsequent class was less so, with the seniors seeming bored, cynical, and interested only in "How will this help me get a better grade?" or "What's in it for me?"

I visited hundreds of schools, thousands of classrooms, and my fascination with our way of educating the young became that of one who views a great disaster. Yes, the schools did manage to pass along a certain amount of our cultural knowledge and to teach the manipulation of symbols and certain other skills — but only with spectacular inefficiency and at great human cost. I even came to be thankful for the schools' inefficiency, for only that, along with the obduracy of certain individuals, could account for the creativity and learning ability that survived after graduation from the present school system.

Then, early in 1962, I investigated a new development in education that seemed to promise an alternative. Programmed instruction, its adherents claimed, would make it possible for students to learn individually and at their own rates through the use of teaching machines or specially written and designed workbooks. Not only that, they could learn most of the basics much more easily and quickly than with conventional teaching.

Programmed instruction had been inspired by the work of Harvard psychologist B. F. (Frederick) Skinner, who was both famous and infamous for his belief that all behavior must be ultimately predictable, controllable, and therefore improvable. It happened that Lillie was studying Skinner in a psychology course at San Francisco State at that time and was finding his work refreshingly clear and commonsensical. I read some of Skinner's articles and a couple of his books, then headed off to Cambridge to see the man himself.

Skinner was a trim, slight sixty-two-year-old with a professorial way of talking and a rather Victorian air about him. He read French aphorisms (mounted on a special rack next to the bathroom mirror) every morning while shaving, and once a year played through the entire corpus of Mozart's piano compositions (with a rather heavy touch, it must be said). But Fred Skinner was by no means stuffy. He had a lively, childlike curiosity about everything around him, especially attractive women. He applied his theories to everything from pigeons to schoolchildren, from weight control to gambling to the sonnets of Shakespeare. I spent two days visiting his home and his laboratory, learning to "shape" the behavior of a pigeon, talking nonstop about his work. It was the beginning of a relationship that was to last throughout the sixties.

According to Skinner, your tendency toward any action — your "character," "personality," "motivation" — has been shaped mostly by the consequences of past actions. How you will act in the future will be further shaped by what happens to you *after* your present or future actions;

in other words, by your interactions with your environment. Skinner by no means denied the influence of genetic endowment as a limiting factor, but he questioned the need for such "explanatory fictions" as "inner drives" or "the subconscious" to explain behavior. And he argued that learning occurs as a result not so much of being told to do something as of what happens *after* you do it. A baby's ability and tendency to say *mama* is developed not so much by her parents telling her to say *mama* as by the smile or the attention she gets when she does successfully voice the word. If the child never received any response whatever for saying *mama,* she would very soon stop saying it. The behavior would be "extinguished."

Through numerous animal experiments, Skinner discovered that not punishment but reward — "positive reinforcement," in his term — is the most effective force for changing behavior. He showed with great precision how different schedules of reinforcement affect the response pattern of the organism being reinforced. An irregular schedule of reinforcement, for example, gets more work out of a pigeon or a person than a regular schedule does. Positive reinforcement can be a grain of corn for a pigeon or a fish for a dolphin. For the human animal, it might be food, money, praise, a kiss, a smile, a fleeting nod of approval. It might consist simply of getting a right answer and knowing it's right, of working out a puzzle, of mastering a skill, of finding new beauty and order in words, music, color. Every culture and subculture, every school, every home has its own way, acknowledged or unacknowledged, of using rewards and punishments. Too often, according to Skinner, people have relied on punishment or the threat of it to control other people. Punishment, however, is less precise than reward in shaping behavior. And it creates aversive side effects — resentment, guilt, neurosis, psychosis. Nor are the results of positive reinforcement invariably positive. It can be crude and damaging, as in the piecework system of certain industries. Skinner considered himself both scientific and humane in wanting to substitute reward for punishment, in relying more and more on the subtle and "beautiful" forms of positive reinforcement.

The programmed instruction movement was an attempt to apply Skinnerian methods to education, and I was struck by how much the new technique differed from the kind of teaching I had previously seen. After two days with Skinner, I traveled around the country visiting the top people in the field, examining their work in action in the classroom, and trying out the programs for myself. Programmed instruction, as I saw it, could be described as follows:

1. The student is given information in tiny, easy-to-digest bits, only a sentence or a short paragraph at a time.

2. The information is arranged in logical order, with each step building

on those that came before. The first steps are very easy. They become more difficult so gradually that the student is hardly aware of the change. This arrangement is called a program.

3. At each step the student writes his or her answer. The student participates actively in the learning process.

4. The student is shown the correct answer immediately, so that he can compare it with his own.

5. Most programs are written and pretested to insure that almost all students will get about 95 percent of the answers right. This, according to programmers, makes learning a pleasure, not a threat, and leads students to learn faster and remember longer.

6. Each student works individually, at his own rate of speed.

7. The program (on paper or microfilm) can be loaded into a teaching machine. This, in the early days, was simply a box about the size of an attaché case. The student turned a knob to bring each step or frame before a window in the face of the box. He wrote in his answer to that frame, pulled a lever to uncover the correct answer, then went on to the next frame. A program could also be presented in book form, by printing the frames one beneath the other, with the correct answers at their side. The answers here were covered with a slider (or a ruler or sheet of paper), which the student slid down after writing each of his own answers.

Educators are usually eager to show the best face of things to visiting journalists, and I witnessed some spectacular applications of the new teaching technique. In Roanoke, Virginia, thirty-four eighth graders finished off a year's ninth-grade algebra in a half year with no homework, then tested out at a ninth-grade level. And one Roanoke senior got so carried away by a solid geometry program that he took it home with him and finished a semester's work in four days.

In spite of these successes, Skinner's claims for his theories seemed excessive. It was almost as if the formulations of Sir Isaac Newton on the motion of physical objects could be applied to all of human behavior. But I did see great possibilities in using some form of programmed instruction — perhaps improved and adapted to the computer — as a way of individualizing the teaching of certain basic subjects and thus freeing students and teachers alike from the tyranny and inefficiency of the conventional classroom. If programmed instruction really worked, it would give teachers a much more creative role in the educational process.

What most lifted my heart, however, was the optimism and ebullience that I encountered among the programmers themselves, which inspired the last paragraph of "Revolution in Education," June 1962:

> Beyond its utilitarian applications, the new movement holds out a rare
> new faith in the untapped abilities in every human being. For several de-

cades, the world's leading philosophers and poets have preached of man's weakness, helplessness and despair. It has been a long time since there has been any serious talk of the perfectability — or even the improvability — of man. Now, a buoyant, busy group of psychologists and educators are refusing to set any limit on what the average human being can accomplish. If they are right, they will give this nation a big boost in what H. G. Wells called "the race between education and catastrophe." And they will prove to the world that the human race has been selling itself short.

The article appeared in *Look* and later in *Readers Digest*. It received an unusually great amount of reader mail, and I couldn't help noticing that more than half the letters referred favorably to that last paragraph. Maybe it was yet another sign of that yearning for hope, for vision, for some transformative action, that I had first sensed early in 1960 at the White House conference. How could I speak to that yearning in my own work, my own life?

Some years later, I found myself under fire from what we call the Establishment for being too enthusiastic, for seeing the world through rose-colored glasses. I could understand this criticism, but didn't really think it was right. From where I stood, I saw my vision as emerging not from a sunny view of the world but from a sense of outrage at the darkness and the waste all around us.

The prevailing literary culture had seen the darkness and waste and had turned to the wise cynicism of Ecclesiastes: Thus it is and thus it was and thus it always will be. But I wasn't willing to accept that. I was well aware of the dark side of human existence. How could anyone be reared in the South with open eyes and not see it? I had seen it in the bicameral dungeon of race, in mutual subjugation, mutual terror. And if that was not enough, I had spent much of my youth (with my grandfather an undertaker) in the presence of death, death not as the final transformation of lives well led but as the shadowy submergence of lives only half lived. And later I had seen it firsthand in war and the preparation for war: our nuclear-armed legions in Europe, our sleek jet planes, our missiles poised to destroy the world (I had done stories on all of these). I had seen it in the Fence that splits the world and in all the other fences that we have erected against each other and ourselves. But maybe more than anywhere else I had seen it in the classroom, in the systematic, relentless destruction of human potential that goes on day after day, year after year, in schools all over the nation and probably all over the world.

I had seen all this and it had burned inside me, and at last the moment came when I was no longer willing to sit back and write about it with the currently fashionable sense of despair. The moment involved nothing as dramatic as a black man in chains, but it was nonetheless an illumination, one of those rare events during which the wiring of the brain seems suddenly to shift.

Paul Fusco and I had been assigned a major story on vocational education in America. A film crew had been hired to produce a documentary on how a *Look* team did a story and how our approach differed from that of the other media. The film would be shown on public television. I had decided to do a little preliminary reporting before the film crew closed in on us, so on the night of January 10 I got Dr. Edward Goldman, San Francisco's assistant superintendent for vocational education, to take me for a look at a local vocational school.

The school was a dreary place with the high windows of an outmoded factory or a prison. Harsh fluorescent lighting gave a pasty look to those who wandered from machine to machine like automata. The machines looked more vital than the humans. I never saw a smile or a spirited exchange.

Dr. Goldman was aware that the situation was grim, and he spoke candidly as he drove me back to California Street. We had seen many students doing sheet metal work, though there was little demand for sheet metal workers in the area. Why? Sheet metal training facilities were there, he said, and thus they were being used. Money was not available for new equipment, so what could you do? Actually, the whole situation was crazy. Industry was changing fast, and most of the skills being taught the students were already outmoded.

We went on talking after Goldman parked in front of my house. I had an idea. Why shouldn't we create a sort of basic training in each major field of the industrial arts? Not to teach specific skills, but to teach the general, overall skills that make for vocational success. Each industry would be expected to do its own specific skill training for new workers. It generally has to do that anyway. The basic training done by the public schools would be kinesthetic, tactile, theoretical. Goldman thought it was not a bad idea, but it would be hard, probably impossible, to change the system.

We sat in silence for a while. Then a short phrase spoke itself in my mind: It doesn't have to be this way. We could do it better.

Then, with no effort on my part, those words shifted from vocational education to cover everything in our society — at which point all I had seen and tried to understand for years seemed suddenly to fall into place.

It doesn't have to be this way. We could do it better.

Those entirely ordinary words somehow gave meaning to the experiences of a lifetime. They decoded the cryptic messages of my "special" childhood and youth. They focused all that I had learned in ten years of studying America as a journalist. Dr. Goldman resumed talking, and strangely enough, though my mind was racing and my body was charged from head to toe with potent but delicious electric current, I was able to respond as if nothing unusual were going on. While some distant part of me continued our conversation, I saw my future: I would write a book about how we as individuals and as a society could do things better. It would be called *A Practical Utopia.* It would be straightforward, down to earth. It would be truly radical. It would clearly demonstrate the tragic waste of human potential in our society. It would show that our society, our whole civilization, was headed in the wrong direction and needed to make a change of course involving new values, new patterns of behavior, new educational methods and goals. Goldman went on talking, I went on talking, and ideas, chapter titles, and even complete sentences for the new book streaked across my consciousness like a shower of meteors.

I stepped out of the car into the cool San Francisco night, hearing the subdued sound of city traffic, feeling the hard pavement of the sidewalk through the soles of my feet. The electric charge that had surged through my body was diminishing, but ideas were still rushing through my mind with no effort on my part. Standing on the front steps of my house, seeing the vapor of my breath, I knew I was on a new path. I had no idea where it would lead.

11

The Trouble with Utopia

UP UNTIL THE MOMENT in Dr. Goldman's car, my journals had been filled with notes for the novels I had been planning to write — first the one about suicide, and then "a New York novel of self-awareness," and finally *The Adventures of a Southern White Girl,* to be based on my cousin Sissy's involvement in the sit-ins and freedom rides. Then everything changed. From January 11, 1963, through the rest of the decade, the novel form might as well not have existed as far as my journals were concerned. Instead, there was material of an entirely different sort, material that had been dammed up for years by my stubborn insistence that I was primarily a novelist working temporarily as a journalist. With that dam broken, the ideas poured forth in a flood.

Increasingly over the past several years, traveling to schools and slums and racial battlegrounds had convinced me that most of the potential of most of the people I encountered was being routinely squandered or destroyed. James Agee had written, "I believe that every human being is potentially capable, within his 'limits,' of fully 'realizing' his potentialities; that this, his being cheated and choked of it, is infinitely the ghastliest, commonest, and most inclusive of all the crimes of which the human world can accuse itself. . . . I know only that murder is being done against nearly every individual on the planet."

Now I realized that it might be just this — the enormous, worldwide glut of what was *not* being achieved — that weighted humanity down. Maybe it was our failure to develop even a fraction of our capabilities that caused much of the world's discontent, neurosis, conflict, and crime. The murder of human potential was being done everywhere. It was not some distant, statistical event. It was close at hand, in my parents and children, my friends and brothers, myself. And wherever I searched, there appeared to be no concerted effort to correct the problem — in fact, very little awareness that it even existed. Maybe it was time to shine a spotlight on this unacknowledged crime, time to put the full development of the human potential at the forefront of our national agenda.

I found myself wanting to turn everything over and examine what was underneath. Consider, for example, the assumption in much of our best literature that the human condition is essentially tragic, that we are finally alone, that we must live constantly under the shadow of unfulfilled desire, suffering, and death. If such is the case, then only detachment or some sort of noble stoicism can save us from despair. Maybe the assumption is right. History tends to affirm the wisdom of pessimism. To assume that the tragic state is "normal" goes a long way toward explaining the injustice and suffering we see all around us, and is thus somehow comforting. For me, however, the tragic view, even if it was "right," seemed too easy, tending to justify acceptance and inaction in the face of injustice and suffering.

I wanted to try out a different assumption, if only for the sake of argument. What if the normal human condition, the normal state of the human organism, is joy? That wouldn't mean that people would be joyful all of the time or most of the time or even *any* of the time. It would simply mean that joy is what's *normal*. If you see a culture as a whole system and then enter this assumption into the system, everything else changes. If the natural state of the organism is joy, then our present mode of schooling is not only inefficient but perverted. And what about the suffocating sexual repressiveness of the South and the whole culture? How much is that repressiveness justified and perpetuated by the assumption that life is a vale of tears? And how about human relations in general, the web of lies, and queasy self-deceptions that serve social stasis and "pride"? I noted that to accept the idea of joy as the normal human condition would be difficult, since it would mean discarding much of the essential framework of our Judaic-Christian-Greco-Roman assumptions. Even the human body would have to change. "How hard it is to find a beautiful American," I wrote in my journal. "In utopia, we'll have many more beautiful people. That inner radiance of joy is what counts — not facial bone structure. Posture, the walk, too, express joy, or its many antitheses."

From the beginning I conceptualized my reformed society in terms of a sort of general systems approach. Skinner's "contingencies of reinforcement" guided me. What are we rewarded for? In what manner are we rewarded? What are the feedback loops between the individual and the society? These questions seemed more useful than a mere study of legislation and mores in analyzing a culture. Interaction was what counted. In this light, the Communist slogan "From each according to his ability; to each according to his need" made no sense at all. In terms of structure and feedback, Adam Smith (disregarding the abuses possible under his system) seemed more relevant than Karl Marx (disregarding the abuses possible under his.) My first journal entry after January 10 suggested that whatever utopia I ended up formulating would not be considered radical in a political sense: "The best test of the efficiency of a governing structure (assuming its purpose to be to maximize the joy and potential development of all its citizens) is the efficiency of its feedback mechanisms. In this respect, capitalism, free enterprise, ranks very high."

Utopias, I knew, had gone entirely out of fashion, to be replaced by such dystopias as *Brave New World* and *1984*. To discover why, I went back to some of the well-known utopias of the past, starting with *The Republic* of Plato. I had encountered that esteemed work previously only through an excerpt assigned in a college philosophy class. Now I tackled it *in toto*, at first with exasperation at the slow pace, then with an increasing sense of horror as the shape of Plato's ideal state emerged. Behind the interminable *reasonableness* of the dialogues were plans for an oppressive oligarchy, its potential for tyranny constrained only by the good will and superior nature of the ruling class, the Guardians.

There is no private property in the Republic. All women are theoretically wives of all men, with matings arranged for by lot among parents who are judged to be of good breeding stock. Children are taken from their mothers at birth and reared by the state. Artists and writers are persona non grata. Artistic expression is silenced or heavily censored. Everyone has his own place, his own status, his own duties. And the duty of the Guardians is to rule, resorting to the "noble falsehood" when necessary — which means lying to the people for their own good. There is plenty of wisdom in *The Republic*, but unless you read it as a strange sort of satire, it adds up to a monstrosity.

From there, visits to Sir Thomas More's *Utopia*, Francis Bacon's *New Atlantis*, and Edward Bellamy's *Looking Backward* confirmed that they were places in which I would prefer not to live. Then there was Skinner's modern utopia, *Walden Two*, which *Life* magazine called "a slander on some old notions of the 'good life' . . . a slur upon a name, a corruption of an impulse." I found it not so much slanderous as dull. Like the other utopianists, Skinner seemed excessively tidy, preoccupied with minor details. To teach delayed reinforcement, parents are told to hang a sugar lollipop around each young child's neck in the morning. If the child resists licking it all day (as evidenced by the absence of lick marks on the sugar coating), he or she is rewarded by getting to eat the whole thing. In Skinner's small, pastoral utopia, Plato's Guardians are replaced by behavioral managers, who arrange the contingencies of reinforcement so that people are effortlessly virtuous and happy; fear, shame, guilt, and punishment are replaced as methods of control with a process of conditioning that begins at birth. In one way, Skinner shapes up as a secular version of Dostoevski's Grand Inquisitor: He offers contentment at the cost of moral choice. I continued to admire Skinner's system of behavioral analysis as a useful tool for change, but I could see in *Walden Two* its dangers when used to control human affairs.

Then there was the problem of insulation. How could you keep a community such as Walden Two from being affected — infected, if you will — by the compelling technological advances and cultural changes of the outside world? In spite of its bias toward science, Walden Two seemed to require a static technology, as did almost all of the utopias. Though technology was relatively stable in Plato's time, today it was dynamic, and its influence was pervasive. In studying the United States as a laboratory of social change, T George Harris and I had concluded that technology was generally a far more potent force than politics in producing that change. And there seemed to be little chance of containing it within community or political boundaries. The time was coming when African and Indian villagers would not only drink Coca-Cola but also watch U.S. television. Any vision for positive social change in the sixties would best be realized by using technology humanely rather than trying to freeze it.

But the real trouble with utopia was its insistence on order at the expense of freedom. From Plato to Skinner, the utopianists seemed bent on controlling human impulse. I wanted to liberate it. The attempt to impose a high degree of order on any human group clearly tends to lead to oppression. To impose total order, moreover, is impossible. The relationship between order and the effort needed to maintain it might be represented by this idealized curve:

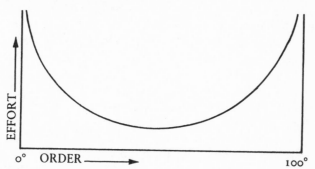

Even in something as relatively simple as a household, it's obvious that a certain optimum amount of order (the middle of the curve) takes the least effort to maintain. As the attempt to impose order increases, the effort required to maintain it rises exponentially. After a certain point on the curve, the cost of achieving order becomes prohibitively high. And finally, to keep every object in a house precisely in place, to coordinate every event precisely in time, to remove every speck of dust instantly

wherever it appears, requires infinite effort, and is thus impossible. Anarchy, the total absence of order, also requires increasing amounts of
effort to approach and is impossible to achieve, or at least to maintain.

Dealing with larger, more complex social organizations — communities, nations — requires even greater amounts of effort for each degree of
order or anarchy. Real-life dictators and utopian theorists alike share an
obsession with order; anarchists simply mirror this obsession, which in
either case is destructive to human beings and all living things. The glory
of America, it seemed to me, lay in its ability and willingness to tolerate
what must seem to traditionalists and authoritarians an alarming lack of
order. On the order-effort curve, the Soviet Union would appear far to
the right of the United States. Our willingness to accept diverse lifestyles,
freedom of individual expression, political heterodoxy, and a high crime
rate is difficult for the Soviet leadership to understand. Yet out of this
seeming chaos comes great energy and creativity.

From the beginning Americans have generally been willing to sacrifice
order for the sake of freedom. But there has always been a certain utopian cast to everything that is most characteristically American. The Pu-
ritan father John Winthrop, first governor of Massachusetts, gave a sermon aboard ship before landing at Salem harbor in 1630, in which he
spoke of "a city upon a hill" — an ideal community based on brotherhood and equality and constituting a reflection of divine order. The
American Revolution itself was idealistic, if not utopian. The American
Philosophical Society, founded by Benjamin Franklin in 1743 and later
centered on Thomas Jefferson and his friends, was less interested in theoretical speculation than in "such subjects as tend to the improvement of
[the] country, and advancement of its interest and prosperity." In the
mid-nineteenth century, hundreds of utopian associations sprang up in
America, notably Brook Farm and the Oneida Community. That these
associations (which attempted to escape rather than incorporate technological advance) eventually failed should not obscure the fact that the
map of America has always included space for utopia.

My ideal society would stand near the middle of the order-effort curve.
It would be democratic and "American" in structure and style. It would
dedicate itself to the full and free development of the individual and social potential of the human race, using technology to enhance, not stultify
or destroy, this potential. It would be by no means a typical utopia —
which made my title, A Practical Utopia, more than somewhat inappropriate. I kept using it (hoping the modifier, practical, would set it apart)
only because I couldn't think of anything better.

All through the winter and spring of 1963 I continued researching and
planning A Practical Utopia. At the same time I completed the vocational

education story, taking the opportunity to spend time with Bobby Kennedy in Washington on the pretext of including him in the documentary film that was being shot on Paul Fusco and me. Kennedy and I drove out to his home at Hickory Hill in his government limousine for lunch and a swim. Our conversation turned more and more to education.

After vocational education, Dan Mich summarily launched me into producing a boating package, one of those splashy summertime features full of beautiful females and scenic locales and the latest in pleasure boats. It turned out to be a logistical nightmare, a tricky chess game involving the interaction of boats, people, cameras, locations, and weather. Finally, in mid-July, I was ready for a month's vacation, the longest time I had taken off since starting to work. During that vacation I planned to write the outline for *A Practical Utopia*.

It was a family reunion on St. Simons Island, Georgia. My mother was there, and my sister and her three boys, and at various times my two brothers and their families — as many as fifteen people staying in a big old beach house with screened porches and that musty, salt-sea smell that houses on the southern coast always have. St. Simons was a magic place for me, rich with memories of childhood and youth. The tourist trade had passed it by, and the old lighthouse, the sleepy village by the pier, the nearly deserted beaches, the marshes on the inland side, the old live oaks hung with Spanish moss, were all just about as they had been before the war.

During the months when I had been preoccupied with imagining a better society, my own life had fallen into disarray. The stresses caused by my constant travels, along with the clash of our egos (both of us wanted so much out of life), had finally frayed the bonds that drew me and Lillie together. I had become involved with a woman who had been a friend, and had moved out for a short while. That fever was subsiding, and Lillie agreed to come to our family vacation, but only for a few days. She left then for a trip to the Northeast to see friends and maybe to visit Fred Skinner and his lab — I really didn't know. Skinner had visited us in San Francisco during a psychological conference and had been charmed by both Lillies. He had spent so much time with us that I worried about all the Skinnerians who had come to the conference to see the great man.

"I hate Skinnerians," he said with a professorial chuckle.

So now I was at St. Simons, alone in the midst of my family. Somewhere inside me was a sadness very deep and very still. I felt that if I disturbed it, it might run over, so I left it where it was. I was quieter than usual. I moved more slowly. I spent hours with my daughter Lillie, a high-spirited three-year-old who could make herself at home wherever she happened to be. And twice a day, at high tide, I rode the waves. At the beginning I would go in early in the morning and late in the afternoon, when the tide came in again. The tides advanced by a half hour or so every day, and I followed that primal rhythm until I was riding the waves at high noon and midnight, and then even later. I missed some of the high tides between two and five A.M., but that was all.

The sea was marvelously warm and sensual after the chill Pacific, teeming with so much life that the water itself was alive. At night it sparkled and glowed with its own phosphorescence. I went to the beach alone in the darkness and my footprints left a ghostly light wherever I stepped in the moist sand. I dived into a wave, not daring to imagine what manner of sea life might be lurking underneath, and when I emerged, my arms and shoulder were bathed in light. I spit out a mouthful of that rich seawater and the stream of it sparkled in the dark. I imagined myself a dragon of the depths emitting a pale and ghostly fire.

The rhythms of the sea captured me, body and mind. There was no television or radio in the house, only the sound of children playing, family laughter. Sometimes we would drive to the pier in the late afternoons, or rent motorscooters and take the winding road through spectral, moss-hung oaks to the ruins of the prerevolutionary fort where the English had fought off a Spanish attack. The dim light that filtered down through gray moss and ancient trees made us want to whisper. The only sound in the ruins was the rustle and rush of the fiddler crabs that lived in the mud on the floor of the dungeon.

The outside world began to fade away. I had short list of things to do: notes and phone calls that would wrap up some *Look* projects. The first few days I kept telling myself that I would do those chores tomorrow. But every day they seemed less important. At least you can phone Bill Arthur, I thought. But when I considered actually walking to the phone to call the managing editor, an unfamiliar lassitude came over me. Within two weeks the thought itself was only a distant memory, a remnant of another life. The rhythms of the sea had captured me: the tides, the clouds and wind and stars, the slap of the waves, the sound of the children. Somehow I managed to work an hour or so now and then on the outline of *A Practical Utopia*. I had all the notes; it was just a question of putting them into a marketable form.

Then something entirely unexpected happened. Back in the spring of 1962, I had had to decide who would replace T George Harris as my chief assistant on the West Coast when he went to join the New York office. Dan Mich told me I could pick anyone on the staff, subject to his final approval. It was a choice assignment, and both Mich and I figured that anyone offered the job would be inclined to take it. I went over the names of the nineteen senior editors listed on the masthead of the magazine. Some of them had special responsibilities: sports, business, copy editing. Others had carved out their own niches and had developed the idiosyncrasies that were encouraged by *Look*'s system, with a hard crust around them that might be hard to penetrate. I foresaw great changes, an explosive decade. It would take a new kind of journalist to cover it. The senior editors on the masthead were known quantities; I was looking for potential, promise.

My eyes kept falling on one name. John Poppy was still an assistant editor but was already doing major stories. And as far as sheer promise was concerned, Poppy had it over anyone on the staff. But my decision went beyond mere logic. Precognition or destiny, if such things exist, would have had to be involved. The fact is that I was drawn to John Poppy from the beginning, just as a well-aimed arrow is drawn to the bull's-eye.

Poppy had been a diligent researcher, and the stories he had written as an assistant editor showed the beginnings of a distinctive style: carefully crafted sentences that read like casual conversation, phrases with unusual word combinations that skirted dangerously close to awkwardness, then came out with surprising grace. There was, in fact, an unpretentious elegance about everything that Poppy did. At twenty-six years old, he was a trim, athletic five-ten and 150 pounds. He wore horn-rimmed glasses, and his sincere, studious look might have made him a fledgling college professor or corporation lawyer. He had attended Phillips Academy at Andover, Massachusetts, on full scholarship, and upon graduation had received a gold medal, the school's highest award, "for best exemplifying the ideals and traditions of Phillips Academy." At Harvard, where he started out, again, on a full scholarship, another side of his persona emerged. Liberated from the monastic prep school regimen, he learned to smoke and drink, shifted his major from Romance languages to pre-med to English, was elected president of the Harvard Dramatic Club as a sophomore, and started skipping classes in his passion for theatrical production. He lost a portion of his scholarship before his junior year, but went on to graduate *cum laude* anyway, with a senior thesis on Graham Greene titled "The Necessity of Sin."

Beneath Poppy's elegant and understated exterior beat the heart of an Eastern European romantic. His parents' marriage was something out of a storybook. John's mother, Anne, went to Prague to study German when she was seventeen, and fell in love with a forty-year-old Czech named Hugo Poppy. Anne's parents, as soon as they found out, ordered her home. Hugo followed shortly, arriving by boat wearing a heavy wool suit in midsummer, barely able to speak English. He took a train to Wilmington and appeared at Anne's door. Her father, a well-to-do Du Pont executive, ordered him away. Hugo then phoned Anne and arranged an elopement. Anne didn't climb out of her bedroom window as in the best tradition of such affairs; she and Hugo simply walked away from the house after a confrontation with her parents, fled across the state line to Maryland to get married, then took a taxi to New York. They phoned from there to give the news to Anne's parents, who called off the state police search and joined their daughter and new son-in-law for a brief meeting before the couple sailed for Prague.

At first the romantic, middle-aged Czech and his teenage bride were supremely happy. They lived a festive life, with good friends, parties, excursions to mountains and lakes. When John was born in 1935, it still seemed possible that this charmed existence might go on forever. But Prague stood directly in Hitler's path. Hugo Poppy got his wife, three-year-old John, and a new infant son out of Czechoslovakia at the end of 1938. He followed six months later on the last train that the Nazis allowed to pass the border. He rejoined his family in America and threw himself on the mercy of the man whose daughter he had stolen away. His father-in-law installed him as manager of a 240-acre dairy farm in Pennsylvania, just across the Delaware border.

John spent his childhood on the farm, doing his chores, making good grades at school, and coming to realize that his gentle, passionate, bottled-up father suffered the domination of his father-in-law. John turned out to be more complex than he at first appeared: a good boy with dreams of Byzantium, a man haunted by borders and shadows and occasional vistas of golden light.

Coming to California was an opening to one of those vistas. John was sitting in his windowless office in New York City when his phone rang. It was Dan Mich's secretary, asking him to come in immediately. In two years with the magazine, he had been in Mich's office only once. He couldn't imagine what was up. As usual, Mich offered no prologue:

"Sit down. I have two things. First, I want you to be a senior editor. And second, how would you like to go out to San Francisco and work with George Leonard for a year?"

From the beginning the two of us worked well together. John might not have been as driven or as daringly original as T George, but he had a passion for human justice and a knack for seeing the personal point of view in the larger issues, a fine eye and ear for character and nuance, and a sense of style in everything he did. Even more important, he was a learner, one willing not only to entertain new and unfamiliar ideas but also to change his ideas and himself.

John Poppy's introduction to San Francisco was a sweet autumnal interlude, but he hadn't traveled west to linger on the edge of the Pacific.

With *Look*'s marvelous disregard for geography, he was soon headed east again, to Atlanta and Greenwood, Mississippi, to do a story called "The South's War Against Negro Votes." In Mississippi he sometimes hid on the floor of a car driven by civil rights workers, because of the fact that the sight of blacks and whites riding together might attract bullets.

I had asked John to give my sister, Julia, a call while he was in Atlanta. She suggested they get together for lunch, and said she would bring her mother.

"How will I recognize you?" John asked.

"Well, you know what George looks like. I'm six feet tall and have iron-gray hair."

John was standing at the elevators at the Top of Peachtree restaurant, so intent on looking for a gray-haired, six-foot-tall woman that he entirely missed the woman who walked up with her mother and introduced herself to him. She was five-five, petite, and very pretty, with dark hair and glowing brown eyes. The three of them had a pleasant enough lunch, then John went back to work. It was a duty call, nothing more.

Before my vacation at St. Simons began, John Poppy had embarked on a difficult and extremely chancy journalistic adventure. The two of us were committed to testing the limits of what was possible in the magazine field. To our knowledge, no general magazine had ever done a major story on homosexuality in America. The subject was taboo to an extent that would be hard for later generations even to imagine. The homosexual communities in the big cities were secret enclaves, unmentioned and unmentionable. Somehow we had convinced Dan Mich to let Poppy go out, contact those communities, and do a full-scale, objective essay on the subject. John had already visited homosexuals in San Francisco, and now he was in New York. When he phoned me at St. Simons, I could tell immediately that he was depressed, and he didn't deny that the assignment, with all the secrecy involved, was getting him down. He had an interview possibility in Jacksonville, Florida, and I suggested that he join us in St. Simons afterward. There was a little airport on the island, and a DC-3 came in every morning at six. He gratefully accepted the invitation. After some high-spirited discussion among the family, it was agreed that Julia would get up early and meet him at the plane.

The airport was only a mile away, but the two of them didn't arrive at the house until ten-thirty. I saw them walking to the back door from where I was sitting at the kitchen table. Both were barefoot. John was carrying his suit jacket and tie over his shoulder, and his trousers were rolled up to his knees. Their faces were flushed, and they looked as if they had been struck by lightning and had miraculously survived. They had had lunch in Atlanta a year earlier and nothing had happened. But now it didn't take a sworn statement or even a word of explanation to see exactly what was going on.

John stayed a week, as oblivious of the outside world as I was, if for a different reason. This was clearly not a trivial or transitory infatuation. Like his Czech father who had traveled to America to steal away his young bride, John was a man of single-minded passion. Though her marriage was shaky, Julia had a husband back in Atlanta, and her three sons, ranging in age from three to fourteen, were with her at the island. What would this development mean to her life, to the family, to John, to our relationship at *Look*? Those considerations passed through my mind, then drifted away. I was so entrained to the sea and the tides that I couldn't really concern myself with that. And even if I had, it wouldn't have made any difference. The question of whether this new thing was wise or unwise, good or bad, was simply irrelevant. It was a force of nature, a fact of existence no less inevitable then the ebb and flow of the tides.

Somehow I managed to finish my outline, typing it out on a rickety old Remington portable. There were to be fourteen chapters, ranging from "A Few Words on Past Utopias" to "On the Human Potential" to "How Fifty Men — or One — Can Change the World." Included were prescriptions for radical change, including two "emergency actions." The first of these would involve a major shift of funds and energy to preschool and early elementary education, even if that meant less for high school and higher education. The second would constitute a massive push against racism at every level of our national life. What I had in the twelve pages of the outline was, finally, not a typical utopia but a series of action programs based on a re-emphasis of human potential and a recontextualization of individual and social values and goals.

I never phoned Bill Arthur, but near the end of the vacation, just as I was getting out of a shower after a midday swim, he called me. Would I be willing to come straight to New York to pick up a photographer, then fly to Paris to pick up a researcher, then on to Brescia in northern Italy to do a story on the new pope's nephew and the nephew's fiancée? I paused before answering. A towel was wrapped around my middle, and a slight breeze through the house felt good on my still-wet body. What Bill Arthur was saying sounded familiar but distant, something out of another world, another time. I made a physical effort to wrench myself into that world and time. I had done it before. I guessed I could do it again.

12

On a Foreign Street,
a Voice from Home

THE BROTHERS MONTINI loved fast cars, fine restaurants, and social status. When their uncle was named Pope Paul VI, both of them
became instant celebrities in the secular world, and perhaps in heaven as
well. Driving on the *autostrada* from Milan to Brescia, Giorgio Montini,
a thirty-eight-year-old Roman lawyer, lost control of his speeding Porsche.
It spun across the median and then across two lanes of traffic coming in
the opposite direction. Three cars had to careen off the pavement to avoid
hitting the Porsche, which ended up on the far shoulder of the *autostrada,* facing the traffic. When Giorgio arrived at his father's house in
Brescia, where we were meeting to start doing our story, all of us had to
come out and examine the car. Giorgio was bursting with excitement.
He showed us the weeds and shrubbery still attached to the Porsche's
undercarriage.

"But look, not a scratch on it," he exulted. "It's incredible, incredible."

Over and over again he described the crazy spin, the oncoming cars,
his conversation with the drivers of the cars he had forced off the road.

"They were not angry with me. They understood. They sympathized."

Finally the torrent of words slowed, and Giorgio became reflective.

"You know, I've never given much credence to this religion stuff. But
now, after what happened on the *autostrada* . . . with my uncle being
pope . . . the grace of God and all that. . . . Maybe there is something
to it after all."

It was not the kind of story I liked to do. Serge Fliegers, the Hearst
correspondent in Paris, had sold the idea to *Look* for God knows how
much money. Fliegers had made an exclusive deal with Giorgio's brother
to do "A Nephew's Portrait of Pope Paul," which would be by-lined "by
Giovanni Battista Montini as told to Serge Fliegers." Photographer Bob
Lerner and I would do a picture story to go along with the text. We
would also visit the pope to get a portrait for the cover.

The next few days consisted mostly of mad drives through the Lombardy countryside, interspersed with multicourse lunches and dinners at expensive restaurants with views of lakes and mountains, during which the discussion revolved almost entirely around food. I found the Montinis to be rather cold. Their attempts at sophistication didn't quite come off. Everything about them seemed mannered, self-serving. But my job wasn't to do an exposé. There was a huge Roman Catholic constituency in the audience of any mass magazine, eager to read anything available on the new pope and to dote on his family. Serge Fliegers, a small pouter pigeon of a man, didn't share my reservations. He enjoyed the interminable meals. He had a vested interest in making sure everything worked out. The fact that he spoke fluent Italian helped. I tried to rekindle my enthusiasm, but it was hard.

Then my stomach began aching. Every day it got a little worse. The dissonance I was feeling about my assignment might have been partly to blame, but the ache was probably due mostly to my personal situation. I hadn't seen Lillie for a month and didn't know where we stood. We wrote long letters analyzing our relationship. The letters pointed toward reconciliation, but I wondered how deep and lasting the reconciliation would be. Basically we admired and cared for each other, but our lives seemed to be out of tune. I had my career, and she wanted a career too, but she didn't know what it would be. Her father still had a folder marked "Signs of Early Genius" in his safe-deposit box. It must have been hard for her to live up to his expectations, and her own. I was happy for her to have any career she wanted; we could both have successful careers as far as I was concerned. What a waste our conflict was. Surely there was something we could do about it, some way to work it out. There had to be hope, and hope was painful.

Sometimes I would become vaguely aware that my shoulders were tense and the muscles of my abdomen were as tight as piano wires. That couldn't be very good for my internal organs. At these moments of awareness I would try to relax, using will power to control my body. Sometimes it would work. But then, before I knew it, the tension would clamp down on my body again. Another waste of human potential. What could be done about it? When I got home, I would go to my doctor. He would undoubtedly prescribe some kind of tranquilizer or muscle relaxant.

One day we were out in the Mercedes owned by the younger nephew, Giovanni Battista, who was called Giambattista. He was driving, with his fiancée, a slightly plump young contessa, sitting next to him in the front seat. Serge Fliegers, Bob Lerner, and I were in back. Giambattista was pushing the car along country roads at a particularly high speed. We came to a village with narrow streets, and he barely slowed down. As he blasted through, the car barely missed a bicyclist and seemed to brush the sleeve of an old woman. I looked back and saw that the bicyclist was on the ground and the woman was cursing us. Shortly after, we stopped for lunch.

I had already made my decision. After lunch I guided Fliegers to the parking lot ahead of the others.

"I'm driving," I said.

"You can't be serious."

"I'm completely serious."

Fliegers stopped. He was turning pale.

"You can't do that. These Italians are very proud of their driving. You'll humiliate him in front of his fiancée."

"I'm sorry. I'm driving."

"It will be the end of the story. The whole thing will go down the drain."

"I'm driving, or I'm not getting in the car."

"Look, he's the chairman of the races at Monza. His driving is his manhood. *You can't do this*." For the first time since we had met, Fliegers was losing his composure. "Do you have any idea how much *Look* has invested in this story?

"I don't know and I don't care. I'm driving."

At this point, Giambattista and the contessa came out of the restaurant. I walked over and forced a smile.

"I'd like to drive the next lap. I'd love to try out your Mercedes. Hope you don't mind."

Giambattista's face went blank, and there was a long moment during which everything was absolutely still. Then he glanced down at his fiancée, shrugged, and handed me the keys.

I knew I would grit my teeth and do a story that would make the Montinis seem what they wanted to be and what millions of readers wanted them to be: "sophisticated, high-spirited, and playful." But we didn't have much to say to each other for the rest of our time together.

Rome. I checked in at the Hotel Imperial and took a stroll on the via Veneto, pretending I was Marcello Mastroianni in *La Dolce Vita*. Bob Lerner and I were to wait in Rome until it was convenient for the pope to see us. It might be three days or it might be ten days. I had never been to Rome. I looked forward to visiting its cultural treasures at leisure. But when I returned to the hotel, there was an emergency telephone message from my ex-wife, Emma Jean, in Paris. She and her husband and my two older daughters were there on vacation. Our sixteen-year-old, Burr, was in the American Hospital with pneumonia. She was having trouble breathing.

It was eight P.M. I quickly discovered there was no way to fly from

Rome to Paris after eight P.M., so I arranged to have the pope's portrait shot without me, took off for Paris early the next morning, and made my way straight to the hospital.

Burr was sitting up in bed playing her guitar and singing. She had a slight fever, but her condition was not at all serious. The story about her trouble with breathing had resulted from my ex-wife's misunderstanding a chance remark Burr had made. I was so relieved that I wasn't angry abut Emma Jean's causing me to stand up the pope. Anyway, it would be good to spend three or four days in Paris with Burr and Mimi.

Later that morning I was walking along a street not far from my hotel, feeling the gratitude and clarity of perception that come when a family member passes the crisis in a life-threatening illness. I had slept little the night before, and now I was open and vulnerable, close to tears. I passed a newsstand and something caught my eye, something familiar yet very strange. The front pages of all the papers were just about the same. There were pictures of a great multitude on the Mall in Washington, D.C. There were bold headlines in French about two hundred thousand marchers, about Martin Luther King.

I had been out of touch with the news. There in the *Herald-Tribune* of August 29, 1963, it was: an unprecedented civil rights march on Washington the previous day, climaxed by a speech by Martin Luther King. I turned to the text and stood there on the sidewalk reading it. Back in my hotel room, I read King's speech again and again.

> I say to you today, my friends, that in spite of the difficulties and frustrations of the moment I still have a dream. It is a dream deeply rooted in the American dream.
>
> I have a dream that one day this nation will rise up and live out the true meaning of its creed: "We hold these truths to be self-evident; that all men are created equal."
>
> I have a dream that one day on the red hills of Georgia the sons of former slaves and the sons of former slaveowners will be able to sit down together at the table of brotherhood. . . .
>
> I have a dream that my four little children will one day live in a nation where they will not be judged by the color of their skin, but by the content of their character.
>
> I have a dream today.
>
> I have a dream that one day the state of Alabama, whose governor's lips are presently dripping with the words of interposition and nullification, will be transformed into a situation where little black boys and black girls will be able to join hands with little white boys and white girls and walk together as sisters and brothers.
>
> I have a dream today.
>
> I have a dream that one day every valley shall be exalted, every hill and

mountain shall be made low, the rough places will be made plains, and the crooked places will be made straight, and the glory of the Lord shall be revealed, and all flesh shall see it together. . . .

How strange it was to be reading this in a foreign country, and how marvelous. King's words sent a chill up my spine. *I have a dream.* I was no longer aware of the ache in my belly. I felt fully alive and ready for anything that might come. Once again I read the text of his speech, and I could hear the music of his voice. That music forgave my flaws, redeemed my uneven efforts, clarified my goals. It somehow pulled together everything I had dreamed of in the sixties thus far. And it was only a beginning. The revolution was real, and now the whole world was reading about it: a revolution not of guns and bombs but of hearts and minds and the music in the voice of an Atlanta boy whose skin was colored differently from mine. I swore to myself that I would further that revolution by every means at my command.

The catharsis ended. I started drawing up my plans. I would make things right with Lillie. I would revise my book outline and send it to a publisher. And as soon as possible I would finish a story I had been toying with since before my vacation.

13

"I'm Gonna Sue You for One or Two or Three Million Dollars"

1964

THE MOMENT of illumination in January had not only given me direction but also freed some material I had written for *The Adventures of a Southern White Girl.* I had expropriated some childhood experiences in Monroe — the story of my grandfather and his tenant farmers and the black man in chains and much more — and given it to my fictional heroine. Deciding not to write the novel had allowed me to take this material back and use it in my own name. Though what I had in mind was probably too personal and too explosive for *Look,* I thought I would write it anyway, just to see how it came out.

At first I hesitated, unwilling to commit myself to this piece without reservation. But after my return from Europe, after Martin Luther King's speech in Washington, I set to work in earnest, determined to write something quite different from anything I'd written before, to hold nothing back, to say exactly what it was like to be a southerner in this revolutionary time.

I shaped my article as a southerner's appeal to the North. "In this time of tragedy and violent change," I wrote "it is strange to be a Southerner away from home.

It is like living an old bad dream all over again. Hardly a day passes without something happening that gives me a start, a small shock of recognition. I am no longer surprised at the sound of the word "nigger" pronounced with a hard "r." But I am dismayed to observe among my Yankee acquaintances the gradual shrinking away from reality that goes along with racial prejudice. I do not want them to suffer the affliction that many of us Southerners have spent lifetimes escaping. I want my friends in the North and West to know, to *feel* what it is like to live as a white man in a segregated society. For I have been there.

I went on to tell about traveling to Atlanta in July and going swimming with a group of my kinfolk in a newly integrated lake that had been one of the favorite haunts of my childhood. On this summer's day, there were just about as many blacks as whites in the water. This scene only a few years earlier would have seemed as strange as science fiction.

The only ominous element was the presence of a scattering of middle-aged, shirt-sleeved men and poorly dressed women standing around the water's edge. . . . Possibly one of them had a pistol or a crude bomb hidden on his person. But it was not violence we read on their faces, or hostility or even horror. It was something far more eerie, something that sent shudders up my spine. They were gripped by an almost hypnotic fascination. Their lips were drawn back, the hard lines in their faces somehow softened, eyelids narrowed, eyes glazed. They were not really *seeing,* yet they could not move their eyes from the dazzling sunlit images before them. Their bodies must have been numb, for they were absolutely rigid; they sat or stood for minutes at a time, motionless.

All of us, North and South, who would understand the phenomenon of racial prejudice must look into those eyes. I had seen their same expression, that same zombie-like posture, at a Ku Klux Klan meeting in 1961 while a grotesque pantomime about the horrors of interracial marriage unfolded on the stage of Atlanta's former Tower Theater. I had seen it on the face of a minister as he told me how happy and contented all the Negroes were in the Mississippi town where Mack Parker had been lynched. I had seen it in Little Rock and at Ole Miss, while men and women spun for me their fantasies of proud old Southern traditions undermined by Communist agitators from the North. And I am beginning to see that expression on Northern and Western faces.

Take it as a symptom, a clue to the true nature of prejudice. Up to now, we have skirted the truth. National leaders and experts have analyzed segregation and racial prejudice as a sociological phenomenon, a political gambit, an economic lever. In limited ways, it is all of those things. But we have got to go a step farther. If we of the white race are to move effectively against the malady that cripples us, we must see it for what it is, and call it by its true name. Start with those glazed, unseeing eyes. What you are looking at is not a political, sociological or economic phenomenon. It is dangerous, self-destructive madness. . . .

Men who would murder a fourteen-year-old because, possibly, he whistled at a white woman, or those who would set a bomb to explode during a Sunday-school service attended by little girls, have lost all touch with reality. But it is not enough to restate the obvious. We must look into the hearts of "reasonable," "moderate" men — those who live in governors' mansions or sit in the U.S. Congress; our friends, our relatives, ourselves.

The madness associated with segregation takes several forms; all involve the failure of perception, the inability to make sense from the information presented to the senses. We have no trouble "understanding" our servants or our friends' servants. As long as a Negro is a servant or a slave — that is to say, not a human being — we can face him. If we should confront him as a human like ourselves, however, we might feel what he feels, and that would be unbearable.

Almost every white Southerner must start from childhood building defenses against the danger of seeing the truth. He walls himself off from one emotion after the other; he draws the shades of his sensibilities. Because he lives in a deficient society, he is not aware of his deficiencies. But to be cured is overwhelming; one realizes then that hardly any aspect of the segregationist's personality has not been damaged. Almost every white Southerner starts out as an emotional, intellectual, visual, aesthetic cripple. . . .

White Southerners need love perhaps more than anyone else. Northerners often cannot believe in "Southern hospitality," but it is real, and it can exist, *must* exist, side by side with slavery, suppression, police dogs, and lynchings. The white minority in South Africa also has a reputation for personal hospitality. Both peoples are beset by a perpetual loneliness. In some far corner of their hearts, they know their treatment of their black brothers is immoral and inhuman. They sense, without conscious awareness, that they have had to block off some of their warmth and feeling in order to endure and perpetuate the system into which they were born. More than other people, they are driven to communicate warmly. They need to show others, and thereby reassure themselves, that they really are human and loving, that their system really is, somehow, not immoral.

Southern hospitality is real, but often takes grotesque shapes. Not long after the Ole Miss riots, Mississippi's Gov. Ross Barnett was involved in an altercation with reporters in Chicago. One of his aides reportedly struck a photographer in the face. Barnett, according to *The Chicago Sun-Times*, "his teeth clenched, took several steps towards reporter Larry Weintraub and, shaking his fist in Weintraub's face, demanded, 'Give me those notes.' " The next day, he turned for a final word to another group of hostile reporters. With a broad, hospitable smile and in a sentimental tone of voice, he said, "Come to see us. Come by the Governor's mansion. . . . Yes, sir, you come to the Capitol." This was no pose. It was precisely what would occur to a Southerner at such a moment.

Southern hospitality is the Southerner's desperate, pathetic outcry. He is saying, "I am not what you think I am. I am not what I think I am." The Southerner needs love, and in love (as some Southern writers have said) may come the solution to the Negro problem. But ahead of that lies much pain for all of us, South and North.

I told of the rides I took with my grandfather to his tenant farms in the countryside around Monroe, and of his reassurances to me that our darkies were really happy, that they wouldn't have it any other way. I told of the young black man in chains in the courthouse square, and of how our eyes met. To the best of my ability, I was honest.

Strange things pop up at us like gargoyles when we are liberated from our delusions. Madness never seems so real as when we first escape it. My own liberation came through fortunate circumstances while I was still in my teens, even before I joined the Air Corps in 1942. When I first began meeting Negroes as equals, I thought I was entirely prepared, emotionally and intellectually. But at the beginning, something happened, so embarrassing to me I have never before been able to tell anyone. Each time I shook hands with a Negro, I felt an urge to wash my hands. Every rational impulse, all that I considered best in myself, struggled against this urge. But the hand that had touched the dark skin had a will of its own and would not be dissuaded from signaling it was unclean.

That is what I mean by madness. Because, from the day I was born, black hands had held me, bathed me, fed me, mixed dough for my biscuits. No thought *then* of uncleanliness or disease.

At the end, I told of revisiting Monroe just before going on my vacation to St. Simons.

When I drove into Monroe at noon on that hot July day in 1963, much was the same. The Confederate monument, inscribed "Comrades," still stood guarding the courthouse square, and the old brick courthouse took me in an instant back to the summer days of childhood. Walton Street, too, seemed unchanged. The clear calls of the bluejay, the cardinal, and the wren rang through the green haze of leaves that once had seemed to shut off the outside world. But there was a strange new silence. Most of my generation, I learned, had moved away, and now there were hardly any children on Walton Street. A new residential area had sprung up on the other side of town; the younger set, some of whom had migrated in with the town's new clothing plants, lived there, in houses almost as expensive and ordinary-looking as those to be found in any suburb of Atlanta or Los Angeles.

A way of life had passed away. The Negro tenant farmers had somehow disappeared. Many of the old farmhouses stood empty; the fields that once had bloomed with cotton now were planted with pines; the rabbit, the possum, and the fox flourished. I learned that our old Marcus had died. His children, so far as anyone knew, had moved to the cities, mostly in the North.

Integration had not come to Monroe. But Atlanta now seemed closer, and the town's citizens knew that, sooner or later, *"they"* would arrive. There were bitter faces in Monroe, especially among the older generation. But there was also a sad sense of inevitability, a reluctant readiness for change, even a wish to have it all over with.

And, everywhere, I found lingering affection for my grandfather, who had died years earlier, followed within six months by my grandmother. He had lived a long life in the esteem of his fellows. He had always loved and had wanted very much to be loved. He had been as good as his society would allow. But I learned a sorrowful thing, and I discovered later that it is common throughout the South. He had not died peacefully. In the last months of his final illness, he had been haunted by terrifying hallucinations. Several men were "after him." He felt he needed a gun to protect himself. The men were Negroes.

I hate violence with a sort of revulsion that is more visceral than cerebral. Yet, when I first read of the Negro "riots" in Birmingham, my primary feeling was elation. From my childhood, I had known Birmingham as an oppressive, brutal, inhuman place. I was amazed that so many Negroes had had the guts to move so soon into its streets.

Uprisings can cause suffering, injury, and death. But, for Negroes, there is worse pain in a life of silence and submission. In the death of the spirit lies the ultimate human defeat. I know James Baldwin was wrong: The fire is not "next time." The fire was *then,* in the past, in the long years of so-called racial peace and harmony in the South, in the years when the madness of segregation burned the hearts and spirits of Negroes and whites alike. Each movement *away* from harmony built on lies is an escape from fire.

The truth can hurt. Not facing the truth can destroy. Face it: The Negro has grievances. They are real and pressing. Setting them right will cause pain and maladjustment in South and North alike. But pretending they are not real will not make them go away. Voting for George Wallace of Alabama will not make them go away. Waiting for everyone to be "ready" will not make them go away, but will only stiffen attitudes on both sides and increase the likelihood of violence.

Let a Southerner who loves the South and all its tortured people say a word to those responsible for upholding our nation's laws: Do not delay. Do not leave us with our madness. Hurry.

It seemed unlikely that the story would ever run in *Look*. What magazine would argue in print that a sizable proportion of its readers — millions of them — were insane? But once finished, the article took on a life of its own and demanded that I at least try to get it published.

Before sending it off to Dan Mich, however, I had my family to think about. My uncle and aunt were living in Monroe, and racial tensions there were fairly high. Shortly after World War II, there had been a ghastly lynching near the town in which two black couples had been shotgunned to death. My uncle had been mayor at the time. Federal agents had swarmed over Monroe and its environs for a while, and though most people thought they knew the killer's identity, no one was willing to talk about it. I was not seriously concerned about my uncle and aunt. I figured they would have little trouble disassociating themselves from their eccentric California nephew.

My mother was a different story. She was still having a great deal of trouble adjusting to my father's death. When he died, the general opinion was that she would never be able to spend a night alone. In spite of her many phobias, she did get her own apartment. Still, every night was an agony, and now she was considering moving to Monroe and living with my aunt.

Even before my father's death, my mother had changed her thinking about race. Once the shift occurred, she, like some other white southerners, had become a dedicated integrationist. She spent considerable time on airplanes visiting me or my youngest brother, who had moved to Westport, Connecticut, to work with a marketing firm. As soon as she took her seat, she would always close her eyes and pray that a black person would sit next to her. When she arrived at the gate for one of her flights from New York, my brother told her she didn't have to worry about a thing; Martin Luther King was on the plane. Before takeoff she got up and walked to seat 19, where King always sat, and introduced herself. He asked first about my cousin Sissy, who was well known in the movement, then about me. My mother was usually terrified of flying, but when she got back to her seat, she was totally happy and at peace. "I knew," she later told me, "that if the plane crashed we would go straight to heaven."

I decided to send her a copy of my story and abide by her decision as to whether I should send it to Dan Mich.

"It's the best thing you've ever written," she told me on the phone. "You've *got* to run it."

I warned her of the possible reaction in Monroe and how this might affect her life. She said she didn't care what happened. "You *have* to run it. This is *very* important to me."

I mailed the manuscript to Dan Mich. "I'm impressed," he said gruffly on the phone. "It's long, but I don't want to change a word."

Still, it was not until July 29, 1964, that "A Southerner Appeals to the North" appeared as the lead piece in *Look*. Around nine o'clock that night, the phone rang in my San Francisco house. It was just the flat, hard, southern voice that we had dreaded hearing after the publication of the Ole Miss story. But this voice was that of my uncle in Monroe.

"George," he said without any preamble, "I've spent the afternoon with my attorney, and we're gonna sue you and *Look* magazine for one or two or three million dollars."

There was silence on the line. My experience had failed to prepare a reaction to such a statement from my uncle.

"Well," I finally said, "I'm really sorry to hear that."

"Yes," he said heavily, "one or two or three million dollars." It was midnight in Monroe. He sounded as if he might have been drinking.

"I'm really sorry to hear you feel that way" was the best I could come up with.

"You've ruined your grandfather's reputation."

"I wrote a lot of nice, affectionate things about him."

"No, we're all ruined. My business is ruined. You didn't have to do that."

"I bet it won't hurt your business at all. People will sympathize with you. Your business might improve because of this."

"You didn't have to do it, George. I'm gonna sue you for one or two or three million dollars."

For the rest of that night and over the next several days, the phone kept ringing. To my surprise, my aunt said she fully supported me. But my mother, who was in Westport, said that my aunt had told her on the phone that she was sleeping with a pistol under her pillow and that there were rumors of impending race riots. A few days later, my aunt (who had a talent for dramatic statements) phoned my mother and said she was considering shooting herself because of the continuing outcry.

I heard nothing more about the lawsuit, but found out that *Look* had been removed from the newsstands in Monroe and banned indefinitely in all of Walton County.

Then the letters started coming, a deluge of them. I opened each one with dread, trying — unsuccessfully — to put on the thick skin of the veteran journalist.

> You are the true died in the wool liberal mushy headed, addled pated, starry eyed do gooder of the type who are so swiftly bringing our Nation to a position of impotience in the world today. You just love every body, how wonderfull, I am sure you must have several lovely white daughters married to some simply wonderful Nigger men.

> God have mercy on your miserable soul, because only He can forgive you for the distorted, hate-ridden, biased editorial in "LOOK" of August 11, 1964. *You* are not a Southerner, Northerner, or even an American! Anyone who spreads hatred as you are doing *should* be treated as a mad dog.

> Why don't you crawl in a hole and quietly rot away? But first lend an ear . . .

> If God had intended for Negro and White to live together, He would have made us all alike. Why don't you try sexual intercourse with a negro woman. I am sure that you would enjoy it. And also, may you rot in Hell with everyone of them and everyone like you. Now cuss me for everything you're worth. Then have a nigger to dinner with you tonight if you aren't one yourself. Your article didn't clearly state what you were.

> I would love to see you whipped til the blood runs down in your shoes.

Though I had expected such letters, they still tended to make my mouth feel dry. But it soon became clear that the favorable letters were going to far outweigh the unfavorable. And I was surprised (though perhaps I shouldn't have been) by how many of them were from white southerners, and how eloquent and revelatory these letters were. But my favorite southern letter didn't come from a white reader:

I am a Negro. I just had to write and let you know how very much I enjoyed reading A Southerner Appeals to the North. So truthful. Surely God has His Hands on your Soul. I only wish that there was more like you. It will be my prayer that God will Watch Over you all the days of your life. God will have to keep watch over you if you continue to speak the truth. May God bless your Precious Soul.

More than anything else, I appreciated the notes I received from my colleagues, the other senior editors of *Look*. I made a file folder to hold the scraps of yellow legal paper, *Look* stationery, and memo pads on which they had typed or scrawled their warm comments. In terms of tone and self-revelation, I had broken the prevailing rules of journalistic expression, but I had done it in a context — race relations, integration — that was familiar and acceptable. I was still one of them. What neither I nor my colleagues knew then was that there exists an unacknowledged but rigid boundary beyond which not even the most well-meaning writer can go, and that my quest was taking me dangerously close to that boundary. In less than two years I would have the occasion to reread those warm comments ruefully.

Shortly after the story came out, my mother, in spite of dire warnings, moved to Monroe to live for a while with my aunt. I considered how much more courageous she was than I in my haven 2500 miles to the west. She arrived in the midst of racial uprisings. Whether they had been triggered by my article was hard to say. There was an eight-thirty P.M. curfew. My uncle was still bitter; he delighted in showing her editorials from southern newspapers condemning my article. Country people pointed her out on the street.

I was worried. I wrote a letter full of good news, hoping to bolster her spirits and make her feel that sacrificing her own ease among her people was somehow worthwhile.

August 15, 1964

Dearest Mother,

All of us here are wondering how things are going with you, since we haven't heard since last weekend. We are hoping, hoping that nothing unpleasant is happening, although we suspect that Uncle Edward and his family just couldn't be entirely without resentment and bitterness at this time. I received a very sad, resentful letter from Ed III, ending on the note that "I hope our paths will never cross."

I plan to write him and Uncle Ed in about a week or so — no need to write now; better to let time heal a little. And I'm convinced it will.

Except for that reaction, I have nothing but remarkably good news about the story. The letters *keep* coming in, and now they are getting to be about ten to one favorable. Many Southerners write with their own "confessions" that the story triggered off. Many people write that it is the "greatest," "most moving," "most perceptive," etc. story they've ever read. As it turned out, you aren't the only one who read it more than once. Many people say they've read it over and over again.

As you know, Gary, Indiana, is the center of the "white backlash" problem. The Gary newspaper asked for and received permission to reprint the story. It appeared, in full, in last Sunday's paper, beginning on the front page with a note from the editor that the story might be a help to the people in that community. . . .

I keep getting phone calls, from people I know well and others I barely know, at all sorts of strange hours. . . . We've now begun to get letters from overseas. . . .

I tell you all of this (and there's much, much more) . . . so you'll realize that this single story is truly having a significant effect on the nation at this most critical time, and you're really the one who makes it possible and you are the only one, really, who's bearing the brunt of whatever unpleasant comes of it, since you're the one directly associated with me — the same name, even. All of us truly admire you, and we just hope that it will not be too unpleasant.

My mother wrote later that she was happy, that it was more than worth it. On her first Sunday in Monroe, she said, she attended services at the Episcopal church, though she had been reared a Methodist. At the coffee hour after the service, a woman said in a very loud voice that she was the mother of the man who had written "that story."

"Yes," she said in an equally loud voice. "I am the mother. That is my son."

At that moment, the women all rallied around her. "From then on," she wrote me, "I fell in love with the Episcopal Church."

14

"We Are Students, Not IBM Cards"

I DIDN'T WANT to believe it.

Cal Bernstein and I were on a school playground in San Francisco. We were doing a story called "Integration in Reverse" about a winsome seven-year-old white girl who, with a few other white children, had recently entered an all-black school. I felt I was on the track again after having been temporarily derailed by the pope's family story. Cal was photographing our seven-year-old trying to learn a difficult form of jump rope called double Dutch when a teacher came out on the playground and walked swiftly up to us, a stricken look on her face. There was a report on the radio, she said, that President Kennedy had been shot in Dallas.

It was November 22, 1963, a crisp, sky-blue day. I didn't want to believe what the teacher said, but the moment she said it the sky seemed to darken. Cal and I left for our homes immediately. The reports on the radio were fragmentary — the newsmen didn't want it to be true — but I soon had to accept the fact that the president was dead or dying. I had met him briefly in the Rose Garden of the White House during a teacher-of-the-year ceremony, and had come away with an overwhelming impression of an extraordinary élan that quite subsumed his well-known intelligence, wit, and charm. Three years after his election, some of Kennedy's flaws were beginning to show, but none of them clouded this shining aliveness, perhaps his finest gift to the nation.

And now he was dead — the victim, it was at first assumed, of a right-wing Texas extremist. The real story turned out to be far more troubling than that.

Our black-and-white television was in the bedroom. Lillie and I sat on the edge of the bed for hours, watching as the bizarre events of the next two days unfolded. Lee Harvey Oswald, the alleged assassin, was captured in a movie theater only hours after the shooting. Oswald turned out to be more left-wing than right-wing. He had been to Russia and to Cuba. What could his motive have been? Was he alone or part of a conspiracy?

Like millions of other Americans, I forgot about my work. I stayed home watching television, hypnotized by a drama stranger than fiction. I watched Jackie Kennedy getting off the presidential plane that had flown her back to Washington, still wearing a suit spotted with the president's blood. She wanted to remind Lyndon Johnson just what his fellow Texans had done to her husband. I saw Oswald shot to death by a Dallas strip-joint owner named Jack Ruby on live television two days after the assassination. What were Ruby's motives? Was he part of a conspiracy to shut up Oswald?

It was as if something demonic had been loosed in the nation. Beneath the grief and horror was a premonition — I felt it in my solar plexus — of unperceived disorder, of questions that would remain forever unanswered; a feeling that something new and uncertain had entered our world.

Almost lost in the turmoil was another news item. Since 1932, when he had published *Brave New World*, Aldous Huxley had pointed to the future. In 1962 he had published a flawed utopia, *Island*. In recent years he had been preoccupied with human potentialities. These included, for Huxley, not only the verbal and the rational but also the "nonverbal humanities" — sensing, feeling, intuiting, creating. He had been giving lectures on this subject to whoever would hear him. His death at age sixty-nine would have been big news all over the world if it hadn't happened on the same day as the president's.

I sent the outline for *A Practical Utopia* to a respected book editor I had met while I was working in *Look*'s New York office. After a few weeks the outline came back. The editor's letter was thoughtful and generous, but he couldn't quite envision my utopia from what I had included in the outline. I realized he was right: I needed more material to bolster my argument, at the heart of which was the assumption that the human organism is endowed with an enormous amount of unused potential.

How could I get the material I needed? I recalled the outpouring of letters in response to that one paragraph about untapped human abilities at the end of the "Revolution in Education" article the previous year. It was simple: I would do a *Look* article called "The Human Potential." I sat down immediately to write my story proposal. I would have to fly all over the country to talk with leading psychologists and brain researchers. The story might take up to six months to do, and might run up to ten thousand words. Dan Mich replied quickly. No problem. Do the story.

But first I would have to pay some dues. The editorial board wanted John Poppy and me to do something, anything, to improve *Look*'s coverage of the entertainment world. So we headed for Hollywood and spent a week visiting sets and meeting movie and television stars. Our guide was Los Angeles editor Stan Gordon, one of the kindest men I had ever known. Movie and television stars were not my favorite subjects. They were at their best, it seemed to me, when the spotlight was on, when the camera was rolling. In real life they seemed to be rather limited, defensive people trapped and partially paralyzed in the glow of a million eyes, like rabbits held in a headlight's gleam. I didn't know what to do to make them shine off-camera. After a number of meetings and discussions, John and I concluded that we should try treating entertainment not as fluff but just as we treated every other subject. John took on a short piece about Mary Tyler Moore and a major feature on the television series *Bonanza*. I did a picture story with Paul Fusco on a bit player and jazz singer named Fran Jeffreys, who was touring with Count Basie, one of my long-time heroes. I felt privileged to join the Basie tour, to sit with the Count on his piano bench, to share brandy from the half-pint bottle he always had with him.

After that, in the marvelous schizophrenia attendant upon the life of a mass magazine journalist, I did a serious essay called "What Is an Extremist?" The unease that had followed Kennedy's assassination was exacerbated by a rather alarming growth of groups that were willing to overstep the traditional limits of U.S. social and political intercourse. Most of them, including the John Birch Society, the Ku Klux Klan, and the Minutemen, were situated on the far right of the political spectrum. I attended the Republican National Convention in San Francisco's Cow Palace, where Senator Barry Goldwater was wildly cheered for justifying extremism "in the defense of liberty" and moderate Republican Nelson Rockefeller was roundly booed simply for appearing at the podium. In San Diego I visited Troy Haughton, the head of the California Minutemen, who spoke of paramilitary operations against the coming Communist takeover of America.

Meanwhile, Lyndon Johnson, in a display of legislative virtuosity unknown in the Kennedy administration, was ramrodding his Great Society program through the Congress — a major education bill, a new tax law, a civil rights act, and an economic opportunity act that declared what he called the War on Poverty. In his campaign speeches for the 1964 election, he argued against widening the conflict in Vietnam, painting himself as the dove, with the Republican nominee, Barry Goldwater, as the hawk.

And wherever you turned there was rapid movement, a sense of swift acceleration. Lillie and I had finally traded our beat-up 1957 Chevy for a sleek white new Pontiac Tempest convertible. It was a car that strenuously resisted moving at less than eighty on the freeway. But no worry; everyone else seemed to be going nearly that fast. The Tempest was equipped with a very strong engine and very weak brakes, which seemed perfectly in tune with the American spirit as of 1964.

It was a good year, a hectic, happy summer. My daughters from New

York were in for extended visits. There was a houseboating cruise on the San Joaquin delta, trips to a friend's ranch, to other friends' beach houses. And there was an unusually heavy influx of *Look* people, including managing editor Bill Arthur, who got the same kind of treatment we gave to Dan Mich. Fred Skinner was also out for a visit, also wined and dined. Whenever I could get him to talk shop, we discussed the subject of the human potential. I looked forward to September, when I figured I could start working full-time on the story I was beginning to see as my *magnum opus*.

It would seem that Lillie and I had everything we could desire: a wonderful place to live, our Frisbee group, good friends, a four-year-old who was everybody's darling, and brilliant, beautiful older daughters who were a continual source of stimulation and amazement. Now we were expecting another baby in September. We had planned it all along, figuring that four years was the perfect interval between children. But the baby was also emblematic of a new commitment. We both wished for love and passion and careers and daily chores all joined in a sort of perfect harmony — an impossible wish. But that summer was so rich and full there was no time for dissonance.

In June my sister and my colleague got married. During one of Dan Mich's staff visits to San Francisco, John had asked to see him alone.

"You probably know I've fallen in love with George's sister and asked her to marry me." There was an implied request for permission in the back of his voice.

After a slight pause, Mich responded with uncharacteristic gentleness. "I only hope that you and Julia will be as happy together as Isabella and I have been with each other."

The wedding was held in Atlanta in June. All of John's family came, but Lillie and I had to stay in San Francisco. The next day John got into the driver's seat of Julia's station wagon and started across the country with her, her three boys, and my mother, who had had all she could take of Monroe. They drove straight to California Street, where Lillie and I toasted the newlyweds. Was this nepotism? It didn't really matter. *Look* was a family anyway.

It is totally dark except for the lights from two slide projectors. It is totally silent except for the whir of the projectors' fans. About twenty or thirty spectators are sitting in a semicircle around a cleared area that serves as a stage in the attic of an old house in Berkeley. On the stage are three young women. They are totally nude except for the patterns of light and darkness projected onto their bodies. Though it is quite obvious that they are nude, it is also as if they are clothed in the patterns (now the sinuous silhouettes of vines, now a matrix of abstract waves and whorls) that cling to their bodies. And now the soft liquid notes of a lute begin to sound, and the young women are moving to the music, not really danc-

ing but swaying slowly, turning slowly, as if on the floor of a fantastical
sea.

Berkeley in the summer and early fall of 1964 was a beehive of innovation, with each new event more daring than those that had preceded it.
The attic show called "Revelations" that Lillie and I visited was only one
of the underground experiments taking place in the old houses that surrounded the University of California. And in late September of that year,
the university itself saw the birth of a new kind of social-political action.

Back in August 1962, a group of radical college students who called
themselves Students for a Democratic Society (SDS) had published "The
Port Huron Statement." Originally drafted by SDS leaders Al Haber and
Tom Hayden, the statement decried the estrangement, isolation, and depersonalization of modern life. Its language was idealistic: "Men have
unrealized potential for self-evaluation, self-direction, self-understand-
ing, and creativity. It is this potential that we regard as crucial and to
which we appeal, not to the human potentiality for violence, unreason,
and submission to authority." Inspired by the southern black Student
Nonviolent Coordinating Committee (SNCC), the SDS radicals called for
a "participatory democracy."

There was also power in numbers. With the percentage of Americans
who were college students the highest in history, the authors of the Port
Huron statement saw the university as the potential base and agency in
a movement of social change. They stated that the "New Left" must
consist of younger people who have matured in the postwar world, and
that it "must start controversy across the land." They called for an alli-
ance of students and faculty that would "wrest control of the educational
process from the administrative bureaucracy" and "make debate and
controversy, not dull pedantic cant, the common style for educational
life."

During the summer of 1964, a good number of white students from
Berkeley as well as other universities had gone South to help register
blacks to vote. They had returned not only imprinted with images of
injustice but also skilled in the tactics of nonviolent civil disobedience.
The universities were primed to explode, and the fuse was first lit, as
usual, in California. What happened at Berkeley that fall was to become
inspiration and model for hundreds of campus uprisings all over the United
States during the next several years, uprisings that eventually would un-
seat a president and help end a war. Through the mysterious magnetism
that draws certain journalists to historic events, John Poppy and Paul
Fusco, without knowing consciously that it was going to happen, were
there at the precise moment when it all began.

Poppy and Fusco were on the U.C. campus shooting a picture story on a first-year graduate student in mathematics named Michael Rossman. Their original idea had been to show a student who would carry the riches of the university out into the world with him — someone who stretched himself in many directions, including the arts, off-campus politics, the coffeehouse scene. After lunch on September 30, John and Paul interrupted a stroll toward Sproul Hall, the campus administration building, to watch a bushy-haired young man stand up on a chair and begin speaking to a cluster of students. The speaker was Mario Savio, chairman of a campus civil rights group. He and four other students had been summmoned to the dean's office for breaking university rules against overt political action on the campus: recruiting members, soliciting funds, organizing off-campus demonstrations. Would *all* of you, he asked, follow us into Sproul Hall in a show of solidarity against these unjust rules?

John figured Savio would get maybe a dozen followers, but at three P.M. Savio led three hundred students into Sproul Hall, where they staged a twelve-hour sit-in and dared the deans to punish them all. Savio and seven others were suspended from the university. The next day, students set about deliberately breaking the rules. Around noon, a dean and a campus policeman told an ex-student who refused to leave an illegal recruiting table in front of Sproul Hall that he was under arrest for trespassing, and led him to a nearby police car. Several hundred students quickly surrounded the car and sat down. Altogether, about three thousand students converged on Sproul Hall Plaza. Several hundred more sat in in Sproul Hall itself. The roof of the police car became a platform for a stream of speakers, with Savio emerging as the most impressive. The students were there to stay until the administration removed all restrictions on "free speech" — that is, political activity — on campus and pardoned the eight suspended students.

University administrators, state officials, and the national media were generally caught off guard. Universities in other countries had served as bases for radical activity, and American campuses had seen a number of civil rights demonstrations over the past four years. But this — a protest of the nature of university education itself — was entirely new. The U.C. administration announced that it would not negotiate with a mob. California governor Edmund Brown declared, "This will not be tolerated." But the demonstrators stayed through the night and all the next day. At dusk, more than five hundred armed and helmeted policemen began assembling behind Sproul Hall. Students began linking arms.

Shortly before a possibly violent confrontation, U.C. president Clark Kerr reversed the administration's decision. Just after dark he signed an agreement that elated the rebels. Not only would the cases of the eight suspended students be reconsidered, but a faculty-student-administrator committee would be created to study "all aspects of political behavior on campus." The army of police left. The demonstrators dispersed. The captured police car, its roof flattened, drove off. But that was just the beginning. On the following day, rebel leaders announced official formation of the Free Speech Movement (FSM).

All fall the battle between students and administrators surged back and forth across the Berkeley campus, with an alarmed faculty trying to make peace. The original demands of the Free Speech Movement were fairly straightforward: first, freedom to use the campus as a base for off-campus political and social action, a place to set up tables and distribute leaflets; and second, the right to make faculty and students the sole judges of educational policy, reducing administrative officers to housekeepers. Behind these demands, however, was a powerful moral disquiet. The members of the FSM saw the universities as having become instruments of cold war politics and the military-industrial complex. There had been a heady rush for government and corporate research grants, for faculty consulting jobs, and students had been relegated to an assembly-line mode of training designed to produce components for the economic machine. Little time was left for true education, for the creation of individual, thinking people, Now the components were rebelling. "We are students, not IBM cards," one of their signs read. "Do not fold, spindle, or mutilate." Students by the thousands were willing to go to jail in order to assert their humanity and to transform the university.

Michael Rossman, the young mathematician whom John and Paul had selected as the subject of their picture story, turned out to be a leader in the FSM, perhaps its most brilliant theoretician and tactician. Whenever he was in San Francisco, he would drop by the *Look* office and give us his version of what was going on. For Rossman, everything was deeper, more complex, and more significant than we could imagine. He was small and well built, with intense blue eyes. Before he would tell us what was *really* happening, he would light a cigarette, roll up his shirtsleeves, sigh, run his hand through his full head of curly hair, push his hair down into his eyes, and then — finally — torture out an eloquent statement in halting phrases that demanded our full attention. One day in early December, nearly 1000 students sat in in Sproul Hall, and 779 were arrested. The next day, as Rossman predicted, a huge number of students — an estimated 9000 — skipped classes to protest the arrests. By that time the aims, if not all the disruptive tactics, of the FSM had the support of most students and perhaps a majority of Berkeley's faculty.

We had other visitors that fall. Among them was a man named Brad Cleaveland, perhaps Berkeley's most famous, or infamous, "nonstudent." (The term was used by critics of the FSM to describe the off-campus radicals who they claimed were fomenting the rebellion.) Cleaveland did have the air of a conspirator. He handed me a broadside he had published before the uprising, calling for "open, fierce rebellion" at U.C. He sat in front of my desk making cryptic statements followed by significant looks.

"We know about you," he said. "We know your work."

"Who's *we*?"

"The ones who are making things happen."

"Who are you talking about specifically?"

"Oh, student leaders. Other people."

"Nonstudents?"

"Maybe some." He paused and fixed me with those gleaming, conspiratorial eyes. "We have copies of your 1960 issue of *Look*. You know, the one about the Explosive Generation. We sit around on the Terrace reading it, studying it."

"Studying it?" I asked.

"Yes."

Studying it? I thought after he left. The thought gave me a slight chill. I had identified the oncoming generation. Maybe I had "discovered" it. Was I also taking a role in furthering it? That had not been my intention. Still, there was no use denying that mass journalism influenced social change. What was real as well as what was important was being validated and in a sense created every day in newspapers, television, and magazines. The most powerful influence was that exerted by the standard version of events that filtered down from the *New York Times*. But since it was so pervasive, this influence was essentially invisible to those who lived under its sway. Only when someone in the media saw a somewhat different reality, then presented it in a way that was corroborated by subsequent events, was it possible to see just how journalism might be shaping as well as showing reality.

Like many other people, I was alarmed by the student rebels' lack of concern for due process, their demands for instant justice. At the same time, I could visualize those huge lecture halls holding hundreds of students, the chairs bolted to the floor, the floor rising in tiers so that students in the rear looked far down at a stick figure reciting stock answers to stock questions, speaking dryly or with self-serving wit and charm but never really touching the students' lives. Where was the dialogue? Where were the feedback loops? Quizzes graded by teaching assistants? Midterm and final exams? That wasn't enough. The university had become a huge, implacable machine, an effective screening device for graduate school or law school or the corporate recruiters, a goad to force ambitious students to learn on their own what was not being taught in the lecture hall.

It was a place where exciting research was being conducted. But how much of that research was devoted to the advancement of knowledge and how much to the advancement of the military-industrial state? It was a place of specialized training. But was it a place of education?

"There is a time," Mario Savio said to the rebels before their December sit-in at Sproul Hall, "when the operation of the machine becomes so odious, makes you so sick at heart, that you can't even tacitly take part, and you've got to put your bodies upon the gears and upon the wheels, upon the levers, upon all the apparatus, and you've got to make it stop. And you've got to indicate to the people who run it . . . that unless you're free, the machines will be prevented from working at all."

My mind was filled with questions and reservations, but my heart rejoiced.

Our new daughter was born at 11:17 A.M. on September 18. We named her Emily Winship, after my father's mother. Like her older sister, she was born by caesarean section, and she was wide awake from the beginning, looking me straight in the eyes with a rather surprised expression. And once again I was elated and filled with an awe that brought tears to my eyes. Unlike her older sister, she didn't sleep through her first night home, or for a long time thereafter. And there was one very strange thing. For the first three months of her life, a startled expression would appear on Emily's face whenever she looked at anyone. There was no question about it — even the photographs show it, she was truly startled. We joked that she had been sent here by mistake from some other planetary system where everyone had one eye and two noses, and she just couldn't get used to faces with two eyes and one nose. In any case, she had decided to be born in a startling time.

15

In Pursuit of the Human Potential

I HAD TOLD Dan Mich that the human potential story would take six months, but I knew it would be all right if it took longer. I crisscrossed the country, taking Paul Fusco with me. It wasn't Paul's usual kind of story; there were few dramatic visual possibilities in store. But he was fascinated with the subject, just as I was. In New Orleans we visited the director of Tulane University's Biomedical Computer Center, a hearty, Zorba-the-Greek type named James Sweeney. In an informal experiment on the human potential, Dr. Sweeney had transformed his janitor into a computer programmer. In Miami we met with Dr. John Lilly, who was trying to understand human intelligence better by learning to communicate with dolphins. If he succeeded, it would be a world-shaking event, the first known instance of true interspecies communication.

But there had been casualties. Lilly had tried anesthetizing dolphins so that he could implant electrodes in their brains. What he learned was that dolphins can't breathe while unconscious. In desperation, he had tried driving electrodes into their skulls without benefit of anesthesia. Now Lilly was full of remorse. He told us he had navy contracts to fulfill, but he didn't like running a concentration camp for these gentle and intelligent creatures. The dolphins, especially one large male named Egar, had never forgiven him. When we visited the tanks, Egar reared up out of the water and drenched Lilly by spitting a copious mouthful of water on him. That communication was quite clear.

Lilly was a bold experimenter, a conquistador. He had been pushing his own limits with drugs and sensory deprivation. He had suspended himself in a tank of tepid water, nude, blindfolded, ears plugged, breathing through a face mask. As much as was possible, he had become a disembodied brain. But even when cut off from sensory input, the brain was not content to rest. It reshuffled past learning and built rich and complex new inner worlds, seemingly more real than the real world. "When I went in the tank," he told us, "I could will myself into the center of a giant computer. I could see the connections reaching out from me in every direction in vivid colors. Or if I wished, I could ski across the top of the Andes, skimming from one peak to another."

We traveled on to the Human Development Institute in Atlanta, the Institute for Behavioral Research in Silver Springs, Maryland, the Child Development Institute at the University of Washington in Seattle, the Behavioral Analysis Institute in Palo Alto, California. All the researchers we met were living in a state of high excitement. There was tremendous stretch in the human system, they told us. All of their work added up to the same thing: The human brain/body/sensory system consisted mostly of unused potential. Why was this so, I wondered? For what incredible destiny was this enormous undeveloped resource provided? Why were we failing to develop it? And how were we managing to stifle it?

Bill Sullivan had an uncompromising answer to that question: School was the culprit. Dr. Maurice William Sullivan was a character out of an Ayn Rand novel. I had first met him while doing "Revolution in Education." He lived and worked with a team of equally driven people at an isolated retreat in the Los Altos hills south of San Francisco, producing dozens of elegant educational programs that he hoped would someday make teachers obsolete. Tall, balding, powerfully built, he jogged, lifted weights, practiced boxing, and kept a pistol to ward off intruders from the outside world. He spoke passionately, in complete sentences.

"In the entire psychological literature," he told me, "you can find no evidence that the teacher per se helps learning. You can find much evidence that the teacher does harm to the learning process. The average school, in fact, is no fit place to learn in. It's basically a lockup, a jail. Its most basic conditions create a buildup of resistance to learning. Physically the child is worn down by the fatigue of sitting in one position for inordinate lengths of time. Mentally he is stunned by the sameness of his surroundings and the monotony of the stimuli that bombard him. Can you imagine the amount of energy it takes just to sit still, waiting, against every impulse, for your turn to respond? Too often, when the organism does break through and start responding, he gets slapped down. He learns to sit still, to line up in orderly rows, to take instructions, to feel guilt for his natural impulses — and perhaps to do a few simple things that he could learn to do in one fiftieth — yes, *one fiftieth* — of the time it usually takes him."

I continued my travels, sometimes with Paul, sometimes alone. I carried news from one lab to another, like a bee with pollen. As I saw it, all the people in those labs were working on the same problem, but they didn't know it. What if all this work on the human potential could be connected and coordinated? I imagined a vast network of human-potential researchers and dreamed of reconciling intellectual enemies, whose ideological differences would be revealed as trivial in light of the great work that might come of their cooperation.

On one of his visits to San Francisco, Fred Skinner had given Lillie and me tapes of the famous Skinner-Rogers debate that had occurred at a meeting of psychologists. Carl Rogers was the founder of client-centered therapy, and perhaps the leading humanistic psychologist. He believed that the human organism has a natural tendency toward healthy growth. If you cut off the leading shoot of a pine tree, it will grow another one, always reaching for the light. Like tree, like human being. Given the proper environment, every person will reach for the light. And for Rogers, the proper environment could be defined simply as "unconditional positive regard." In client-centered therapy, the client (not *patient*) defines and seeks his or her own goals; the therapist serves merely as a "facilitator." This therapeutic mode is vulnerable to parody; the therapist always seems to be repeating the client's words, or just saying "Mmm-hmm." In any case, it stands at a far remove from the theory and practice of archbehaviorist Skinner, who argued that nothing is unconditional and who had a great deal of wicked fun analyzing the reinforcement powers of the therapist's "Mmm-hmms."

I could understand the differences between the famous behavorist and the famous humanist, but beneath the acrimony of the debate I could sense an incipient commonality of purpose that was worth nurturing in view of the stakes involved, which were nothing less than the development of human potential. To attempt a reconciliation between Skinner and Rogers might make tilting at windmills seem a reasonable activity, but I had always been willing to accept Cervantes as coauthor of my life's work if no one else was available. So in my talks with Carl Rogers in La Jolla, California, I took the opportunity to tell him of the many humanistic qualities in Skinner's life. I pointed out, as diffidently as I could, that behavioral analysis might be useful in the helping to understand and clarify the interactions in the intensive small-group experiences he was experimenting with.

Rogers seemed pleased to hear something positive about Skinner. "I've discovered in my own work," he said with a smile, "that children and the mentally retarded experience conditional love as more loving than unconditional love." For Rogers, this was a concession, a generous statement, and I repeated it to Fred Skinner shortly thereafter when I again visited him in Cambridge. Skinner too was pleased but unyielding.

On that occasion Paul Fusco and I sat with Skinner in his study for

seven straight hours while he talked almost nonstop, explaining the sub-
tleties, the implications, and the further reaches of Skinnerian theory. I
filled up two yellow legal pads with notes, and Paul finally stopped taking
pictures and sat motionless — his face dazed, his eyes bloodshot — as he
tried to follow Skinner's disquisition.

Skinner made a powerful case for the significance of particular schedules of reinforcement. When a reinforcement or reward (a grain of corn
in Skinner's example) is given randomly, on what is called a variable
schedule, the subject (a pigeon) reacts faster than when the reward is
given regularly. When the variable schedule is stretched — that is, when
the grains of corn are given at longer and longer random intervals — the
pigeon pecks faster yet. A pigeon can also be given an electric shock
through the grid it is standing on, along with the grain of corn. Then the
food reward can be gradually withdrawn, on a variable stretching schedule, leaving only the shock. Here you end up with a pigeon working, and
working frantically if the schedule has been skillfully stretched out, for
the "reward" of a painful shock.

My mind flashed to those people who seem bent on masochistic, self-
destructive behavior. I thought of children who work hard to get hit or
yelled at by their parents, thus receiving the attention and contact that
once was associated with love. Maybe you didn't need complicated
Freudian explanations to explain their behavior later in life.

Back at the University of California at Berkeley, while student protests
echoed outside, we visited the laboratory of psychologist David Krech,
where for several years he and his associates had been rearing matched
sets of rats in two sharply contrasting environments. One set of rats lived
in a sealed room. Each animal was isolated in a separate cage and kept
in complete darkness and silence. The second set of rats, litter mates of
the first, were kept in a rich and varied environment. They learned to
explore mazes. They were taken out and handled every day.

Krech had come up with stunning results. Starting out the same at
birth, the enriched rats developed a higher concentration of a key brain
enzyme than the deprived rats did. Not only that, their brain cortexes
became larger and heavier, because of the life they had led. The deprived
rats, when tested for learning ability, lagged far behind their more richly
educated litter mates. They were mentally crippled.

One brief glimpse into the silent, darkened room in which the deprived
rats were isolated was like a blow to the solar plexus. I thought of the
big-city ghettos I had visited. The rather cool term "cultural deprivation"
took on new force and immediacy. I remembered classrooms in which
children were quelled, silenced, placed in rigid psychic isolation. Were
those children being robbed of their potential brain tissue?

Paul Fusco went on to other assignments, and I continued my studies, reading everything I could on the brain, visiting the labs of top researchers at Berkeley, Stanford, and the University of Southern California. I was particularly attracted to the chief of the Brain Research Institute at U.C.L.A., a tall, rawboned Australian named W. Ross Adey. Many researchers tended to see the brain as a sort of computer, with each brain cell or neuron having the capacity to fire or not to fire. Given the various combinations available among billions of active neurons, this alone could account for the behavior exhibited by John Milton in composing *Paradise Lost* or by Einstein in formulating the general theory of relativity. For Ross Adey, however, this was only the beginning. Using a huge computer and a tiny electric probe that pierces a single neuron, Adey and his colleagues had discovered hitherto unsuspected electrical happenings deep within the brain. They had found complex wave patterns during learning and recall. They had measured the changing resistance to electricity across certain key brain areas and had found significant patterns during the learning process. The electricity, these waves, were found to flow not through the neurons themselves but through the softer neuroglial cells that surround them and the jellylike substance that fills the space between the cells. Adey suspected that such activity might constitute a subtle means for influencing the *probability* that neurons would fire across a relatively wide area of the brain.

"The brain," he said, "is not a telephone switchboard that operates only when signals arrive from outside. The switchboard is always flooded. It's altered in the whole. And it's altered by subtle, qualitative changes in the incoming signals — not by the presence or absence of lights on the switchboard, but by shifts of brightness or color."

I visited Adey several times, even after I had started drafting my article. I was fascinated by his model of the brain, and he was pleased when I showed him what I had written:

> With enough poetic license, we may view each neuron not merely as a computer-like cell with a single function, but as a versatile, complex personality in miniature. It may have a specialty, but is also able to participate in a multitude of memories, moods, perceptions and actions. It interacts directly with its neighbors, but also tunes in to news of distant events in the brain, ready to add its vote or its influence when the moment is appropriate. It has a stable, recognizable character, but is willing and able to change, to learn from experience.
>
> A brain composed of such neurons obviously can never be "filled up." Perhaps the more it knows the more it *can* know and create. Perhaps, in fact, we can now propose an incredible hypothesis: *The ultimate creative capacity of the brain may be, for all practical purposes, infinite.*

I started drafting "The Human Potential" in December, and by the middle of January it had grown to more than fifteen thousand words. That was already far too long for a *Look* article, and it was not nearly finished. I had already interviewed thirty-seven people, and had more material than I could possibly use. But the most important meeting, the one that would change my life, was still ahead of me.

I had heard stories during my travels about what was described as "a funny little institute on the Big Sur coast" that was holding seminars on the human potential. There was a faint air of mystery and intrigue around these stories, but nothing in the way of hard information. Somebody had given me a flyer for Big Sur Hot Springs Seminars, which I assumed was the organization people were talking about. The flyer was headed by the words "The Human Potentiality," but seemed vague as to topics, methods, and credentials. I was briefly tempted to look into this matter, but never got around to it.

With the article getting longer and longer and no end in sight, Lillie and I took off for a weekend at Bob and Nancy Morse's ranch some 150 miles south and east of San Francisco. Bob was a large man with an enormous voice and a rich sense of drama. He was an Episcopal priest, and he believed that the modern church had made a fatal error in renouncing mystery and ritual. He was fond of saying that nowadays the last place in town you'd go for a mystical experience was your neighborhood church.

I had met Father Morse at a Pacific Heights cocktail party. I heard his booming voice quoting from T. S. Eliot's *Four Quartets*. "A condition of utter simplicity," he intoned, then paused. "Costing not less than everything," I shouted across the room. We rushed together and embraced. It was the beginning of a close friendship. Morse was strenuously nonphysical and never joined our Frisbee group. His favorite playing field was the dining room table, and we met regularly for lavish dinner parties and well-lubricated restaurant meals with hours of good talk about the Christian mysteries and the earthly delights made available by the Holy Spirit.

Nancy Morse was slim and patrician, with a somewhat severe exterior. She was the widow of an heir of the Miller-Lux fortune. Use of the organization's Delta Ranch was one of the benefits bequeathed to her two young children, who of course had to be accompanied by adults. The Morses enjoyed having authors to the ranch, and they had invited Eugene Burdick, Dennis Murphy, and their wives for the weekend. Burdick had written *The Ninth Wave* and was coauthor of *The Ugly American*. Murphy was writing the screenplay for his critically acclaimed first novel, *The Sergeant*.

Lillie and I arrived at last light of a cloudy winter's day. I unpacked quickly and went to the living room, where the guests were to meet for drinks. Standing in front of a roaring fire, holding a drink in his hand, rocking slightly forward on the balls of his feet, was one of the handsomest men I had ever met. He was six feet tall and solidly built, with dark eyes and that flashing, slightly ironic, slightly quizzical smile that goes with the Clark Gable model of masculine charisma. He introduced himself as Dennis Murphy. There was no one else in the room. I poured a Jack Daniels and water, and we stood by the fire, talking.

From the beginning I noticed that Murphy was watching me intently, checking my movements, measuring me. After about two minutes, grinning matter-of-factly, he said, "We're going to have to fight."

"Fight?" I said. "Who?"

"You and I."

"Why?"

"I can tell just by looking at you. Before the weekend's over, we're going to have to fight."

I examined Murphy more closely. He seemed to be in excellent shape and exuded the confidence of a practiced street fighter. I was by no means a fighter, but on this occasion I felt completely calm and at ease.

"All right," I said. "I don't want to fight. I'm not going to start a fight. But if you want to fight, so be it."

Murphy smiled. "Good. Now that we've got that straight, let's have another drink."

After dinner that night, Murphy got into a literary argument with Burdick. The argument grew in intensity, and Murphy's language became increasingly insulting. Burdick had recently had a heart attack, but he held his ground, puffing steadily on a long cigar. Murphy pulled his chair directly in front of Burdick's and began making physical threats. It appeared that he might pounce on him at any moment. I didn't mind Murphy's playing Hemingway, but given Burdick's obviously weakened condition, this bullying was inexcusable. I decided that if he made a move toward Burdick, I would hit him with a flying tackle. I moved my chair around so as to gain the perfect angle of attack. It was an interesting evening, divided between preparing for a physical brawl that never came and enjoying a first-rate literary brawl.

There was a pheasant hunt the next morning — it was one of the activities available at the Delta Ranch — and Murphy kept everyone laughing by tramping across the field ahead of the hunters, helping the dogs flush the pheasant while swigging from a bottle of scotch. Nobody took the hunt very seriously, although Lillie made a nice overhead shot with the 16-gauge pump shotgun her father had given her when she was sixteen. Afterward, Morse and I took a leisurely stroll, and I told him how

I had planned to intercept any Murphy attack on Burdick. We agreed that however boorish Murphy's behavior had been, his discourse had been quite brilliant.

"He has a brother who's even more brilliant," Morse said. "Dennis's brother Mike spent almost two years in an ashram in India. He meditates eight to ten hours a day."

This was before trips to India and visits to gurus had become commonplace. It was the first time, in fact, I had ever heard of an American making such a pilgrimage.

The Murphy brothers, Morse explained, came from a well-to-do family in Salinas, California. Both were intellectually gifted and both were natural athletes. Except for that, however, they were as different as night and day, with Dennis a manifestation of the darkness, Mike of the light. It was rumored that the Murphys were the models for the two brothers of John Steinbeck's *East of Eden*. Steinbeck, also a resident of Salinas, was a friend of the Murphy family's and knew the brothers well; he had been brought into the world by Dennis's and Mike's grandfather, who was the town's leading physician. Dennis was obviously the brother played by James Dean in the movie version of the book. I asked Morse what the "good" brother, Mike, was doing now.

"He's trying to start some kind of institute down at Big Sur on his family's property. I don't understand exactly what he's up to. I don't think anybody does."

The weekend passed without a fight between Murphy and me. As Lillie and I got ready to drive off, in fact, he walked to the car and leaned down to shake my hand. "You're all right," he said, flashing that incredible smile. "I like you."

By the first of February I had just about finished "The Human Potential," and to my despair it was more than twenty thousand words long — a small book, not a magazine article. My assignment had certainly provided all the material I needed for *A Practical Utopia,* and more. Now I needed an informed and sympathetic reading, so I sent a copy to Lois Delattre. Lois worked at a brain research project in San Francisco's Mount Zion Hospital, a project at which Lillie was currently working. I knew Lois to be a woman of warm and generous spirit as well as one with broad knowledge of brain research. I asked her to come have lunch with me at the Garden Court after she had read my oversized draft.

We met on February 2, and she was generally enthusiastic about "The Human Potential." Her first criticism was unexpected: I had come down too hard on LSD and other psychedelics. At that time psychedelics were legal, and those who used them were by and large responsible, mature professionals who were seeking to broaden and deepen their consciousness. Street use was practically unheard of. Nevertheless, I had argued that in changing the brain for the better, both drugs and electrical stimulation were crude prostheses compared to the manipulation of the environment. I had quoted U.C.L.A.'s H. W. Magoun, an elder statesman among brain researchers: "We don't need a crutch to get around on if we have our legs. In our sense organs — eyes, ears and so on — we possess the most beautifully controlled, delicate and effective access to the brain. If we want to change a brain, we can best do it through our natural senses. That is what we *are* doing every day, what society has always done. The puzzle for the future is how to do it better."

Lois accepted that argument, but asked me if I would do a little experiment. "Just take a minute to look around at the faces in this room and then tell me if you think they could use one session with LSD."

I looked around. The light floating down from the dome of frosted glass above us softened the overall contours of every face while bringing out facial lines and wrinkles in sharp relief. The mayor and his party of visiting dignitaries were sitting just two tables away. And there were businessmen and professional people and elegantly dressed older women. I let my eyes slowly sweep around the room. The smiles I saw seemed strangely fixed. The gestures of attention and agreement seemed false and manipulative. On not a single face could I discover the expression of an authentic emotion.

I turned back to Lois, to her soft, warm, genuinely caring smile. "You've got a point," I said. I told her I would look over the section on psychedelics, but actually I doubted that I would change it significantly. Our society, through its values, its organizing principles, its methods of enculturation, its mode of schooling, had put those masks on the faces in the Garden Court. We needed to change those things, not just give people a glimpse of another reality through psychedelics.

Lois's second comment was as unexpected as her first. "I've been thinking a long time that you and Mike Murphy should meet," she said. "When I read this manuscript, I realized you *have* to meet."

"Is this the Murphy with the institute at Big Sur Hot Springs."

"Yes. They've changed the name to Esalen Institute, after the tribe of Indians who used to live there."

"I met his brother."

"They're not at all alike. Anyway, I've decided you two have to meet, and I'm not going to let you get out of it." She paused, beaming like a mother giving her child a wonderful present. "Mike's driving up from Big Sur today and he's having dinner at my house, and you're coming too, and you can't say no."

I hesitated for a moment. "You're right. I can't say no."

16

A Shot Heard Round the World

1965

I DROVE to Lois Delattre's flat in the North Beach district with that spicy feeling of anticipation that comes just before the curtain goes up on a play. By this time Michael Murphy had begun to fascinate me. I had never met anyone who had meditated an hour a day, much less eight to ten hours. Then there was that mysterious institute on the Big Sur coast that was devoted to human potentialities. Maybe it would fit into my article in some way. Lillie had taken little Lillie and my aunt Emie on a short trip to Lake Tahoe, leaving me with four-month-old Emily and a temporary live-in baby sitter, so I had asked Merla Zellerbach, a friend from our Frisbee group, to come with me. Lois's young daughter let us in and we went back to the kitchen, where Murphy was eating cheese and crackers while Lois cooked.

He had a winning smile and a firm handshake. If I had expected to meet a pale and introspective mystic, I couldn't have been more wrong. "In addition to his other gifts," Calvin Tomkins was to write in a 1976 *New Yorker* profile, "Murphy is endowed with a warm, responsive nature, extravagant good looks, and a wild Irish charm." But *New Yorker* profiles were still years in the future. The first thing I noticed on February 2, 1965, was that Mike had his brother's dark, sparkling eyes and athletic carriage but none of his *machismo*. He was an inch or so shorter and a bit slimmer, with long legs. My perceptions were to undergo several drastic shifts over the rest of that evening, but my first impression of Michael Murphy — as a typically likable Salinas high school student body president and Stanford fraternity man — was only to be subsumed, never contradicted.

We started talking right there in the kitchen. I told him of my meeting with his brother. Mike ruefully confirmed Dennis's tendency to brawl.

The boy's father, an attorney who had briefly fought professionally as a young man, had taught both of them to box. Though Mike was two years the elder, he quit boxing with Dennis when they were teenagers.

"He was too fast," Mike said. "He'd hit me — boom! — and I never saw his fist coming. It would just *be there*. I could never see it coming."

It was hard to resist joining Murphy's infectious, rather high-pitched laughter.

Our conversation opened with a discussion of my research on the human potential, the travels I had made, the scientists I had met. With each name, each new finding I mentioned, Mike's eyes would get even wider. His attention was total and complete. I was surprised at how easily my words were coming, how very well I was explaining things. I asked about his institute, and he told me how he and a friend named Dick Price had gotten it started. Murphy and Price had been classmates at Stanford, though they didn't know each other in college. In 1960, three years after Murphy returned from India, the two of them met in San Francisco and became good friends. In the spring of 1961, Murphy and Price moved down to Big Sur to live on the Murphy family's old seaside vacation property, on which there were several houses, a motel, and hot springs. They began writing letters to people such as Aldous Huxley about their ideas, and these people almost always responded warmly and favorably. In July they decided to open some sort of center there for the exploration of new ideas: the synthesis of Eastern and Western thought, of the ancient and the modern, of science, religion, and art. The Murphy family agreed to let them have a try at it, and Murphy began firing off letters asking people to come lead seminars. For some inexplicable reason, almost everyone he invited, including Huxley, Alan Watts, Linus Pauling, Paul Tillich, Harvey Cox, and Arnold Toynbee, accepted the invitations, traveling sometimes over great distances to an unknown institute that offered the most modest of fees.

It was as if some giant magnet were drawing just the right people to the new institute. Abraham Maslow, for example, was the man who had turned psychology upside down by studying exceptionally healthy people rather than the mentally disturbed people who were the subjects of most studies. Out of this came a radically different and far more hopeful picture of human possibilities. In the summer of 1962, Maslow and his wife, Bertha, were driving down the coast road, which turned out to be more tortuous than they had expected. When darkness fell, they started looking for a place to spend the night. They spotted a light and drove off the road toward what they took to be a motel. What had happened was that they had ended up at the institute. They were astonished to find that almost everyone there was reading Maslow's *Toward a Psychology of*

Being; Mike had bought a dozen copies of the newly published book and distributed it among the staff. Beginning with this improbable meeting, Maslow became a strong supporter of the new institute.

"That had to be synchronicity," Mike explained, using Jung's term for events that seem merely coincidental but are actually more than just that. Maslow's descent *ex machina* was only one of a number of such events. "I'm keeping a journal of synchronicities," Mike said. His smile was self-deprecating and amused, but it held the promise of delightful and unanticipated mysteries.

I told Mike about Ross Adey's model of the brain, and it was as if I had handed him a marvelous gift he had been wanting for years. His eyes sparkled. The light came not just from the surface but also from somewhere inside. Beneath the persona of the genial fraternity man was a sort of inner radiance that I had never seen before.

Lois served dinner, but I hardly noticed it. Both of us kept talking nonstop, breaking in on each other in a rhythm that was counterpoint rather than interruption. Murphy offered — diffidently, boldly — a short course in Eastern thought. It was a gap in my own education, yet there was an attraction. Lillie and I had visited a Zen temple in San Francisco, and rarely missed Alan Watts's radio talks on the subject. I was especially drawn to the idea of essential, eternal truth that was confirmed not through scripture or doctrine but through direct experience. As Mike talked of the sweep of history, of armies and ideas, his voice took on a rolling cadence. I was awed by his command of names and dates and Sanskrit terms. All of this, he said, all of history, was part of the divine play. Existence is consciousness is joy: *sat-chit-ananda.*

Mike had spent eighteen months in the Aurobindo ashram in Pondicherry. Relatively unknown in the West, Aurobindo (who had died in 1950) was a giant figure in Indian history. He was born in Calcutta in 1872, but lived in England from the age of seven until he was twenty; he was educated at Cambridge and was well versed in English and French literature as well as the Greek and Latin classics long before he could read Sanskrit. When he returned to India, he joined the struggle for independence from British rule. For thirteen years he risked the gallows; he was tried three times by the British for subversive activity; once he was jailed for a year. Even when he turned to things of the spirit, he never deserted those of the world.

Aurobindo was, in fact, a master synthesizer — of Western and Eastern thought, of contemplation and action, of matter and spirit. In his concept of time he was more Western than Eastern. He saw not endless cycles but evolution. God or spirit, he argued, has descended into matter, in a process he called involution. "In every particle, atom, molecule, cell of Matter," Aurobindo wrote, "there lives hidden and works unknown all the omniscience of the Eternal and all the omnipotence of the Infinite." With the eternal and the infinite already locked in matter, the evolution of life, of mind, of a higher consciousness, is simply the manifestation or unfolding of something that already exists. (*"God is waking up!"* Mike said, almost as if it were a football cheer.) This formulation leaves room for something beyond our present limited mind, another stage in human evolution, something Aurobindo called the supramental state or the supermind.

I was enchanted. My surroundings, all the physical world, seemed to recede. I was only vaguely aware of Lois and Merla, of their rather amused smiles. With all the power of his knowledge, Mike was unfailingly deferential. If I so much as breathed as if to say something, he would stop talking. But I only wanted him to go on. For a long time I had been an explorer thirsty for new knowledge, and now I had discovered an inexhaustible fountain.

Sometime around eleven, Mike, Merla, and I drifted off to my house and continued our marathon conversation. I told him of my discovery of the sixties generation and of my growing conviction that we were living in what might be a watershed era in human history. He agreed. I outlined the evidences of cultural change that T George Harris and I had uncovered in working on the California issue, of the transformed consciousness that would be necessary to control the enormous power that had come into human hands. He agreed again. He told me of the emergence of humanistic psychology, a third force beyond psychoanalysis and behaviorism. Based on the ideas of Abraham Maslow and Carl Rogers, this new psychology was beginning to spawn promising techniques for developing the nonverbal aspects of the human potential; some of these were being tried out at Esalen. I told him of the book I wanted to write, and of the difficulties I was having putting it into a viable form. Without hesitation, he gave me a couple of ideas. He invited me to come down to Esalen and see the work being done there.

Around two A.M., the realization came over us that everything we had been doing and thinking dovetailed like the pieces of a fine woodwork. There was only one more piece to fit. I started talking about the civil rights movement, about what it was like to have been brought up in the South, about the intractability of the southern mind, the rigid customs and laws and quasi-legal understandings that kept segregation in place. It was deep and firm, this way of life. Almost all the men of my father's generation and most of my own were convinced that it would never yield. And yet under pressure of the civil rights movement, it was yielding — more swiftly, more decisively than even the most optimistic southern re-

former might have dreamed. Blacks who had been reared in utter degra-
dation, the descendants of slaves, people who until very recently wouldn't
have dared to look a white person in the eyes, were now marching through
southern streets, eating with white people, going to classes with them,
swimming with them. If this was possible, then what was not possible?
The civil rights movement had shown me something. Now people of all
races, all of us, needed to start liberating ourselves from the unacknowledged, unseen oppression that keeps us from achieving our potential,
that robs us of our very brain tissue . . .

I paused. It was very late and very still. Even the city traffic had stopped.
Mike and I were standing by the marble fireplace in the high-ceilinged
living room. Merla was sitting on the couch watching us. I had built no
fire, and I suddenly realized it was getting cold.

Mike leaned on the mantelpiece, looked at me with those extraordinary eyes (quite serious now), and said, "George, let's fire a shot heard
round the world."

"Okay, Mike," I said matter-of-factly. "Let's do it."

17

Into Outlaw Country

FIVE DAYS LATER, early on the morning of Sunday, February 7, Lillie and I left the children with my aunt and headed south to Big Sur. We drove down Highway 101 past San Jose, Morgan Hill, and Gilroy, then took 156 west past Castroville ("The Artichoke Capital of the World") over to Highway 1 at the point where it followed the long, gentle curve of Monterey Bay. It was one of those dazzling blue and green days of California's premature spring, chilly in the early morning but warming as the sun ascended. We drove through a part of Monterey, then past Carmel. We were tempted to turn off the highway and go down to the beach at Carmel, but something was drawing us southward. We stopped along the highway for gas, then pushed on past a few stores and scattered houses and a Carmelite monastery out onto the more than hundred-mile stretch of Highway 1 known as the coast road.

The coast road! To the right, beyond seaward-sloping meadows of vivid green, the endless glittering inky-blue Pacific surged against dark and jagged rocks. To the left, the Santa Lucia Range cascaded up to nearly five thousand feet, a rugged wilderness, a place of bobcat, mountain lion, and wild boar. As we moved southward, the space between ocean and mountains narrowed, and we could smell the chill freshness of the sea, the salty, iodine-tinged, nose-tingling redolence of kelp forests, tide pools, starfish, abalone.

Now there were few houses to be seen, or any other signs of human habitation. The coast road began to climb. We crossed one bridge, then another, and there in the distance was a magnificent sight: a graceful arch that would take us across a vertiginous gorge at the edge of the sea. Just before this bridge was a large yellow highway sign with bold black letters:

> HILLS AND CURVES NEXT 63 MILES
> DANGEROUS IN BAD WEATHER
> ROAD NOT PATROLLED AFTER DARK

I had driven past that sign before, but now it was somehow different. Officially, this was a business trip; it would go down on my expense account under "human potential story." I would interview Mike Murphy and others, and check out his institute. Some of what I found might go into my already oversized manuscript. And that might be all.

But I doubted it. The previous week's meeting with Murphy had been decisive, the taking of a pledge, a marriage of a sort. When we drove past the sign, I had a strange feeling that I was leaving a certain sureness and comfort behind. In a way I couldn't quite define, I was moving into out-law country, into a new world where the old, familiar rules might not hold true, where wonderful and dangerous and unheard-of things might happen, a world that was not patrolled after dark.

Now the mountains pressed directly against the sea and the road wound upward along a mountainside, then curved down again, threading a nar-row edge between mountain and ocean, sometimes going along the edge of a cliff, sometimes swooping downward to trace the concave edge of an inlet. The road hypnotized us. We rarely saw another car. Now and then I had to swerve to miss a large rock that had tumbled down from the steep slopes to the left of the road. It was easy to imagine a landslide that would obliterate us, sweep us down into the sea.

Then the road leveled and went inland a half mile or so past the town of Big Sur, which wasn't a town at all but only a few rustic stores and campgrounds sheltered beneath redwoods and eucalyptus trees. A long uphill stretch of road took us out to the edge of the coast again. Another twelve miles of hills and curves and many bridges, and we came to a sign — it would have been easy to miss — announcing Esalen Institute. I turned sharply right and started down a steep driveway. There it was: a few buildings and a swimming pool lying on a plateau between the coast road and the Pacific. The pool was built on a deck that seemed to jut out over the edge of a cliff above the ocean. The buildings — a redwood lodge and a few cabins — might be taken for a rustic motel. At the bot-tom of the drive was a parking lot in which new-model sedans took their places next to dusty old junk cars and trucks converted to makeshift campers.

We got out and wandered over toward what appeared to be an office. Lounging on the bench just outside were two tall, deeply tanned, bearded men who might have been nineteenth-century western outlaws. I started to say hello, but there was a heavy silence around them that was impen-etrable. Lillie and I went in the door and walked up to a counter. We stood there for what seemed a long time while two young women behind the counter went about their business, completely ignoring us. Both were slim and suntanned. They had long hair and wore intricately patterned blouses and floor-length skirts of rich colors. I noticed that neither of them was wearing a bra, something that struck me as both erotic and aggressive. When I announced that we were there at the invitation of Mike Murphy, they were unimpressed. They had no record of our reservations. They had no idea where we were supposed to stay.

I was beginning to feel sweat breaking out on my forehead when I sighted Mike Murphy out of the window. He had on a bright red cardigan sweater and was bounding through the parking lot with exuberant, long-legged strides. As he burst into the office, everything changed. Here again was the genial Stanford fraternity man with the sparkling eyes, welcoming us as if we were the most important people who had ever come to his institute. He had arranged for us to stay at the house of a psychologist named Joe Adams, just a couple of miles up the coast. But first he would show us around the property. And then there was lunch.

As we walked over to the pool, to the edge of the cliff, I began to realize just how isolated this place was. At the point of land where we stood, the Pacific Ocean stretched out beneath us on two sides. Looking to the left, southward down the coast, I could see other points of land jutting distantly out into the Pacific like the prows of enormous ships. Behind us were mountains rising to more mountains to a distant sun-struck peak. This small area of habitable land was entirely bounded by water and wilderness. I asked Mike about communications with the outside world. Television and all other microwave signals were blocked by the mountains. AM radio reception was poor. Newspapers could be received in the mail, but delivery was unreliable; not many people ordered papers or magazines. There were telephone lines, but they were likely to go down during the big winter storms. Landslides sometimes closed the highway, cutting Esalen off from the north or the south or both.

We walked down a sloping path to a lively stream that coursed down a canyon from the wilderness. We entered the canyon by ducking under some long-hanging branches and vines. It was a different world, a world of veiled light and deep silence beneath towering redwoods. We went back out to where the creek plunged in a waterfall down to a rocky beach. We climbed over giant boulders that must have been washed down from the canyon during the wildest of the storms.

Back in the lodge, lunch was already under way. The dining room was filled with an unlikely assortment of people. Mountain men and Old West characters mingled with bearded psychiatrists wearing thick glasses. And there were men in sweaters with women wearing makeup and high heels, along with college students and a few people in sweat suits. Light poured in from large sea-fronting windows and gleamed off the polished surfaces of redwood tables. Long-skirted waitresses swept haughtily around the room, bringing food and drink. Everybody seemed to be talking at once. Lillie loved it. While waiting to be served, she struck up an enthusiastic conversation with the other people at the table, and I asked Mike questions and made notes on a legal-sized yellow pad.

The first seminars the institute had held had been didactic, but now more and more of them were "experiential." It was a new word for me. What it meant, Mike explained, was that the seminarians (those who came to the seminars) wouldn't just hear about or talk about something but would actually experience it. Psychotherapist Robert Gerard, for example, would both discuss psychosynthesis, a meta-Freudian theory and method developed by Italian psychologist Roberto Assagioli, and also lead his seminarians in guided imagery and visualization exercises.

Then there was Frederick S. Perls. Mike pointed out a man sitting alone at a table near the door. With his bald head and pointed white beard, he could have been a Viennese psychiatrist or an Old Testament prophet. He saw us looking at him and fixed us with large, formidable eyes. We turned away. Fritz — that was what he insisted everyone call him — was the founder of gestalt therapy. He was seventy-two. He had known Freud and had worked with Wilhelm Reich. Just a few months earlier, he had decided to come live at Esalen. His sessions, Mike explained, were highly experiential. He believed that therapy could happen only in the here and now, and that endless analytical explorations of a person's past were not only a waste of time but a fraud. People at his seminars took turns in what Fritz called the hot seat. Everything in the "victim's" life would be brought into the present. The victim would talk to and for his dead father, for example, who would be located in an empty chair. The victim would *become* aspects of his own life. If he was an angry man, Fritz would insist that he exaggerate his anger. The sessions, Mike said, were spectacular. You could watch Fritz cutting to the core of a neurosis like a surgeon, sometimes in a matter of minutes.

I listened to all this as if I were a European of the age of exploration getting the first news of unimagined worlds. Everything Mike said had the shine of newness about it.

After finishing lunch and getting unpacked in Joe Adams's house, Lillie and I returned to the deck just outside the dining room for our first experiential session. Our teacher was a man named Bernie Gunther, and what he taught was called sensory awakening. Gunther wore tight pants and a tight T-shirt that showed off a weight lifter's muscles. He spoke in a soft, gentle, hypnotic voice, asking us first of all to close our eyes and simply become aware of our surroundings: the sounds and smells, the feeling of the air on our skin.

We stood facing the sea. The day was cool, but the low February sun was pleasantly warm on my face. The sound of the surf seemed to come from everywhere, rising, falling, circling from left to right and back again. Somewhere behind me and to the right I could hear the high, questioning chirp of a bird, and to the left, far away but almost painfully distinct, the measured notes of a flute. Gunther suggested we relax our bellies and our shoulders and then again become aware of our surroundings. I felt him coming around behind me and putting his hands gently on my shoulders. There was a strange melting sensation and a feeling of tension draining away. My shoulders seemed to drop by an inch or two.

With my eyes shut, I again opened my senses to what was around me. I took a deep breath, and there it was, that bewitching smell that would always be Esalen for me: the freshness of the sea, the camphor of euca-lyptus buds, a faintly sulfurous odor rising from the hot springs, a trace of wild sage drifting down from the mountains — all of this tingling in my nostrils, tantalizing me with the promise of new experiences, a new life.

Gunther had us open our eyes. He showed us how to let our fingers bend at the joints. He asked us to tap the top of our heads with all five fingers, at first gently, "using a lilting motion like rainfall," then more vigorously, all over the top of the head, the back of the head, all around the ears, the side of the head, and the forehead. When we finished, he asked us to close our eyes and report what we felt.

"Well," I said, "your head feels bigger — "

"*My* head feels bigger," he interrupted.

The correction pulled me up short. "My head feels bigger," I said. "I'm more aware of it."

Gunther gave each of us a small flat polished stone. He asked us to hold it in our right hand, with eyes closed, and explore it fully with our fingers. Then we were merely to hold it in our right palm and feel its weight. After that, he had us open our eyes, put the stone down, extend both arms directly in front of us, and again close our eyes.

"What are you experiencing?" he asked.

I was surprised by what I felt. "Your right arm feels longer," I said.

"*My* right arm feels longer," he corrected me again.

Again I was caught up short. But this time, instead of simply going blank, I felt the sudden click of a new connection in my brain. My eyes flew open and I looked directly at Gunther. He laughed.

It was seemingly such a small thing, this shift in the case of the personal pronoun — trivial, even. But for me it was significant. By the habitual use of *you* or *one*, I had been avoiding responsibility for what I felt. I had been abstracting something that was personal and unique. I had been making unwarranted generalizations that were ultimately depersonalizing.

Gunther continued his exercises and my body relaxed, my senses seemed to expand. But my mind kept coming back to the question of *I* versus *you* or *one*. Maybe the achievement of human potential involved not just the way we manipulated symbols and physical objects but also the way we experienced the world. Our ability to abstract and generalize had obviously produced beautiful structures of order and understanding, and had gained us great power over nature. But could it go too far?

After dinner we went to the hot baths. It was a rite of passage, and I looked forward to it with excitement and dread. If people knew anything about Esalen, they knew the baths were coeducational. Mixed nudity in those days was extremely daring. It was this more than anything else that gave the place its aura of danger and sensuality. But as Mike, Lillie, and I took our clothes off in the poorly lit, rather cold dressing room with its concrete floor, I felt anything but sensual. There were outdoor baths on either side. We went to the one on the right, the one still marked MEN.

We walked through a short passageway and out into an area that was partially roofed, entirely open on one side to the sea and the stars. My eyes were both eager and reluctant to register the scene that came within my field of vision. Wisps of steam danced in the light of two candles. Nude bodies, strange classical sculptures in male and female form, leaned against the railing, lounged on massage tables, or sat in the baths. Entering that area was crossing a boundary, one of those invisible lines that separate *before* from *after*. For me, it was a boundary not of sensuality but of vulnerability.

The three of us stepped into one of two large square tubs made of concrete blocks, into hot mineral water that at first took my breath away but soon became as softly warm and gently caressing as I had ever felt water to be. I stole glances at the bodies around me. It was a fantasy that mocked itself in the very act of coming true. It was utterly outrageous. It was completely ordinary.

I looked out into the night. The air was still, the sky incredibly clear. My eyes adjusted to the darkness. The stars were close and very bright. I stretched my legs out in the water and rested my head against the back of the bath. The nude figures were there, but it was the endless depth of the night sky that held me. I became aware there was nothing, nothing at all, between me and the most distant galaxy. Right side up could be upside down; there was really no difference. Again I was overwhelmed by the sense of *newness*. We had come to a magical place on the edge of a continent, on the edge of the world. The sound of the surf rose from the rocks below us; hot water murmured up from far beneath the earth. I felt completely happy.

The next morning I was at the baths again for a session of shiatsu with a man named Gia-fu Feng.

"Shiatsu is Japanese art, but I am Chinese!" he said, then laughed hilariously.

Mike had told me that Gia-fu had come from China to study at the Wharton School of Finance and had migrated to Big Sur to serve as accountant (he used an abacus), sometimes cook and keeper of the baths, teacher of tai chi, practitioner of shiatsu, and resident Oriental mystic. I was lying nude on one of the massage tables at the baths in the morning sunlight. Gia-fu, also nude, was pressing his thumb rather firmly into what seemed to be the most sensitive points of my body. Gia-fu was small and skinny, and he had a wonderfully droll and mischievous face.

"I am pressing into acupuncture points," he said, "but I am using thumb, not needle. This will open up your meridians and increase the flow of ch'i throughout your body. Maybe!"

Again he laughed uninhibitedly. I willed myself to feel the flow of ch'i, whatever that was, but all I could feel was the pain of Gia-fu's thumb. Now and then I regretted letting myself in for this session. I wondered what it had to do with the human potential. Lying there under these strange probings as men and women walked in and out of the baths was more an exercise in vulnerability than it was an energizing experience. But I couldn't help liking Gia-fu, and I found myself laughing along with his explosive, unpredictable cackle. And after we got dressed and started up the rather precarious path at the edge of the cliff that led back to the lodge, I did feel energized and exuberant, if only out of relief that the ordeal was over.

Except for the times that we were in the baths or having experiential sessions, I spent my every moment at Esalen with Mike Murphy, continuing the conversation we had begun on the night of our meeting. I filled up one yellow, legal-sized pad and began another. I was taking notes for the human potential article, but it was also more than that.

After dinner on Sunday night, Mike brought out one of his journals. He said he had never before shown it to anyone. I opened to a page on which he had listed similarities between the new humanistic psychology, as represented by Maslow and Rogers, and the main line of Eastern philosophy. Maslow's concept of the peak experience (an episode of egoless delight and heightened clarity during which all things seem to flow in perfect harmony) was similar to the Eastern ecstatic experience of *samadhi* or *satori*. Maslow's notion of self-actualization was similar to the Eastern notion of *yoga* or *tao*, the lifelong path of mastery that involves self-development and good works but that is not narrowly competitive or goal-oriented. Both the humanistic psychologists and the Eastern sages were open to a wide range of mental and spiritual experiences. Both agreed that consciousness was not, as hard-line scientists would have it, a mere epiphenomenon, but rather a vast *terra incognita,* a rich territory for exploration. Both agreed that human nature was not fixed and flawed, as Freud would have it, but multidimensional. And given the right environment, it was essentially good.

I made notes from Mike's notes. He seemed pleased. I turned pages. It was clear that Mike was interested in making connections, tearing down fences, building bridges. Analysis for him was not an end in itself but rather a means toward synthesis. He saw possibilities everywhere. Even our quirks and neuroses, he wrote, could be valuable. (This was an idea, he told me, that he had first hit upon when he was sixteen.) Turn a quirk around and it can become a virtue. "Somehow," he had written, "we hook ourselves onto a transcendent order. We are all stumbling toward a yoga." Some Eastern holy men had found enlightenment through the full expression of what Westerners would call neurosis; the Indian saint Ramakrishna had lived for a while as a woman, and then as a monkey. The new psychology also took a benign view of a wide range of human desires and impulses, which Freudian psychology tended to see as threatening.

And there was the body, which was generally ignored or denigrated by the great religious thinkers and philosophers of both East and West. But not, Mike noted, by Aurobindo, who argued that a transformation of the body must be an integral part of any total transformation of the person. Mike's journal was sprinkled with references to the importance of sports and the body. "The redeeming of the emotions, senses, body," Mike had written. And then, "The *body* as a vehicle of the mysteries."

My second yellow pad was almost filled. I felt it was I who was privy to the mysteries. " 'Joe Kamiya — mind/body,' " I read aloud. "Who's Joe Kamiya?"

Mike's eyes sparkled. "You really should go see his work. After Kamiya, no one can doubt the connection between mind and body."

Mike explained that Kamiya, a researcher at San Francisco's Langley Porter Neuropsychiatric Clinic, was working on an amazingly simple way of teaching people to control such inner states as brain-wave patterns. In his experiments, Kamiya had his subjects lie in a quiet room, eyes closed, with electrodes attached to their scalps. He told them only that a tone would sound when they were "right." The apparatus was hooked up so that if he wanted the subjects to increase a particular brain-wave pattern, the appearance of that pattern would automatically set off the tone. At first the tone would sound only when, more or less by accident, the desired wave form appeared. Merely by reacting to the reinforcement of the tone, the subjects gradually learned to make it sound more frequently and thus to increase the desired brain wave. When they learned to enhance the alpha-wave pattern, the subjects told of reaching a state of heightened awareness. They became relaxed and serene, almost as if they were in a state of profound meditation. Once the subjects learned to influence their brain waves or blood pressure while using the apparatus, they were likely to be able to do so on their own, thus demonstrating voluntary control of bodily systems that present medical science considered autonomic — totally beyond such control. It was brand new work, Mike said. What would later be called biofeedback didn't yet even have a name.

By the time, three weeks later, that Mike came up from Big Sur to visit me and Lillie, I had already interviewed Joe Kamiya and was rewriting the last section of my human potential article to include news of his experiments. I had also talked on the phone to another researcher Mike had recommended to me. Frank Barron of the University of California at Berkeley was a leading authority on creativity. His studies had shown that creativity often went along with the ability to yield to impulse and tolerate ambiguity, and that everyone could learn to be more creative. I was beginning to realize that if I followed up on all the names Mike had given me, I would never finish the article.

Mike arrived in time for dinner on a Friday night and stayed until Tuesday morning. Since my aunt was using our only guest room, he slept on the large cushioned window seat in the living room. He had a few other appointments in San Francisco, but for the most of those three and a half days the two of us continued the dialogue that had begun almost a month earlier. I showed him the outline of *A Practical Utopia*. I had just about decided that the book was unsalable, but Mike's enthusiasm gave me new heart. He was particularly interested in the attention I had given Skinner and his work. Skinner was considered to be the archenemy of the humanistic psychologists. Now it was my turn to make unexpected connections. I told Mike of my flights back and forth between Skinner and Rogers, and of their common interest in developing the human potential.

"Do you think we could get Skinner to come to Esalen and give a seminar?" Mike asked.

"Sure," I said jauntily. "When do you want him?"

"Really? Carl Rogers is giving a seminar from October first to the third. How about the next weekend? Do you think he would come?"

"What are the dates?"

"October eight to ten."

"Why not? I'll give him a call."

"Skinner and Rogers back to back! *Whoooo.*"

Infected by Mike's exuberant spirit, I went to the phone and called Cambridge. I told Skinner briefly about Esalen, dropping the names of some of the more distinguished previous seminar leaders. Then I described Esalen's physical charms — its beautiful masseuses, its hot springs. I said I would pick him up at the airport and drive him down. There was only one problem: I hoped he wouldn't mind the fact that there was mixed nude bathing. Fred Skinner cleared his throat and said he thought he could make it.

Mike was beside himself with glee. He had planned the fall of 1965 to be, he said, "our biggest show of firepower." He had already signed on such leaders as Rollo May, the existential psychologist; James Pike, the controversial bishop of the Episcopal Diocese of California; Gardner Murphy, director of research for the Menninger Foundation; Virginia Satir, a founder of family therapy; S. I. Hayakawa, a leading general semanticist; J. B. Rhine, the pioneering parapsychologist; Maurice Friedman, the principal interpreter of Martin Buber in the country; Alan Watts; Frank Barron; Carl Rogers; and now B. F. Skinner.

The fall 1965 brochure, Mike told me, would have a new, larger format. He saw its publication as the raising of a flag in the culture, a flag announcing a vision of expanded human possibilities. Inside the front cover of the brochure would be a quote from *A Sleep of Prisoners,* by Christopher Fry. Mike recited it from memory:

> Dark and cold we may be, but this
> is no winter now. The frozen misery
> of centuries breaks, cracks, begins to move,
> the thunder is the thunder of the floes,
> the thaw, the flood, the upstart spring.
> Thank God our time is now when wrong
> comes up to face us everywhere,
> never to leave us till we take
> the longest stride of soul men ever took.
> Affairs are now soul size.
> The enterprise
> is exploration into God. . . .

The passage both thrilled and sobered me. Were the rigid strictures of centuries beginning to break apart? Were these years, these vivid years of the sixties, really to be a time of thaw?

Mike told me that he wanted the opening statement of the brochure to be an eloquent one, a small manifesto of "the big vision." He showed me some notes he had made. They were fragmented, not particularly well expressed.

"If you like, I'll take a crack at it," I said, hardly noticing that I was becoming a volunteer worker for Esalen.

For a long time I had been viewing America as a huge cultural laboratory. I had crossed the nation so many times that I could glance down from 38,000 feet almost anywhere and generally recognize where I was. But the business of looking for a cultural transformation had never before seemed quite so much fun. Just being with Mike Murphy was fun. His extraordinary enthusiasm empowered me to drop all my inhibitions, to be totally free and open in the realm of ideas.

I suggested we do a brainstorming session on any signs or symptoms of current or impending change in the culture. Both of us could call out anything that came to mind. In line with the rules of brainstorming, we wouldn't censor ourselves in any way, nor would anything be questioned. I would write each idea on a separate slip of paper. We would evaluate them later. The ideas came in a rush. I scrawled each one and threw it on the floor:

Significant changes in young people — the Explosive Generation
Emergence of humanistic psychology
Changes in family structure
Growth of Zen practice
Popularization of Zen and other Eastern ideas in the culture
Previously unthinkable changes in southern race relations
New research showing complexity of brain — the human potential
Programmed instruction — possible revolution in education
Psychedelics
Emerging sexual freedom — the birth control pill
Radical youth movement — SDS
The Free Speech Movement in Berkeley
Development of body disciplines
Communications revolution — the transistor
McLuhan and the global village
Automobile culture, new suburbs — breakdown of old values
Ad hoc communities
Growth of volunteerism
General systems thinking
Human power vs. nature — need to control power, transform
  technology

As the floor around the living room couch became covered with slips of paper, my mind kept coming back to the civil rights movement. It was my most reliable beacon of hope. It affirmed the possibility of profound change.

"There's a civil rights movement," I said, "and a free speech movement. Why not a human potential movement?"

I wrote "human potential movement" on a slip of paper and threw it on the floor, and we went on brainstorming. Neither Mike nor I had any idea I had just labeled a "movement" that over the next five years would be interpreted and misinterpreted in hundreds of articles, that eventually, in one way or the other, would affect the lives of millions of people, and that ultimately would be taken for something that neither of us had intended.

Though we were to use that term off and on over the next three or four years — long enough for the media to take it up — we were never entirely serious about it. As it turned out, we were always willing to laugh at our most grandiose plans while at the same time pursuing them for all we were worth. We took ourselves both seriously and lightly. In the spirit of play, we dedicated ourselves to changing the world.

18

Midnight Plane to Alabama

MONDAY, MARCH 8, 1965, a week after Mike Murphy's visit, Lillie and I were in the living room watching the six o'clock news. For days we had been following the voter registration campaign in Selma, Alabama. There had been police violence during a march there on the previous day. We had heard radio reports and read of the event in the newspapers. We knew that tonight there would be film reports on national television.

The pictures were not particularly good. With the sky overcast, the black-and-white images took on the quality of an old newsreel. Yet this very quality, vague and half silhouetted, gave the scene the immediacy of a dream: We see a column of blacks striding along a highway. A large force of Alabama state troopers blocks their way. As the marchers draw to a halt, a toneless voice drawls an order from a loudspeaker. The blacks are told to turn back "in the interest of public safety." A few moments pass, measured out in silence, as some of the troopers cover their faces with gas masks. Then a powerful phalanx of troopers charges straight into the column, bowling the marchers over.

There is a shrill cry of terror as the troopers lumber forward, stumbling on the fallen bodies. The scene cuts to charging horses, their hoofs flashing over the blacks who have fallen to the ground. Some lie motionless; others struggle to get up and get away. Another quick cut: A cloud of tear gas billows over the highway. Periodically the top of a helmeted head emerges from the cloud, followed by a club on the upswing. The club and the head disappear into the cloud of gas and another club bobs up and down. The motion is mechanical, unhuman.

The picture shifts swiftly to a church. The bleeding, broken, and unconscious pass across the screen, some of them limping alone, others supported on either side, still others carried in arms or on stretchers.

I could hear Lillie sobbing next to me. "I can't look anymore," she said. She got up and walked away. The television announcer was saying there would be another march on Tuesday afternoon. Martin Luther King and other civil rights leaders would be there.

I turned off the set and sat in stunned silence. Then I got up and walked aimlessly around the house. Over and over I heard the same phrase in my consciousness: "I should be there tomorrow." The sound that had come out of the speaker, the cries of terror — I had never heard anything like it on television. It was utterly terrifying. I corrected myself: I was terrified.

Yes, I was terrified. I didn't want to be gassed, trampled, and beaten. I didn't want to go down there. I didn't have to. But the thought wouldn't go away: "I should be there tomorrow." I paced back and forth. I felt as if I were bursting.

There was a knock on the door. It was Price Cobbs, a black psychiatrist who had become a good friend. He had seen the news and had driven straight over. He came in and sat on the window seat. I had never seen him so somber. We said a few words but mostly just sat looking at each other. That was enough. I said I thought I'd better get down there. He nodded gravely. I went to the phone and made a reservation on the first flight to Alabama. Then I phoned Bill Arthur at his home. I knew I was going anyway, but if I could make it a *Look* assignment, maybe I'd have something to write for the magazine. Arthur said by all means go.

At midnight the San Francisco airport was nearly deserted. Three men stood at the Delta Air Lines counter, a black man and a white man in business suits and a tall, fair Episcopalian priest in clerical garb. The priest's companions seemed especially solicitous as they helped him through some complex negotiation with the ticket agent. I introduced myself and learned that the priest was going to Selma, that he had decided to go only that night, and that he had no idea how he was going to get from Birmingham, where the flight ended, to Selma, ninety miles south. I told him I had wired both Avis and Hertz for cars at Birmingham. Somehow I would get him to Selma.

As we started toward the plane, I realized why the priest's companions had seemed worried. Father Charles Carroll of St. Philip's Episcopal Church in San Jose, California, walked with a cane; it was an effort for him to maintain our rather slow pace down the concourse. The march was planned to go from Selma to the state capitol at Montgomery, fifty miles away.

Flight 808 to Dixie rose into a cloudless night sky. Father Carroll was sitting next to me, and when the plane reached cruising altitude, he started telling me of his student days in Germany in the 1930s. "It was the voice of Sheriff Jim Clark on the radio that brought it back to me — that strange feeling in the pit of my stomach. I remembered my apartment in Berlin, the Jewish family with whom I lived, the steel that was to be used to bar the front door when 'they' came, the bottle of cyanide in the medicine cabinet. Everybody knew why it was there. I remembered my German cousin who had turned Nazi. He came home one night in 1938 and was asked by his wife what was burning in town. He said, 'The synagogues,' and she replied, 'What synagogues?' " Father Carroll paused. *"Could this be happening here?"*

"I went about my rounds today wondering how I could get to Selma and what I would do if I got there. Then I saw the news, just as you did, and at that moment I *knew*. It *is* happening here. I had no more doubts as to what I had to do."

Dawn came in Dallas as we waited between planes. The night had brought other flights from the West. Each had its cargo of pilgrims. All of us trooped aboard a rakish, shining Convair 880 for Birmingham: a score of clergymen both black and white, a lawyer from Palo Alto, a psychiatrist from Los Angeles, a San Francisco Bay Area matron who had had too much to drink, a young couple from Berkeley.

Inside the plane, a plump black minister from Los Angeles kept leaping to his feet to introduce himself and everyone within earshot to each new passenger coming down the aisle. Most of them were bound for Selma. He told us that the previous night he had been wanting to go "more than anything," and that the phone had rung at about ten-thirty with news that he had been given a ticket, at which he had murmured, "Oh, He's answered my prayers so quickly!" One of the minister's companions admitted that "when I told my wife, all she said was buy as much insurance as possible."

There was a stir at the plane's door as a group of rumpled students entered. They were preceded by a bushy-haired young man who immediately caught everyone's attention. Mario Savio, leader of the Free Speech Movement at Berkeley, was at that time a familiar figure in national magazines and on television. He and his girlfriend sat across the aisle from me, the door was closed, and we took to the sky. Savio and his friends, I learned, had decided to come after watching the eleven o'clock news. They had raced from Berkeley to the airport to catch the flight after ours. Now they were all over the plane, bursting with curiosity. Someone said Governor Wallace and the state of Alabama had been enjoined from interfering with the march.

"Looks like someone may be walking fifty miles today," I said, glancing down at the high heels worn by two of the students, a sophomore and a junior.

"We didn't have time to change," one of them said.

"We'll have to march without shoes," added the other.

"Oh, no," said Savio, no doubt considering past criticisms of his group's appearance, "we'll buy you shoes."

"How about your shirttail?" the sophomore said to Savio.

"I'll put it in."

"And your face," she went on, indicating what appeared to be a two-day growth of beard.

"I'll shave," Savio said.

Dark clouds grew into the morning sky and shook our plane as it passed over Texas and into Louisiana. No matter. I was buoyed up by the presence of so many Selma pilgrims on this plane. Could it be that there were other planes from all over the country, all filled with people bound for Selma? I looked out of the window at my country, the laboratory of change. There, up ahead, was the Mississippi Delta, the lazy, graceful loops of the river. My hopes soared.

In Birmingham we learned that a federal judge had enjoined Martin Luther King from marching to Montgomery that day. Whether he would march anyway remained in doubt. But nothing could slow our momentum; we who had traveled so many miles were not going to stop now. The airport was in turmoil. People from all over the nation were streaming in. Many others, we heard, were landing in Atlanta, still more in Montgomery. I picked up the rented car, loaded it with passengers, and started out for Selma.

Father Carroll sat to the right of me, calm and serene. In the back seat was another Episcopal priest, Thomas Steensland. He had left his home in the rural California town of Paso Robles at the last minute, driven south more than a hundred miles to catch a plane from Santa Barbara, missed that plane by ten minutes, and kept going another hundred miles to make a one A.M. flight from Los Angeles. Father Steensland also faced a difficult march; as an infantry lieutenant in World War II, he had stepped on a land mine and lost part of one foot.

Also in the back seat was an older couple who had sat in front of me on the plane from Dallas. I had heard the name, William Morris, and the hometown, Malibu Beach, California. (*That's* a strange parish, I had mused, assuming Morris to be a clergyman.) Getting in the car, I noticed that Mrs. Morris wore a particularly expensive-looking suit and carried a Malaysian Air Lines travel bag. Now I turned and asked lightly: "To what aspect of human life do you minister?"

"Oh, I'm not a minister," Morris said. "I'm in the theatrical business."

A quick realization: He was William Morris of the venerable and prestigious William Morris Agency, which represented many of the top stars of music, the movies, and the theater.

"We watched the news," Ruth Morris said, "and then we went in and sat down and were eating dinner. Our home is right on the ocean. It's a very pleasant place to live, rather gay in color. Our dining room is warm and gay and we were sitting down to a very good dinner. We felt sort of guilty about being there enjoying ourselves after what we had just seen on TV. We both said it at the same time — it just seemed to come out of the blue: 'Why are we sitting here?' Then I said, 'I'll pack,' and Bill said, 'I'll call for the reservations.' "

The day was more Indian summer than late winter. We were driving south at a careful fifty miles an hour about a hundred yards behind a bus from the Pilgrim Hill Baptist Church of Birmingham. Church members had explained to me the procedure for traveling in Alabama in 1965. We were not to have any integrated cars ("Might attract gunfire"). We were to gas up at a black station in Birmingham; no stops would be made along the way. We were to stick to the speed limit. In fact, if the sign said 15 mph, we were to go 14. Two cars loaded with blacks would scout ahead, returning if necessary to warn us of danger. The most vulnerable vehicle was the bus, for it carried most of those, black and white, who had been on our plane. We of the all-white car were to follow it at a good distance. If the bus was stopped, we were to pull up behind it and witness whatever happened. The driver of the bus had sketched the route on my map and had shown me the "bad" communities along the way where we might expect trouble. He would warn me if anything went wrong by turning on his blinking yellow loading lights.

Now these lights were flashing. The bus turned off the superhighway we had planned to follow and started down a narrow rural road. We had no way of knowing what the trouble was. We just stayed behind the bus, moving with a turn of the steering wheel into another world, the hazy, dreamy southland of my childhood. After a night without sleep, I was particularly susceptible to the aching loveliness of the land. But there was a terrible evil in that loveliness, a lingering decay. We passed rundown black tenant shacks, the kind that my grandfather had owned. It was easy not to see them clearly, or to see them merely as elements in a picturesque landscape, like an old oak or a stand of pines on a rolling hill. I had a sudden compulsion to point them out to my West Coast passengers.

"Look at that shack," I said, "the holes in the roof, the broken windows, all the children. It gets cold down here."

We turned again. The road became even lonelier. I switched on the radio for news from Selma, but it was difficult to pick out any clear station from the sizzle and static and hillbilly music. At last a faint voice told us Martin Luther King was marching. The march would start in an hour. We could make it.

We never found out why we had followed such a circuitous route, but we entered Selma without ever passing a roadblock or even a city limits sign, and we stayed on dirt roads all the way to the black church district that was our destination. As we pulled to a stop, three slim young black women walked past our car. One of them leaned over to us and said with absolute simplicity, "Thank you for coming." Tom Steensland said quietly, "The trip is already worth it."

The scene inside the church burst upon me. Every seat, every aisle was packed. They were shoulder to shoulder: the Princeton professor and the sharecropper's child, the senator's wife and the elderly black woman. I had been watching scenes from this place, the Brown's Methodist Church Chapel, for several days on television, but the pictures had been in black and white. The same scene in all the richness of its colors took on a power that was surreal. The balcony at the left side of the church was like a fresco by a great Renaissance painter. The classic, dizzying angles formed by those who leaned to view the altar were fixed forever, it seemed, against the glowing hues of the stained glass windows.

It was almost more than my eyes could comprehend, for there at the altar, all gathered in this one place at this one time, were most of the leaders of the civil rights movement: Charles Evers of the Mississippi NAACP; James Farmer of CORE; James Forman of SNCC, whom I had met on several occasions at my Aunt Maggie's apartment, a troubled young activist who bore more battle scars than all the rest, now dressed as a poor country boy in overalls; the Reverend Ralph Abernathy, Dr. King's trusted lieutenant; and in the center, King himself.

But now a doctor from New York was speaking. He was giving us, with scientific enthusiasm, our medical briefing. "Tear gas will *not* keep you from breathing. You may *feel* like you can't breathe for a while. Tear gas will not make you *permanently* blind. It may blind you *temporarily*. Do *not* rub your eyes." I looked around at the amused but somber smiles. The doctor's enthusiasm was carrying him away. "If you become unconscious, be sure somebody stays with you." A delighted, outraged laugh rose through the church. The doctor laughed too. "I mean, if you see someone become unconscious, be sure to stay with him." The doctor received an ovation.

Martin Luther King stepped forward to the microphone. His eyes glistened in the glare of the television lights. A faint smile, both humble and triumphant, came and went. "Now we have a problem here in Alabama," he said with restraint and regret. He did not try to stir his audience; they didn't need that. He outlined the situation that faced us matter-of-factly. He talked of the decisions all human beings must make. Next to me, a tweedy man with a pipe and a large moustache wiped tears from his cheeks. All the faces around me were radiant. "Perhaps the worst sin in life," Dr. King said with a kind of majestic sadness, "is to know right and not do it."

Outside, in hazy sunlight, the marchers formed. I stood on a grassy bank and watched the first ranks of four go past. I exchanged smiles with

Jim Forman, who walked arm in arm with Martin Luther King in the front rank. Not far behind them were those with whom I had traveled. Tom Steensland went by with another white minister and two blacks. Bill and Ruth Morris were together and Charles Carroll was with them, supported on the right by a strong black minister. I fell into a rank behind them, realizing with some shame that I was more cautious than they, near enough to the front to see what was happening but far enough back to avoid the first charge of the horses.

We marched through Selma, a small southern city like so many others. The streets were nearly empty. We marched across the Edmund Pettus Bridge and out onto the Montgomery highway. The highway was also empty; there were no cars to be seen. We moved silently into the countryside, which seemed lonely even in the presence of this great throng. I looked back. The line of marchers poured over the bridge and onto the highway. It was endless.

Then up ahead I saw the flashing lights, the roadblock. We kept marching until the front rank came to a stop; then we inched forward, crowding the ranks. I hadn't slept for thirty-two hours, but felt totally awake and alert. We stood there on the highway as Dr. King negotiated with Sheriff Clark. I couldn't hear what was being said, but word moved swiftly back to us. The talk was legal, of court orders, injunctions, appeals. A good half hour passed, then word came that we were returning to Selma. The march to Montgomery was being postponed, pending further court action.

I felt both relieved and disappointed as we marched back to the church to get the news that there definitely would be a march to Montgomery, but probably not tomorrow. There was no place in Selma for so many people; most of us would have to leave for Birmingham or Atlanta.

It was a strange feeling. We had traveled so far, only to be turned back. But something spontaneous and unprecedented had happened. Maybe in later years wearier people would find some way to discount what at that moment seemed almost miraculous. More than anything else, those of us who had journeyed to Selma had made a point: The black people in this lonely corner of America were not alone against the forces of oppression. We were not like the Germans of the thirties. In Germany, people from all over the country hadn't left their homes without a change of clothes and traveled all night to walk with the oppressed.

Our group spent the night in Birmingham. The next day I flew to New York and wrote an article on my experiences. Another *Look* team had been assigned to cover the march to Montgomery. It started on March 21, and my friend Price Cobbs, along with hundreds of people from all over the country, joined it on the day it entered Montgomery, four days later. Afterward, he said that as he had walked up to the state capitol, white people as well as blacks along the sides of the street had shouted encouragement and appreciation. Price had put on dark glasses to hide his tears. It was then that he had had an almost mystical glimpse of something that might transcend our clumsy language (conservative, liberal, radical) and reveal at last the meaning of the words *love* and *brotherhood*. It was only a glimpse, but it had opened to him in the deepest part of the Deep South.

As it turned out, my article was pre-empted by a dramatic picture story on the march to Montgomery. And anyway, maybe it was a bit too emotional, too melodramatic, even for *Look*. It eventually appeared in *The Nation*. Here's how it began:

> When the wind was right, a peculiar odor spread over the towns that lay near the great crematoria at Auschwitz, Belsen, Dachau. The good people who lived there learned to ignore the stench. They ate, drank, sang, prayed, gave moral instruction to their children. To deny reality, however, is no simple act. Conversation becomes conspiracy. Reality, though denied, always waits nearby, a silent intruder on every group around the fire, every child's bedtime story, every scene of love. In the end, even the senses themselves must join the conspiracy. The people who lived near the gas ovens taught their noses to lie.
>
> Americans, too, have learned to deceive their senses. Sermons have been preached, crusades launched, books on ethics written, systems of morality devised, with no mention whatsoever of how American Negroes are treated. When the senses lie, the conscience is sure to sleep. The chief function, then, of the current Negro movement has been to awaken a nation's conscience, which is to say its ability to smell, see, hear, and feel.
>
> Such an awakening is painful. It may take years to peel away the layers of self-deception that shut out reality. But there are moments during this process when the senses of an entire nation become suddenly sharper, when pain pours in and the resulting outrage turns to action. One of these moments came, not on Sunday, March 7, when a group of Negroes at Selma were gassed, clubbed, and trampled by horses, but on the following day, when films of the event appeared on national television. . . .

19

A Turning in the Road

DAN MICH'S HEALTH was failing. By the fall of 1964 he was missing days from work. He and Isabella spent a couple of nights in San Francisco on their way to Hawaii in December, and I was shocked by his appearance. His normally pale, almost transparent skin was even paler, and there was an unfamiliar aura about him, something withdrawn, almost furtive. When I arrived in New York from Selma, he was again home sick. I phoned, and he asked me to have dinner with him and Isabella at their apartment.

The trouble, he said, was with his liver. He had been to two doctors and they couldn't seem to get together on anything. One told him he should never drink again, the other disagreed. I noticed he was sipping gingerly on his beloved Grant's Eight-Year-Old. "Remember this, George," he said. "Doctors don't know anything about the liver." I didn't know how to respond.

Back in San Francisco, I went over the twenty-thousand-word human potential manuscript for what seemed the fiftieth time, then mailed it to Bill Arthur. I was happy with the way it had turned out, and assumed it would be accepted. Still, I was anxious enough about the editor's response to jump up from my desk and rush to the teletype machine in the corridor when it started chugging out a message one morning about a week after I had mailed the article to New York.

The message from Bob Meskill, one of the assistant managing editors, began, "Congratulations." I felt my chest and shoulders relax. Meskill, the magazine's most fastidious and bookish editor, went on to say that the article would elevate *Look* to a new level of excellence and importance. About a half hour later, the machine typed out an equally extravagant message of praise from the other assistant managing editor, Patricia Carbine. When John Poppy and I came back from lunch, our editorial assistant, Marilyn Kelso, with a big smile, handed me another TWX, this one from Bill Arthur, who said that the article would set a new standard for all future *Look* features. Marilyn asked if she should go out for a bottle of champagne. It seemed an appropriate time for a celebration, but I said we'd better wait to see how we were going to manage to get twenty thousand words into two successive issues of *Look*. I also considered the fact that Dan Mich, who was still home with what was obviously an increasingly serious illness, wasn't in on the decision.

While waiting for the editors to find space for my article to run, I flew to Seattle to do another schooling story, this one on business education, and then to the *Look* Los Angeles office for a staff visit. There I got a phone call from Dan Mich, who was back at work, feeling much better. As usual, he quickly got to the heart of things.

"George, sit down."

"All right," I said with a sort of laugh.

"Are you sitting down?"

"Yes."

"I've read your human potential story, and I'm not going to run it." There was a brief pause. I didn't know what to say. "It's too long and too theoretical."

"It could be cut," I said, grasping for straws.

"No, it shouldn't be cut. You've done a good job. It just isn't right for *Look*. It's too theoretical, not personal enough."

I started to mention the reaction of Meskill, Carbine, and Arthur, but thought better of it. He seemed to read my mind.

"I know the other people here think highly of it, but I've outvoted them, one to three."

He sounded a little tired, but he was his old self. I knew it would be useless to argue. I had always admired Mich's decisiveness. I had told people how liberating it was. If he said no quickly, then you were free to go on to other things. But on this, the human potential story?

"You've got good stuff," he continued. "I'd like to see a picture story on Sullivan, your educational programmer. I'd like to see a picture story on Sweeney, the guy who made his janitor into a computer programmer. I'd like to see something personal and specific on John Lilly and his dolphins. But I'm not going to run this story."

"Well . . ." I said.

"All right, George. Now go out and buy yourself a drink."

I hung up the phone and sat there. I had no desire for a drink.

At this point, it might make a better story if I could say that I was terribly shattered, that I went into a prolonged depression. But the truth is that I felt strangely cleansed and clear, as a person might feel after some absolutely conclusive and irrevocable disaster. I shook my head, wondering why I couldn't get this one idea out into the world. Maybe something — fate, whatever — was blocking me. Was I the unknowing inno-cent in a case of dramatic irony? Did somebody know something I didn't know?

I set about rethinking my book proposal. I cast around for new titles: *An American's Guidebook to the Future, Solving the Insoluble, A Road-map to the Future.* Mich's rejection of the human potential article made writing the book seem that much more urgent. My new literary agent, Sterling Lord, asked that I send him a completed opening chapter along with summaries of the other chapters.

But before I could finish, Dan Mich summoned me to New York. His office seemed more hushed than usual, and his face was wan. But he was still regal behind his desk, and his eyes were intense. He wanted a full issue on the South. The issue would answer the question "Is the South really changing?" Everyone else on the editorial board, he told me, was against the idea. The South had been done to death, especially in *Look.* But once again he had outvoted them.

"I know you can do it, George."

I took this statement as a command, yet, uncharacteristically, it was also a plea. I had a sudden premonition: *He'll never see this issue.* My heart went out to this tough, forbidding, vulnerable man. So he had killed my magnum opus. Maybe, in some way I couldn't fully understand, he was right. I could feel tears behind my eyes. But I responded with a grin: "Consider it done."

The first step to getting it done was to fly to Atlanta to talk with family and friends and with contacts in the Southern Regional Council, on the *Atlanta Journal* and *Constitution,* at *Newsweek,* and in the civil rights movement. Almost everyone agreed that the South still had a long way to go on racial reform but that it was changing at breakneck speed, far faster than anyone would have dreamed even five years ago.

But there was something more impressive than all the words of the experts: Atlanta looked as if it had been bombed. Construction crews swarmed everywhere. The Atlanta that I had known in my childhood was being wiped out, to be replaced by gleaming downtown high-rises and residential subdivisions marching out across the surrounding pine forests and cotton fields. As late as the 1950s, the South had still had most of the characteristics of an underdeveloped nation, along with the raw materials, cheap labor, good weather, and recreational sites needed for fast and substantial development. All it had to pay for prosperity was a set of social beliefs and customs that most southerners had thought they would die to maintain. In 1961, under pressure from federal court orders and black civil rights demonstrators, Atlanta's city fathers had decided to pay that price. Now they were reaping their reward. Atlanta was the leader, but it was not alone. All over the region that was once called

Dixie, southerners were making the painful, previously unthinkable decision to turn from the gods of segregation to the gods of commerce. Could it be — an incredible thought — that the South would join the West as the fastest-growing region in the nation, the seat of national political dominance?

By the time I returned to San Francisco, I was ready to send a plan for the issue to Dan Mich. It would involve putting twenty-four *Look* photographers and editors into the field. And unless our reportage indicated otherwise, it would answer Mich's question, "Is the South really changing?" with a resounding yes. Historic developments, once they have occurred, tend to seem obvious, but at that time there was something marvelously daring about the words that would appear on the cover of the southern issue: "A Surprising Report on THE FAST-CHANGING SOUTH. Its Booming Business . . . Its Boiling Politics . . . Its Courage and Its Cowardice . . . Its Unsung Resorts. AND WHY IT MAY SOLVE ITS RACIAL PROBLEMS SOONER THAN THE NORTH OR WEST."

Over the next four months I flew six times to New York and the South. I pulled together what I considered the best of *Look*'s editorial staff, long-time journalistic comrades-in-arms. T George Harris did a lead story called "The Boom Man" on the Memphis-based head of the Holiday Inn chain, and another story on a courageous Mississippi editor, a woman. Fletcher Knebel analyzed "The Changing Face of Southern Politics." Jack Shepherd and photographer Doug Gilbert followed an unknown young SNCC field worker named Stokely Carmichael to Lowndes County in southern Alabama. Chris Wren did an article on one of Alabama's "New Politicians," then went out with photographer Art Kane to produce a portfolio of pictures illustrating the civil rights movement's freedom songs. The picture for "We Shall Overcome" was simply two babies against a white background. One of the babies was white, one was black. The white baby was touching the black baby's foot.

It was a dangerous time for anyone from a national magazine. The New South was in the works, but the Old South was not dead. Some white southerners, especially those not yet benefiting from the new prosperity, were filled with murderous rage, not so much at the blacks as at the reporters who had told their story and helped create incomprehensible changes in their lives. Several of us were roughed up or threatened as our paths honeycombed the South. Chris Wren and Art Kane were nearly killed.

It happened when they drove into Bogalusa, Louisiana, at noon of a typically scorching summer day. They were surrounded by a cluster of white youths, who told them they could get killed if they didn't get out of town. When they quickly drove off, the toughs jumped into cars flying Rebel flags on radio antennas and gave chase, darting in front of them to block every escape route. This nightmarish game of cat and mouse continued for a good half hour, until Wren and Kane managed to get on the highway to New Orleans. Some ten miles out of town, they were driven off the road by three cars and jammed between two of them.

The young toughs emerged from their cars screaming obscenities. Wren tried to back out of the trap. The motor stalled just as a bottle crashed into the windshield, showering Wren and Kane with glass. One of the pursuers ran up with an iron pipe. Wren got the car started as another bottle hit the windshield, and smashed his way out onto the road, barely missing an attacker who lunged in front of the car. Once more the chase was on, this time at speeds up to 85 miles an hour.

For nearly twenty more miles, with wind rushing in from the shattered windshield, Wren stayed ahead of his pursuers; then he finally lost them. At last he spotted a state police barracks and stopped there. A police lieutenant told Wren and Kane they would have to go back to Bogalusa to report the incident. They drove on to New Orleans.

Just two days earlier, Wren had spent several hours in a Natchez, Mississippi, jail on a trumped-up traffic charge, during which time the tires of his rented car — parked next to the police station — were slashed. Wren had just returned from covering the war in Southeast Asia. His southern assignment, he told me, was "worse than Vietnam."

Our bad moments generally occurred in the small towns, on the lonely flatlands of southern Georgia, Alabama, Mississippi, Louisiana — wherever the white southerner's confrontation with himself was just beginning or moving toward a climax. But most often we were received — sometimes after a period of initial suspicion — with the most touching and eager courtesy. In our wanderings through the South, we saw the undeniable physical evidence of racial progress: integrated swimming pools, playgrounds, hotels, restaurants, private parties. We sensed the subtle changes that can never be verified by polls or statistics: Black southerners seemed to hold their heads higher; white southerners, for the most part, seemed more relaxed and confident. And everywhere, in every meeting, in every conversation, we felt the special kind of longing that comes from pain, from a desire to be understood. The words poured out. The interview scheduled to last an hour took three or four. "Listen to us. Be kind to us. See what the odds are against us and what we have accomplished in the face of them."

A new South was being born. At the same time, something shameful and terrible but — how can I say this? — strangely lovely was dying. John Poppy went out to find the kind of sleepy little southern town that had not yet been touched by the passage of time. It wasn't easy. After driving through much of Georgia and South Carolina, he and photographer Bob Adelman finally settled on Camden, Alabama, but even there a civil rights demonstration had recently occurred. Adelman's pictures and Poppy's words captured something soon to be lost forever:

"You have to be born here not to be a stranger," said a lady in Wilcox County, Ala. Her white neighbors have grown up under each other's scrutiny, generation upon generation, blending their many histories into one. They love their homeland without needing to know precisely why — perhaps because they share the sweet familiarity of its rhythms. Fall is turkey-shooting time. Winter's icy damp yields to planting time, spring. Then comes the Southern summer. Heavy, liquid heat hugs the body, its lingering pressure slowing human motion while it forces cotton, okra, timber from the red earth of the fields. "We are the people who have jelled here," the lady said. Around Camden, the county seat, people recall the Southern past as if it were just last night — which, in a sense, it was. No fresh factories have come to this country town, yet, to stir the dust. Each day is a hushed wait for tomorrow; life seems suspended. The words on the county's monument to its Confederate dead reveal an attitude toward living: "The manner of their death was the crowning glory of their lives."

I spent much time alone. I drove country roads in rented cars. I ventured into hotel lobbies in small towns in south Alabama. There was change everywhere. Even far out in the country, the mule was giving way to the tractor, and biplanes were spewing pesticide over freshly plowed fields. There were great red gashes in the earth where new superhighways, new shopping malls, would be built.

One night in the middle of July, I was driving on a lonely road between Tallahassee and Mobile in a Mustang convertible with the top down. To the left, toward the Gulf of Mexico, lay a marsh with occasional stands of gnarled and twisted trees. No lights, no signs of human life, were to be seen, only the pulse of lightning out over the Gulf, illuminating a distant line of clouds. And just above the clouds there hung a dusky yellow moon. The day had been hot, but now a coolness rose from the marsh, a sweet smell of life and decay. I leaned back and let the car take me along the blacktop, let the soft tropical air sweep over my face. The sweetness of this night reminded me how much I loved the South. There was an inescapable resonance between this land and something essential at the heart of my being. I had hated the South and I had disliked it. But mostly I had loved it. Now I knew how very much I loved the southern land, the southern sky, the lonely roads, the wooded hills, the endless southern plains.

But this South was finished. All that I had hated and loved would be destroyed — something shameful was to be replaced by something merely ugly. A faint odor of pesticide blended with the fragrance of the marsh. The South was selling its soul to commerce, no holds barred. I had talked with business and civic leaders, and had heard nothing whatever about controlling growth or mitigating the dehumanizing effects of a runaway technology. The unlimited human power about which Aldous Huxley had warned me was to be unleashed in full force on this lovely, tragic land. In 1961 Atlanta had called itself "a city too busy to hate." Maybe it, along with the rest of the South, was also too busy to love. Maybe it was just too busy.

Wasn't there some better way? Driving on that lonely road in south Alabama, I found my mind going back to the overriding concern that never left me for long. Surely there was some better way of educating people, of dealing with matter and energy, of creating value. Surely there was some way to achieve prosperity without destroying the land. Surely human intelligence could come up with a set of values better than racial oppression on the one hand and unbridled greed on the other. There *had* to be a better way.

When I returned to San Francisco between trips to the East and South, I finished the first chapter of my book proposal and sent it, along with a revised outline of all the other chapters, to Sterling Lord. He replied within two weeks. The sample chapter just didn't quite do it. He couldn't see in it what the book was going to say — a serious problem, since it was obvious that the book wasn't going to fit into any easily recognizable category. He suggested I write at least one more chapter, and then maybe he could send it out to publishers. His letter was kind and thoughtful but not very hopeful.

What was going on? During my years with *Look,* almost every story I had written had run in the magazine. And my stories and special issues had been, by every indication, very popular. I took pride in being a popular writer. But now, with what I considered the most important and fascinating subject I had ever investigated, I was completely stymied. Well, maybe I could condense my human potential article into a manageable chapter for Sterling. But that would have to wait. For now, there were no minutes to spare. I had to get back to New York, then down South again, then back again to New York to lay out the southern issue.

By the time all the layouts were done, Dan Mich was seriously ill again, and there was talk that he would never return to work. I asked the art production department to make full-sized photocopies of every page that would run in the issue. I taped the pages together and took them to Mich's apartment after work. Isabella opened the door, gave me a significant look, and led me to the bedroom. Mich was in bed in his pajamas, propped up on pillows. He was very weak, but also very eager to see the layouts.

I pulled a chair close to the bed and started through the issue, beginning with the cover. All the pictures and headlines and other display type were just as they would be in the magazine, but the body type was dummied in. As was customary with *Look,* the articles would be written after the layouts were made.

So I talked Mich through the issue, telling him what the *Look* staffers had experienced down South and what their articles would probably say. I spun out every story, trying to give Mich its flavor as well as its facts, explaining how each related to the others and to the overall theme. As he had suggested, I had managed to get at least a piece of the human potential reportage into the issue; there was a short picture story on the New Orleans computer executive who had helped a poorly educated black janitor become a computer expert. I showed him the obligatory features on sports (Coach Bear Bryant of Alabama), fashion (high-fashion cotton dresses), and food (a Savannah oyster roast). I took him step by step through the closing essay, which would nail down the issue's outrageous cover lines. I told him of my long talk with Martin Luther King. I had asked King if laws could change the human heart. "Laws don't change men's hearts," he had said. "They do change men's habits. Once the habits are changed, the hearts change." And King had also said, "If the North is not eternally vigilant, the South will outrun it in race relations. Wherever the Negro looks in the South, he sees progress, In the ghettos of the North, he often sees retrogression. He sees no way out of his dilemma. His problems are more difficult because they are more subtle." I ended with my own conclusion: There were still troubles ahead and there was a dark side to what was happening in the South. But the flow of human understanding was irreversible. As the old Confederate colonel said, "The South will rise again." But it would be a South the colonel wouldn't recognize.

I had talked for nearly an hour. Mich had asked very few questions. His weakness, his resignation, was apparent. But as I had warmed to my subject, I had sensed that he was pleased, satisfied, even happy.

"I knew you could do it, George," he said, holding out his hand.

We shook hands, and neither of us let go for a while. His hand was warm and surprisingly gentle.

The next time I got back to New York, late in October, Mich was in the hospital. It was now clear that he might never come home, much less return to work. Bill Arthur, Mich's long-time number-two man, was running the magazine, with the increasingly effective help of assistant managing editor Patricia Carbine. I went to see Mich several times. On one occasion Isabella asked if I would sit with him for a couple or three hours while she went to a movie. He had a comfortable private room. He was not in pain, but he was already turning away from this world. We sat mostly in silence. His eyes were often open, but he was somewhere else. Now and then he would speak. "I have a wonderful staff," he said; then, after a long while, "It's hard to go. It's very hard." He reached out and I took his hand. We sat there, holding hands in silence, just that.

Dan Mich died on November 22. I was not deeply shaken; we had already said goodbye. But I wondered what would happen to the magazine without him. Bill Arthur was a good man all the way through, but he had played the loyal assistant so long and so well that he might have trouble changing roles. Maybe he was too kind and considerate to be a king. The magazine had already been operating without Mich for a number of months, however, and its senior-editor/producer method had its own energy and momentum.

A few weeks after Mich's death, T George Harris and I had dinner in New York. He followed me to my hotel room, took off his suit coat, and sprawled across the bed while I sat in a chair. After a pause he said, "George, let's take over the magazine."

That suggestion caught me totally off guard. Before I could say anything, he continued. "Just think what you could do with a magazine of almost eight million circulation."

"Wait a minute," I said. "Even if we wanted to take over *Look,* I don't think we could. There's a team already in place, and they're doing a good job. Anyway, Cowles isn't the kind of guy to rock the boat."

But T George was adamant. He argued that we actually could take it over and that I would be the editor. "Think of the fun we could have," he said. I argued that I enjoyed my situation, that I liked the perspective I got from working on both coasts, that I could do more good by producing articles and special issues than by being trapped in an editor's chair.

T George kept pushing for me to be the editor, but as we went on debating the subject, I realized that *he* was the one who should and undoubtedly would be the top editor of a magazine someday. He had strong ideas about journalism. He had a powerful conditioned need to serve the culture, to help people, to make important statements. I wondered how long he would stay at *Look.*

When T George realized I couldn't be swayed, he dropped the subject. What I hadn't told him was how rich my life outside of *Look* had become. I had reached a turning in the road. The explorations I had started with Michael Murphy were taking me more deeply into outlaw country, into a *terra incognita* of the body and spirit. Then too, at about the time of Dan Mich's death, as a result of a surprisingly simple and even obvious change of emphasis in my outline, I had signed a publisher's contract for the book I had been wanting to write for almost three years.

20

Another Reality

WHENEVER I WAS on the West Coast during the spring and summer of 1965, during the time I was working on the southern issue, more likely than not either Lillie and I were in Big Sur for the weekend or Mike Murphy was with us in San Francisco. It might seem that my life was split between political, social, and journalistic matters on the one hand and esoteric concerns on the other. But for me it was seamless. Mike and I were engaged in tireless speculations about nothing less than a transformation of social values and individual modes of being, and both of us viewed what was happening in the South and the rest of the nation as entirely relevant to this transformation. The challenge as we saw it was summed up in the introductory statement I wrote for the fall 1965 Esalen brochure:

> Within a single lifetime, our physical environment has been changed almost beyond recognition. But there has been little corresponding change in how we, as individuals, relate to the world and experience reality. Such a change is inevitable, however — indeed, it is imminent. New tools and techniques of the human potentiality — generally unknown to the public and to much of the intellectual community — are already at hand; many more are presently under development. We stand on an exhilarating and dangerous frontier, and must answer anew the old questions: "What are the limits of human ability, the boundaries of the human experience? What does it mean to be a human being?"

The brochure, with its array of eminent seminar leaders, listed me as a member of the executive committee of the Esalen Institute. Mike had asked me to join the board, and I had told him I would always donate my time; I wouldn't even accept reimbursement for travel. Esalen would be my Good Work.

One July afternoon at Esalen, after a walk up the canyon, Mike and I went to his room in the large, rambling, shingled house across the creek from the Esalen lodge. Lillie was getting a massage at the baths. The room overlooked the sea, and we sat watching it for a while, feeling no need for conversation. Finally I brought up the subject we hadn't yet discussed head on.

"What about God? Do you believe in God?"

"Well . . . of course."

"I mean," I said, "a personal God."

"God is at least personal."

"And more than that?"

Mike turned to Aurobindo to explain that God is both transcendent and immanent. God is the source, God is the goal, and God is the process. But if God is immanent in the world, in each of us, we are also involved in the expression of God. The divine spirit, according to Aurobindo, descended into matter and thus is present in every atom of the universe. Now, through the process of evolution, the divine spirit is manifesting itself, is showing its face: "God is waking up." Each unfoldment — from matter to life to mind to supermind — reveals another aspect of God's glory. Throughout this process, God is always available to our deeper knowing as an unwavering presence, an Essential Ground of All Being.

"How can you be sure?" I asked.

"I'm absolutely sure, because I directly experience it when I meditate. The Essential Ground breaks through in countless ways — during certain moments in music, poetry, friendship, love, in nature. But the only way you can experience it consistently is through a consistent practice, such as meditation."

"So if I meditated, I could be sure too?"

"Yes, but not immediately. It would take time." He paused. "There's a quicker way. Some people — Huxley, Heard — have been using LSD to experience the Essential Ground. If you and Lillie are interested, I know a psychologist who's very good and who could serve as your guide."

A couple of days after returning from Big Sur, I got a phone call. It was a man's voice, deep and rather conspiratorial.

"I hear you're interested in taking a trip."

I had never before heard *trip* used in that context, but the way the man, the San Francisco psychologist, said it let me know that what he had in mind was truly a journey, an adventure. He said he would bring a woman to assist him. We would have to lodge our children elsewhere from noon of the day of the trip until noon the next day, and agree not to leave our premises during that period. We would meditate, or at least be still and silent, for two hours before the session began at three in the afternoon. The fee would be a hundred dollars.

At that time LSD was not yet illegal. Respected psychiatric institutes as well as government agencies were still experimenting with its therapeutic use. (It was later revealed that the government was also conducting covert chemical warfare experiments with LSD on unsuspecting subjects.) I had examined the LSD phenomenon in my human potential research. Street use, which was just getting started, was not part of the equation at that time. What I had heard of was adventurous scientists and intellectuals using LSD to explore their own psyches and to enter new states of consciousness, which were said to be akin to ecstatic religious experiences. And there were also the highly publicized experiments of Professors Timothy Leary and Richard Alpert, which had gotten them fired from Harvard in 1963.

It was a journey. There were dangers. I had heard tales of terrifying as well as ecstatic experiences under LSD: walls that seemed to waver, feelings of claustrophobia or paranoia. Lillie and I were told that whenever anything terrifying appeared, say a fire-breathing dragon, we should move toward it in our consciousness. If we did this bravely and resolutely, the dragon might well turn into a prince or princess. If, however, we attempted to escape or resist what terrified us, it would persist and most likely become even more terrifying.

The psychologist, a man with a slightly receding hairline and the air of a professor, arrived with a stack of classical records. He was accompanied by a soft-spoken young woman with long, straight, dark hair. After a brief talk on our responsibilities, he gave us two white pills. Lillie and I looked at each other with the smiles of parachutists about to jump, and swallowed them.

For the next fifteen or twenty minutes we sat quietly, enjoying the mild euphoria of those who have willingly taken a fateful and irreversible step. Then I began getting occasional flashes of something very large and very wonderful happening inside me, along with deeper twinges of anxiety. Lillie reported she felt thousands of champagne bubbles lifting her arms and shoulders. The psychologist seemed unduly preoccupied with the records. The one that was playing seemed extremely scratchy. He removed it and began rubbing it around and around with an electrostatic record-cleaning pad. How annoying! It seemed he would never stop cleaning the record. At last he put it back on the stereo. It seemed scratchier than ever.

By this time I could hardly bear to sit still. I squirmed from one position to another. I tried walking back and forth, but that didn't help. Lillie went over and lay on the cushioned window seat before the bay windows at the front of the room. I lay in the middle of the room, sweating all over, feeling uneasier than I had ever felt. Again and again I tried to get control of myself. Each effort at control made things worse. I began to understand my situation: I was going to have to relinquish all control. There was no alternative.

This knowledge terrified me. Since earliest childhood, I had learned in countless ways — from my father, from my southern white culture, from flying combat missions — that a man must always maintain control. To give up control would be like dying.

Premonitions of another reality were beginning to intrude on my consciousness. In this new reality, each of the four of us in the room knew what the other three were thinking. The intrusion was anything but gentle. The new reality was thrusting itself into me crudely and with overpowering force. It was the reality, I thought, of a schizophrenic. The psychologist and the young woman were busy with Lillie at the window seat. She was obviously further along than I was — more adventurous, less constrained by the need for control.

I wondered how long the terrible unease was going to last. Now the psychologist was cleaning another record, scrubbing it so hard it seemed he might go right through it. I need help, I thought. I wish he would come over here. With my unspoken words, he turned and walked over. *Of course!* He kneeled and leaned down over me, his face kindly.

"What's the trouble?" he asked.

"You know," I answered, convinced he could read my mind.

"Yes, but tell me anyway."

"I'm afraid," I said, trembling all over.

"What are you afraid of?"

"You know," I whispered.

"Tell me anyway."

I waited for what seemed a long time, afraid to say it, ashamed to lose control. I tried one more time to think of some other way out. There was no other way. At last I said it, softly but clearly.

"Death. I'm afraid of death."

With those words, the world stopped. Just as action is frozen on a movie or television screen, everything in the room stood stock-still. And the face that was frozen above me was a ghastly green. I turned as cold as ice. The psychologist had become a cadaver. He was death. I wanted to turn away, but I knew I had no real choice except to look at him, at death, full in the face. I looked, and instead of fear I experienced release. Everything let go. My self-control was gone. "Manliness" was simply irrelevant. I burst into tears. I cried without shame or any other consideration. And with this release, this giving up, I found myself in another reality.

In one sense, nothing at all had changed. Everything in the living room was just the same as before. There was Lillie on the window seat at the large bay windows. Our guides were sitting nearby on the rug, watching me with great compassion. And there, just as before, were the chairs and the couch, record player, lamps, tables, fireplace. Everything was exactly the same, *but much, much more so.* I looked at one of the chairs as if I had never seen a chair before. Its very *chairness* stunned me. Far from being blurred or confused, all the objects of my daily life were startlingly clear and unequivocal, so *real* that I could hardly bear to look at them. The room resounded with incredible vitality, power, and meaningfulness.

As for the music, the static was completely gone, and every note was brilliant and immediate. The room was not big enough to hold it. A horn call on the stereo seemed to emerge from our bedroom three rooms away. There was no question that the horns were there, enormous gleaming golden horns many times more powerful and resonant than the instruments we now know, not so much frightening as fateful: hunters' horns calling to me from our bedroom at the back of the house.

How can I say it? If you should bring to mind the single most poignant moment you have ever experienced in all the movies and plays you have seen, then multiply it by ten, you would have some idea of what I was feeling *all the time.* It was like Emily's experience in *Our Town,* when she returns from her grave to witness her own twelfth birthday party and finds it more beautiful than she can endure. "Humankind cannot bear very much reality," T. S. Eliot wrote in *Four Quartets,* and I knew now that he was right. My own existence, reality itself, was unbearably beautiful and poignant.

Was this the Essential Ground of All Being? Something was missing. I looked over at Lillie. She was lying on her back on the window seat, holding a red rose in her hand, now and then smelling it. I wanted her to come to me. With the thought (*again!*) she got up and started walking over to where I was lying on the rug. She opened her arms and came to me in slow motion. It seemed to take a long time, bringing to mind those sentimental and archetypal commercials on television in which a beautiful woman holding a flower runs in slow motion through high grasses toward the viewer. It was like that, except that Lillie seemed infinitely more beautiful, her face as supernaturally white and pure as the imagined faces of those thirteenth-century ladies of whom the minstrels sang. She fell into my arms and my tears overflowed. I cried with relief that I would no longer have to hold anything back. I cried for our every misunderstanding, every lost opportunity to love each other. I cried for the foolhardy bravery of what we were attempting just by being married and having children. We had come together seven years earlier with the passionate certainty of the young. The birth of our first daughter had brought joy and an inexplicable change in our relationship. Our intensity became dissonant. Our passion turned to bewilderment. Our bewilderment became a complex contest over sex. Now all of this was unimportant.

After what seemed a very long time, the tears stopped and I lay in absolute silence and clarity. The music was Rodrigo's haunting *Concierto de Aranjuez,* and I was that music. Lillie and I lay on the rug next to each other. She handed me the rose. I held it for a few moments, then gave it back to her. This simple interchange seemed immensely significant to me. I closed my eyes and found myself in some other kind of time and place. I felt myself drawn downward into the vortex of a powerful, primal experience which I recognized as the act of love. There were no pictures of this act, or any sensation of carnal passion, but rather the feeling of an inexorable force. It was like experiencing the silent impulse that underlies music, or the essential, nonmaterial relationship of forces that makes a suspension bridge possible. I realized that the underlying structure of the act of love was infinitely more powerful than the act itself, that it could ultimately destroy anything that got in its way.

Shaken, I returned at last to my living room and reached over for the rose that Lillie was holding. When she gave it to me, I was grateful and reassured. I gave it back and went away again, now for a much longer journey. And now somehow Lillie was part of the experience, involved with me and with the experience of countless ancient lovers — re-enacting the experience, *becoming* it. I was away so long on this journey that I began suffering all the bittersweet longings of homesickness. I returned and reached for the rose. That it was still there seemed a miracle and a validation as well, a symbol of our connection, a tiny lifeline to the familiar world of matter and energy, space and time.

This process continued for some two hours, which for me were entirely outside of ordinary time. With each exploration I relinquished more and more of the appurtenances of ordinary life — sight, hearing, and all other sensory input, language, ego, maleness, time, space, gravity, mass, even the sense of having a separate body. With each giving up, I came closer to the Essential Ground I had been seeking. I have no idea how many times I brought myself back to the room to exchange the rose with Lillie. But in the end, as we were to discover, nothing remained of it but a two-inch-long fragment of the stem, polished to a fine gloss by having been passed from hand to hand so many times.

And what was left when all that was unessential had been discarded? For me, there was still a sense of I-ness, of a personal identity that could somehow survive every possible loss. There was as well a sense of unity, of all existence as a single, ultimately indivisible entity. And underlying this paradox, making up the Essential Ground, recreating it every instant, was Eros: a relentless, ineluctable force that would go on forever creating form out of chaos. At the heart of existence was love.

The effects of the drug gradually wore off. Lillie and I helped each other up. We hadn't noticed that night had come. The room had returned to its former dimensions. The electric lights dazzled. We walked around regaining our balance. Our guides were all smiles. We ordered a large Chinese dinner. It was wonderful to be there drinking beer and eating Chinese food after having traveled so long out in the winds of eternity. I told my story with great enthusiasm. All along, I assumed that Lillie had in some way shared my travels. After all, we had the polished stem of the rose as proof of our connectedness.

But Lillie had a different story. She had been aware, she said, that I very much wanted her with me, and she quickly realized the importance of the rose. But passing it back and forth every few seconds was quite distracting. With all her heart, she said, she wanted to be available to me. At the same time, she was eager to embark on her own exploration.

"So I got ready to leave my body," she explained, "though I had no idea how that might happen. But first I wanted everything to be right for you. I made sure my body was warm and a smile was on my face. Suddenly I was looking down on the two of us as we lay on the living room floor. You seemed fine, so I knew I could leave. Instantly I was in outer space, moving just as if I were under water. I could see all the brilliant galaxies and in one corner the Earth, also brightly lit. I was comfortably at home, swimming in the universe. Then I realized that I and the cosmos were actually located inside my head. All of that, the whole universe, was there — enough space so that I knew I could never again feel crowded or pushed into a corner.

"Coming down, I saw some kind of structure. It had seventeen levels and each of the levels was performing a separate function. I realized those seventeen levels were parts of my personality and that they weren't integrated. It was funny. I laughed to myself at the rightness of it. Then each of the levels, one by one, came down onto my body. Each one fit perfectly, like a layer of skin, putting me back together again. As each layer landed, I said, 'There comes another one.'"

I felt a brief stab of disappointment, then a quick, somehow reassuring fall back into the realm of ordinary consciousness, into what our culture calls objective reality, that useful, disillusioned state defined by consensus and measurement. So my perceptions of telepathy and synchronicity had been delusional; Lillie and I had not been journeying together. Instead of a miracle, we had gained the dubious rewards of irony: our diverging paths would make a good story to tell our friends.

But eventually that divergence couldn't be laughed away. All of our efforts, our high mutual regard, our love and concern for each other couldn't override a profound dissonance at the deepest level of our relationship. We tried hard; we were to keep trying for many years. But it was an exuberant and impatient decade, a time for adventures and explorations. What we couldn't find with each other — the moment of absolute connection, the apprehension of Eros — might just be available with someone else. That was one of the things the sixties said.

Still, I had gained the sure knowledge that other realities do exist, whether or not they follow the rules of logic. When I was fifteen, my cousin Ed encouraged me to read *The Varieties of Religious Experience,* written by William James at the turn of the century, and I had never forgotten his descriptions of those exalted states that quite transcend the limitations of our normal walking consciousness. There was one statement from the book that I was to hear again and again throughout the decade:

> Rational consciousness as we call it is but one special type of consciousness, whilst all about it, parted from it by the filmiest of screens, there lie potential forms of consciousness entirely different. We may go through life without suspecting their existence; but apply the requisite stimulus, and at a touch they are there in all their completeness, definite types of mentality which probably somewhere have their field of application and adaptation. No account of the universe in its totality can be final which leaves these other forms of consciousness quite disregarded.

Now I saw more clearly than ever that the human potential included the ability to enter unusual states of consciousness. On the day I had met Mike Murphy, Lois Delattre had asked me to look around at the people having lunch at the Garden Court and decide whether they could use one session with LSD. With all the qualms I might have had, my answer would still have to be yes — if only to break through the narrow dogmatism I had seen on those faces, to show those automatized people that there was something beyond their smug, ultimately self-destructive notions of "success." LSD was dangerous, but so was first grade. From the moment of birth, parents, teachers, friends, and media tirelessly conspire to put us on a dualistic trip, during which we are forced (at the risk of missing out on "success") to perceive of the mind as separate from and generally opposed to the body, of the self as separate from and generally opposed to nature, essentially alone, trapped in the prison of the skin, eternally at war with the world. Our objective consciousness is useful, but it is also limiting. The time had come, I thought, for breaking through limitations.

As for me, I was glad I had taken the LSD trip, but I had no desire to take another one. Whatever the power and poignancy of the experience, there had been something in the nature of psychic rape about it. I had not slipped through the filmiest of screens. I had not gained some sort of enlightenment through long and consistent practice. I had been slammed through a wall. There was value and richness in alternative states of consciousness, a whole new world to explore. But there must be better ways, natural ways, to make that exploration.

21

A Seven-Second Reverberation

1 9 6 6

EVERYTHING SEEMED to be happening at once. Early in September 1965, Richard Kennedy, an editor from Delacorte Press, came to San Francisco on a scouting tour. He read the outline of the book I wanted to write and noticed one interesting fact: Exactly half the chapters were about education. Why not change the emphasis just a little bit? Add a couple more chapters on schooling, and condense some of the stuff on society outside of school. Put something about education in the title. Then I would have a book that would fit into a recognizable category and thus would be marketable. I could still say what I wanted to about the reform of society.

I revised the outline under the tentative title *Education* and sent it to Sterling Lord. What had previously seemed impossible now was easy. Lord came up with a contract and gave me all sorts of rights I wouldn't have known to ask for, plus two that I would — full approval of the title and the cover — and an advance of $17,500, which seemed fair enough for one who hadn't yet published a nonfiction book. When the contract arrived, just before Christmas, I waited for Mike Murphy to come to town. I signed it on the marble mantelpiece where we had agreed to fire a shot heard round the world, and Mike witnessed the signature. Now there was only one problem: With all the work I was doing for *Look* and for Esalen, how the hell was I going to find time to write a book?

Also in September 1965, a brochure inviting applications for Esalen's first residential program went out. Esalen was to be a college of a sort, but unlike any college we knew. Around twenty graduate-level fellows would take up residence for nine months, starting in September 1966. Their curriculum would include meditation, encounter, sensory aware-ness, inner imagery and dream work, peak experience training, and expressive physical movement. The fellows would study "those basic capacities — sensory, emotional, interpersonal, and spiritual — which current education neglects or entirely fails to recognize."

More than a hundred people applied. James F. T. Bugenthal, first president of the American Association for Humanistic Psychology, reflecting the extravagance of the times, called the program "the equivalent of the Mercury or Apollo Projects, solidly grounded, all-out efforts to explore entirely new regions of human experience. From among the 'psychonauts' may come the first real breakthroughs into 'inner space' that may well change the entire conception and nature of the human experience."

Tuition of $3000 would cover less than half the cost of the proposed program, but maybe money wasn't going to be a problem. At about that time, August Heckscher, head of the Twentieth Century Fund, offered to put on a series of luncheons in New York to introduce Esalen's ideas on the human potential to the top people in about thirty of the nation's major foundations. Mike lined up the speakers for these luncheons — Maslow, Skinner, Rogers, Frank Barron, Rollo May, Gardner Murphy. He asked me to speak at the luncheon featuring Skinner. The human potential movement, it seemed, was on its way.

Early in October, Paul Fusco arrived to work with me on two stories for a special issue on women that was being produced by Patricia Coffin of *Look*'s Special Editorial Department. One of the stories was a portfolio of color photographs. The other was a black-and-white picture story on a twelve-year-old girl and her best friend. We chose Lois Delattre's daughter to be our heroine.

One afternoon Paul came into my office with an incredulous expression on his face. He had been walking around in Golden Gate Park looking for candid shots of women, and had come across a young man with hair down to his shoulders sitting on the grass watching birds flying from one tree to another. He asked Paul if he could see the jet trails behind the birds. He said he had taken LSD. Paul sat and talked with him for a while, then accepted a ride on the back of his motorcycle to go to his "pad." It was in the Haight-Ashbury district.

"You've got to see this, George. There are girls walking around giving people flowers. The guys all have long hair. Something's happening."

That night Lillie and I drove to Haight Street. Paul was right. A neighborhood in decline had been reclaimed and turned into something entirely new that hadn't yet been discovered by tourists and the media. We were charmed and bemused. We returned several times that fall, bringing our young daughters to wander through the exotic shops, showing what seemed a permanent carnival to our out-of-town visitors. It was a time of grace, lasting from that October of 1965 to the summer of 1967, when all in life that had been gray and two-dimensional seemed to explode into unexpected color and depth, rich with new smells and sounds and the imminence of miracles. Almost overnight a new culture had sprung up, with its own dress and art styles, its own music, its rituals and incense and bells. It was true that beautiful young women dressed in swirls of color would give you flowers as you walked by. And it was also true that for a while the crime rate in the district (with the exception of drug arrests) dropped to practically zero. I had no thought for my daughters' safety.

The inhabitants of this new world were called hippies. The word came from *hipster,* but these young people were soft and warm and a little fuzzy where the hipsters had been hard and cool and a little cynical. Every Saturday afternoon the hippies spilled out of the Haight-Ashbury into the nearby panhandle of Golden Gate Park, where free rock concerts materialized as if by magic. While we waited for the bands (some of which were soon to become so successful that they were unavailable at any price), the anticipatory rustle of tambourines seemed to evoke a mythic presentiment of transcendence.

In October one of two brothers who ran a psychedelic shop on Haight Street phoned me at my office and asked that Mike Murphy and I come meet with them on "a matter of great importance." We were ushered into a small office at the back of the shop, where four chairs were arranged in a tight circle.

"We want you to know," one of the brothers said, "that what's happening here" — he gestured vaguely around him — "has international significance."

The two of them went on to explain that the hippie movement represented a turn away from materialism by a small but influential group of young middle- and upper-class Americans at the very time when material prosperity was on a strong upswing. This movement could easily spread throughout the world. They showed us astrological charts, and pointed out that what was happening in the Haight-Ashbury could be the first sign of a new age, the Age of Aquarius, when materialistic striving would be replaced by communal love and the exploration of consciousness. When I asked what they wanted of us, they shrugged and said they just wanted us to know.

Mike and I were put off by the brothers' grandiosity and conspiratorial air. Still, there was something in what they said. Perhaps the sudden emergence of this new subculture out of the matrix of the middle class was a sign of some sort of transformation that was trying to happen. The important thing, it seemed to me, was to give it time to develop without attracting public attention. That meant protecting it from the media.

Back in 1957, I had done the first major article on the beatnik subculture that was just emerging along upper Grant Avenue in San Francisco. Within three weeks of the article's publication in *Look,* the Gray Line sightseeing buses were making the beatnik scene a regular attraction. A week after that the Hell's Angels descended. Within two months, upper Grant Avenue was awash with tourists, and the subculture was destroyed beyond repair.

The hippie subculture was very young and very fragile and far more appealing than the beatniks had been. It needed time to mature. I shuddered to think what would happen in the wake of a major article or television show. What was now growing organically, totally unknown to the larger public, would be subjected to the beguiling, disorienting glare of the media. Young people from all over the country — all over the world — would swarm in like locusts and destroy not only the Haight-Ashbury but also themselves. I didn't see the media as totally value-free; I wasn't going to be part of that destruction.

I picked up Fred Skinner at the airport on October 8 and drove him down to Esalen for the weekend we had arranged. More than a hundred people, many of them hard-core Skinnerians, had come to see and hear him. Skinner, as usual, spoke brilliantly and persuasively. But he was far more interested in Esalen's baths and abounding natural beauties than in the Skinnerians.

"There's a place in some corner of Walden Two for an Esalen Institute," he said after the last session of the seminar.

"I've been thinking the same thing," I said, "but in reverse order."

November 29: a chance to try out my education ideas in the real world. I was giving the keynote speech at a planning conference for a new town being built by Goodyear Tire & Rubber Company at Litchfield Park, Arizona. My topic was schooling in the year 2000.

Looking at an audience of community planners, educators, corporate executives, and officials from the U.S. Office of Education, I asked them to consider that "in a time of dramatic technological and social change, U.S. education for the most part exhibits a remarkable resistance to innovation. If the rate of educational change over the thirty-five years between now and the year 2000 is going to be the same as during the past thirty-five years, we might simply turn the schools over to the technicians, the consolidators, the time-and-motion men. There would be, in such a case, no room for innovation."

Were we willing to sit around and see that happen? Drawing on my book proposal, I outlined a three-point program for schools of the future.

First, the present system of educational priorities, giving the most money, attention, and status to the upper grades, would be completely overturned. Second, the present subject breakdown of knowledge and techniques would be reshuffled. Many new areas of learning, having to do with aspects of human functioning that were then neglected or completely ignored, would enter the schools. A significant proportion of what would be learned in A.D. 2000 did not even have a commonly accepted name in 1965.

Third, the traditional one-teacher, thirty-student presentation situation would no longer exist. There would be no exams as currently conceived and utilized, and no regular, fifty-minute class periods. Most of the commonly-agreed-upon factual knowledge of our culture, as well as the most useful techniques and skills, would be learned through programs, probably presented by electronic devices requiring little help from teachers. Teachers would spend most of their time in individual or seminar instruction. Ways would be worked out to utilize the most wasted educational resource in our system: the capability of students to teach other students. At the end of fourteen years of public schooling, tomorrow's students would outscore today's college students, even on the severely limited and unperceptive achievement tests currently in use. The university would have a new function: Higher education would not stand apart from life, but would be the chief substance, the very center of existence, the communication-work-recreation unit, of each community. The demarcation between "student" and "non-student" would blur and finally fade away; every member of the community would be to one degree or another a member of the university.

Expanding on these three points, I discussed my human potential research and urged community participation in the schools. The planners listened for more than an hour, and then surprised me with applause that sounded genuinely enthusiastic.

Their work was not just theoretical. They were planning a real town with real schools and real people. How could I not be encouraged?

December 17 [from my journal]: I wake up at 8:30 in the Élysée Hotel, make the Washington shuttle by minutes. Run into radical journalist Paul Jacobs on the plane. We take a cab to the Mayflower Hotel. From there to Cosmos Club at 12:15 for lunch with James Carr, executive director of the National Education Association. I give him my idea for an Office of Innovation in the NEA. I sell it hard: The time is ripe; schools have to change. He loves the idea: "It's so simple and right that it would seem something must be wrong with it — or else why hasn't somebody thought of it?" At 2:15 he drives me to the U.S. Office of Education in his black Continental. From 2:30 to 3:30 chat with and interview Fritz Lanni and his PR guy for a story to be called "Testing vs. Your Child." From

3:40 to 4:30 interview U.S. Commissioner of Education Francis Keppel and tell my ideas on educational reform. From 4:45 to 5:45 drop in on Paul Jacobs seminar at Peace Corps, then talk with old friend Bob Hatch (now at Peace Corps) and four of his colleagues. Barely make American flight to NYC. In *Look* office at 8:15. T George is still there. Go to his house. Heavy conversation about possible staff changes at *Look*. Back to hotel at 10:45. Phone Lillie. Sleep from midnight to 7:30. Breakfast with August Heckscher of the Twentieth Century Fund at 8:30, selling Esalen and the human potential movement. In *Look* office by 10 . . .

Was it a movement or a revolution or just a cluster of ideas? The occasion finally presented itself for Mike and me to put together a statement, a manifesto of sorts, through which we could make public at least an outline of what we often called simply "this thing." Esalen was sponsoring a lecture by Abraham Maslow at Grace Cathedral in San Francisco on January 6, 1966. The cathedral is a classic Gothic structure at the very top of Nob Hill, with seats for a congregation of twelve hundred. Very little money was available to promote the event — no newspaper ads, just a few posters placed here and there around the city — and there were times when we marveled at our own chutzpah in selecting such a grand setting.

Nonetheless, we decided to prepare a joint statement on behalf of the Esalen Institute, which I would present at Grace Cathedral prior to Maslow's talk. For much of the two weeks between Christmas and the event, Mike and I sequestered ourselves in my living room at 1818 California Street to discuss what I would say at Grace Cathedral. There was nothing somber about these deliberations. The living room opened to an entrance hall which in turn opened to a large dining room, and that extended interior space, with its high ceilings, was conducive to large statements. Sometimes we stood at opposite ends and threw a Frisbee back and forth faster and faster, barely missing lamps and other breakable objects as we shouted our ideas at each other. Lillie drifted in and out, adding her ideas, as did my brother Edward, who taught political science at the University of Texas at El Paso and who had spent Christmas with us. Just to summarize our wild outpouring of thoughts and speculations would be impossible, but there were certain principles to which we returned again and again.

From the beginning we insisted that if there was to be a movement, it would be open and nonexclusive. "It's a big party, everybody's invited." Nor would there be adherence to any single, narrow doctrine or discipline. Mike had already seen efforts by leaders of specific schools of thought or practice to make Esalen their private domain. Fritz Perls, for example, wanted to turn the institute into a "gestalt kibbutz." But Mike's deferential geniality had a stubborn streak. He was determined that Esalen should never be captured by any single discipine or doctrine — and neither should this movement. Both of us saw informed eclecticism as a virtue and dogmatism of any stripe as a danger.

Our basic concern was, simply and literally, the human potential. The fact that almost everyone possesses enormous reserves of untapped abilities stands as one of life's greatest mysteries and one of any culture's greatest opportunities. Anthropology had already shown that different cultures had successfully reinforced and developed radically different aspects of the human potential — seemingly with plenty to spare. The Bushman could track an eland with exquisite accuracy through trackless deserts. The Hindu could enter an ecstatic religious trance. The medieval European architect could conceive and design a cathedral, the modern technologist a spaceship. There were biological limitations, of course, but my research as well as the anthropological record strongly suggested that if a new society needed new human abilities, the potential was there to fill almost any such need.

Social transformation requires individual transformation, and individual transformation requires social transformation. The two are inseparable. Aurobindo's philosophy is based on the evolution of a higher consciousness; Aurobindo was also a social activist. Mike and I agreed (though social and political change was a more immediate concern on my part than on his) that a transformation of self and society was not only needed but already under way. Technology was speeding up human interaction, was weaving the world together. It was also threatening human survival. For the first time in history, "progress" could conceivably destroy the world.

The history of the nation-state was one of exploration, the conquest of territory and other people, and the exploitation of physical resources. Such pursuits were now becoming increasingly maladaptive, even in a narrow, selfish sense. This situation alone demanded some radical revision of our values. Until now, for example, a high degree of aggressiveness and competitiveness had appeared to be adaptive for the survival and furtherance of a given society, and thus was seen as a positive value. Our present and future situation, however, seemed to call for collaborative, empathic relationships. A society bent on conquest and domination would naturally value tight emotional control, mind-body dualism, single-mindedness, sexual repressiveness, and the like. But these old values were now bringing the world closer and closer to destruction.

The future as we saw it called for a turn to the exploration of consciousness, the deepening of relationships, and the full development of human resources. We saw this as the real frontier. For a while we considered using the Grace Cathedral statement as a call for a NASA-scale program for the development of human potentialities.

Our view of the human individual and of the universe was thoroughly holistic, long before that word gained currency. We saw mind, body, and spirit simply as different manifestations of an underlying unity. Nor did we view the human individual as separate from and at war with the world. All of existence is interconnected, and the whole is reflected in every diverse part. Reality consists of relationships rather than objects and events. At the heart of all this, at the heart of the atom, is pure spirit, the Essential Ground of Being.

The purpose of life? To manifest the divine spirit as best we can through the full development of our potential — the potential not just to memorize facts and manipulate symbols but also to expand the senses, to develop the body, to explore consciousness, to create new form, to deepen relationships and serve others. To put it another way, life's purpose could be seen as lifelong learning in the broadest sense. Education would take on immense importance in any viable future society.

From the time I had first imagined *A Practical Utopia*, I had seen no immediate need for basic changes in governmental structure. Our constitutional system had the potential for safeguarding individual rights and providing an arena for benign innovation. Recently, in fact, the federal government had demonstrated its power as a court of last resort in the matter of civil rights. The values and behavior that we favored could exist, it seemed to us, without expanding government's role. We looked to private and voluntary organizations as agencies for change. Even corporations might be helpful; already a number of them were using Maslow's and Rogers's ideas in their management training groups.

Perhaps most important of all would be the media of communication. People couldn't very well choose to support new ideas if they had never heard of them. If the nationwide print and electronic media could simply introduce the new ideas — neither sensationalizing nor ridiculing them — then people could begin to make their own choices. But that would be very hard for journalists to do. Generally liberal in the narrow political sense, they tended to be quite conservative where changes in perception and basic values were concerned. The reason for this is simple: It's far easier to write in terms of categories and concepts that the reader is already familiar with than to try to explain new ones. I knew that Esalen or a human potential movement would be tough for any journalist to understand and deal with.

Mike would do well never to refuse coverage by a responsible media person, I told him. Meanwhile, he could count every day golden that didn't bring a gaggle of reporters to Esalen. Still, the word eventually had to get out, and how it got out would be a key to the future of the new movement. In any event, there would probably be no representatives of the media at Grace Cathedral on January 6.

We went around and around trying to decide what to include in the statement. It would have to be short. Anything more than five or ten minutes in length might upstage Maslow. Yet we felt it would be difficult, if not impossible, to summarize our ideas in that short a time.

Then one day Mike happened to mention the cathedral's unique acoustics: There was a seven-second reverberation. Why not *use* that reverberation? Instead of trying for a systematic, programmatic presentation, why not make the statement something like a brief sermon or prayer — something appropriate to the setting?

With this in mind, I sat down to the typewriter and drafted a three-page, double-spaced statement, imagining a pause between every few words to get the full effect of the reverberation. I read it aloud to Mike. He made suggestions for changes. I rewrote it, practiced it a few times, and awaited Maslow's arrival.

January 6, 1966. A huge storm had blown in from the Pacific, turning umbrellas inside out, ripping branches off trees, sending waves of rain racing along California Street. The wind made my car shudder as John Poppy and I drove from our office up to the Mark Hopkins to have lunch with Maslow. Mike Murphy and Pat Felix, the woman he was going with, were there, along with a young psychologist named Ed Maupin and two people from a local FM station. The previous night a group of us had had drinks in Maslow's room, and I had found him to be one of the most nonphysical people I had met, one given to gravitating toward any object on which he could lean, lounge, or lie. By no means could you call Maslow a handsome man, nor was he an elegant phrasemaker; his words came out rather dryly, in standard academic terminology. But there was something about this very ordinariness, along with the dazzling brilliance of his mind, that made Abraham Maslow not only fascinating but charismatic as well. He was a fearless warrior in the realm of ideas, and just being in his presence accelerated the beat of my heart.

After lunch I drove through the rainstorm to the FM station to be interviewed. I was so full of ideas about the new movement that I talked passionately and almost nonstop for the better part of two hours, and discovered after the interview that I had lost my voice. How stupid could I be? The Grace Cathedral event was less than four hours away.

Back at 1818 California, I lay in bed and sucked on a lemon, saying not a word to anyone. I had a sick feeling in the pit of my stomach. Even if I could recover my voice, the whole affair, including our pretentiousness in writing the statement, began to seem ridiculous. There had been hardly any publicity. And who would venture out in this storm anyway? I had a vision of reading the statement to a nearly empty cathedral. How would the seven-second reverberation sound with only a few people scattered throughout that cavernous space?

Grace Cathedral was a five-minute drive straight up California Street. The event was to start at 8:00, so Mike and I left my house at 7:15 in a driving rain. As we crossed Van Ness Avenue and started up Nob Hill, the rain suddenly stopped. California Street slanted sharply upward, and before we knew it the clouds had parted, revealing a full moon. The street gleamed; the cable-car tracks reflected the light of the moon. We hardly dared speak. By the time we had parked in the cathedral lot and stepped out of the car, our world had been transformed. Everything was wet and fresh, a blustery wind was blowing, and up above were only stars and a triumphant moon, incredibly white, making the cathedral so pale, so silvery bright, that it might have been a dream.

At the door we had to push our way past a long line of people waiting to enter. By 7:45 every seat in the cathedral was filled, and David Barr, the chaplain, was working frantically to have more than four hundred extra chairs brought in. Still more people came. A large platform had been set up at the altar, and I was seated to the left of Maslow, the two of us in grand, purple-cushioned chairs at a large table before two microphones. At 8:10 people were still arriving, finding places to stand in the back, around the edges. Where had they come from? How had they heard of this event?

At last Barr took a microphone and introduced me. The huge space and all the two thousand people in it fell absolutely silent.

"On this night of the festival of Epiphany, we gather to celebrate a new *kairos,* a joyful and awesome moment in mankind's long day . . ."

The sound system was more powerful than I had expected. At first the reverberation shook me, but then, realizing I had my voice back, I let it support me, lift me up, as I sang out the words that Mike and I had put together in my living room.

"Those who dismay at humanity's condition have had their turn upon the stage. They have offered intricate critiques, sinuous analyses of everything that is wrong with mankind, leaving unanswered only the questions they have almost forgotten how to ask: What do we do now? How do we change it all? How do we act to make our society and ourselves whole?"

Standing in the back, Mike noticed that many people, thinking I was offering a prayer, had knelt at the pews. Others had not. No one knew exactly what to make of what I was saying. I went on speaking, becoming more and more confident, my voice stronger and stronger as I went along.

And when I ended, no one knew quite what to do. Some applauded. Most did not.

Maslow spoke for some forty-five minutes, restating his theory of self-actualization as if he were lecturing a college class, paying no attention whatever to the seven-second reverberation. The discussion session was much livelier. We collected written questions from the audience. I sorted them out and read to Maslow those most frequently asked: How do men and women differ in peak experiences? (Women often have peak experiences during childbirth and child rearing.) What do you think about psychedelics? (He was sympathetic but quite cautious.) How does sex fit into self-actualization? (It's a part of it.) How can a parent best fulfill the hierarchy of needs in three- to six-year-olds? (He didn't know.)

Afterward, Maslow, Mike Murphy, Pat Felix, David Barr, and my friend Bob Morse, the Episcopal priest, came home with me and Lillie. Maslow lounged happily on the window seat, celebrating the success of his lecture. A friend named Neil Smith blew in, barefooted, from a dance class. Smith had his own architecture firm, and soon the conversation turned to a long discussion of how to transform the firm into what Maslow called a eupsychian organization, one that would bring out the best in the individual as well as the group.

The party broke up at two A.M. At three I was still lying awake, letting the events of the day wash over me. There was the image of the moon breaking magically free of the clouds. There was the rhythmic sound of the seven-second reverberation. And there was the strange, deep silence that had greeted my statement. I wondered if anybody had heard what I was saying, or if that even mattered. What mattered, I thought, is that I had said it, especially the last three paragraphs:

> Tonight we speak for scientists, religious leaders, educators and interested citizens who have cast their lot with the future. We believe that all men somehow possess a divine potentiality; that ways may be worked out — specific, systematic ways — to help, not the few, but the many towards a vastly expanded capacity to learn, to love, to feel deeply and to create. We reject the tired dualism that seeks God and human potentialities by denying the joys of the senses, the immediacy of unpostponed life. We believe that most people can best find God and themselves through heightened awareness of the world, increased commitment to the eternal in time.
>
> We believe, too, that if the divine is present in the individual soul, it must be sought and found in men's institutions as well; for people will not readily achieve individual salvation without a saving society. We envisage no mass movement, for we do not see people in the mass; we look instead to revolution through constant interplay between individual and group, each changing the other.

The revolution has begun. Human life will be transformed. How it will be transformed is up to us.

The words went around and around in my consciousness. At one point before I finally drifted to sleep, I wondered what those words would mean in the future. But I didn't spend much time in the future, or the past. At that wonderful, magical moment, the present was good enough for me.

22

Euphoria

THE NORTHERN CALIFORNIA SPRING came even sooner than usual in 1966. By early January the acacia trees were bursting into bloom, splashing the vibrant winter green of the countryside with gold. I always wondered about those trees: How impulsive, how illogical it was for them to put out such delicate lacelike flowers when the worst of the winter storms were still ahead of us. Maybe they were like California itself: fast-growing, shallow-rooted, vulnerable to the wind. After every big January and February storm, acacia boughs with their golden flowers would litter streets and sidewalks, and you could see whole trees cracked at the trunk or entirely uprooted. But they seeded very fast, and the following year even more of them would be blossoming on the hillsides, impatient and extravagant, always leading the way, possessed of a vital force that finally would not be stopped. And then there were the plum trees, exploding into blossom within the span of a day or two it seemed, and the cherries and magnolias and azaleas, and crocuses thrusting up out of the earth and clematis sending tendrils out and the urgent tip-growth of the evergreens.

But it was not just the forests and meadows and hillsides that were sending out new shoots. Everywhere I looked I could see growth and change. An unfamiliar feeling of openness was in the air, an eagerness to embrace every new idea. The explosive decade was in full flush, but with far more dash and diversity than I had imagined five years earlier. The civil rights movement had achieved its goals at a rate beyond the most optimistic projections. Campus activism, with Berkeley's Free Speech Movement in the vanguard, was a commonplace rather than a rarity. An Experimental College with student-led classes in a wide variety of subjects had opened at San Francisco State, and the concept would spread rapidly across the nation. Then there was the sudden emergence of the new hippie culture in San Francisco. It too, for good or ill, would surely spread. Meanwhile, young people from all over the country were vying for positions in the Peace Corps. In the early spring of 1966, it was hard to believe that a Gallup poll five years earlier had predicted that a young person of the sixties would be "most unlikely to rebel or involve himself in crusades of any kind."

Young people, and California young people in particular, were spearheading the change, yet the nation's exuberant frontier mood was not limited to any single age group or locale. The economy was expanding; corporations had the money and the confidence to start experimenting with such things as encounter groups. The space program was on track. As incredible as it had once sounded, the United States might actually land a man on the moon by the end of the decade. And educational reform was an increasingly popular topic in the media. My own ideas on education were finally achieving acceptance wherever I presented them. Instead of being shocked by my proposals at Litchfield Park, the U.S. Office of Education officials there had told the group that they were going straight back to Washington to see how they could put the proposals into effect. Only later would I recognize the enormous gulf that separated such enthusiastic statements from implementation, especially where schooling was concerned.

Still, there was no denying the explosive expansion in acceptable discourse and behavior among large numbers of Americans. Things that only a few years ago people had rarely talked about except in whispers were now being openly discussed. With talk came action. In 1960 it had been unthinkable, except in the bohemian districts of certain large cities, for unmarried couples to live together. Now unmarried couples throughout much of the country were openly sharing apartments and hotel rooms. Few people were willing to go as far as the Sexual Freedom League in Berkeley, which held regular meetings at which participants were urged to do anything they wished with anyone in attendance as long as it was mutually agreeable. But with birth control and VD seemingly no problem, the notion of sexual freedom was very much in the air, along with a rage for expressiveness in every aspect of life. It was a time when things once only dreamed of were constantly coming true and when very little seemed entirely impossible.

There were shadows, however, all the darker for the dazzling light of that euphoric spring. After Selma, the fragile coalition between the young civil rights radicals of SNCC and the generally older ministers of Martin Luther King's SCLC had started coming unraveled. The SNCC people considered King too conservative and cautious. They wanted action and exclusive black leadership, and they even began to question the sanctity of nonviolence. "I've been hit on the head one time too many," SNCC leader Jim Forman had told me the previous year. "I can't take it much longer." Sitting on the screened porch of my aunt's second-floor Atlanta apartment at twilight, Forman had suddenly dived for the floor. He was reacting to the sound of a car racing its engine as it sped by; he thought somebody was going to throw a bomb at him.

In August, unexpectedly, the Watts section of Los Angeles had exploded with riots instigated by blacks. Before it was over, whole blocks had been burned to the ground, and troops had had to be called in to contain the violence, which had left thirty-three dead. Was Watts a preview of things to come in the black ghettos of our large cities?

Then there was Vietnam. At first it had been only a small, distant shadow. Most Americans thought it would soon go away. Surely the American technology, know-how, and spirit that had been irresistible in World War II could take care of black-pajama-clad irregulars in a small Southeast Asian nation, even if our involvement was misguided and essentially immoral. But in July 1965 President Johnson doubled the draft and sent fifty thousand more American troops to Vietnam, and even then the problem wouldn't go away. Instead, a peculiar thing started happening: War itself — the gory reality of it — came into the living rooms of America in vivid television images. With everything else being revealed, why not young American soldiers with their guts exposed, Vietcong prisoners shot in the head at close range?

Could domestic transformation proceed alongside this horror? Maybe the revelation of war's true face would make a transformation seem even more urgent. Now everyone with a television set could see the consequences of our culture's devotion to power, prestige, dominance, and aggressiveness. In a society devoted to the full development of human potential, I thought, there could be no Vietnam War.

The winter-spring Esalen brochure listed me as a vice president of the institute. Cofounder Dick Price was the other vice president, the real one as far as I was concerned. I had no duties or responsibilities except perhaps to advise Mike Murphy, which I would have done in any case. But Mike wanted me as an officer, so I accepted. From January 21 to 23 I led my first Esalen seminar, under the title "Some First Steps Toward Utopia." The opening session, on Friday night, was rather perfunctory. Not good enough, I thought at the end of the evening. Fifty people have driven the coast road to talk about utopia. It's spring. This is Esalen. I decided to hold nothing back. Saturday morning I got up early and made a new set of notes for the ten A.M. session. When I started talking, my voice was high in my chest with excitement:

In chapter six of *The Prince*, Machiavelli made a statement that sounds kind of ominous, but I still think it's true. "There is nothing more difficult to take in hand, more perilous to conduct, or more uncertain in its success than to take the lead in the introduction of a new order of things." In spite of that, in spite of the limitations of words and definitions, I'd like to make the following three propositions:

One. It is possible to put forth a tentative working model of a vastly improved human life, or even a better and changed human being.

Two. It's possible to outline some practical steps that will start changing our present society in a way that's necessary to achieve these human goals. The two always go together. We must never forget that.

Three. Present-day American society is not only amenable to change, but is eager for change, is hungry, thirsty, and desperate for change.

In the previous night's session, I pointed out, several of the seminarians had despaired of achieving an improved society, feeling themselves shackled by history. It just can't be done, they had said. Look at history and you'll see.

"Among the battle cries of what Mike Murphy and I have come to call the human potentialities movement," I continued, "in addition to a sort of animal cry of joy, is . . . 'Fuck history!'"

There was a burst of outraged and delighted laughter from the audience. I went on to argue that history was not a very good teacher, being mostly a record of wars and exploitation; that maybe the past several thousand years, ever since the agricultural revolution, had constituted a bad trip for humankind; that the early nation-states had controlled human individuals mostly by the threat of punishment; that "reason," in the sense of being opposed to emotion, was often used, even by the most civilized societies, as a way of internalizing the whip; that now we had a chance to change all this, to offer a reward rather than punishment, to create new values, to build a society in which "reason" and "emotion" would not be seen as opposites, in which individual and social impulses would be as one.

Michael Rossman, one of the Berkeley FSM's leaders, was there as a guest of the institute. He sat on the floor in front of me, occasionally snapping pictures. "I know what you're doing," I told him during the break. "You're clicking the shutter every time I make a particularly oratorical gesture. You're making me look like a southern preacher." Rossman just grinned.

After the break, as I outlined the instruments of change in American society, the stuff that Mike Murphy and I had formulated in our brainstorming sessions, I saw Fritz Perls slide out of the big easy chair at my left in which he always sat during seminars, get down on the floor, and start crawling in my direction. He was a gifted mime, and it was immediately clear that he was acting the part of a baby. He gave Rossman, who was still on the floor with his camera, an infantile smile, then slowly, slowly turned his head and looked up at me: a wide-eyed baby in awe of his daddy. I kept on talking, and after a while he went back to his chair.

"What's up with you, Fritz?" I said at lunch.

He looked at me fiercely, no infant now. "Giff me no blueprints," he said in his best German psychiatrist accent. "Change must occur spontaneously."

I sat at a table with Rossman and asked him what he thought.

"You make it sound too easy. I agree with much of what you say, but it's not going to happen without bloodshed. I'm talking about major bloodshed, man."

I was taken aback.

"What you're talking about would cause major shifts in the power structure, and the power structure's not going to roll over and play dead for you. You're talking revolution."

I explained that I was looking for a new kind of revolution, a nonviolent revolution, a change in values and behavior involving no change in the form of government. I would resist ideology and dogma to the death. There was no detailed blueprint, in spite of what Fritz had said, nor was one needed. What was wrong with a society dedicated to freedom, dignity, and happiness through the full development of the human potential? Wasn't that what the Founding Fathers had been talking about? Rossman said I was being naive.

"What about the civil rights movement?" I said. "There've been tremendous changes in the South in a very short time with relatively little violence."

"Yeah," Rossman said, "and how much change would there have been without federal troops or the threat of federal troops? Look, the top guys in government and in the big corporations and the unions — they don't want the development of the human potential. They want passive consumers who will keep the economy going and keep them in power. Look, if a lot of people got smart and got in touch with their feelings and their bodies, they wouldn't go for things like the Vietnam War. They wouldn't be marching out and buying a new model of a huge, overpowered car every year or two. They wouldn't let the universities make robots out of their kids. You're too optimistic. You're not looking at the dark side of our society."

"But will you grant me one point?" I protested. "I won't argue that it's likely or probable, but will you agree that the kinds of changes I'm talking about are *possible* without bloodshed?"

"I doubt it, seriously."

"Okay, how about this — could we make a *start* in that direction without bloodshed?"

Rossman squirmed in his seat, hunched his shoulders, ran his hand through his hair. "All right," he said finally. "I can see the Establishment letting the change continue as long as it's fairly trivial, as long as it doesn't threaten their power. Maybe they'll see things like Esalen as aids to consumerism, as opiates, ways of diverting people from political action."

"I'm not just talking about Esalen. Changes in first grade are much more important."

"Yeah. Right. But as soon as *any* change, wherever it happens, begins to interfere with their exercise of power, or threatens to, watch out. They'll come down harder than you can imagine. Just watch out."

Rossman's warning shook me. But then, he had always been given to dramatic statements. And anyway, look at how much the FSM had accomplished, and how the idea had spread to universities and colleges all around the country — without bloodshed.

Then two words spoke themselves silently in my consciousness: "So far."

Now that it's gone, how can I recreate that time, that spring of 1966? The dazzling light, the ferocious, incandescent release of energy, the renunciation of all the repressions of the past, the crazy sense that each new day might bring something unexpected and wonderful. It was the season of Eros, when the only sin was to say no. And as for the shadows, they only made the light more vivid, more poignant. Sometimes I had a hollow feeling in my stomach. Maybe I was going too far. Maybe there would be retribution and pain; people I loved could be hurt in the pell-mell rush for transcendence. But maybe not. The air was filled with hope, and if we were falling, we were falling forward too fast to stop.

It was during this season, at this high point in the high sixties, that I was asked to produce another issue on the state of California, to engage again in a complex marathon of planning and persuasion, to become journalist and entrepreneur, writer and salesperson, artist and handyman in an enterprise that would touch more than 30 million people. Another California issue! The whole editorial board was hot for it. Bill Arthur — he was seated firmly in the editor's chair now — told me to get it done as soon as possible. Why not? The last California issue had been the biggest seller in the magazine's history up to that date. Now *Look* was closing in on an 8 million circulation. As incredible as it would have seemed only a few years back, *Look* was now bigger than *Life*. Another California issue would probably bring in even more readers.

We couldn't do a repeat of the 1962 California issue. So why not go a step beyond it, or *ten* steps beyond it? Shortly after Christmas, at the same time I was working on the Grace Cathedral statement with Mike Murphy, John Poppy and I took two days in the office to come up with twenty-seven story ideas, twenty-one of which were accepted by the board. I was just finishing up the education story called "Testing vs. Your Child" on January 17 when Paul Fusco arrived to start work on the issue. Over the next two months, eighteen New York staffers flew to California for several days or weeks. Fusco stayed the whole time.

Almost all of us had worked together before. We had done the southern issue a few months earlier. We were like a repertory company, players who knew each other's favorite moves. John Poppy set out to do a story with photographer Doug Jones on educational programmer Bill Sullivan, as Dan Mich had suggested when he killed the human potential story. John also teamed up with Art Kane on a photo portfolio called "California: A Vision of Hell and Heaven," and interviewed Minuteman Troy Haughton for another essay. T George Harris came out to do a piece called "California: The First Mass Aristocracy Anytime, Anywhere." Chris Wren, always the adventurer, tackled "Climb Beyond the Possible," a picture story about men who scaled the sheer granite walls in Yosemite Valley. And there was a picture story about a liberated Berkeley graduate student who shared an apartment with her boyfriend, and one about a Black Nationalist street worker in burned-out Watts, and one about Joan Baez and her school for nonviolence, and stories on food and fashion and country houses and politics.

I assigned myself the opening essay, "California: A New Game with New Rules," and a picture portfolio with Fusco called "The Turned-On People," as well as the concluding essay, "Where the California Game Is Taking Us," also to be illustrated by Fusco. The theme of this, of all the words and pictures in the issue, was the hidden stuff coming up into the light, the search for new ideas and alternative values, the expressiveness, the euphoria, and more than anything else, the human potential.

To produce a special issue is usually a hectic job beset by an unimaginable variety of problems. This time everything was easy. The New York staffers were transported from a place of biting winds and dirty snow to a place where it seemed that spring might last forever. The green hills and flowering trees mocked the whole idea of self-denial and limitation. The weather played happy tricks for us, providing sunlight to filter down through a forest of redwoods as backlighting for a portrait, and then, when needed, sending a ceiling of fog over bare hills for a long shot of a runner.

We were colleagues and good friends. We got together whenever we could. One night thirteen of us had dinner around a large round table at Johnny Kan's Chinese restaurant in San Francisco and entertained each other with stories of our adventures. I was more a host than a supervisor of a special issue. The issue didn't need supervising. It was doing itself.

Another night Lillie and I, Paul and Pat Fusco, John and Julia Poppy, and Art Kane and his assistant, a stunning blond model named Missy, met at Esalen. No seminar was going on and the place was uncrowded, so after dinner Mike Murphy and the eight of us took over one side of the baths. Mike had several bottles of chilled champagne sent down, and we lay in the steaming mineral baths popping champagne corks out into the darkness while John, Julia, Art, and Missy entertained the rest of us with stories of their experience earlier in the week at the Sexual Freedom League.

John and Art had arranged to photograph one of the league's meetings for "California: A Vision of Hell and Heaven." They might have wondered how they could run pictures of an orgy in a family magazine, but part of our plan for the issue was to press the limits of what had been previously revealed. Maybe Art Kane could apply his genius as an illustrator to coming up with something more artistic than lewd. (As it turned out, the lighting was poor and the pictures expressed neither heaven nor hell but just something rather seedy, and were unusable in any case.)

Art and John were invited to take off all their clothes like the rest of the guests, but declined. "Can you imagine anything more ludicrous than a naked man with three cameras hanging around his neck?" Art asked, laughing. While he shot his pictures and John sat on the floor talking with nude men and women and taking notes, Julia and Missy, also fully clothed, stood in the entry hall. Julia told us how she had been repeatedly propositioned by men who were seemingly inflamed by the very fact that she was wearing clothes. As the propositions became increasingly insistent and even hostile, she found herself pulling her turtleneck higher and higher, until finally it covered her mouth and ears.

"It was the only time in my life," she said, "when I wished I'd worn gloves."

We found it amusing that she said this while nude in a hot bath with eight other nude people. Context is all.

The LSD genie was out of the bottle, and the authorities were becoming increasingly alarmed. Ken Kesey and his Merry Pranksters had been going around California holding "acid tests," all-night happenings at which large groups of people took LSD and danced or simply grooved to the music of the Grateful Dead and other groups while psychedelic light projections were played on the walls, ceiling, and floor. In late January, on the weekend of our utopia workshop at Esalen, Kesey teamed up with a young cultural innovator named Stewart Brand to put on a huge event at Longshoremen's Hall in San Francisco. The "Trips Festival" was supposed to give the effect of LSD without LSD. But many of those who came took the drug anyway. Paul Fusco covered the festival for our issue. The next week he showed John Poppy and me about a hundred of the three thousand or so pictures he had shot, and told us what had taken place. Some ten thousand people had attended — students, businessmen, SNCC workers, fraternity boys, teenagers, motorcyclists. They wore everything from business suits to "ecstatic dress," a form of hallucinatory, do-it-yourself costumery that already was beginning to influence fashion on both coasts. The senses took a beating from flashing strobe lights, dazzling film projections, electronic rock music, taped noises, screaming whistles, and wafting incense. Couples tried to dance, but all the dances got mixed up, and people pressed together in clumps, reaching upward as if appealing to some unknown spirit. One young woman staged a topless dance; another chose to lie motionless while the crowd covered her with confetti.

Beginning two weeks later and regularly thereafter, Bill Graham, who had managed the original event, produced his own version of the Trips Festival at the Fillmore Auditorium, a funky old dance hall in the black district. The idea of the psychedelic ballroom was soon to spread across the United States, and eventually throughout most of the world. Lillie and I started going to the Fillmore that spring. We found it hard to believe that people could take large doses of LSD and still walk around, much less dance. That this was happening, that young people were dropping acid and then going to a dance hall or an amusement park, pretty well destroyed the concept, which I had shared, of LSD as strictly a sacramental drug.

Still, for a while the Fillmore events seemed amazingly loving and benign. The admission charge was between two and three dollars, and got you a free apple and a poster of the next event, done in the psychedelic–art nouveau style of the Haight-Ashbury. We loved the music and light shows and the dancing. But more than anything else we loved the *newness,* the spectacle of an unfamiliar world unfolding before our eyes. Maybe this strange new culture of the young, LSD and all, was a symptom of a larger transformation trying to happen, a breakdown of the rigid, fragmented old consciousness in preparation for a society of diversity and community and lifelong learning. In a sense, the hippie rebellion was more thoroughgoing than any political rebellion could be. These young people were rejecting the old order, not through demonstrations and signs and slogans and political activity but through overnight changes in their own minds and bodies and ways of living. Only in science fiction could changes happen so fast. But changes *were* happening fast, and there was a science-fiction feeling in the air.

*

A man named Myron Stoloroff had made some millions as a founder of Ampex, then had retired to start an organization he called the International Foundation for Advanced Studies, which was devoted to LSD research. Jim Fadiman, a psychological researcher for the foundation, phoned and asked if I had a specific creative problem that I was working on; if so, he would like Paul Fusco and me to participate in an experiment on creative problem solving under psychedelics. Well, there were the picture portfolios that would go along with the opening and closing essays for the California issue. That should do it, he said.

I liked Fadiman's faintly ironic tone. He was on the California frontier but had all the Establishment credentials: nephew of the literary critic Clifton Fadiman, Harvard undergraduate, recent Stanford Ph.D., with a dissertation on psychedelics and creativity.

California officials, alarmed by the explosive growth of the psychedelic culture, were beginning to crack down on LSD. But Fadiman told us the foundation held a federal license to use LSD in creativity research. We would be, he said, serving the cause of science. Not only that, the foundation put on one of the most elegant trips to be had anywhere.

I was not eager to take that trip, no matter how elegant. I had already been slammed into another reality, and it had been almost more than I could bear. But it was the spring of 1966, and new worlds were bursting open all around me. Adventure was becoming almost obligatory.

"You can ask Mike if you wish," Fadiman said, perhaps sensing my reluctance. "He's a pretty good creative problem solver."

On the night before the experiment, we met at the foundation's rather luxurious suite of offices and conference rooms not far from Stanford University. Stoloroff, a serious, somewhat humorless man, and Willis Harman, his equally serious associate, briefed us on the research project and our part in it. Stoloroff and Harman would supervise. Fadiman would take a small dose of the psychedelic drug so that he could serve as a bridge. Paul, Mike and I would take a full dose. The three of us signed a paper agreeing, among other things, to stay on the premises and to give our full attention to our particular creative problem when asked to.

We spent the night in a nearby motel and reported for the session at 7:30 in the morning. Both Stoloroff and Harman wore white lab coats. After another briefing, Stoloroff left the room and came back with four miniature silver cups on a small silver tray. The cups held small white pills. The four of us trippers toasted each other with the cups and threw the pills down. We were then led into a room with couches and cushions. On one wall was a painting of an Indian mandala, on another Jesus and his disciples. We were fitted with stereo headsets, and then lay on a carpeted floor that was itself like a cushion.

For the next four hours we listened to a program of music taped for this session: flute sonatas by Bach, Rimsky-Korsakov's *Scheherazade*, a series of Indian ragas. The fall into another reality was less traumatic this time. When the Indian music came on, I experienced the dark sinuosity of the sitar as the interconnectedness of everything in the universe, and the constant drone of the tamboura as the Essential Ground from which the endless weaving rose. My own independent existence became a mere spark among an infinitude of similar sparks, or not even that, but simply a sort of generalized awareness entirely independent of time and place.

Then — suddenly, unexpectedly — a brilliant major chord, a series of ascending major triads, the full-throated sound of a church organ: a Handel organ concerto! And there I was in a great Gothic cathedral with golden sunlight streaming in through golden stained glass windows. All the darkness, all the sinuosity was gone in the wink of an eye, and there was only this clarity, this golden light. At that moment I realized that I belonged to the culture of Europe and the New World, not of the Orient. I was Western and always would be. Tears of understanding and gratitude ran down my cheeks. How brave it was, how poignant: this attempt by the West to redeem the self from timelessness or from endless cycles of ultimately meaningless time.

The rest of the program was all Handel and Bach, the alternation of major and minor, the harmony of light and dark, the celebration of God who was a *self,* a God of time as well as timelessness. I reveled in the golden light, the experience of time as alive and crackling with energy and purpose. The music ended, and we took what seemed a long time to stretch, sit up, and get ready to work. Mike had already made a few notes. Paul and I got our notepads and layout sheets, and we were ready to begin. The six-hour conversation that followed was recorded on audio tape.

In the few minutes before we started talking, I had already visualized the whole layout: three two-page spreads of color pictures, with only one or two very large pictures on each spread. The first spread expressed the theme "All men are brothers," and consisted of one large picture, almost monochromatic, of black and white people. The second spread had the future as a theme. On the left side was a huge fire consuming swastikas, guns, bombs, and missiles, while on the right, in dark plum tones, was a picture of all races living in harmony. The theme of the final spread was "The joy of now." On the left was a beautiful young woman, nude, in a bed of greenery and golden flowers. On the right was a crucifix superimposed on an indistinct face that represented death, with golden light streaming from behind it. Joy and death seemed somehow to go together, in either a contrasting or a complementary relationship.

My colleagues greeted this vision with something less than enthusiasm. It gradually dawned on me that it was pretty bad, which only made me defend it more vigorously. Finally Paul roused himself and told me just how corny my layout was. I argued that the greatest ideas were always corny. Paul said that the pictures had to stay in human terms, not symbolic ones. Especially not those clichés I had suggested. I yielded; my premature solution was not just bad, it was terrible.

Mike Murphy came up with home as a metaphor. He pointed out that America has never really found a home. The only home is in God. Not knowing that, Americans are forever trapped in a polarity between comfort and security on the one hand and adventure and expansiveness on the other. But we can never find either until we realize that home is God. Good enough, but what pictures did that suggest? Paul saw the concept of home less in God than in family. At least you could take pictures of a family.

Our conversation began moving in wider and wider circles — to the adventure and expansiveness of the space program; to the pill, which was making the birth of a child a moral choice; to the overwhelming power of technology, which was potentially making almost every choice a moral one; to the possibility of a police state in reaction to the explosive changes in mores and morals; to new ways of involving the reader — including feedback cards in the magazine, for example. The title of the issue was "California: A New Game with New Rules," but strangely enough, we kept circling back to the most basic themes: home, family, God. Once, when Mike repeated one of his favorite statements, "God is waking up," I said that that would make a great headline in the morning newspaper. Jim Fadiman provided the wording: GOD WAKES UP. STOCK MARKET FALLS. Our conversation devolved into an old-fashioned bull session. Anyone listening to the tape might never suspect that any kind of psychedelic agent was involved. Paul Fusco kept bringing up the importance of the most fundamental of relationships. "I keep getting back to the fact that George and I have to make it," he said. "Before talking about 'All men are brothers,' I have to learn to get along with my wife, my children, my friends." That was where it started, he argued. That was the New Game.

In midafternoon, just as our session was about to break up, Jim Fadiman's wife, Dorothy, came in. She was a lovely woman with particularly striking eyes. When she first looked at Jim, Paul saw something in her expression, a sort of ecstatic intimacy, that as far as he was concerned completely solved the problem of the picture portfolio. He spent the next day shooting pictures of Dorothy alone, and then with Jim. Two days later he came to the office with a selection of slides. Everyone there, including the ad people, gathered in a darkened room to view them. There were close-ups of Dorothy looking at golden acacia blossoms, eyes wide with wonder, Dorothy in a field of golden mustard flowers embracing Jim. The pictures were stunning. The blossoms burned like molten gold on the screen. The expression on Dorothy's face entirely justified my reckless line "The joy of now."

I sent out for champagne, and we toasted Paul, the California issue, and the future. Our session on psychedelics and our six-hour creative problem-solving session hadn't really been necessary for Paul to get those pictures of Dorothy Fadiman. Or had it? In any case, things had worked out perfectly. It seemed we were operating in a state of grace, and nothing, absolutely nothing, could go wrong.

When American Airlines Flight 14 started down the runway shortly after nine on Sunday morning, April 17, the Hallelujah Chorus was playing on the audio. Mike, Susan and I exchanged glances. It figured.

Mike had been planning to go to New York to meet with August Heckscher of the Twentieth Century Fund, and I had suggested he make his trip at the same time as mine. I was going to spend a week or two putting together the final layouts for the California issue. A skydiver named Susan was a last-minute addition to our party.

Just a few days earlier Paul Fusco had come into the office and announced that he had photographed a girl who could fly. She was twenty-two and not only a first-rate athlete but also one who claimed psychic powers. Paul said she should be on the cover. He showed us his pictures: Susan in free fall, Susan checking her equipment, Susan crowded in the back seat of an airplane. Dressed in jump boots, white coveralls, and helmet, she had an angelic smile, delicate features, and the slightly feline eyes of the movie star Audrey Hepburn. I asked her for lunch at the Garden Court on the Friday before I was to leave for New York.

She showed up wearing high heels, a straight, light tan skirt, and a white ruffled blouse, her long dark hair done up. After the photographs with boots and jumping gear, the effect was startlingly feminine. She didn't deny that she could fly. "It's not like falling, ever," she told me. "For a long way, you're not aware of the ground coming up. Your time sense changes. Thirty seconds is a half hour — or an eternity." Whether or not Susan was, as she claimed, a white witch, she was certainly bewitching.

I had just finished reading *Stranger in a Strange Land,* a science-fiction novel by Robert Heinlein that tells of an Earthman named Valentine Michael Smith who has been raised from infancy on a planet inhabited by beings of a far more advanced culture than ours. Smith returns to Earth, still genetically a human but with extraordinary abilities — telepathy, erotic virtuosity, the ability to make objects disappear into another dimension — that he has learned from the alien culture. This assumed stretch in the human system made the book an underground favorite among those who were interested in human potential and human transformation. Some people were even given to the speculation that Michael Murphy was the real-life model for Valentine Michael Smith. In any case, the fictional Michael teaches his followers on earth a brief ceremony, the completion of which joins them together for life.

When our second gin-and-tonics came, I lifted my glass to Susan, and without asking whether she had read the book, spoke the first line of the ceremony: "Share water?"

Without hesitation, she lifted her glass and responded, "May you never thirst."

As we put our glasses to our lips, our eyes met, and something happened. If it had to do with the two of us, it also had to do with that particular moment in history, when old boundaries were there only to be crossed. When I asked her to come to New York, I realized that what I was doing was crazy, but I was unable or unwilling to stop.

On Monday morning, Susan, Mike and I walked into the *Look* offices to join up with T George Harris and Paul Fusco in putting the final touches on the issue. Within a couple of days, Mike had been integrated into the *Look* operation. That this was possible was due not only to the informal, free-swinging nature of the magazine but to his unusual charm. Mike made friends with most of the top editors, especially Patricia Carbine, who shared his Irish gift of laughter and warm sociability. What the other members of the staff thought about this was not clear. But after all, it was a new game with new rules.

Actually, things were in great shape. If we were a bit on the far side of euphoria, we were also very well organized; all the stories were in the house and laid out ahead of schedule — a rare situation for any magazine. In effect, this gave the members of the editorial board two easy weeks, and everyone on the eleventh floor was in a holiday mood. As for our little group, it seemed that we were under a charm, that we could walk through fire, that all of life was a wonderful game.

One day I was chatting with Paul Fusco in the room set aside for photographers. A large conference table stood in the center of the room, and rows of locked doors lined the walls on either side. Each of these doors opened to a spacious walk-in closet with shelves for cameras, tripods, lights, and film. I heard a large group of people slowly approaching in the hall. The group had come through the editorial conference room earlier — about twenty journalism students from a midwestern university being led on a tour of *Look*'s offices by administrative editor David

Maxey. Paul and I quickly decided on a plan to blow their minds.

"Would you mind if I gave your group a little talk?" I asked Maxey as he herded the students into the photographer's room.

I spoke very seriously to the students for a few minutes about *Look*'s editor-and-photographer system and the advantage this gave us over other picture magazines. I gestured toward the large table: "This is where the photographers can spread out their prints and make choices before going into layout." Then I walked slowly over to Paul's closet door. "And this," I said as I opened the door, "is where we keep our photographers."

Paul was standing in the closet facing us, his body rigid, his eyes fixed straight ahead like a zombie's. I left the door open until everybody could get a good look, then closed it, leaving Paul inside, and walked toward the photographic studio.

"Now if everybody will just come through this door," I continued in the same matter-of-fact tone, "I'll explain how we do our studio shots."

The students filed dutifully into the studio. None of them smiled or asked a question or looked back at the closed door to Paul's closet, but there were puzzled and strangely melancholy looks on many faces. I glanced behind me in time to see Dave Maxey staggering out into the hall, bent double with silent laughter.

On Saturday morning Susan and I were sitting at the bar at the Barberry Room talking with Ray, the bartender, when Bill Arthur walked in and sat next to Susan. There were only the three of us and Ray.

"Would you like to go on a trip?" Susan asked Bill.

He gave her a startled look, then said, "Sure."

"Okay," she said. "Order a gin-and-tonic with a piece of lime."

When he had his drink, she leaned close to him and began talking in a low voice about what it was like to be alone on an arctic iceberg. She spoke for two or three minutes, her voice finally dwindling to a whisper in his ear. Then she said, "Now lean down, put your nose very close to the ice in your drink, and breathe in deeply."

Bill Arthur did as he was told. Then he sat up straight and stayed that way for a few seconds, his eyes fixed. Suddenly he hit the bar with his palm and shouted, "Ray! Ray! For God's sake, close the door. It's *freezing* in here!"

The last two days of our stay, we kept somebody on guard at all times in the main conference room, where the layouts of the entire issue were displayed on racks all around the walls. The process had come off without a hitch, and we wanted to make sure that nothing would be changed before the layouts were shipped to the printer. We saved our biggest celebration for the flight home. As the plane rose, our spirits rose much higher. We could barely restrain our exuberance and joy. Not long after takeoff, Mike managed to squeeze into the space between my seat and Susan's and the seats in front of us. He stood there facing us as we talked about the incredible days that had just passed and the more incredible possibilities ahead of us. We made up scenarios of the future: We would run Price Cobbs for president in 1980; America would be transformed. Our voices rose. We hugged and kissed each other with passion and belief. After about two hours, we became aware of the other passengers. Surely they were shocked and outraged by our behavior. But as we glanced around we could see no strained looks, no hostility, nothing out of the ordinary. It was as if we were encased in clear plastic, immune from the constraints of ordinary life, maybe even from the law of gravity.

As the plane made its final approach to San Franciso, the "Kyrie" from Bach's B-minor Mass was playing on the audio. It was obvious that God or one of his favorite angels was programming the music on American Airlines.

Why couldn't it be this way forever?

23

Penance

BACK IN THE SAN FRANCISCO OFFICE, I had three weeks to write two essays as well as the captions for two photo portfolios. The photographs and layouts had already been shipped to the printers. The words, as usual, had to fit precisely in the space allocated for them. It was hard to settle down to work, but finally I got some momentum going. The opening essay called for definitions:

> The Game is no longer to explore and conquer your physical environment, nor to build empires on the face of the earth, but to explore and expand yourself, your institutions and all of human possibilities, to seek ever-receding frontiers in the infinitely rich and varied common countryside of humanity. The Rules include a surprising openness in personal relations, a new intensity of personal commitment, a radical shift in the morally admissible, an expanded definition of education, a whole new array of learning techniques and a heavy reliance on direct action and direct experience rather than theory and talk.

I was writing for *Look* magazine, for more than 30 million readers. I was writing about California. What I was writing was true. The trends were there, no doubt, in the minds and the actions of real people in a real state. But I was also writing a personal dream that I hoped would resonate in the minds of millions of other people all over the country: a dream of barriers dismantled, of human potential tapped as it had never been tapped before, of a new society, a new world. Three weeks and thousands of words later, as I neared the end of the closing essay, I was flying high again, and ideas I had thought about for years were pouring out:

> Pursuit of the human potential could become a national goal worthy of the original American dream, something we could offer the world not as a threat but as a gift. Too often now, we give the bewildered people of underdeveloped nations guns, wheat, money and vague verbalisms about "freedom" that make no sense whatsoever in lands that have neither our tech-

nology nor our traditions. Perhaps there is a more effective approach. What if we could give them a vision large enough to stir the longing for commitment in everyone, a practical message of faith in humanity that every human being could understand? What if we could show a poor Asian farmer the almost infinite genius within him and his children? What if we could offer him simple, specific techniques for achieving, almost overnight, *in his own terms,* new literacy, culture, ability to cope with technological change? What if we could suggest alternative ways for him to build utopian communities far bolder than anything the Communists, with their doctrinaire view of human potentialities, could conceive? If we do not lose our nerve or imagination, all these possibilities are nearly upon us.

As I typed out the closing paragraphs, I had a totally unexpected vision of a checkered flag waving in front of me, signaling a victorious finish.

Since the French Revolution, choruses of theological and philosophical voices have sounded against the notion that men can be "perfected" or even significantly improved. Human nature, the argument goes, is immutable; any attempt to change it involves the sin of pride.

Some of this argument is just reaction, sanction for the status quo. But much of it springs from humane motives. We have seen what mischief and suffering can follow half-cocked, idealistic revolutions in which only the hangmen change, the gallows remain the same. And so pessimism about the potential of man has become not only humane but highly respectable as well.

Against the challenges of the present and future, however, these arguments fall apart. They are simply irrelevant. We will continue to expand our capacities — or go down the drainpipe of history.

A spirit of hope is in the air. What comes of it depends not only on the wisdom of national leaders but on the acts of all who read these pages. Those who turn away still cannot escape the challenge. Those who have the courage of their humanism will rejoice.

A day after mailing the last of my copy to New York, I drove south for a weekend at Esalen, not to take a seminar or give a seminar but to relax in the hot baths and visit with Mike Murphy. The next morning, shortly after breakfast, I was summoned to the office for an urgent phone call. It was T George Harris. He was calling from the *Look* office and his voice was grave.

"Sam Castan's been killed in Vietnam," he said. "Somebody's got to go over to Hong Kong and bring back his wife and baby to New York."

There was a long silence, during which I sensed a curious shift in the momentum of my life.

"I'd be very happy to go," he continued. "I mean that, George. But you're three thousand miles closer, and time is important."

I knew he meant it. T George was born to self-sacrifice. I wasn't. I asked a few questions, giving myself time to consider the situation. Sam Castan had been a driven, what-makes-Sammy-run kind of guy who always wanted to be where the action was. He had pressured Dan Mich relentlessly until Mich had agreed to send him and his family to Hong Kong so that Sam could cover Vietnam. I could imagine nothing I would more dread doing than flying halfway around the world to bring his widow and baby back to New York. But I was also aware of the California issue, the past several months of euphoria. A terrible sinking feeling in my stomach told me that somehow I owed *Look* a trip to Hong Kong. There was a symmetry in the universe, some sort of balance between privilege and duty. It was my turn to be dutiful.

"I'll go," I muttered.

For the next hour I was on the phone with Bill Arthur in New York, with contacts in Washington who arranged for somebody in the passport bureau in San Francisco to open up that Saturday afternoon, with the British consul to arrange for a visa, with a doctor to give me the necessary shots. T George stayed on the job with Bill Arthur in New York, ringing up Far Eastern contacts, arranging for Chase Manhattan to transfer funds to me at the Mandarin Hotel in Hong Kong, working out funeral arrangements, checking on Castan's insurance. I drove back to San Francisco. After a hectic afternoon and evening of making arrangements and phone calls, I got a few hours of sleep. The next morning at nine I was on Pan Am Flight 1 westward from San Francisco.

Bill Arthur had been very explicit in his instructions. I was to do everything in my power to make Fran Castan's return comfortable and dignified. I was to go out of my way to be of service. Anything she asked for was hers. Money was no object.

The plane landed in Hong Kong twenty-four hours later, after stops at Honolulu and Tokyo. I might have slept an hour on the plane, no more. Bob McCabe of *Newsweek* met me at the airport and drove me to the Mandarin Hotel.

"The bad news is that Fran is blaming *Look*," he said.

"What's the good news?"

McCabe shrugged. "Things are pretty tense at her apartment. I'm afraid you're in for a hard time."

"How could she blame *Look*?"

"I think Sam told her *Look* made him take the assignment."

I couldn't believe it. Mich had told me that he had said no to Sam so many times that Sam had finally come in and threatened to set fire to all his old stories and immolate himself right outside of Mich's office unless he was assigned to the Far East.

Things at the Castan apartment were even tenser than I had expected.

I felt my very presence was an intrusion. I had never before met Fran Castan, but now I offered myself to her body and soul. I said *Look* would pay any outstanding bills and that I would immediately deposit $500 in her account to take care of incidentals. She wouldn't have to worry about subletting the apartment. In fact, she could keep it at *Look* expense if she would like to return to Hong Kong for a while. *Look* would take care of shipping anything she wished to New York. I had arranged for Pan Am to grant her full courtesies on the flight home.

She accepted all this without comment. She was concerned about an education for her one-year-old daughter, Jane, what with Jane's father killed so young. She wanted to be absolutely sure Sam's body would not be cremated. She would not leave Hong Kong until the body was on a plane from Saigon. I told her that *Look* was checking on Sam's insurance, that Sam's body had already been embalmed in accordance with Jewish rites, and that I had already phoned a military contact in Saigon, Lieutenant Colonel Dianzi, and a State Department contact, Barry Zorthian, and a media contact, Jack Lawrence of CBS News at the Hotel Caravelle, so that we would know exactly when the body was on a plane. I conveyed to her the deepest regrets of Bill Arthur and the entire *Look* staff, and said that I was there to serve her to the best of my ability.

The next forty-eight hours passed with no clear distinction between night and day. Both nights I was up at two A.M., which was the best time to get calls through to New York on the overseas lines. From my hotel window I could see the bay crowded with sampans, and other exotic scenes that I would have no chance to visit on this trip. I paid a call on the Pan Am public relations director to make sure that we would have special treatment all the way back to the United States. I checked in by phone with U.S. State Department representative Conrad Abramowitz. I spent Tuesday afternoon and $21 buying baby food and bottles and a sedative and diarrhea medicine and toys for little Jane. On Tuesday I sent a cable to Bill Arthur:

WILL DEPART HONGKONG WITH FRAN WEDNESDAY VIA PAA FLIGHT 2 BUT ONLY IF CASTAN REMAINS HAVE LEFT SAIGON BY THEN STOP WE ARRIVE NEW YORK 6:35 AM THURSDAY VIA AMERICAN 18 STOP PLEASE PHONE ME 7 PM EST IF I HAVE NOT REACHED YOU BY THEN CIRCUITS BUSY REGARDS

The Castan remains left Saigon on a military air transport plane bound for Travis Air Force Base, California, in time for us to make Pan Am Flight 2. We took the first two seats on the left in first class, just behind the lounge. We were to spend most of the next two nights so close together we could touch. Yet during this entire period, Fran rarely looked at me and spoke only when telling me what to do. I kept reminding myself that perhaps as she saw it, *Look* had killed her husband, and that I was an embodiment of *Look*. To try to attempt to correct her version of how Sam got to Vietnam would have been not only inappropriate but useless. I had my job to do, my duty to fulfill.

And that job, it turned out, was mostly caring for the baby. All the other seats were taken. Sometimes Jane slept in my seat while I sat in the lounge, and sometime she slept in Fran's seat while Fran went to the lounge. But for hours on end she stayed on my lap. I had helped raise four daughters and I knew the territory. Jane had a round face and was larger than my girls had been at that age, but she had the same magical ability to be totally present. We played games with the toys I had bought. There was all the time in the world, so I made the games last as long as possible, exploring the subtlety of movement, of approach and with-drawal, of acceleration and deceleration, that is the special province of those not yet seduced by language. We played very slowly and very seri-ously, for even a hint of laughter seemed to draw Fran's disapproval. But this only increased the secret warmth between the two of us. Sometimes in the night, when Fran was asleep in her seat and Jane was asleep in my lap and I was sitting there with eyes wide open and burning with sleep-lessness, I prayed that I could enter her one-year-old consciousness, where there were no words and no expectations and no judgments, only the eternal present.

Once during the first night, when Jane was asleep in Fran's seat, I heard angry words from the lounge. I went forward to see what was wrong. Fran was having some sort of argument with a man who was holding a drink. The man was annoying her, she said, and I should do something about it.

"What's the problem?" I asked the man.

"Nothing," he said with a grin. "We're just having a little talk."

His face was flushed and he obviously had been drinking heavily. When Fran and I got back to our seats, she told me that Sam would have han-dled it differently. I nodded and said I imagined he would have.

The trip seemed interminable, the tension unrelenting. At San Fran-cisco, still sleepless, I changed planes with my charges and we flew away to the east. After all the distance we had spanned, the five hours to New York seemed to pass swiftly. But I was near the end of my resources. When we landed early Thursday morning, Bill Arthur was waiting for us at the gate. Before he even spoke to Fran, he looked at me with a startled expression.

"My God, George," he said. "You look *terrible*."

He didn't have to tell me. I was too empty to feel happiness or relief or anything else when I turned Fran and Jane over to Bill. I just gave him the information I thought he had to have, got my baggage, and took a cab to the Hotel Élysée. I thought I might never get to sleep, but when I did, I slept for hours. I awakened to a strange sort of depression. Was this whole episode an omen of future difficulties? Would this joyful revolution someday join all those other hopeful movements that ended up merely increasing the sum of human suffering? The world was still out there, and the war.

A few months later, *Harper's* magazine ran a lead article entitled "Men Facing Death: The Destruction of an American Platoon." Military historian Brigadier General S. L. A. Marshall pieced his story together from accounts of the four survivors of a platoon that had been overrun by units of the North Vietnamese army.

The twenty-two men of the platoon were guarding an oval-shaped perimeter on a slope in Vietnam's central highlands. They were accompanied by a war correspondent, Sam Castan of *Look* magazine, who on this occasion was seeking the thoughts of men facing death. The soldiers were hidden in foxholes, and the flanks of the perimeter were screened by tall grasses. Castan, however, was moving from position to position, standing erect, taking photographs, asking questions, and, according to a survivor, disclosing the limitations of the force to any enemy who might be watching.

The Vietcong attacked suddenly and with overwhelming force. Castan was one of the last of those killed. He took a bullet in one arm and several grenade fragments in his back, saying nothing. He died of a bullet drilled through his left temple.

24

The Day
I Was Drummed Out
of the Establishment

UP TO THIS POINT, the ferment of ideas and activities centered on Esalen and other California institutions had achieved no significant degree of public knowledge. Millions of people would first learn of it through the June 28, 1966, issue of *Look* magazine. If that issue was reportage, it was also manifesto, and I might have guessed that it would occasion a certain amount of controversy. But I had no idea of the storm it would whip up. Years later, when something called the human potential movement became a favorite whipping boy for Establishment critics who had only the vaguest, most symbolic notion of what they were attacking, I recalled the *Look* California issue as a Distant Early Warning signal. In any case, June 14, 1966, the day the issue went on the newsstands, was to be a milestone in my life.

The summer weather had returned to San Francisco. The mornings dawned beneath a solid low overcast — high fog, we San Franciscans called it — so dense and damp it seemed the sun would never shine. But sometimes as early as ten and sometimes as late as one or two, the fog would retreat, revealing a brilliant sky and a vertical sun that would make you want to shield your eyes no matter which way you turned. At night the fog would come back again, chilling the city, causing the city lights to glisten.

Waiting for the California issue to come out, I took some days off to go to the beach, to play Frisbee in the park, and at last to get started on the education book. The New York escapade had left a residue of guilt and unease that even the euphoria of the times couldn't entirely override. The Hong Kong ordeal had helped balance the scales. And now I was relieved to respond to the pull of my conservative side: family, loyalty, safety. It was one of those rare periods when Lillie was neither working nor taking courses, and she and I found ourselves at the center of a large and rather complex family group. My elderly maiden aunt Emie was living in a nearby rooming house and spending as much time as possible with her namesake, twenty-month-old Emily. Five-year-old Lillie was in nursery school. Seventeen-year-old Mimi was soon due from New York on her way to Esalen, where she was going to spend the summer as part of the crew that cleaned and straightened the cabins, and nineteen-year-old Burr was planning an extended visit later in the summer.

As for me, there were no immediate plans except to go out and promote the California issue when it hit the stands. The *Look* promotion department had set up a full schedule of newspaper and radio interviews and, most important of all, television appearances for that week. If the decade had shown one thing so far, it was the power of television. The 1960 Kennedy-Nixon TV debates had turned an election around; vivid coverage of the civil rights movement had awakened the nation's conscience; and now television was bringing the Vietnam War home. There was no escaping the power of the new electronic medium to influence opinion and create instant celebrity. A few months earlier, a waitress in a small restaurant in San Francisco's Japantown had asked my name. When I told her, she said, "You on TV!" She had seen me on the noon news, promoting the southern issue. She came back with a pad for my autograph. I suggested she go two booths over and get Herb Gold to sign her pad. "He's a famous novelist," I said. "Just got the top French literary award for the year." She looked at him, then shook her head. "He no on TV."

The big general magazines still had the advantage over television of being able to run ads in full color, but advantage was clearly temporary. U.S. households with color TV sets had increased from less than 1 percent in 1960 to nearly 10 percent in 1966, and the percentage was rising fast. It didn't take a futurist or a seer to realize that television was the mass medium of the future. But if this was the twilight of the general magazines that competed with television for advertising, you wouldn't know it at *Look*. Our circulation had grown from 6.2 million in 1960 to 7.7 million in 1966, and surveys showed our readership now to be 34 million. Our advertising revenue had increased from $59 million in 1960 to $80 million in 1966.

What's more, the magazine that had started out twenty-eight years earlier on cheap paper with lurid pictures and sensational words now stood at the pinnacle of prestige. Awards for editorial excellence were coming in so fast that it was hard to keep track of them. In March 1966, in fact, *Look* received the highest possible honor. It was in that year that the Magazine of the Year Award was first established. The award was sponsored by the Graduate School of Journalism at Columbia University, at the invitation of the American Society of Magazine Editors and under a grant from the Magazine Publishers Association. The very first of these awards would always hold a special significance, and it was given to *Look* "for skilled editing, imagination and editorial integrity, all of which were reflected particularly in its treatment of the racial issue during 1965."

In accepting the award, *Look* founder Gardner Cowles quoted Dan Mich, who, Cowles said, had felt that magazines must deal with the tough and controversial issues of our time, and who had believed that "the hottest places in hell are reserved for those who, in time of moral crisis, maintained their neutrality." As far as I was concerned, the award belonged to Dan, and it was too bad he wasn't around to receive it. But it felt good that I had been reporting on race since 1957, and that the southern issue had come out near the end of 1965.

Actually, I gave little thought to awards and prestige and "position." Such things had little significance out in the field of action. But if someone had asked me, I would have had to answer that I simply assumed the esteem of my editors, my colleagues, my readers, and what might be called the journalistic Establishment as well. Then, in the course of one day, everything changed. The first indication that something extraordinary was going on came in a phone call from T George on Wednesday.

"It's pretty lonely here," he said. "I wish you were in town."

He told me that of all the New York staffers who had worked on the California issue, he alone was in the office that week. It happened that the others were away on assignment. He was the only one available to defend it.

"Defend it?" I said.

T George allowed that there was quite a bit of controversy, but for him that was all to the good. He had always believed that a certain amount of abrasion makes whatever is under attack shine more brightly.

I left early Thursday morning for radio and television appearances in Los Angeles. On Friday, Bill Arthur called the L.A. office.

"This is the most exciting week of my twenty years at *Look*," he told me. "People are shouting in the corridors. I never thought people would shout in the corridors at *Look*, but they are."

The place was in an uproar, he said. Everybody was outraged about the California issue. It was hard to get any work done. The new issue, as usual, had been delivered to the desk of every *Look* employee on Tuesday. The attacks had started then, and had grown in intensity ever since. Arthur seemed amused as well as bemused, and I couldn't believe the situation was serious. With its senior-editor/producer system, *Look*'s grouping of separate dukedoms had a long tradition of noninterference.

Anyway, I considered the other senior editors and the photographers, even those who didn't usually work on my special issues, as friends. Surely they would phone me personally if they wanted to discuss a problem. They certainly wouldn't complain about me to members of the editorial board.

I was wrong. Back in the San Francisco office the following week, I received a steady stream of phone calls from New York, not from my attackers but from members of the editorial board, who were kind enough to tell me what was going on. One senior editor had scrawled obscenities on the issue with a red grease pencil and tossed it on Pat Carbine's desk. Another, a tall, elegant, fastidious man who was sometimes referred to as our Princess Grace editor, had returned from one of his numerous trips to Monaco just in time to pick up a copy of the issue on the newsstand. He appeared in co–managing editor Bob Meskill's office, pale beneath his Riviera tan, his hands trembling. According to Meskill, this normally gentle man threw the magazine on his desk and shouted, "We're through! We're finished! We'll be out of business in six months, like the *Literary Digest*." He was referring to the enormously successful magazine of the thirties that collapsed a few months after forecasting that Alf Landon would defeat Franklin D. Roosevelt in the 1936 general election.

Carbine and Meskill tried to maintain an air of detached amusement in their talks with me, but it was obvious they were concerned. The negative reaction, except among those who had worked on the issue, was nearly universal. And according to senior copy editor Martin Goldman, it was virulent. "They didn't just want you fired," he told me later, "they wanted you immolated."

The hurt I felt quickly turned to indignation that my detractors wouldn't confront me directly but persisted in attacking me behind my back. I couldn't resist mentioning this cowardice during my talks with Arthur, Carbine, and Meskill. When Joe Roddy sent me a copy of a memo he had written to the three of them, I felt relief, even gratitude. Roddy was a cultured man with a wicked wit and a sense of irony that he rarely let you forget for as long as two minutes. One of his hobbies was choir-crashing. He would put on the appropriate robe and sneak into a dressing room before a choral performance, then go on stage with the rest of the singers. He was a good enough musician to get away with it, and he had performed with some of the nation's best choirs.

"The California issue embarrasses me," he wrote. "If you care to know precisely why it embarrasses me in ten words, a hundred, or a thousand, I will set them down for you on request. Before you answer I will rush in with one question anyway, just to get the discussion going. Question: If the state of California asked a skillful PR firm to draw up a promotional brochure, would it not find that this issue of *LOOK* was in substance and tone the near-perfect fulfillment of its needs?"

I wrote him immediately, thanking him for sending me the copy of his memo, then arguing that he had it all wrong. The revolutionary happenings I had reported on were certainly not what any Chamber of Commerce group would want promoted. Anyway, everything I had reported on in California was actually happening, whether we liked it or not. I had also heard from Bill Arthur that Joe had called the issue evangelism, not journalism. I reminded him that neither he nor anyone else at *Look* had called it evangelism when I had beat the drum passionately for a quick end to southern segregation and extolled the civil rights movement to the skies. *Look* was a journal of opinion, not just news.

He answered by return mail with further arguments. I was about to respond to his response, and indeed to mount an attack against all my attackers, when it occurred to me what an enormous waste of time that would be. Instead, I settled back and tried to figure out what had created such a violent and unprecedented response from people who had previously been friends and admirers. I pulled out the file I had kept for years containing laudatory comments from my colleagues. I shook my head as I read notes of praise from the same people who now wanted to immolate me. John Poppy and I went through the issue searching for sections in particular that might have provoked such a murderous rage. We looked for the worst, and found two or three passages that might have been considered provocative. There was, for example, a paragraph in the opening essay:

> The Californians you are going to meet move in the fields of education, art, science, and the like, or in fields so new they have no commonly accepted names. These people are excited and enthusiastic. They are turned on by life. Because of this, they sometimes baffle the Eastern sophisticate. ("I've decided that anyone who's enthusiastic," a New York lady magazine editor recently said, "is either selling something or is simply naive.") But the sophisticate has been too long squashed down by the soot and grime of worn-out ideas, the sheer difficulty of living, the endless torrent of words, words, words that cannot but dull the natural sensibilities. . . .

Such passages, however, couldn't account for the scale and intensity of the reaction. Provocation had appeared before in *Look*. I had previously written that segregation was "a dangerous, self-destructive madness" and that "almost every white Southerner starts out as an emotional, intellectual, visual, aesthetic cripple," and had received only warm applause from those who were now attacking me.

No, it was something else, something more fundamental than a few provocative statements. Maybe it had to do with irony. The bitterest attacks were coming from those who prided themselves on the possession of that sense. Irony required detachment, perspective, and I couldn't deny that it was useful in journalism. Ironic perception involved taking an obligatory backward step, seeing things in a larger context. It was, in a way, the opposite of enthusiasm, offering the journalist protection against phonies, con men, and snake oil salesmen. But it was also, in the words of novelist Wallace Stegner, "that curse, that armor, that evasion, that way of staying safe while seeming wise." On a scale of a hundred, the California issue had undoubtedly moved eight or ten points away from irony and toward enthusiasm, and maybe that alone was enough to get me drummed out of the Establishment.

More important than that, I figured, was the matter of category. The human mind works ceaselessly to discover or impose order on the stuff of the senses. It works metaphorically, making comparisons, matching the new with the old, perceiving the unfamiliar in terms of the less unfamiliar. The mind, and especially the Western mind, separates reality into categories, so as to narrow the number of comparisons that need to be made in the ordering process. But categorization, however useful, can come to dominate perception and define reality. When something new arises, the mind runs it past abstract categories rather than specific references. Categories thus precede and sometimes take precedence over direct experience in the process of ordering sense perceptions.

What happens when the mind confronts a new experience or description of a new experience or set of experiences? First it tries to fit it into some old category. What if the fit is difficult to make? The mind goes right on trying to shoehorn the new experience into the old container. In some cases this leads to frustration, anger, and finally (if the fit turns out to be impossible) disorientation. It's possible, of course, to deal with the uncategorizable data by creating a new category. But this is a difficult and adventurous process, requiring considerable mental strength, stability, and courage. It's far easier to dismiss or ridicule the new data, or to attack whoever or whatever presented it. Sometimes it's easier just to blank out.

There's still another possibility, and that is to create a pseudocategory. Take the case of a new kind of massage that was being given at Esalen. Both the person giving and the person getting the massage are nude. They are likely to be of opposite sexes. The masseur or masseuse is sensitive and caring. The veteran journalist observes or hears about or reads about such a massage. It takes less than a second for his or her mind to find a category. It's sex, of course.

The proponent of the new massage tries to explain. The purpose is not to arouse. Arousal is always possible but unlikely, and it would only get

in the way of the real purpose, which is to produce nonerotic, unconditional tactile pleasure for both the giver and the receiver, and perhaps to
compensate, if only a little, for the endemic deprivation of nonhostile,
nonseductive touch in this culture. The journalist, if he or she is willing
to investigate further, observes that there are absolutely no signs of sexual arousal during such a massage. Interviews with people who have been
massaged yield a consensus that the experience is sensuous but not sensual. The journalist might even have such a massage (but don't count on
that) and be not in the least aroused.

Will the journalist write a report pointing out that the massage is not
erotic, and then go on and try to describe the experience honestly and to
place it honestly in a new category? Maybe, but that would be very unusual indeed. Back in the editorial office, the journalist finds the actual
experience fading against the powerful field of predisposition that sur-
rounds him or her. How embarrassing it would be to face the ridicule of
colleagues and editors. Then too, think how hard it would be to create a
new category that the reader would be asked to take seriously. It might
help to cite Prescott's cross-cultural studies for the National Institutes of
Health showing the correlation between societal aggressiveness and the
lack of touch in childhood, and Harlow's studies at the University of
Wisconsin showing the disastrous results of touch deprivation in mon-
keys. However, it would take a lot of research and thought and many,
many words to explain, and it would still invite ridicule. How much
easier it is to stick tongue firmly in cheek and write a short, witty description of the massage along with sly intimations of suppressed sexual feelings.

And if not sex, what? Ah, here we have the pseudocategory, the real
purpose of which is not to describe and define but to disparage and dismiss. How about "touchy-feely"? *Perfect!* "Touchy-feely" can be applied
not only to the Esalen massage but to any and all experiences in which
human beings touch each other in a nonsexual, nonaggressive way. It
provides a convenient box in which to dump everything about touch that
is not explainable in traditional terms. Thus, neither the journalist and
the editor nor the readers have to deal with the new class of experience,
and the status quo is preserved.

There was little in the California issue that would fit the pseudocategory "touchy-feely." With its discussion of new modes of living, new
values, and even a new consciousness, it was even more difficult to pi-
geonhole. Suffice it to say that the producers of the issue had committed
the sin of dealing seriously with previously uncategorized material that
normally would have been disparaged, ridiculed, or dismissed. I began to
realize how disorienting this must have been to the senior editors who

were mounting the attacks. On my first trip back to New York after the issue came out, a senior editor walked up to me, her eyes darting from side to side with genuine agitation, and said, "You know I've always liked your writing, but I have to tell you that I read whole paragraphs of the California issue and I don't have the vaguest notion of what you're getting at." For one who prided himself on writing clearly, without the fashionable mystification of some of the more ironic writers, that hurt.

But at least I was beginning to understand the cause, nature, and vehemence of the disorientation, and the attacks. For quite a while, however, I didn't know what to do about them. I wasn't considering retreat. Something was happening in the world that needed to be reported on, and I was determined to keep writing about it. I would have enjoyed a fight, an all-out confrontation with my attackers. But as I have said, that would have been time-consuming, and I had work to do.

The answer came to me in a flash. It was so perfect that I couldn't keep from smiling for most of that day.

I would forgive them.

I wrote Joe Roddy an understanding and conciliatory letter. In subsequent discussions with Arthur, Carbine, and Meskill, I never quite said, "I forgive them" — that would have been too obvious — but I did let it be known that I could understand and even sympathize with the attackers' point of view. My tone was patient and kind.

At this point, I wish I could report that I was motivated solely by compassion and a desire for harmony. There might have been a little of that in my actions. But to keep the record straight, I must say I was rather fiendishly delighted with this tactic. I could imagine the dismay and frustration among my detractors when they realized they were being forgiven. And that did turn out to be the case. I could hear the gnashing of their teeth all the way from New York to California.

For the moment I was in a pretty good position. The issue was selling very well. Letters were pouring in, running slightly more favorable than unfavorable and vehement on both sides of the question. The three top editorial people continued to support the issue, as did most of the members of the editorial board. They really had to, since they had approved of the plans all along. Then too, the top editors were less ironical people than were the bulk of the senior editors.

The truth of the matter was that my detractors were closer in their views and sensibilities to the Establishment, if the journalistic and critical Establishment could be roughly characterized as the *New York Times* and the *New York Review of Books,* than were Arthur, Carbine, and Meskill. The members of the Establishment were generally smart, good, liberal people. But the reaction among the smart, good, liberal people on the *Look* staff provided me with information that would stand me in good stead for the rest of my life: The good people of the Establishment are willing to give plenty of running room to those with differing ideas and opinions. They are quite genial in honoring freedom of inquiry and expression. But only up to a certain boundary. Step across that boundary — which has to do with new categories, new ways of perceiving and ordering reality — and the geniality vanishes in the wink of an eye. The traditions of tolerance are suspended. The rules of evidence are off. You have become an outlaw, more threatening by far than those who merely carry guns, and thus fair game for any kind of attack, no matter how unfair.

As the summer of 1966 deepened, I realized with increasing certainty that June 14 had been a pivotal day in my life. In producing an issue on a new game with new rules, I had uncovered some of the unwritten rules of the old game. And I had created a new game with new rules for myself. I didn't know then that before the decade was over, I would attract disapproval from the national administration and *Look*'s editor-in-chief would be offered a million dollars to fire me, but I did know that nothing would ever be quite the same.

The new game was war, and I could smell the approaching battle.

PART THREE

BREAKDOWN IS BREAKTHROUGH

25

The Night Fritz Perls
Spanked Natalie Wood

WORD OF THE NEW MOVEMENT was getting out of California and into the country at large. There were the Twentieth Century Fund luncheons in New York, and there was also the California issue, which never mentioned "human potential movement" as such but treated many of its ideas. But what if the American entertainment business should take up the cause? That was the question on Jennifer Jones's mind when she decided to give a large party on July 29, 1966, to introduce leaders of the new movement to some of Hollywood's top executives, directors, and stars. The Academy Award winning actress, widow of producer David O. Selznick, had been coming to Esalen since the earliest days and was fully committed to its people and ideas. Her party was to be a West Coast equivalent of the Twentieth Century Fund luncheons.

Before the party, psychologist Carl Rogers, John Levy of the American Association for Humanistic Psychology, philosopher Abraham Kaplan of the University of Michigan, and I met at a coffee shop on Sunset Boulevard to discuss what we should try to accomplish that evening. Richard Farson of the Western Behavioral Sciences Institute and Mike Murphy were already with Jennifer Jones. She was still agonizing, as she had been for the past two days, over seating arrangements for dinner. Fritz Perls was due to arrive later. Esalen cofounder Dick Price had decided to skip the whole thing.

Mike wanted me to give a small talk at the party to describe the aims of the movement and introduce the members of our contingent, and I already had some notes on three-by-five cards. But when someone brought up the question of just what we were going to *ask* for, everyone was stumped. A sudden vision horrified me.

"What would it be like," I said, "if Hollywood stars were driving up the coast road to Esalen every weekend? They'd take it over."

We talked for a while, considering various possibilities. Finally we decided that the best thing would be to make our presentation, mingle with the guests, and ask for absolutely nothing. It turned out to be a fateful decision.

I drove up the winding road to the Selznick mansion around sunset. The car was taken away by one of a corps of red-jacketed parking valets, and I walked to the house up a long curving path hung with Japanese lanterns. Jennifer Jones looked ethereal and lovely in a pale green silk gown. A number of people were already there with their drinks in a living room as large as a small theater. Jennifer introduced me to Rock Hudson, Glenn Ford, Eddie Albert, and several directors, including George Cukor. Shirley MacLaine was charming Mike Murphy and Dick Farson. The guests kept arriving — producers, directors, and stars. To me it looked like half of the film industry. It was impossible to finish a drink without having a waiter appear at your elbow with another. Around dark, Fritz Perls made a dramatic entrance. He was dressed in a tuxedo, the only person there to be so attired. Fritz loved the theater and the cinema. How would he act in the presence of so many stars?

The plan was for me to give my talk in the living room. But no sooner had the servants begun arranging chairs than Jennifer Jones changed her mind. It was a lovely night; we would go to a lawn area behind the house. Amid much confusion, servants and guests carried folding chairs up a narrow walkway to the lawn. By the time everything was set, darkness had fallen. Some eighty guests took their seats. Jennifer Jones welcomed them nervously, then introduced me. Subdued lights glimmered around the periphery; I could barely see my notes.

Just as I started to speak, Jason Robards, Jr., staggered up next to me and announced that he had a few things to say first. Someone tried to get him seated, but he was insistent. If he couldn't speak, he would do his gorilla imitations. He proceeded to give a sample. I stood there, bemused but strangely calm. Let him do what he would.

Finally someone led him away into the shrubbery, and I began my talk. I described recent work on the human potential and the development of techniques and practices to tap it. Then I began introducing each member of our delegation. When I introduced Fritz Perls, he stood in his tuxedo with an expression of benign majesty, turning slowly in all directions to receive the admiring gaze of stars he had so often gazed at admiringly. As all of us were being herded down to the house after this little ceremony, Fritz thanked me for the introduction. It was the first time he had ever spoken to me with any warmth whatever.

We repaired to tables for ten in a spacious solarium, where dinner was served along with wine, champagne, and liqueurs. Dennis Hopper dominated my table with descriptions of a movie he was planning about young people of the sixties. It was already quite late when the entire party gathered in the living room to see the rough cut of a documentary film entitled *Journey into Self*, about an encounter group led by Rogers and Farson. Something was wrong with the projector, and refreshments again made the rounds while it was being fixed.

The film finally began rolling, a low-key, black-and-white record of people sitting in a circle talking about their feelings. From having experienced encounter sessions, I knew how explosive they seemed from the inside. Viewed from the outside, however, they could seem merely interminable. Though the documentary would go on to win an Academy Award in its category, this showing was more conducive to sleep than to high honors. How embarrassing it was, I thought, to show such an amateurish effort to a group that included many of the top filmmakers in the world.

When the showing ended, Carl Rogers stood up and announced that he would now lead an actual encounter group. Anyone who wanted to participate should follow him into the next room. He walked through the door, followed by one individual, a small, nondescript man in a dark suit with thick glasses.

It was now around midnight. After the documentary the Apollonian phase of the party ended, and the Dionysian began. Jennifer Jones, who had been missing for a while, reappeared like an apparition, newly radiant in a simple white silk gown. In spite of her beatific presence, things became increasingly boisterous. Jason Robards's gorilla imitations grew in popularity. Oskar Werner, the nation's current romantic heartthrob, accosted me, his deeply misunderstood eyes now clouded with a sort of dumb rage.

"You goddam psychiatrists," he said. "You goddam psychiatrists — telling us what to do. The trouble with everything in the world is *you.*"

I tried to explain that I was not a psychiatrist, nor was anyone else in our group except Fritz Perls. Werner slumped back on a couch, his eyes glazing over.

"You goddam psychiatrists," he called after me as I walked off.

I wandered around, trying to find somebody who was in a condition to talk. There, standing alone, very erect and seemingly alert, was James Coburn. I walked up and told him that I had admired his performance in *Our Man Flint*, that I had preferred it to Sean Connery's James Bond. Coburn was indeed fully alert, an island of clarity in a sea of inebriation. Somehow we got onto the subject of the martial arts, about which I knew nothing and about which Coburn seemed quite knowledgeable.

Later I went outside. Fritz Perls was giving a session of gestalt therapy by the pool. A group of people were gathered around in chairs, and Natalie Wood, very aware of her youth and sparkle and desirability, was in the hot seat. It was another part for her to play, and she was enjoying herself immensely. Fritz tried to get her to admit she was acting. She skillfully slipped out of his verbal traps. Then Fritz let her have it.

"You're nothing but a little spoiled brat," he said in a voice harsh enough to stop time, "who always wants to get her own way."

She gasped and her mouth fell open. A moment later Fritz somehow had her over his knee, spanking her. It was a brief episode, hard for the senses to register or credit. Natalie flounced away, and her friend Roddy McDowell offered to fight Fritz. Fritz ignored this offer. About two minutes later, Natalie marched out of the party with no goodbyes, her nose angled sharply upward.

Not long after that, Tuesday Weld sat in the hot seat, with approximately the same results, minus the spanking. She too stormed out, her long blond hair streaming.

Fritz was undeterred. One of our contingent, Abe Kaplan, got in the hot seat. Kaplan was a philosopher of some repute and was not to be so easily routed. Like Fritz, he was a bearded, patriarchal figure, less forbidding but equally dramatic in appearance. I glanced away at one point during the session, and when I looked back, Kaplan had left the hot seat and was sitting with Fritz in his chair, his arm around Fritz's shoulders. The two men's faces were so close that their beards touched as they shouted at each other.

"I can understand the first and the second levels of self-deception," Kaplan said heatedly. "But what about the third and the fourth and the *fifth* levels of self-deception?"

"*Shut up!*" Fritz said.

The party was still going strong when I left around two A.M. The next morning I got reports of how it had turned out. Mike Murphy's brother, Dennis, had arrived at about three in high spirits. He had been charming, hadn't challenged anybody to a fight, and had helped keep things going. Many of the guests had still been there to have breakfast and watch the sun rise. In terms of Hollywood parties, it was a great success, and that's probably why so many people stayed so long.

But I later wondered if they had stayed partly because they were waiting for something that never happened. Hollywood people were accustomed to going to parties at which they were asked for something — money, votes, pledges of support, invitations to further events. In this case, they were asked for nothing at all. They weren't even invited to Esalen. It must have seemed a little strange.

After that, Hollywood luminaries would occasionally show up at Esalen for a weekend seminar, but there was never to be a large influx, nor did Hollywood have any significant influence on the perspectives and practices that grew out of the institute's work. Maybe it was only coincidence that later, during the time that Esalen and human potential were fair game for satire, Natalie Wood starred in the satirical *Bob and Carol and Ted and Alice* and Tuesday Weld starred in the equally satirical *The Serial.* In any case, for good or ill, Jennifer Jones's party was an opportunity not taken, a turn of large or small importance in the garden of forking paths.

26

Jamming with McLuhan

1967

THERE WAS LITTLE TIME for the education book. I was often away weeks and weekends. When I was in town, I would try to get home in time to play with Emily and Lillie before dinner, then tell them a bedtime story afterward. By then it was eight-thirty or so, and I was very reluctant to start work on the book after nine. Sometimes it would be five minutes to nine before I went down the stairs to the basement room I had set up as a study, a gloomy place with iron-grilled windows just above ground level. I would sit at my portable typewriter, yawn, rub my eyes, and fight off the urge to call it off for tonight and try to get started a little earlier tomorrow night. I would stare vacantly at the blank white page in the typewriter, lean back, and yawn again. My life was filled to overflowing. My work at *Look* alone could occupy every waking minute. And then there was Esalen and Mike Murphy and our plans to bring new teachings and new interactions into the world. It was much more fun to do things than to write about them. But here I was, so I might as well write.

Teachers are overworked and underpaid. True. It is an exacting and exhausting business, this damming up the flood of human potentialities. What energy it takes to make a torrent into a trickle, to train that trickle along narrow, well-marked channels! Teachers are often tired. In the teachers' lounge, they sigh their relief into stained cups of instant coffee and offer gratitude to whoever makes them laugh at the day's disasters. This laughter permits a momentary, sanity-saving acknowledgment, shared by all, that what passes for humdrum or routine or boring is, in truth, tragic. (An hour, of which some fifty minutes are given up to "classroom control." One child's question unanswered, a hundred unasked. A smart student ridiculed: "He'll learn better." He learns.) Sweet laughter, shooting up like artesian water, breaks through encrusted perceptions and leaves a tear in a teacher's eye. A little triumph.

Sometimes I would keep writing until after midnight, until the words blurred and the lines wavered on the page. Making my groggy way to bed, I could only vaguely recall what I had written. When I went down the next morning to read the evening's output, I was often surprised to discover it was all right. But maybe there was an advantage in my being so exhausted: I was too tired to censor myself. I didn't have any mental energy left to worry about what the critics or the educators or the literary Establishment would say. I didn't write defensively. I just let it fly.

"If you'll notice the placement of the skylight, here, on the side of the room away from the windows, you'll see that the illumination is perfectly balanced at every desk." The principal is happy and I rejoice with him about the delicious, perfectly balanced flow of outdoor light into a room filled with beautiful children. But something disturbs me, a vinegary tingle at the back of my neck. *There is a witch in this room.* I see her near the back of the fourth row — milk-white skin, black hair falling onto a faded blue blouse, a band of freckles across the bridge of a small, sharp nose. Dark eyes with dilated pupils are fixed on me now, bold and direct, telling me that she knows, without words, everything that needs to be known about me. I return her stare, feeling that this girl, with an education she is not likely to get, might foretell the future, read signs, converse with spirits. In Salem she eventually would suffer the ordeal of fire and water. In our society she will be adjusted.

"When it gets dark outside," the principal is saying, "an electric-eye device — here — automatically compensates by turning on the lights to the requisite illumination." The girl's eyes never leave mine. She is a sorceress, too, for already she has created a whole new world inhabited only by the two of us. It is not a sexual world. What she has in mind — she could never put it into words — bypasses the erotic entirely. But later, when those talents of hers which do not fit the scientific-rationalist frame are finally extinguished, she may turn to sex. And she may become promiscuous, always seeking the shadow of an ecstasy and knowledge that by then she will remember only as a distant vibration, an inexplicable urge toward communion.

"You see, a classroom such as this can never become dark. The illumination will always be even." The principal, I realize, is telling Miss Brown that we are leaving. The girl has no intention of releasing my eyes. The principal is moving toward the door. For a moment I grow dizzy, then break the connection and follow my host out of the door, quickly reassuming the disguise we all must wear to travel safely in the world that I and the principal and most of us customarily pretend is real.

I compliment the principal but I know the illumination in that room will never be even. A classroom, any classroom, is an awesome place of shadows and shifting colors, a place of unacknowledged desires and unnamed power, a magic place. Its inhabitants are tamed. After years of unnecessary repetition, they will be able to perform their tricks — reading, writing, arithmetic and their more complex derivatives. But they are tamed only in the manner of a cage full of jungle cats. Let the right set of circumstances arise, the classroom will explode.

Progress came in fits and starts, but it came. In the first chapter I went back to fundamentals, expanding on a three-part definition of education:

1. To learn is to change. Education is a process that changes the learner.
2. Learning involves interaction between the learner and his environment, and its effectiveness relates to the frequency, variety, and intensity of the interaction.
3. Education at its best is ecstatic.

The second chapter was called "The Human Potential" and was adapted from the unpublished *Look* article. Just as I was starting the next chapter, Bill Arthur assigned me to collaborate on an education article for *Look* with the man who was perhaps the most provocative and controversial thinker of the times, a man known by some people as the herald of a new age.

The first time I met Marshall McLuhan, we talked for thirteen hours straight. We started at his house in Toronto at ten A.M. on Saturday, October 8, 1966, and didn't stop until eleven that night. We went out to lunch and dinner together, and as it happened visited the men's room at the same time, never once breaking the flow of our conversation.

In 1964 Lillie had seen a small review in *Harper's* of McLuhan's prosaically titled book *Understanding Media,* and had immediately bought a copy. We had both read and reread the book with fascination. Many people knew *Understanding Media* only for one of its phrases: "The medium is the message." But that one phrase was paradigmatic; even McLuhan's severest critics had to agree that he clarified the human situation by stressing that the effect information produces is determined not just by the content of the information but also by the medium through which it is communicated — whether that medium is a television set or an elementary school classroom. McLuhan theorized that technology was bringing on an Electric Age, pervasive and all-involving, its instantaneous two-way circuitry joining the world into a global village. The Electric Age contrasted sharply with the fading Mechanical Age, which was linear and fragmenting, with a genius for stamping out products, including human components, in the mass.

"The Future of Education" was the title of our proposed collaboration. I was already fully prepared to write about the future of education without McLuhan's help. He, in contrast, had given little thought to elementary and secondary education. But he wasn't long in focusing the wild brilliance of his mind on that subject.

McLuhan was tall and rather stiff physically, and he spoke in professorial tones — appropriately enough, since he was a professor and director of the Center for Culture and Technology at the University of Toronto. McLuhan lived almost entirely on the mental plane. Though he reacted with excitement to ideas and to the information about schools that I brought to the dialogue, he rarely, if ever, asked about my personal life. He told me his mind never stopped. Sometimes, he confessed, he could hear his friends' ideas in his head through a kind of telepathy. "It's a great bother, really," he said.

However abstract, McLuhan's mind was a marvel to behold. Among the mental tactics for which he was known were his "probes" — sudden, unexpected leaps of thought. During our nonstop conversation, we kept coming back to the subject of competition. Why did schools use so much competition in the educational process when research showed that it generally failed to improve performance and often produced negative side effects? Late in the afternoon, while we were talking about something else, McLuhan suddenly raised his finger.

"I've got it," he said. "Competition creates resemblance."

For a moment this went right past me. Then I got it. In order to compete with someone, you must agree to run on the same track, to do the same thing, only faster or better. This "probe" was to figure in a section near the beginning of the article devoted to a critique of present-day schooling:

> Specialization and standardization produced close resemblance and, therefore, hot competition between individuals. Normally the only way a person could differentiate himself from the fellow specialists next to him was by doing the same thing better and faster. Competition, as a matter of fact, became the chief motive force in mass education, as in society, with grades and tests of all sorts gathering about them a power and glory all out of proportion to their quite limited function as learning aids.
>
> Then, too, just as the old mechanical production line pressed physical materials into preset and unvarying molds, so mass education tended to treat students as objects to be shaped, manipulated. "Instruction" generally meant pressing information onto passive students. Lectures, the most common mode of instruction in mass education, called for little student involvement. This mode, one of the least effective ever devised by man, served well enough in an age that demanded only a specified fragment of each human being's whole abilities. There was, however, no warranty on the human products of mass education.
>
> That age has passed. . . .

The ideas bounced back and forth between us, gaining velocity and momentum with each bounce. I flew back to San Francisco with the notes of our conversation and wrote "The Future of Education" with relatively little effort. It was a thoroughgoing criticism of conventional education and a brief for the use of modern technology, especially computers, to create self-paced, individualized learning, to break down the rigid walls between school and the world. "The Future of Education," the lead story in the February 21, 1967, *Look,* had plenty of McLuhan in it, but was essentially, as one critic later pointed out, a précis of my book-in-progress.

The senior editors who had objected to the California issue were by now fully alerted, and quickly registered complaints with the top editors. What made it worse was that the same issue had an article by John Poppy allowing rebellious and disaffected young people to have their say. There was a lot of talk then about a "missile gap" between the United States and the USSR. John's title was a play on that term. At first he wondered whether to call it "generation gap" or "generational gap," but he finally decided on "The Generation Gap." Within weeks the term was in common use, even in ad copy. John didn't mind when his title was widely used with no credit to him, but was somewhat miffed when advertisements appeared with whole phrases lifted out of his story. (It was about this time we discovered that the opposition editors were beginning to watch the teletype machine in the New York office for TWXs from San Francisco, in order to gain knowledge of our future plans. Maybe, I told John Poppy, we should install a system of cryptography.)

McLuhan loved "The Future of Education." He began phoning, often late at night, with ideas for other articles. We had dinner in San Francisco in late November; then, in early January, I dropped by Toronto on my way to New York to lay plans. We brainstormed future topics. I suggested "The Future of Sex." He liked "The Future of War." ("War," he said, "is speeded-up education.") I came back with "The Future of Power." What we were planning seemed far more than a series of *Look* articles — another book, another whole career. What was I letting myself in for?

At the end of March we talked again in Toronto about "The Future of Sex," and again we had a wonderful time, a jam session in ideas. We agreed that sex as we now think of it might soon be dead. I described sexual customs in primitive cultures, something I had come across while doing research for my book. McLuhan pointed out that the Romans had coined the word *sexus,* probably deriving it from the Latin verb *secare,* "to cut or sever," and we agreed that that was exactly what civilization had done to man and woman, especially in the industrial age. I brought up the idea of the narrow-gauged, specialized male, a creature who is essentially hard, domineering, and unfeeling. McLuhan speculated that the narrow-gauged male of the industrial age produced — in ideal, at least — the specialized woman, the one who is passive yet armed with feminine wiles. We foresaw the end of this specialization, the cooling of hot sex, the creation of a world in which all of life is erotic.

"The Future of Sex" was longer and somewhat harder to write than "The Future of Education." And by this time I was getting desperate about completing my book. The deadline was May 15, about six weeks away, and the book was less than half finished. I had never missed a deadline at *Look,* but it was clear I would have to ask for an extension on the book.

In mid-April McLuhan and several members of his family visited San Francisco. With them was Father John Culkin, a communications expert from Fordham University, which had awarded McLuhan the $100,000-a-year Albert Schweitzer Chair in the Humanities, beginning the next September. We all went to a peace march at the panhandle of Golden Gate Park at noon on Saturday. The marchers were mostly members of the Haight-Ashbury hippie community. Price Cobbs joined us. We stood next to McLuhan at an intersection and watched them go past, their faces painted, their bodies adorned with beads and feathers and a wild variety of improvised psychedelic clothes.

McLuhan was fascinated and bemused. He kept shaking his head.

"There's no question," he finally said in his most professorial voice, "that this is a result of the new tribalism of the Electric Age. Whether I can deal with it is another question."

I suggested that if he really wanted to see the Electric Age in action, we should all go to the Fillmore ballroom that night. He seemed strangely reluctant. I insisted, describing the all-around, all-involving sound and light, the coolness of the medium, the tribalism of the dancers.

"It's everything you predicted," I said. "The Fillmore is pure McLuhan."

Still he demurred. During lunch at the Cliff House, his wife, Corinne, quietly explained that Marshall had hypersensitive hearing. Any loud sound was extremely painful.

That afternoon we all went out to John and Julia Poppy's house in Marin County — Marshall and Corinne McLuhan; their son Eric; their daughter Mary with her husband, Tom Colton; John Culkin; the Poppys and their three boys and my mother (who was living with them); plus me and Lillie and our two young daughters. We went up to a hill behind the house and flew kites, then came down and became involved in one of those wonderful conversations during which nothing particularly important is discussed and everyone is happily involved.

The Poppys were not expecting such a large crowd but somehow managed to scrape up dinner. Afterward, McLuhan insisted on doing the dishes. It was his job at home, he told us, a sort of meditation. I had never seen him so relaxed and happy. Corinne had a long talk with my mother and ended up inviting her in all sincerity to come visit them in Toronto. After the children went to sleep, we stayed up talking past midnight, and even then we didn't want to say goodnight.

I felt warmer toward McLuhan that night than ever before. I had enjoyed working with him. I liked the two articles we had done together. I knew he was eager to get started on "The Future of War." Yet it was precisely then that I began pulling back. There was the matter of my work overload, which was truly overwhelming. But there was something else, perhaps even more decisive: McLuhan's name was listed first in our joint by-line, and I could tell from the letters in response to "The Future of Education" that almost all our readers assumed that the ideas were his, that I was simply the writer who put them down. Quotes in the newspapers from our article were attributed to McLuhan alone. Not that such an assumption wasn't understandable; he was famous for his ideas, whereas I was not. But in truth we shared in the production of the ideas in these particular articles, in addition to which I did all the writing. The time had come, I thought, to make my own statement and put my own name on it.

Later I was very sorry that I didn't talk frankly to McLuhan about my feelings on this matter. What made the omission worse was that I was then engaged in encounter groups based on the free and candid expression of feelings. Instead, I just faded. When McLuhan phoned with ideas for our next article, I pleaded schedule problems. That was the truth, but not the whole truth. Finally he stopped phoning. His son Eric came to the West Coast for a while and joined our Frisbee group, and two of his daughters occasionally visited Lillie and me. But Marshall McLuhan and I gradually lost contact. A couple of years after the day we flew kites, I wrote "The Future of Power" for *Look,* alone.

In retrospect, I can see that my brief but intense relationship with Marshall McLuhan was more valuable than I then realized. His ideas — on the importance of the media of communications, on the Electric Age, on the global village — might have been expressed in neon rather than sober scholarly tones, but he was essentially right. Only in the late 1980s can we clearly understand just how right he was.

27

Racial Confrontation as Transcendental Experience

MIKE MURPHY burst into my office with an exuberant smile.

"I escaped," he said.

I just looked at him from behind my desk.

"I escaped," Mike repeated, completely delighted with himself. He threw himself in a chair, leaned back, and told me his story. Pat Felix, the woman he had been going with for over a year, had been driving him to downtown San Francisco. Before he knew what was up, they were headed across the Golden Gate Bridge instead, then up Highway 101, bound for the high sierras or for God knows where — Reno, Mike suspected. Pat was a large, passionate woman with a spectacular body who saw all of life as melodrama. Mike was strongly attracted, but he had come late to the joys of the flesh and retained a share of the ascetic. Their relationship was explosive.

When Mike told Pat he had appointments back in town, she kept driving. But the car was low on gas. She stopped at a service station just off the freeway, and Mike grabbed the car keys. A furious wrestling match ensued next to the gas pump, with the attendant looking on in horror. Pat was a powerful woman physically, and even more powerful in her intentions. When she got the keys back, Mike bolted. He ran straight across all six lanes of the busy freeway, vaulting a high steel fence in the middle. He raised his thumb to hitchhike, and the very first car, a white Buick convertible, stopped and picked him up. Hearing Mike's tale, the man in the Buick drove him all the way to my office.

It was lunchtime, so we walked up Post Street to Drake's Tavern. By this point in 1967, even downtown was showing signs of becoming a carnival. Women's skirts were shorter, men's hair was longer. An occasional hippie passed by. It was the beginning of what was being called the Summer of Love. Young people by the thousands were pouring into the city to join the hippie movement. The Haight-Ashbury obviously couldn't hold them. The whole of San Francisco probably couldn't hold them. But if a disaster was ahead of us, everything was still on the upbeat and our spirits were high.

In January, *Time* magazine had chosen the twenty-five-and-younger generation as its Man of the Year (only six years after *Look*'s Explosive Generation issue). Also in January, the first Human Be-In had drawn twenty thousand people to the polo field in Golden Gate Park to listen to music by the Jefferson Airplane and the Grateful Dead and to hear talks by Allen Ginsberg, Gary Snyder, Timothy Leary, and other avatars of the sixties, with the Hell's Angels serving as security forces. What had most impressed me that day was the sight of Zen master Shunryu Suzuki, who sat in impeccable, undisturbed meditation on the stage through the entire event.

Like everything else in that setting, the music was freshly minted, and there was beginning to be talk of a San Francisco sound. Actually, the Jefferson Airplane, the Grateful Dead, Country Joe and the Fish, Quicksilver Messenger Service, Sons of Champlin, and Big Brother and the Holding Company (with Janis Joplin) sounded quite different from one another. If there was anything they had in common, it was ear-splitting amplification, a powerful, often raucous beat, and a meandering, psychedelic lead guitar. Entirely gone were the romantic, moon-June lyrics of the old standards and show tunes. The words of the San Francisco groups, like those of the Beatles and the Stones before them, were aimed more at scrambling than soothing the mind. The new music was one more signal of the breakdown of the old culture. Though we listened carefully, we could make out no clear message about what was to come.

On that day, however, Mike and I had our own agenda of cultural change to discuss. After toasting Mike's narrow escape, we turned to our most pressing current project: the inauguration in September of Esalen's San Francisco operation. Mike had sat through more than two hundred seminars in Big Sur over the past four years, and was close to burnout. He enjoyed coming to the city to visit Lillie and me. He was ready to expand Esalen to an urban area, and I strongly supported the move. New modes of education might prove most useful of all among the underprivileged. More than anything, I wanted to apply human potential methods to the racial problem. In spite of the many victories of the civil rights movement, true understanding between blacks and whites still had a long, long way to go. Anything I could do toward this end, no matter how small, stood as a top priority.

In fact, I had already planned an interracial seminar for mid-July at Esalen in Big Sur. It had occurred to me that we might use some of the encounter techniques Esalen was refining to break through the wall of conventional discourse that was keeping blacks and whites at arm's length. As it was, black-power militants screamed their hurt, anger, and hatred. By revealing themselves and speaking the truth, they begged for encounter. White leaders responded with conventional language, cautious words. How could there be understanding without self-revelation? Didn't the whites feel outrage, fear, repressed prejudice? The measured, judicious response seemed a lie. Nor was there real encounter in the biracial committees formed in some cities. Blacks and whites sat around tables, mouthed slogans, established positions, and made decisions of an intellectual and political nature. They generally left the meetings unchanged. What would happen if blacks and whites ventured into the dangerous territory where nothing is hidden?

When I got the idea of holding an interracial seminar at Esalen, I immediately phoned Price Cobbs. Lillie's and my friendship with Price and Evadne (Vad) Cobbs went back to 1962. At that time Price was a new psychiatric resident at the University of California at San Francisco. The son of a physician, Price had been reared in comfortable circumstances in Los Angeles. Vad Cobbs had spent her childhood in the black aristocracy of Savannah, Georgia. She was a physical education teacher in a San Francisco high school. When they and their two small children, Price, Jr., and Renata, had moved into a rather desolate housing tract just south of the city in 1961, they had been greeted by coldness, then insults. When rocks were thrown, Price wasted no time in contacting the Council for Civic Unity, the NAACP, and the *San Francisco Chronicle,* which did a story on the situation.

I saw the *Chronicle* article back in the fall of 1961 and wanted to do something for *Look* on the Cobbs family. The Iron Curtain story had me tied up, though, so Chandler Brossard came out from New York. Before going back east after completing his reportage, Brossard got me to promise to meet the Cobbses. Brossard was a man noted for his dark and cynical vision, but this time he was effusive. Both Vad and Price, he said, were brilliant, and we would get along wonderfully.

A few months later, when Brossard's story came out, I remembered his enthusiasm and phoned Price. We met at the Old Ritz Poodle Dog, a favorite downtown lunch spot. Price walked up to me with a ready smile and a gracious handshake. His physical presence was impressive. He was six feet tall and solidly built, and I later learned that he had run the 880 on his high school track team — a race that's run on sheer guts as much as anything else. We went to our table and spent the first few minutes establishing our credentials: I as an apostate southerner deeply committed to the civil rights movement, he as a promising youth psychiatrist at one of the nation's most prestigious teaching hospitals.

But Price was not one to dally with formalities. He had a way of glanc-

ing aside, then returning his gaze to my face just in time to uncover any
self-deception or pretense. Then too, his quick, infectious smile suggested
a wild sense of humor. It was a waste of time trying to impress this man.
I took a swig of my vodka-and-tonic and began telling him about our
Frisbee game. He responded with a full-bodied laugh that drew the eyes
of those at nearby tables, and we were off and running, talking and laughing
and carrying on like old friends. We discovered a mutual passion for the
blues, and compared our feelings about some of the great blues shouters:
Jimmy Rushing, Joe Turner, James Witherspoon. That brought us back
to the matter of race, and we agreed that it was the touchstone in any
new American revolution. To transform the racial situation would transform the society. But there would be no easy way around it, Price warned.
We would have to deal with years of injustice that could never be fully
redressed, with persisting prejudice, and with rage. We would have to go
right through the middle, be willing to endure the pain that would accompany the recognition of the truth.

The Cobbses invited Lillie and me to a Sunday brunch. Vad Cobbs was
no echo of her husband, She had a dazzling smile, a clear, strong voice,
and if anything was the fierier of the two. But there was no competition
between them. Each deferred to the other in a kind of mutual respect that
I had never seen in a married couple. Neither Price nor Vad hesitated to
invoke black street talk to make a strong point. The rage was there, but
it was clear and true and honest, and mitigated by compassion and laughter.

When they came to our house for dinner, our friendship was cemented.
The young Dr. Cobbs, it turned out, was not only an aficionado of the
blues but a pretty fair blues shouter on his own. After dinner I played
piano and he sang some of the best old ones: "Going to Chicago," "Sent
for You Yesterday," "Fine and Mellow." His voice filled the room. The
coffee cups rattled in their saucers.

The Cobbses joined our Frisbee group. We went on picnics. Our children attended each other's birthday parties. We were not tokens of racial
reform but two families who enjoyed doing things together and were
more and more committed to touching each other deeply.

When I phoned Price early in 1967 about doing an interracial seminar
at Esalen, he agreed about the need for real encounter. He was writing a
book with his colleague William Grier, to be called *Black Rage,* and he
could see the value of the full and clear expression of even the most
negative feelings. But Price was somewhat reluctant to become identified
with Esalen. I told him I wouldn't do it without him. First, it wouldn't
work with just one leader, especially a white leader. Second, his experience and credentials as a psychiatrist would be a necessity in a high-

intensity group experience. When he finally agreed to colead the workshop, I figured it was mostly out of his friendship for me.

We got together to do the write-up for the Esalen catalogue several months before the event was to occur. The title, "Racial Confrontation as Transcendental Experience," came more from my reckless enthusiasm than from his considered judgment:

> Racial confrontation can be an example for all kinds of human encounter. When it goes deep enough — past superficial niceties and role playing — it can be a vehicle for transcendental experience. Price Cobbs, a Negro psychiatrist from San Francisco, and George Leonard, a white journalist and author born and raised in Georgia, will conduct a marathon group encounter between races. The group will try to get past the roles and attitudes that divide its participants, so that they may encounter at a level beyond race.

Mike's enthusiasm for the racial workshop matched mine for the Esalen San Francisco operation. Both of us wanted the institute to address itself to the major social issues of the times. We never considered the possibility of failure.

Values, interpersonal relations, race, schooling — all my ideas for a reformed society were coming together in the education book. It was as if I were writing at the best possible time, when so many of the hopes born of my apostate southern background were being matched in the culture around me. I wrote in high belief and deep exhaustion, and I realized finally that the book was never going to be finished if I kept trying to write at night and on weekends. It was clear as well that I was neglecting my own family in the process of writing a book aimed at making education better for other children. Lillie complained that we never had time to do anything together, and it seemed to me that I headed downstairs to my study every night accompanied by her darkest look of disappointment and disapproval.

In desperation I took three weeks of vacation and put them together with a five-week leave of absence to get nearly two months of clear writing time so that I could meet my revised deadline of September 15. The vacation-plus-leave began July 1, just three weeks before the racial confrontation. The book was at a critical point: the description of a school of A.D. 2001. I had not planned that school, but a moment had come early in the summer when I had heard the vehement, insistent voice of *Look* senior copy editor Martin Goldman in my head. While I was working on "The Future of Education" with McLuhan, Goldman had said, "Don't just write *about* it. Make it *happen*. You owe that to your readers. Make it *real*. Make it *come alive*."

I knew Goldman was right, but for a while I resisted his phantom command. Then one night, sitting at my old typewriter, I was suddenly *there*. A spring morning in the year 2001, visiting day at Kennedy School in Santa Fe, New Mexico. Gleaming geodesic domes and translucent tentlike structures scattered randomly among graceful trees. Children wandering happily from one learning environment to another. The school was both sensuous and highly technological, dedicated to human freedom and ecstatic learning through an intricately interrelated computerized educational system.

Everything came together in this imaginary school — my lifelong interest in science and technology, my twelve years of education reporting and my three years of human potential research, my work with Esalen and my tireless brainstorming with Mike Murphy, and, maybe more than anything else, what my own children had taught me. A whole technology of learning created itself as I wrote: Computer-Assisted Dialogue (CAD), Ongoing Brainwave Analysis (OBA), a wireless Electronic Identification Device (EID), Communal Interconnect (CI), Cross-Matrix Stimulus and Response (CMSR).

And there in my mind's eye was my fictional three-year-old daughter, Sally, sitting at a keyboard in the Basics Dome, creating vivid words and images on a hologrammatic display in front of her and interacting through Communal Interconnect with the displays of children on either side of her. And it was clear that Sally was not just practicing spelling (she could already read and write very well) but dialoguing with CAD to create *alternative* spellings, as a form of creativity training.

> CAD: A cat is a kat is a katte.
> Sally [quickly]: A katte is a kat is a cat.
> CAD: Copy cat.
> Sally: Koppy Kat.

I was there. I could see the cat image on Sally's display gradually fading, could hear its purring mingling with sweeping electronic music, could see the lovely visual symbols of calculus on the display to the left of Sally's blending with a spinning bicycle wheel moving across grassy fields, deserts, down winding mountain roads. Though I had never actually worked with computers, I knew beyond any doubt that this system was right, that it would work, that it or something like it eventually would be built, that children would someday sit at its consoles, laughing happily, as Sally was now, about the endless, endlessly varied delights of learning.

My fictional wife and I walked on through the campus of Kennedy School, looking for our nine-year-old son, Johnny; through the Quiet Dome, where children could meditate or just rest without being disturbed; through the Water and Body Domes, devoted to the education of the body and senses; into one of the Discovery Tents, where a group of young children were replicating the 1831 electromagnetism experiments of Michael Faraday; into another tent in which children were living the life of a primitive tribe of the Malay Peninsula; on past the playfield, where children were engrossed in new kinds of games, including something that looks very much like our version of Frisbee. Finally we found Johnny with a group of older children in a grassy clearing surrounded by shade trees. They had been acting out a section in Thucydides' *History of the Peloponnesian War,* not just memorizing dates and other facts but experiencing the world of the Athenians of 415 B.C., learning to feel as they must have felt during those tragic times.

Shortly after finishing the section on school in the year 2001, I realized that the name of my book was *Education and Ecstasy.* I quickly fired off a letter to my editor in New York, telling him the good news. He was not entirely pleased. How about *The Joy of Learning?* That, I responded by return mail, sounded too much like a cookbook. Anyway, there was now no question about the title. It was not *The Ecstasy of Learning* or *Education as Ecstasy.* It was *Education and Ecstasy:* two seeming incommensurables linked forever (no less than particle and wave, matter and energy) in a paradoxical but inevitable marriage. And if critics and academicians should say the title seemed a contradiction in terms, I would tell them that it was only because of this society's false assumptions about the nature of learning.

According to Walter Truett Anderson in his history of Esalen, *The Upstart Spring,* the racial confrontation was "very likely the toughest encounter session that had ever been convened at Esalen." Price Cobbs and I weren't expecting a picnic, but we didn't know how tough it was going to be. The thirty-five participants were for the most part liberal, well-educated whites and blacks plus two very bright Japanese-Americans. All of them had taken the trouble to drive to a remote place on the Big Sur coast to transcend superficial niceties and role playing on the matter of race. Before the weekend was over, Price and I were to gain our first understanding that even in such a group as this, no white was entirely free of prejudice and no black was entirely free of rage.

I drove down on Friday with my sixty-five-year-old mother and eighteen-year-old daughter, Mimi, who had moved out from New York. That night the group gathered in a circle of chairs in the lodge, warmed against the cool sea air by candlelight and an open fire. After introductions all around, Price and I led the group in an encounter microlab. This process was designed to introduce the group to the three basic principles of encounter: (1) Be completely honest and open. Forget about conventional politeness and reserve. Express anything you wish, no matter how shocking it might seem. (2) Relate on the level of feelings. Don't theorize or rationalize. (3) Stay in the here and now. Don't escape into past events or future plans. Only one prohibition: no physical violence.

We broke the group into four circles of eight or nine each, then led them through the five stages of the microlab, each of which would encourage greater candor and closeness. These were the kind of people who knew how to follow instructions, even when they were instructed to forget about politeness and reserve. The microlab started at 9:25 P.M., and by the time it ended at 10:30 P.M. a few barriers between the races had been crossed and a few eyes were moist with the wonder or relief that often accompanies such crossings. Afterward most of the participants drifted down the steep seaside path that leads to the hot baths. Up to my neck in steaming water with members of the group, I felt comfortable and content. Here were people of good will who were willing to be close. How could they harbor calamitous hostilities?

The next morning we began to find out. Contrary to usual practice, we held the whole group together. This was mainly Price's idea. He wanted to keep the two of us in the same encounter. The example of our relationship, he thought, might prove useful, especially if the group reached an impasse. Price was still a little divided about his decision to come to Esalen. Many of the big city ghettos were under siege. He had been invited to address a black-power meeting in Newark this same weekend, and had been tempted to cancel his part of the workshop. Once again our friendship had prevailed.

The first real confrontation began not between black and white but among the blacks. The morning was shattered by bitter accusations. "Racist," "Uncle Tom," and "fink" were among the milder words that went slashing back and forth across the room. "When they come with machine guns and barbed wire," one black asked another, "all I want to know is, baby, are you for me or against me?" By lunchtime the atmosphere was electric.

After lunch the marathon began. We would stay in uninterrupted session through the night. Dinner would be brought to us. We would keep at it until the conventional defenses against feeling were broken down, even if it took until noon the next day.

We had planned to begin the marathon with a period of sensory awakening led by Bernie Gunther. He intended to have us keep our eyes closed during the entire session. Prejudice, he felt, is visual. When we touched an unseen stranger, we would have to deal with him or her in a way that would bypass racial stereotypes. But many of the group were eager to get on with the encounter, and only about half went out on the sunlit deck to do the exercises. I accompanied them. Price stayed with the ones inside.

It was a bizarre experience for me. As I went through Gunther's exercises, I could hear the voices but not the words from the meeting room. Eyes closed, we walked slowly around the deck and found a partner. Touching hands only, we followed instructions to get acquainted, have a quarrel, make up, try to express love or liking. At the same time, the counterpoint from inside rose: excitement, anger, pleading, and finally a burst of loud sobbing. The real encounter was obviously under way. Sweat ran down my chest and sides. I wanted to continue Gunther's experiment and at the same time be inside. At last the outside group ended with a long, unrestrained shout. To those inside, that too was counterpoint, equally bizarre.

We crowded back into the meeting room to find that everything had changed. The faces looked different. The dialogue had moved to an unfamiliar level. The people from outside were intruders, yet grudgingly accepted as the encounter rushed on. What had happened was this: A young Japanese-American named Larry had driven up from Los Angeles with his friend, a light-skinned black named Cliff. Both of them were college students in business administration, making it in the white world, and they had tried to numb themselves to racial hurt. They were cool and cynical. They wore their masks well. But all the vehement racial talk, and especially the attacks among the blacks, had turned something upside down. Larry had begun talking. He had not realized how deeply he had felt racial prejudice or how much it had ruled his life. But now he knew he was a yellow man, a "Jap," and was ready to admit it. He declared himself to be a soul brother. With this declaration, all of his reserve collapsed and he burst into tears. The dikes were down then, and several of the blacks poured out their hurt.

"How many of you people can realize," a mother asked, "what it's like to send your children off to school and know they'll probably be called *nigger* or spat on? And there's nothing, *nothing* you can do about it?"

When the outside group came in, Larry's friend, Cliff, was locked in a bitter encounter with an attractive young white schoolteacher named Pam. She had told him she wanted his friendship, and he had responded scathingly, denouncing her "pitiful, condescending" overtures. Now her eyes were filled with tears.

"Please. What can I do? I'm trying. Please help me."

Cliff rocked his chair back and forth, looking across the room at her with contempt.

"No, baby, I'm not going to help you. I'm not going to take you off the hook. I want you to feel just what I feel. I want you to feel what I've felt for twenty-one years. Go on. Cry."

"Please," she begged. Tears streamed down her cheeks.

Cliff kept rocking back and forth, his eyes fixed on hers. No one came to her aid. We sat in silence. Somehow it seemed right that this interval in time should be fully realized by everyone in the room. The silence intensified, became in itself a powerful medium of communication. Pam's tears stopped, and we were talking again, the exchanges crackling around the room faster than the mind could follow.

The main theme through dinner and for some time thereafter was the hurt and anger and despair of the blacks, their absolute distrust of all whites. Several times Price said he did trust me, which had the effect of taking me out of the line of fire — a situation fervently desired in the heat of battle, but regretted afterward. At one point I suggested that whites too have their problems, their tragedies. But "I just can't buy that," Vad Cobbs said, her eyes flashing. "Whatever's wrong with you, you can do something about. But I can't do *anything* about the color of my skin — or my children's. Compared to us, you've got it made."

Mimi joined the fray with the vehemence of youth and the experience of a veteran. The previous summer she had impressed the Esalen staff during a gestalt session by standing up to and perhaps even bettering Fritz Perls, something almost no one ever accomplished. For my mother, however, the experience was shattering. She was proud of her attitude on race, which truly was rare among her generation in the South. At one point she told the group how much she loved blacks and how she considered Vad her best friend.

"Oh bullshit, Julia," Vad said. "You just want to be congratulated on your racial tolerance. There's something else going on. Why don't you get down to it?"

My mother was shocked by what she considered a betrayal. She looked to me for help, but there was nothing I could do for her. It was something we all had to go through. Before we could really tear down the barriers between the races, we had to feel and acknowledge and reveal every shred of our own masked prejudice, our own buried resentment and rage. During the afternoon the blacks had been merciless in exposing their own masks: the "Oreo cookie" (black on the outside, white on the inside), the "bad nigger" (out to terrify white and black alike), the sensitive black man (out to make white chicks), the militant dude. Now they had coalesced against the whites, whose revelations came haltingly, with none of the fire and conviction of those of the blacks.

A heavy fog moved in from the sea and pressed against the windows.

It seemed the night would never end. We grasped at anything that might bring a moment of relief. At about 2:30 A.M., a tall engineer with a thin moustache, excoriated earlier as the last of the old-time white liberals, began boasting about his numerous social contacts with blacks. Then, with a faint smile of self-revelation, he said, "Actually, I collect Negroes."

That was all it took. We whooped with laughter. "Do you have a good connection?" someone asked. "Oh, yes, the very best." "What's your source?" someone else asked. The engineer named a ghetto near San Francisco. "I collect Negroes too," a black woman shouted over the laughter. "My source is my uterus."

The laughter died away. We looked at each other and sighed. We still had work to do, and there seemed to be no end to it. Beneath the stark icons of racial prejudice — the Ku Klux hoods and burning crosses, the "whites only" signs and police dogs and sheriffs' clubs — lay another whole realm of bigotry. The suppressed rage, the unspoken resentment, the secret fear, were as deep as the ocean. For me, and for Price too, this was truly a dark night of the soul. Before morning came, it seemed we had revealed all there was to reveal, and still there was more. Maybe we would never get past the barriers that divided even the most liberal and humane blacks and whites. Maybe we had made a terrible mistake.

Some hours after dawn, its resources drained, its hope all but gone, the group took an unexpected turn: The whites began revealing themselves, baring the most tragic and painful moments of their lives. The sun had broken through the fog, and in the peculiar clarity of sleeplessness, everyone seemed strangely illumined. We sensed we were on the verge of something momentous. The way it finally happened is described in Anderson's *The Upstart Spring*:

> It began with a white woman who said she dated black men exclusively. This was taken by black and white alike to be another sleazy piece of white liberal trickery, and the members of the group, especially some of the black men, were pressing her for an explanation of why she *really* did this. She began to cry, and said, "Because I've given up on white men." She sat there, weeping and alone in a roomful of tired people, and then a black woman went across the circle and embraced her. They wept together and everything changed in a simple, non-political moment of human compassion. For some minutes there was absolute silence as a feeling of something powerful beyond words welled up among them. People looked around the room and saw other faces with eyes that were full of tears. Somebody hugged somebody else. Then the whole room was full of weeping and embracing people. Tears and hugs were often in plentiful supply at encounter groups, but there was nothing facile about these; they were hard won and real. The whole development was enormous and astonishing, and perhaps the most

unexpected thing of all was that the blacks were weeping for the whites.

They had another hour or two in which to come back down and attempt to make sense of what had happened. They knew that all the old problems were still there, but somehow the ground had shifted. They had glimpsed a commonly shared substratum of humanity. . . . They had had, in fact, a transcendent experience.

I drove back home that afternoon with my mother and daughter, still stunned by the outcome of the encounter. Late that night, while I was trying to explain the whole thing to Lillie, I got a call from Price and Vad. They had never stopped talking from the moment they started their drive north. They were convinced that we had tried something of great significance, something seemingly impossible, and that it had worked. On that same weekend, the worst riot in America in the twentieth century had broken out in Detroit. Thousands of looters were still roaming the streets. The biracial committees, the polite expressions of racial grievances, had not worked. Maybe what we had done in Big Sur could help prevent such tragedies in the future by allowing the true revelation of feelings. Price proposed putting on a series of similar events in San Francisco and in cities throughout the nation. "George," he said flatly, "we've got to take this to the world."

Shortly after that, Price and I met with Mike Murphy, who had rented a small apartment in the city. We agreed that race was a touchstone. If racial attitudes could be transformed, a society could perhaps be transformed. The interracial marathons would be an important element in Esalen's San Francisco operation, which by then had found a home. The kinds of symposia and seminars and workshops that now were available only at Big Sur would soon be held at the top of Nob Hill in the meeting rooms of Grace Cathedral. The opening event would take place in less than two months.

28

No One Had Said
It Was Going to Be Safe

By SEPTEMBER 1967, 13,500 Americans had died in the Vietnam War, and God knows how many Vietnamese. But thousands of deaths in the abstract are less vivid than the sight of one human being's blood and suffering. Television was changing the noncombatant's ideas about war, especially about a questionable war. In spite of Lyndon Johnson's powers of persuasion, public support for the Vietnam adventure was beginning to erode. At the same time, more and more of the nation's educated and privileged young men were finding ways to avoid the draft — educational deferments, phony psychiatric excuses, emigration to Canada, even jail.

When the television screen wasn't showing burning villages in Southeast Asia, it was showing American cities in flame. Civil rights leaders were moving north: Martin Luther King, Jr., to encourage nonviolent protest, Stokely Carmichael and then H. Rap Brown of SNCC — according to news stories — to encourage protest at any cost. Carmichael and Brown became victims of their own rhetoric. T George Harris believed that the headline writers were playing with them like yo-yos. B. F. Skinner might have analyzed their behavior in terms of reinforcement theory: Carmichael makes an outrageous statement, and is reinforced by headlines all over the country. But to get the same reinforcement the next time, he has to make an even more outrageous statement, and so on, until at last he is saying things that even he has no idea he is going to say.

The Haight-Ashbury, some said, was the only sane place in a nation gone mad, a place of gentle young people who eschewed materialism and gave flowers to policemen. But among the estimated twenty to thirty thousand who came to join the Summer of Love, more than a few were less interested in transcendence than in free sex and cheap drugs. By the end of summer the sex had produced an outbreak of venereal disease and the drugs had attracted the underworld. On August 3, LSD dealer John Kent Carter was found dead in his apartment with his right arm severed. Three days later a black acid dealer known as Superspade was found at the bottom of a 250-foot cliff in Marin County with a bullet in his head. Crowded conditions made the Haight a haven for viruses and bacteria. Young people who came to San Francisco for love ended up with flu or hepatitis.

The overflow from San Francisco moved south. As Mike Murphy was later to write: "Thousands of young people from all over the United States were coming down the coast highway looking for some final Mecca of the counterculture, and during the summer of 1967, the 'Summer of Love,' it seemed that most of them wanted to camp on our grounds. They came with dazed and loving looks, with drugs and fires, swarming into the redwood canyons and up over the great coast ridges, many of them polluting and stealing along the way. The air was filled with a drunken mysticism that undermined every discipline we set for the place."

With plans for Esalen's urban center moving apace, I dug in to make my deadline for *Education and Ecstasy*. My next task was a tentative outline of practical steps for present school reform, starting with the creation of six model early education schools located in various parts of the country, three of the six in ghetto areas. Meanwhile Lillie and I were providing what we could of the new education for our young daughters. We moved our dining room table into the large entrance hall. What had been the dining room became a "happening room" in which Lillie, seven, and Emily, three, could create any kind of learning environment they wished. The room was filled with toys of many kinds, books, a barrel of fascinating junk, various percussion instruments, a stereo, and a high-quality tape recorder. The girls spent hours alone or with friends building elaborate "environments," doing taped interviews, and performing plays. We were pleased with the seeming chaos in our high-ceilinged dining room. School was dull compared to that richness.

I had noticed earlier in the year that Lillie's artwork was becoming tight and cramped, and that in fact she had almost entirely stopped drawing and painting. She was in first grade at a private school in Marin County. When I questioned her about her art instruction, she said, to my horror, that when she wanted to draw, say, a cow, she had to go ask her teacher for the cow stencil. The next Sunday afternoon we went to a dance at the Fillmore Auditorium. On my shoulders in the middle of the dance floor, she had a good view of the extravagant, swirling images projected on the walls all around. Ten or fifteen minutes passed before she spoke, and then it was one word: *"Wow!"* When we got home, she started drawing with an entirely new sweep and freedom.

Hippies were everywhere, even at our Frisbee games. The field where we played lay between the Haight-Ashbury and an area of the park known as Hippie Hill. All during our play, we could see a stream of hippies walking along the edge of our field on their way to or from the gathering place where they openly smoked marijuana and dropped acid. One Sunday after Frisbee, Bill Kelley suggested we challenge a group of hippies to a touch football game. We put together our team, then tried to pick six opponents who were not completely stoned. That in itself took some doing. The hippie team would be the "skins" and we would be the "shirts." They lined up — rather wan young men with flowing hair and bare chests — and fumbled the kickoff. What began in complete confusion quickly descended to low comedy. The hippies had been unenthusiastic from the beginning, and after Bill Kelley leveled one of them with an inexpedient body block, they withdrew from the field of play, telling us that football didn't serve the state of consciousness they were seeking.

One of our newer players was a tall twenty-four-year-old with Nordic good looks named John Luce. He was not related to the Luces of Time-Life, and indeed was intent on landing a job as a writer for *Look*. Luce was a Stanford graduate, a frequent contributor to local journals, and a contributing editor for *San Francisco* magazine. I had assigned him a *Look* picture story on the Jefferson Airplane, and was campaigning hard for him to become an assistant editor back in New York.

Earlier in the year I had succeeded in getting a young writer named Bill Hedgepeth hired to open an Atlanta editorial office. Hedgepeth wasn't just a man who played at being a character; he was a real character, a consistently droll individual who sometimes wore a white linen suit with a black string tie and always wore an eyepatch — the result of a terrible car accident in which he had lost the sight of one eye and suffered head injuries. Hedgepeth would tell you that he had steel plates in his head that could give way at any time. "I might be walking down the street," he would say, "and just go out like a light." He was a colorful, inventive, madcap writer who was obsessed with someday doing the ultimate book on hogs. People wondered whether Hedgepeth was serious or just putting them on. After getting to know him, I concluded that the answer was both. Most of the time we were together, I found myself smiling. I also knew that he, and John Luce as well, would support my side in the war within the magazine, which by this time had settled into the routine of trench warfare, with rolling artillery barrages and bayonet charges only on the publication of articles from the West Coast office.

Luce had joined wholeheartedly into all our activities. He never missed a Frisbee game, was one of the participants in the racial confrontation at Esalen, and was welcome to use a spare desk in the *Look* office. One

Sunday in June, he and his good friend Bill Hatch, who had the sardonic voice and good looks of Jack Nicholson, appeared at the Frisbee green grinning broadly.

"This is a special occasion," Luce said. "We have here one of the first copies of *Sergeant Pepper's Lonely Hearts Club Band*."

After Frisbee and a quick lunch at Enrico's outdoor café, a dozen or so members of the Frisbee group dashed to 1818 California to play the record over and over again.

Music had been near the center of my life since I was nine. I had had a swing band at age seventeen, had written the music for two soldier shows during the Korean War, had come late to a passion for Mozart. Several times I had considered working at music full time. In all my experience, *Sergeant Pepper* stood out as sheer genius, the mastery of a new genre, as significant in its own way as Ellington or Mozart. Luce and his friend were right; the day was memorable. And if *Sergeant Pepper* had a message for me, it was a reaffirmation that in spite of all the failures and false starts and ugliness involved in social and cultural change, something immensely exciting and ultimately valuable was trying to burst into being. For the human potential to be released, there were still fences to be broken down, perceptions of reality to be set in a new context. Somehow the Zeitgeist had touched four young men from Liverpool with the prescient breath of a new and untried freedom — and much of the world was listening. There would be more failures, but there would also be more change.

The seventies were to see a virulent backlash against human potential ideas but could not stop the quiet, pervasive spread of many of those ideas through the culture. *Sergeant Pepper*'s twentieth anniversary in June 1987, celebrated in a burst of media nostalgia, brought back sharp memories of that first afternoon, of a time very young and fresh and innocent. But not entirely innocent. I knew then — the evidence was already in — that some very rough days were ahead.

Esalen's San Francisco operation opened on Thursday, September 14, with a celebration led by Sister Mary Corita, a Catholic nun of the Order of the Immaculate Heart, a noted artist, and one of the "turned-on people" pictured in our 1966 California issue. That night there was a lecture by Abe Maslow on "The Farther Reaches of Human Nature." The following night Alan Watts held what he called an ecumenical liturgy at the First Unitarian Church, and preached a sermon on "Joy to the World." The liturgy included Hindu, Buddhist, and Gregorian chants, Indian music, conga drums, incense, and fire. Among Watts's robed assistants was Timothy Leary, who had been going around the country preaching a much shorter sermon. "Tune in, turn on, drop out."

These events were followed by three nights of panel discussions on

"The Scope of the Human Potential" at Gresham Hall in Grace Cathedral. Fred Skinner had flown out to be a featured speaker. The other speakers included Dick Farson of Western Behavioral Sciences Institute, Joe Kamiya, the biofeedback researcher, and me. Price Cobbs moderated.

The fireworks began before a capacity crowd of six hundred on the first night. Skinner spoke at length in a rather dry and scholarly manner on operant conditioning and programmed instruction. At the end of his presentation, Price Cobbs turned to him and said in a calm but somehow ominous voice, "Dr. Skinner, I want you to tell us how your methods can help solve the current crisis of racism in America."

Skinner was momentarily taken aback. Then a smile appeared on his face and he launched into a short speech. During World War I, he said, scientists had been told they should stop their basic research and leave their labs and go do something of immediate and practical value to help defeat the Huns. During the 1930s, he continued, scientists were told to leave their labs and create immediate practical solutions to the problems that were causing the Great Depression. It was the same thing in World War II: scientists should leave their labs and their research and help defeat Hitler. In spite of all that, scientists had stayed in their labs and continued doing basic research, which was fortunate for science and for the future of the world.

Skinner's smile became increasingly secure as he went through his recitation, as if what he said was irrefutable and would surely silence Price Cobbs's impudent question. But Price was unimpressed.

"I hear what you're saying, Dr. Skinner," Price said. "Now let me ask you again: How can your methods help solve the crisis of racism in America? I'm not talking about World War One or Two or the Great Depression. I'm talking about right now."

Skinner hesitated, then began a rather ineffectual explication of his previous statement. Price interrupted him. "Let me remind you, Dr. Skinner, that as we sit here cities are burning in America. As we sit here."

Skinner looked at me in confusion. After all, I was the person who had persuaded him to fly to San Francisco. He hadn't expected this kind of attack. I was sitting between the two of them. I looked over at Price, trying to catch his eye and somehow signal him to take it easy. But Price wasn't interested in taking it easy. He wanted to bring everything, including Skinner's feelings about race, into the open. The situation was obviously on the verge of an explosion. Skinner loved theoretical debates, no matter how abrasive. But what Price had in mind was more complex than that. He wanted to take B. F. Skinner into unfamiliar territory, back to those secret, unacknowledged predilections that precede theory. I reached over to touch Price's arm. He moved his arm away.

Now the two of them were talking at once, their voices rising. I couldn't believe it was happening, but it was. The confrontation was not so much about race as about the boundaries of relevant discourse. Skinner was comfortable in the area he would call objective, where certain data are subjected to certain methods of observation and measurement. Cobbs didn't deny the power and validity of this area; as a physician, he was trained in the scientific method. But he wouldn't stop inviting Skinner to broaden his perspective, to open up the territory of observation. I caught Mike Murphy's eye. He was, as usual, ranging around the edges of the audience, and he looked worried. But there was nothing I could do, so I sat there trying my best to stay calm and keep my mouth shut.

Then it became clear: Fred Skinner, as I saw it, wasn't just angry, he was frightened. It wasn't physical fear he was experiencing but intellectual fear. Where Cobbs saw an area fertile for exploration, Skinner saw a chasm. He didn't know what to do, so he began shutting down. His lips tightened; his body became rigid. He continued participating in the panel discussion, but almost as a robot.

After the event ended, Skinner complained bitterly to Mike Murphy. Still, the audience had loved the fireworks, and eventually we had talked about the scope of the human potential, and all in all it was just about as exciting as a panel discussion could be, an appropriate and prophetic beginning for Esalen's urban center.

Shortly after that Carl Rogers was scheduled for three lectures at Longshoremen's Hall, and Lillie came up with something new. We expected a large turnout, and Lillie's idea was to make the audience less anonymous, to give Rogers immediate, ongoing feedback while he was speaking. Each person coming in the door got a letter-sized piece of stiff paper, red on one side, green on the other. When the person wished, he or she could hold either the red or the green side up to Rogers. Green meant "I understand. I'm with you. Go on." Red meant "I don't understand. Slow down."

I was in New York during the series. Lillie sat on the stage with Rogers, monitoring the process. He loved it. The founder of client-centered therapy and basic encounter had never liked the disconnected feeling he had had while giving formal lectures. Now everything was different. Often he looked out on a sea of green with only a few specks of red, and he would push on confidently through his notes. Sometimes the sea would turn red, and he would slow down, repeat himself, find a different way of explaining the same thing. The most striking outcome, he later told me, was that he had moved through his material much faster than he had planned. What normally would have taken three lectures had taken two, and he had been forced to come up with new material for the last night.

It was one of those experiments that worked even better than expected, that improved the communication between speaker and audience, and that everybody involved liked very much. But we never tried it again. We were simply too busy. Too much was going on. Events were moving too fast.

Ed Maupin came into the faculty dining room at Stanford wearing a white shirt, sleeves rolled up, with his suit jacket slung over his shoulder. He walked with the jauntiness, the slight swagger, of an astronaut. (Maupin in fact came from the town in Ohio where John Glenn had been born.) He sat at the table with me and Mike Murphy and started out with no preliminaries.

"It's incredible. Schutz has seen encounter groups all over the country. In the six weeks since this program began, Schutz says, this group's already gone further and deeper than any other group in history. And we've got seven and a half more months to go."

Maupin, a psychologist who had been on the staff of the Neuropsychiatric Institute at U.C.L.A., was then the coleader of Esalen's nine-month-long residential program. Mike and I had driven down to Stanford to talk to an Esalen-at-Stanford student group. Maupin had driven up from Big Sur to brief us on the progress of the program during dinner and to join in our talk with the students. The first residential program, which had started a year earlier, had achieved none of the shining success Mike and I had foreseen. The original leader, Virginia Satir, a distinguished family therapist, had simply packed up and left after a few weeks. The program had continued under the informal leadership of Maupin, who had started out as one of the fellows.

This year's program promised to be entirely different. For one thing, the twenty-two new fellows were a lively and adventurous bunch with interesting credentials, and they were fully prepared to push out to the further reaches of the human psyche. Most important, however, was the presence of a man who was to become a major figure both at Esalen and in the public's perception of the human potential movement. On paper Ed Maupin was coleader, but once things got started, there was no question but that Will Schutz was in charge.

Schutz had received his Ph.D. in psychology at U.C.L.A. in 1951, had gone on to do research at the University of Chicago, had created a classic personality test for the navy, had taught at both Harvard and the University of California at Berkeley, and had done pioneering developmental work on small-group interaction. More recently, while working at the Albert Einstein School of Medicine in New York, he had made a grand tour of that city's thriving therapeutic underground, acquainting himself with psychosynthesis, bioenergetics, psychodrama, gestalt therapy, and rolfing. He joined these methods with his own group work to create what he called open encounter, which he described in *Joy: Expanding Human Awareness,* a book written in New York but published after he came to Esalen. Some of Schutz's East Coast colleagues were shocked when he relinquished his post at Einstein to take up residence at an inexplicable institute on the West Coast. But Schutz was entirely sure of himself. Esalen would be the base from which he would eventually achieve far more than he could have at the Albert Einstein School of Medicine. As Walter Truett Anderson pointed out, "Schutz may well have been interested in scholarly prestige, but he gave it up in favor of simpler things, such as money, fame, happiness, sex, and power."

Will Schutz exuded confidence. His solid, mesomorphic build, along with his shaved head and prominent eyes, lent him the air of Yul Brynner playing an Olympic wrestler. Though he was soft-spoken and given to flashes of self-deprecating humor, his extraordinary masculine physicality tended to dominate any group of men. He encouraged a considerable amount of physical confrontation in his groups — arm wrestling, even body wrestling — and was fast and strong enough to intervene decisively just before the confrontation got out of hand. I had worked with Schutz before he came to live at Esalen, and had applied some of his methods to my own workshops. For his part, Schutz was wholeheartedly enthusiastic about the human potential movement and eager to take it to the culture at large, immediately and without reservations.

Freud once described himself as being primarily a conquistador, and it would be hard to find a better word for Schutz. He wanted to rip down all the fences, without any exceptions, that separated people from each other. He longed to make complete openness and honesty the absolute rule rather than a rarity in human relations. He was unwilling to place any limits on what human beings might do or become.

Mike and I had planned a full and diverse curriculum of the nonverbal humanities for the residential program. There would be guest instructors in a number of areas. There would be research. Each fellow would submit a final project. But it was becoming clear that under Schutz's tenacious leadership, open encounter would be the heart and soul of the curriculum for this year's group of fellows. We listened to Maupin's briefing with a mixture of excitement and trepidation. On the third day of the program, the group had done away with all the chairs and started sitting on large cushions on the floor. At the end of the week, one group member had stood up and taken off his clothes. There had been marathon sessions, physical fights, agonizing episodes of emotional catharsis. Nothing was deemed off limits. Schutz was determined to strip away every last vestige of convention, secrecy, defensiveness, and social conditioning, until finally, beneath all of this, the pure and shining gem of unadorned human nature would be revealed for all to behold.

"We see this program in terms of the space program," Maupin said in his matter-of-fact astronaut's voice. "We figure that to reach our goals would be worth one death and two psychotic breaks."

I felt the hair at the back of my neck standing on end. Mike and I exchanged glances. It was thrilling to be a part of such a momentous quest. But one death and two psychotic breaks?

Friday afternoon, November 3. I heard a knock at my door and opened it to find a stranger there. He was smiling as if he knew me. Several seconds passed before I realized I was looking at one of my closest friends, Leo Litwak, who had just finished a five-day workshop with Will Shutz at Esalen and had driven straight from Big Sur to my house. I embraced him and he came in and sat in the middle of the living room rug.

Leo's early years as the child of a Detroit labor leader had been far from tranquil. His World War II combat experience had been by all odds the most harrowing I had ever heard of. Maybe it was those formative experiences, along with his long study of Western philosophy, that contributed to his habitual expression, which lay between skepticism and sadness. But now his face was soft and vulnerable, and his eyes — there's no other way to say it — were like stars. He began talking and the words poured out without consideration, as pure and transparent as words could be. Leo had been assigned by the *New York Times Magazine* to do an article on Esalen, and I had advised him to participate in one of the public workshops Schutz was giving at the time of the residential program. Without the *Times* assignment, he probably wouldn't have done it.

Leo's transformation was contagious. As he continued talking, telling Lillie and me every detail of his experience, I felt my own face softening, my body relaxing, a warm, happy glow suffusing all of me. I, the enthusiast, had been to a Schutz workshop and had been moved. Leo, the skeptic, had been transformed. What a miracle this was! What power there was in this work!

The atmosphere at Big Sur was charged. Schutz and his residential fellows, his "astronauts of inner space," were the center of all eyes. What they were doing was not only significant but dangerous. Hardly a day passed without news of some new breakthrough. Fritz Perls wasn't quite sure what to do; a new bull, a formidable one, had entered his pasture. Schutz was quietly confident. Mike and I had come down to see what was going on, and the first thing he did was ask us to spend the afternoon with the group and give them an inspirational talk.

"What we need right now is perspective on the human potential movement," he said. "You're the guys with the vision, more than Maslow. I want you to give us the big vision."

Maslow had spoken to the fellows on their first day and had been disappointingly dry. We would not be dry. Mike started out with the scope of Esalen's work and the institute's plans for expansion, followed by a vivid rendering of Aurobindo's boldly transformational vision. I had recently finished *Education and Ecstasy,* and I presented its thesis of a future learning society: specialization, standardization, and narrow competition would give way to an interactive, highly responsive, and self-regenerating human ecology, and human individuals would be free to explore possibilities, to create, to *learn* from birth to death. I emphasized the importance of the body in all learning, an emphasis that was hardly needed in this setting. It was an article of faith among Schutz and almost all the other Esalen leaders that the body had been neglected and ignored in the modern West, that it was a sensitive and wise teacher rather than a dumb brute that generally stood in opposition to the imperial mind. This re-emphasis on the body was to spread throughout most of the culture in the mid-seventies. In the late 1960s, however, it was a truly radical idea, which as much as anything else marked Esalen and the human potential movement as outlaw country.

The futurist Herman Kahn also attended that afternoon's meeting and gave a short talk. Kahn was an unlikely Esalen pilgrim. As head of the Hudson Institute, perhaps the toughest-minded think tank in America, he was a leading proponent of *realpolitik.* His books *On Thermonuclear War* and *Thinking the Unthinkable* were monuments to cold calculation. He was reputedly the model for Dr. Strangelove in the movie of the same name.

Still, Kahn, like the equally tough-minded Fred Skinner before him, was charmed by Esalen's human and natural environment. We had dinner in the Esalen dining room that night. He was bald, wore glasses, and must have weighed over three hundred pounds. He would tackle any subject that came up and surround it with swarms of statistics, talking so fast it was hard to follow his line of thought, spicing his discourse with a genuinely funny sense of the ridiculous that made him very likable. Later that night he went to the hot baths with a group of young people from *The Oracle,* an underground newspaper put out in the Haight-Ashbury.

The next day Mike and I and Herman Kahn were walking across one of Esalen's lawns when, apropos of nothing in particular, Kahn said, "There's no question but that you guys are going to change the world."

He never looked at us, but kept his eyes down on the unusually thick, springy grass. "Actually, it's easy to change the world," he continued. "The only problem is, it probably won't come out the way you planned it."

On the first night of the new year of 1968, Lois Delattre died of a reaction to the psychedelic drug MDA. It was Lois who had introduced me to Mike Murphy. She was a graduate of Esalen's first residential program. After graduation she had worked for a while at the institute's San Francisco office. In spite of those connections, Esalen wasn't directly involved in the episode. In fact, David Barr, the manager of the San Francisco office, had refused to help her find MDA when she had asked him, and the three people who had taken the drug with her were not associated with Esalen.

Lois was a warm, loving person, a good mother, a good friend. No one would call her irresponsible. The drug that killed her was not known as a street drug. It supposedly produced no hallucinations, just a euphoric feeling of love and closeness. But one of Esalen's aims was the exploration of consciousness, and Lois was an explorer.

No one had said it was going to be safe. Still, I was shocked and sick at heart.

29

In the Center of the Storm

1968

IN AN AGE OF MCLUHAN, the particular way a new trend or movement was carried to a culture through the nervous system of its communications media had become a matter of no small importance. No national medium had focused specifically on Esalen or on something called
the human potential movement as of September 1967. But within a year
these subjects were commonplace in newspapers and magazines, and Will
Schutz was a familiar figure on most of the major talk shows.

It started rather quietly with an Associated Press story on the inauguration of the San Francisco Esalen center in September. Not long after
that, *Time* ran an Esalen piece in its education section. Both of these
treatments were favorable, if a bit tentative. Then, on Sunday, December
31, an event occurred that opened the floodgates of media coverage: The
New York Times Magazine carried Leo Litwak's major article, entitled
"A Trip to Esalen Institute: Joy Is the Prize." The article was by any
standards a superb piece of reporting and writing; over the next few
months and years it was to be reprinted and anthologized again and again,
appearing in such volumes as *Best Magazine Articles: 1968*. But the very
fact that the *Times* had done the story, and a favorable story at that,
certified Esalen and the movement as worthy of serious attention.

Leo had lived in a state of grace for two weeks after returning home
from Esalen, unwilling to do anything that might bring him down to his
customary state of consciousness. Finally, goaded by his deadline, he had
sat at his desk and had finished the four-thousand-word article in less
than a week.

The *Times Magazine* at first didn't know what to do with Litwak's
manuscript. They asked for more material, to be boxed within the body
of the story in several places. These boxes, they hoped, would explain

what Esalen was up to, fit the institute into a recognizable category. Leo complied, but the boxes didn't help. If the story hadn't been such a compelling one, it probably never would have appeared; yet in the end it ran just about as Leo had originally written it, with only one rather short and straightforward box.

The genius of the article lay in the fact that it started out from the point of view of a skeptic. The *New York Times* reader could easily identify with Leo's reservations about Esalen's grand vision, his suspicions about Schutz's techniques, and his initial dislike of some of the other members of the group. (The strategy of the skeptical beginning has been used by numerous other writers since then; a cover article in the *Los Angeles Times Magazine* in late 1987, for instance, rather closely follows Litwak's format.) The expression of qualms, however, was by no means a mere tactic on the part of a skillful storyteller; it represented Leo's true feelings. When Leo finally approached his moment of revelation and transformation, even the most cynical reader was likely to be drawn along with him.

In order to provide an understanding of the impact of Litwak's article on other writers as well as on readers, I must quote its ending section at some length. In his story, after being deeply moved as the members of the group express their hidden grief and are eased, Leo wakes up one morning feeling that everything has changed. He walks to the cliff edge with one of Schutz's assistants, a woman called Brigitte.

> We lay beneath a tree. She could see that I was close to weeping. I told her that I'd been thinking about my numbness, which I traced to the war. I tried to keep the tears down. I felt vulnerable and unguarded. I felt that I was about to lose all my secrets and I was ready to let them go. Not being guarded, I had no need to put anyone down, and I felt what it was to be unarmed. I could look anyone in the eyes and my eyes were open.

Later that day, Schutz asks Leo if he would be willing to take a fantasy trip.

> It was late afternoon and the room was already dark. I lay down, Schutz beside me, and the group gathered around. I closed my eyes. Schutz asked me to imagine myself very tiny and to imagine that tiny self entering my own body. He wanted me to describe the trip.
>
> I saw an enormous statue of myself, lying in a desert, mouth open as if I were dead. I entered my mouth. I climbed down my gullet, entering it as if it were a manhole. I climbed into my chest cavity. Schutz asked me what I saw. "It's empty," I said. "There's nothing here." I was totally absorbed by the effort to visualize entering myself and lost all sense of the group. I told Schutz there was no heart in my body. Suddenly, I felt a tremendous pressure in my chest, as if tears were going to explode. He told me to go to

the vicinity of the heart and report what I saw. There, on the ledge of the chest wall, near where the heart should have been, I saw a baby buggy. He asked me to look into it. I didn't want to, because I feared I might weep, but I looked, and I saw a doll. He asked me to touch it. I was relieved to discover that it was only a doll. Schutz asked me if I could bring a heart into my body. And suddenly there it was, a heart sheathed in slime, hung with blood vessels. And that heart broke me up. I felt my chest convulse. I exploded. I *burst* into tears.

I recognized that heart. The incident had occurred more than twenty years before and had left me cold. I had written about it in a story published long ago in *Esquire*. The point of the story was that such events should have affected me but never did. The war in Germany was about over. We had just taken a German village without resistance. We had fine billets in German houses. The cellars were loaded with jams and sausages and wine. I was the aid man with the outfit, and was usually summoned by the call of "Aid Man!" When I heard that call I became numb, and when I was numb I could go anywhere and do anything. I figured the battles were over. It came as a shock when I heard the call this time. There were rifle shots, then: "Aid man!" I ran to the guards and they pointed to bushes ten yards from where they had been posted. They had spotted a German soldier and called to him to surrender. He didn't answer and they fired. I went to the bushes and turned him over. He was a kid about sixteen, blond, his hair strung out in the bushes, still alive. The .30-caliber bullets had scooped out his chest and I saw his heart. It was the same heart I put in my chest twenty-three years later. He was still alive, gray with shock, going fast. He stared up at me — a mournful, little boy's face. He asked: "Why did you shoot? I wanted to surrender." I told him we didn't know.

Now, twenty-three years later, I wailed for that German boy who had never mattered to me and I heaved up my numbness. The trip through my body lasted more than an hour. I found wounds everywhere. I remembered a wounded friend whimpering: "Help me, Leo," which I did — a close friend, yet after he was hit no friend at all, not missed a second after I heard of his death, numb to him as I was to everyone else, preparing for losses by anesthetizing myself. And in the course of that trip through my body I started to feel again, and discovered what I'd missed. I felt wide open, lightened, ready to meet others simply and directly. No need for lies, no need to fear humiliation. I was ready to be a fool. I experienced the joy Schutz had promised to deliver. I'm grateful to him. Not even the offer of love could threaten me.

Leo goes on to tell how hard it was to repair all the wounds in his body. He calls on his young daughter to help him get out.

She stood near my heart and said: "Come on out, Daddy," and led me out. I ran to a meadow in my chest. I ran through long grass, toward a gate, directly toward the sun. There I lay down and rested.

On the final morning, the entire workshop met to say goodbye, and Leo found himself "hugging everyone, behaving like the idiots I had noticed on first arriving at Esalen." He sums up his experience in the article's last paragraph.

> The condition of vulnerability is precious and very fragile. Events and people and old routines and old habits conspire to bring you down. But not all the way down. There is still the recollection of that tingling sense of being wide awake, located in the here and now, feeling freely and entirely, all constraints discarded. It remains a condition to be realized. It could change the way we live.

During the week after Litwak's article appeared, queries about Esalen Institute were fired off by editorial offices in New York, Boston, Washington, Chicago — wherever the *New York Times* set the standard and decreed what was worth reporting on. By the end of the week, Mike Murphy was getting phone calls from editors and producers who wanted to do their own versions of the *Times Magazine* piece. The media blitz was under way.

I was, of course, still doing stories for *Look*. In September the famous *Vogue* photographer Irving Penn had come out for several weeks to memorialize San Francisco's new tribal culture in classic black-and-white photography. John Luce and I coproduced the eight-page Penn portfolio — "produced" in the sense that our work was mostly logistical: finding a studio with north lighting to rent, having a heavy concrete platform and backdrop built, negotiating with Hell's Angels, rock bands, hippie communes. One day I drove the five members of Big Brother and the Holding Company, including Janis Joplin, to the studio. The marijuana smoke in the station wagon was so thick I could hardly see the road. When I stopped at the Golden Gate Bridge toll plaza and opened the window to pay the toll, the smoke shot out like the first puff of an old steam locomotive. The toll taker coughed and waved us on.

The Hell's Angels brought their motorcycles to the studio on a freight elevator, urinated out of the window, and stole several items. As the Angels were revving up their motorcycles to leave, Luce nodded toward the one car they had brought with them.

"They've stolen stuff from the studio and put it in the trunk. Do you want to confront the Hell's Angels?"

I said we could surely think up a better way. The Angels were known for wreaking revenge on anyone who crossed them. Later I negotiated with the Angels for the return of the studio owner's irreplaceable personal items, notably an antique bamboo birdcage, and had *Look* pay him for the rest.

Shortly after this, managing editor Pat Carbine got the idea of having my seven-year-old Lillie review the new movie *Dr. Doolittle,* starring Rex Harrison. Lillie and I attended a screening, then I asked her for her opinion, transcribing her words as faithfully as I could to fit a five-page layout of color photographs from the movie. "At least *they* won't be able to attack you for this story," Pat said with a rueful laugh. She was wrong. When the story came out, Carbine got a number of complaints. Why should my daughter get to write for the magazine? The story was too "cute" and put forward ecological views that must have been prompted by me. This was untrue; Lillie's statement on extinction was all hers: "Once, my teacher told me that someday most animals would be extinct and that was the saddest thing I've ever heard about. A lot of the children were crying that day and I was crying when I went home and told my mommy about that."

Clearly, there was to be no truce, no letup, in the war. Everything I (or my seven-year-old daughter) did was to be closely scrutinized by the cabal of senior editors who wanted me out, or if not out, at least muzzled.

"A New Liberal Manifesto," written in January and published in May, raised their outrage to a new pitch. The cabal probably took it as a direct attack on them, though that was by no means its purpose. Actually, I never had the feeling I was writing to be confrontational or "different." A part of me always longed to be a member of the journalistic Establishment, to relax in the warm bath of my colleagues' approval, to be invited to appear on *Meet the Press* and wisely mouth those slight variations on conventional thought that pass as controversy. I sometimes tried, in fact, to write more conventionally. And if what I was writing seemed to veer away from the safe channel of received wisdom, it was only because a deep inner current was turning it to a new heading.

I had been playing with the idea of "A New Liberal Manifesto" for about a year, and it had crystallized after the black-white marathon encounter. In the light of the sixties, the liberalism of the New Deal years appeared to me not only as moribund but actually as more conservative than liberal. Many of the current liberals suffered what seemed a disabling flaw. Their liberalism did not extend below their eyebrows. That is to say, they were liberals of doctrine, ideology, and the intellect. Too often they were reactionaries of the feelings.

The article called for a politics of absolute honesty and open encounter. It proposed tackling issues that were being largely ignored — the abrogation of individual rights possible in a computer technology, the development of new educational methods. It asked for relatively less reliance on the federal government in matters of social reform, an idea that was unfamiliar then in liberal circles. It also proposed that "the new liberal will not do things to or for other people, but will help create conditions in which people can do things for themselves." This applied to welfare reform and to the overhaul of foreign policy, especially to the Vietnam War.

On January 31, 1968, at the time of the Vietnamese festival of Tet, the Vietcong and the North Vietnamese army launched a major offensive. Troops that U.S. officials had been saying didn't exist materialized as if from nowhere and overran U.S. and South Vietnamese forces in many areas. There were battles within the suburbs of Saigon. The Tet offensive was finally contained, but not until it had done its work on public opinion in America, producing a deep and irreversible distrust of the official version of the conflict. Six weeks after Tet, President Johnson's popularity rating had dropped from 48 to 36 percent, and on March 31 he shocked the nation by withdrawing from the presidential race. Earlier, fifty thousand people — a patchwork throng of peace activists, student radicals, hippies, and ordinary citizens — had marched on the Pentagon and surrounded it, chanting, singing, giving flowers to the troops guarding it, getting arrested, and going to jail.

It was a moment balanced precariously between hope and despair. In Czechoslovakia, a gutsy experiment in liberalization, the "Prague Spring," was taking place in the shadow of Soviet guns, tanks, and planes. Throughout the West, peace activists and student radicals were demonstrating against U.S. involvement in Vietnam, against the bomb, against the military, and in favor of a world more open and free and joyful. Would the fences start coming down, or would there be some terrible new repression? Or would there be some unforeseeable combination of the two?

At the beginning of April, Paul Fusco and I went south to do a cover story in words and color photographs on Mexico. We didn't intend the usual travel piece. For background reading, we chose Octavio Paz's *The Labyrinth of Solitude*. We spent a couple of days interviewing people in Mexico City, then drove to Cuernavaca to seek guidance from our old friends Fletcher Knebel and Laura Bergquist Knebel. Fletch and Laura had met and married while working for *Look*, Fletch in the Washington office and Laura as a senior editor in New York. He was a seasoned, well-connected political reporter, and she had done many stories on the Kennedy family, in addition to general assignments. When one of Fletch's extracurricular books, *Seven Days in May*, became a best seller and was sold to the movies, the two of them went on a contract basis with *Look* and began spending winters in Mexico.

Fletch and Laura were eager for us to meet the well-known activist Catholic priest Ivan Illich, so they arranged a dinner party at their rented house. Father Illich brought his brother Sascha, a businessman. The Knebels also invited three other friends. No sooner had dinner begun than the subject of Esalen came up. Everyone there had read either the *New York Times Magazine* piece or some other article on the institute. Ivan Illich in particular was burning with curiosity. Illich ran his own institute devoted to social reform in Cuernavaca, and his essays were attracting the attention of literary critics. He had a dramatic, hawklike presence sharpened by his eagerness to understand any new social or cultural trend. I answered his insistent questions as best I could, but seemed unable to satisfy his curiosity.

"Say, George, here's what you can do," Fletch suggested. "After dinner you lead us all in a little encounter group — a demonstration."

No, no, I said, that would be entirely inappropriate. Encounter often produced powerful emotional states that had no place in a social setting.

"Yes," Illich and the rest of the group insisted. "Yes, you *must* give a demonstration."

"But listen," I warned, "anything we could do will be trivial compared to a real, all-out encounter group."

For at least ten minutes I fought them off. I gave in only when I realized there would be no conversation at all if I didn't.

After dinner we drew our chairs up in a circle on the Knebels' tiled, screened patio, and I listed the ground rules for encounter. I would use Schutz's microlab format, hoping to frame it in such a way as to keep the emotional voltage rather low. We went through the first two stages smoothly enough, practicing the expression of totally honest, here-and-now, personal discourse. Then came the third stage. The group would stand. Each person in turn would go around confronting each other person in the circle. He would look him in the eyes, touch him in some honest way (a handshake, a finger in the chest, whatever), and tell him what he felt about him at that moment. In this one-to-one situation, theorizing would become more difficult.

Laura had been ill at ease from the beginning. She kept asking questions instead of making statements. This was what we called the reporter's cop-out. It created the illusion of dialogue while keeping the "reporter" safe from true intimacy. As Laura went around the circle, she kept up her questioning. I didn't stop her and offer an alternative, as I would have in a real group. I was eager to keep things cool.

As it happened, Fletch and Paul were the last to go around the circle, and when they did, all hopes for an uneventful, reasonably trivial experience blew up. As Fletch moved from person to person, it was clear that he was saying exactly what he felt. When he came to Sascha Illich, who had been chattering amiably during the entire session, he shook his hand in a friendly manner and said, "You're a hell of a good guy, Sascha, but you talk too damned much." This simple statement had a profound effect on Sascha. He turned pale and his eyes opened wide with what seemed to be either fear or illumination. He stood there, stunned and motionless, as the session continued.

Paul Fusco, like Fletch, had a knack for honest expression, a way of cutting straight to the heart of things. When he came to Ivan Illich, he paused for a moment, then spoke vehemently. "What I feel is, I can't connect with you as a human being. When you came up to me and everybody else, it was like you were blessing us. You didn't see us as individuals. We were objects. You're detached, cut off. It's not real, Ivan, it's not real." Illich looked as if he had been slapped in the face. He was a man known for his compassion for the wretched of the earth — almost a saint in some people's eyes.

Illich remained obviously agitated as I led the group through the two remaining stages of the microlab: a period of nonverbal communication followed by the circle's moving slowly inward until everyone touched. We went back to our chairs and sat in silence for a moment.

"I've got to figure this out," Illich said, breaking the silence. "There's something terribly wrong with this, and I don't quite know what it is yet. I've got to think."

I realized I had made a big mistake in doing an encounter demonstration in this setting. Fletch rose to the defense of the process, and for a while he and Ivan had a heated debate. But Ivan couldn't be swayed. He just kept repeating, "I can't quite figure it out, but there's something terribly wrong."

Illich might well have had a point. Later Mike Murphy and I, among others, came to question the long-term value of immediate, unearned intimacy. But on that night I heard myself thinking, Maybe what's really bothering you, Ivan, is that Paul Fusco nailed you — and you know it. In any case, on the basis of this dinner party experience alone, Esalen and the movement with which it was associated had probably gained one more enemy.

As for Ivan's brother Sascha, I hardly noticed that after the microlab he spent the entire evening in silence. A couple of weeks later he sent me an impassioned letter. For him the experience had been a blessed one. He had not spoken a word since Fletch had touched him. He had been living in a state of grace. He had seen into the predispositions that had prevented his happiness. He was deeply appreciative. A few weeks after getting his letter, I ran into him on Madison Avenue near the Look

Building. We embraced. He was speaking again. He seemed happy.

For the Knebels too, the experience provided a powerful opening. They went on to become deeply involved in human potential activities. Fletch and Laura! I could hardly believe it.

News of Martin Luther King's assassination came while we were in Cuernavaca. It ripped through my body like shrapnel. I felt I could hardly breathe. I phoned Bill Arthur and asked if I could come straight to New York to write a memorial piece. As I flew north, the cities were burning again and people were being killed — twenty-nine in the riots following King's death. I got to the New York office and wrote as fast as I could. If I finished quickly, the article might run in the issue that was already going to press. I wrote of King's life and deeds and historical significance and my memories of him. But I didn't stop there. I wrote that we shouldn't just memorialize him, but that we should *do something* about racism. We should call a moratorium on all educational programs in the country, from kindergarten through graduate school, for a week, during which every student and every teacher would confront the racial crisis and his or her own feelings about it. We should hold a continuing series of interracial marathon encounters at all levels of the public and private sector. I knew I was being extravagant and impolitic, but if there was ever a time to let go and try for a miracle, that was it. In two days the article was done.

Bill Arthur and Pat Carbine didn't know what to do with it. We went to Bill Attwood, editor-in-chief of all Cowles publications. Attwood had served as *Look*'s European editor. When he came back in the mid-fifties to be national affairs editor, he moved to New Canaan, Connecticut, where I lived, and we became friends. A leave of absence from *Look* to work for the Kennedy campaign resulted in the ambassadorship to Guinea and then Kenya; in both places he distinguished himself as an American ambassador who wore shorts and drove a Jeep and got to know the people. After Dan Mich's death, Mike Cowles had brought in Attwood as editor-in-chief of all Cowles publications.

When he finished reading my piece, he looked at me and grinned.

"This is terrific," he said, "but you know we can't use it."

He had another job for me. *Look* was going to run an editorial against the Vietnam war. It would be only the third editorial of any kind *Look* had ever run. Other Americans had spoken out long before, but this would be the first such statement in a major U.S. magazine. I sat down and drafted the piece. Attwood rewrote it, and it ran in the May 14 issue at the end of a portfolio of brutal and moving combat photos. It was signed, "The Editors."

Look publishes these photographs to remind you of some things many Americans seem to have forgotten: that people and nations make mistakes; that people and nations can learn from their mistakes; and that in the process of rectifying a mistake, a person or a nation can grow in wisdom and strength.

The Vietnam war has been a mistake, destroying something precious in the word "America."

America is not just fields and forests, cities and towns. From the beginning, it has been for all the world a great experiment, a moral force, a dream. "To be an American," said the philosopher George Santayana, "is of itself almost a moral condition, an education, and a career."

America's genius lies not in war but in peace. The American influence in peace has become the most pervasive in history. It reaches every corner of the earth, crossing national and ideological boundaries, creating the kind of goodwill that can never be imposed at gunpoint. . . .

So let us learn to be useful to the world without trying to be its policemen, or to make its rules. Let us strive, in John F. Kennedy's phrase, to keep the world safe for diversity. Let us work strenuously to create an international environment where all can flourish. Millions of Americans would like nothing better — students, teachers, Peace Corps volunteers, technicians, businessmen. This band of irregulars, backed by the moral force and example of America, can help bring prosperity and build friendship and understanding all over our impoverished and endangered planet. This is an American victory that *can* be won.

That is why we at *Look* believe that the most important national business before us in this year of political debate is to wind up our involvement in the Vietnam war as quickly and as honorably as possible, and to go on from there to the creation of a world order in which America's ingenuity will truly serve the cause of peace.

Paul Fusco had stayed in Mexico. I rejoined him to finish our story. We traveled to Acapulco, Zihuatanejo, Villahermosa, Palenque, Oaxaca, Mitla. Lillie was with us for a part of our travels, and as it turned out, Paul's picture of her sunning in a hammock in a two-piece bathing suit ended up on the cover. Paul's most stunning photo, though, revealed how he felt about bullfighting. It showed a bull's carcass plowing up a wake of sand as it was dragged from the bull ring.

Not long after I returned home, I got a call from William Orrick, a prominent San Francisco attorney and an active Democrat. Bob Kennedy was going to be in town in a couple of days, Orrick said, and wanted me to have dinner with them. Kennedy's campaign had gotten a late start. Eugene McCarthy had already gained momentum among the antiwar constituency. But Kennedy and his team had hit the ground running with an approach to the issues that seemed even more innovative than that of McCarthy. There was a wild, spontaneous quality about the Kennedy campaign. And there was something mythic in the television coverage of the candidate himself as he sat up on the back of a convertible, sunlight catching his shock of hair, and reached out to touch hands with the people who crowded up to the car and almost stopped its progress. His brother had been shot and so had Martin Luther King, and here he was, as vulnerable and fearless as a child, or as a knight who possessed a magic charm. There had been ups and downs, but it now appeared that if he could win the California primary on June 4, he would get the Democratic nomination, and in all probability, the presidency.

I made reservations at L'Étoile, a restaurant in the Huntington Hotel on Nob Hill, across the street from Grace Cathedral. We met at eight. Kennedy came in with Orrick and a woman who represented Indians' rights groups. The change in Kennedy was truly amazing. If he had been tough and ruthless, all that now seemed to be gone. As we ordered drinks, I was struck by a new softness and openness. The glow I had always seen in him was even brighter and clearer. His smile made no demands on me.

I started talking about the campaign, but it soon became clear that Kennedy wanted to talk about me, and especially about my education book. I told him the basic ideas of the book as best I could, sometimes stumbling over my words. He said he would like to see a copy. My mind raced. I had just finished doing the changes my editor had asked for, and had posted the only clean copy. I had a working copy, considerably scrawled upon. I asked Kennedy when he wanted it. He smiled and said tomorrow morning would be fine. If he was elected, the schools would be a top priority. He was eager for all the ideas he could get his hands on.

We lingered for a long time over coffee. He had recently visited an Indian reservation, and he began telling us about the conditions under which the Indians lived. As he talked, I saw tears in his eyes.

I drove home in a happy daze. It seemed a miracle: Here was a man who had grown and changed, a man with real access to his feelings as well as political acumen, a man who was clear and open, who had compassion for the oppressed and a belief in the human potential. And here also was a man who would very likely be our next president. It was almost too good to be true.

The next morning I got up early and wore out several erasers making my working copy of *Education and Ecstasy* presentable. My secretary ran off a photocopy. Around noon I took it to Kennedy's suite at the Fairmont. Kennedy was out campaigning, so I gave it to one of his aides and asked him to put it directly in the hands of the candidate. About a week later, the aide called from Los Angeles. Kennedy had read most of the manuscript, liked it very much, and wanted to talk about it after the California primary.

Maybe there would be real education reform, I thought. And if the schools changed, the whole society would surely be transformed. My dream of a nation devoted to the development of human potential had never been brighter.

During the month of May, college campuses all across the nation were in chaos. In New York, protesters took over the Columbia University administration building. From the media capital of the country, pictures flashed: a student sitting at president Grayson Kirk's desk, smoking one of Kirk's cigars. The picture made me wince. I supported the students' demands but felt such gloating wouldn't help their cause. Young people by themselves, I realized, couldn't create a lasting transformation of society. We needed activists and visionaries of all ages. Then the police were called in to clear the buildings. Using clubs and fists and feet, they injured around a hundred students and faculty members and arrested nearly seven hundred. In response to this show of naked force, the university community — people of all ages — went on strike, shutting Columbia down for the rest of the semester.

Look's art director, Will Hopkins, came out for a West Coast visit. Hopkins, who had taken over when Allen Hurlburt kicked himself upstairs to be Cowles's corporate art director, was a striking figure — slim, with a handlebar moustache and glimmering eyes. I thought he was simply the best art director in the world. Lillie and I showed him the sights around San Francisco, then took him to a ranch north of the city where we went on trail rides and he admired the "formal" quality of the California landscape.

On Tuesday, June 4, I cast my vote in the primary, then took off for Los Angeles with Hopkins. We had dinner with Cal and Roz Bernstein at a restaurant on Sunset Boulevard. The election was close, but by the time dinner was over, it appeared Kennedy was winning. Cal and Roz suggested we go to the Ambassador and join the crowd celebrating the victory, but Will and I decided to go back to our hotel and watch the celebration on television.

We drove to the Bel Air and went to our separate rooms. I turned on the television set, propped up my pillows, and lay back on the bed. There was Bob Kennedy at the microphone, accepting the ovation of his supporters, thanking people, looking a little tired, I thought, and acting a little silly. But that didn't matter to me. Kennedy's last words as he left the stage were "On to Chicago."

A few minutes later, something strange happened on the screen. All order and meaning drained away. The camera wandered aimlessly over the crowd. There were screams. Someone was saying meaningless words over the sound system. There was a knock on my door. Will Hopkins didn't want to be alone. We stayed there, barely speaking, as the horror of that night unfolded.

30

"Twelve Psychiatrists Have Broken My Legs"

IT WAS ONLY DURING THE REQUIEM MASS that I realized the extent of my grief. The picture on the television screen of Teddy Kennedy trying to control his quavering voice as he spoke of his third lost brother broke through the numbness. What an effort he was making to hold back his tears! It was hardest when he quoted Robert F. Kennedy's favorite passage: "Some men see things as they are and say why. I dream of things that never were and say why not?" My tears came at last for Teddy Kennedy and his dead brother, for the country's loss, and mine.

At times of deep grief and great joy we are informed by the wisdom of clichés. The death of an individual is not the death of hope. Bob Kennedy had urged all of us onward. There was nothing to do but continue to work on every possible front for social justice and racial equality and the full development of human potential.

The summer of 1968 was an apocalyptic time. The horror of the recent assassinations still haunted the air. Sometimes it seemed that the nation had come to a precarious edge; one step beyond was an endless fall into chaos. At the same time, a wild, nearly delirious sense that some kind of deliverance was close at hand spread among those seeking transformation. There was no time to waste. New ideas were translated into immediate action, with little thought of the long-term consequences. It was a summer of extremes, of foolishness and cruelty, of madcap beginnings and grotesque endings. Some people actually entertained the thought that the Pentagon might be levitated.

As for me, I was totally and passionately committed — to *Look,* to school reform, to Esalen, to the interracial groups — in a way that might be hard for later generations entirely to comprehend. The intense dialogues with Mike Murphy that had started three years earlier had never stopped. Esalen's San Francisco operation as well as its Big Sur center were going full bore. Will Schutz's resident fellows were exploring the outer limits of human intimacy. Other centers modeled on Esalen were opening all around the country. *Education and Ecstasy* would be published in the fall, and the signs were good.

On the matter of race, perhaps more than anything else, I dreamed of things that never were. Race was clearly a powerful searchlight that could illuminate individual neurosis and penetrate to the core of our national sickness. Through heartfelt confrontation and understanding, integration could become a two-way process. Black Americans could gain a fair share of the rewards of the mainstream culture. White Americans could tap into the richness of the black culture, could recognize the spontaneity, the joy, even the ability to perceive reality that we had kept hidden somewhere in the sterile suburb of our senses.

That possibility, in any case, is what I saw in our interracial marathon sessions, which were continuing at Esalen and spreading around the country, especially among church groups. John Poppy and Ron Brown, a doctoral candidate in psychology at Berkeley and friend of Price's, had formed a second team, and now were doing more groups than Price and I. We held some of the marathons at Big Sur but most of them in meeting rooms in the Diocesan House of Grace Cathedral. Even when we varied the format with new techniques, the fundamental dynamics that had revealed themselves at Esalen remained the same: First the blacks would attack the blacks, then they would coalesce into a powerful force and attack the whites. The whites would recoil in confusion, fearing not so much that they would lose power as that they would have to acknowledge the prejudice hidden in even the most liberal. There would be a time of utter despair, a dark night of the soul. Then, sometime after dawn, the whites would begin revealing themselves as individuals rather than as the impenetrable Establishment against which the blacks had been able to do nothing but rage. And somehow the miracle of understanding at a level barely dreamed of would again occur. I would drive home Sunday afternoon drained but exalted. After all, not everyone had something worth staying up all night for.

The media blitz was in full swing. On July 5, 1968, *Life* magazine came out with a feature entitled "Inhibitions Thrown to the Gentle Winds." The article ran through eighteen pages and was written in snappy, sometimes rather breathless prose. Though centered on Esalen, it was presented as a words-and-pictures report on the human potential movement. The writer, Jane Howard of *Life*'s New York staff, had done her homework. She surveyed the broad and hard-to-define scope of the movement, touching on the influence of Maslow, Rogers, Huxley, Paul Tillich, Erich

Fromm, Teilhard de Chardin, and the Zen Buddhists. She cited human potential applications to business and government by the National Training Laboratories, the Western Behavioral Sciences Institute, and the Human Development Institute in Atlanta. She mentioned the interracial marathons and an Esalen program for the drug-free treatment of schizophrenics at California's Agnews State Hospital, as well as Dr. George Brown's pioneering experiments with affective education at Esalen and the University of California in Santa Barbara. She listed, and dealt with, eleven putative criticisms of the human potential movement ("The movement is anti-intellectual"; "The movement breeds a kind of 'emotional elitism' "; "The movement constitutes a massive invasion of privacy." . . .)

Despite its attempt at comprehensiveness, the article by and large, once again, was an account of the writer's experience in a Will Schutz encounter group — the true confessions of an uptight East Coast journalist learning to feel deeply, to touch strangers, to take a fantasy trip ("I was to picture myself being very, very tiny and entering my body any way I chose. I went in by the mouth . . ."), and finally to shed public tears. The accompanying picture story was even more selective, showing people dancing and hugging in Schutz encounter groups and other people in the hot baths. Sandwiched gratuitously in the middle of the feature was a picture spread of a nude marathon held in Los Angeles that had nothing to do with Esalen. *Life* magazine, in the spirit of the times, was obviously being "bold," but at the cost of creating an emphasis that would mislead millions of readers. The original idea of a human potential movement had had nothing whatever to do with nudity. Mike Murphy, in fact, had always been opposed to mixed nude bathing, which had been initiated by the early guests of Esalen, and indeed had been a part of the bohemian Big Sur culture. He and Dick Price had fought it for a year before giving in to the inevitable. As for encounter groups, they were an important aspect of the movement, a useful tool for the development and expression of human potential — but only one tool among many. Now the public was being led to believe that the human potential movement and encounter groups (along with a lot of mixed nudity) were one and the same.

This public confusion was compounded by the success of Schutz's book *Joy,* which was being widely promoted on radio and television. Willing to be outrageous in the cause of absolute openness and honesty, Schutz made a choice guest for Johnny Carson, Phil Donahue, David Susskind, Dick Cavett, and Merv Griffin. He was called back for encore appearances by almost all of them, four times by Griffin. In a calm and confident voice, Schutz would say exactly what he felt about each host, and urge them, the other guests, and the audience to do the same. With his shaved head, muzzle beard, and powerful presence, he was easily recognizable. For a few months in 1968, people on the street stopped him and asked for autographs.

Schutz possessed the single-mindedness and purity of heart of a warrior. He could laugh at himself for doing the kinds of things that would clearly make people laugh at him, then go right on doing them. In the name of total openness, for example, he removed the doors from the bathrooms in his house. Most people didn't know whether to laugh or cringe when they heard of this development.

There was no middle ground for Schutz. One Saturday night at Esalen, the lodge was cleared for a dance to the music of the Big Sur Mountain Men. I expected some kind of country rock with a powerful, earthy beat. But when these Big Sur heavies with their outlaw garb and menacing scowls began to play, the rhythm came out jerky and mechanical and very, very *white*. Nevertheless, the dancers struggled to be uninhibited and to bring on the Dionysian surge appropriate to the place and the era. About an hour into the dance, when the band was reaching a crescendo of volume if not soul, I saw Schutz strip off all his clothes. A few other dancers joined him; most did not. And there was the intrepid psychologist, bounding around to the mechanical beat of the Mountain Men, looking utterly miserable.

The attempt to raise a new flag of human liberation was clearly producing a maddening literal-mindedness. "Lose your mind and come to your senses"; "Get out of your head and into your body"; "If it feels good, do it" — whatever truth was encoded in these phrases was vitiated by uncritical acceptance and careless repetition. It was almost as bad as the established culture's own slogans: "If somebody pushes you, push back"; "Real men don't cry"; "Winning isn't everything; it's the only thing."

It was about this time that Mike Murphy and I tried to unname the human potential movement. We went around telling people there was really no such thing. We quickly learned that just as it was much easier to change the world than to change it the way we planned, it was much easier to name a movement than to unname it.

At the height of the July heat, three couples set out from the Big Sur coast to hike twenty-five miles through the Los Padres National Forest to the Zen Mountain Center at Tassajara. The party included Mike Murphy, Pat Felix, Dick and Ginny Baker, and Lillie and me. Owing to exceptionally hot and dry conditions, the entire area was closed to hikers. But Dick Baker, the chief organizer of the Zen center, was officially a fire marshal and thus able to get us a permit.

Baker was a tall, dominant man with an exceptional will and a feeling for service and power. Had he not become a Zen student, he might well have made a formidable corporate president. We were probably the only people within hundreds of square miles of wilderness. Our equipment was clumsy and heavy: old-fashioned army canteens and bedrolls. By the time I had humped my forty-pound pack to the three-thousand-foot ridge on which a segment of our trail ran, I was already becoming dehydrated. We hiked on in 90-degree heat, swigging from our canteens as we went. The maps showed plenty of water at the site where we planned to spend the night.

We arrived at dusk to find that the streams had all run dry. We dug for water, with no success. The next water on the map was four miles farther along, on the other side of a fifteen-hundred-foot ridge. We decided to spend the night and start before dawn the next morning. We split our remaining water, which came to half a cup each. We ate nothing. I lay sleepless on my bedroll, hearing outrageous animal sounds all around. Something huge was gnawing on a tree, just to taunt us, it seemed. Other creatures were breathing heavily and snorting — wild boars, perhaps. They sounded as big as rhinos. The stars were bright and merciless and as thirsty as I was. All night I had vivid hallucinations of swimming pools and ice-cold Coca-Cola.

The air was still and hot even in the hours before dawn. We were very quiet as we worked our way up the steep grade that would take us deeper into the wilderness. We climbed to meet the sun, and it touched us like the blast from a furnace. There might be no water at the next site, and if that was the case, we would be in very big trouble. The trail at last sloped downward and we walked faster, lips parched, throats dry, not saying a word. We would soon know.

A mile from the site, we all smelled it. It was unmistakable: the fresh, delicious, healing odor of water. I realized at that moment how animals could find a tiny spring in a parched wilderness. At first there were only brackish pools in dry streambeds. We filled our canteens anyway. But as we moved farther downstream, we came upon running water, the loveliest sound under the sun. After drinking our fill, we discovered a perfect place to rest and eat and drink some more: a flat, bare area with a small hill on one side and the stream on the other. We broke out our freeze-dried food and our utensils and prepared a feast. It was like Christmas and Thanksgiving and Easter all put together.

In this festive spirit, Pat told Lillie a secret, and Lillie told me, and Mike admitted that it was true. Pat and Mike had been married for six months. One night they had gone to see *Zorba the Greek*. Infected by Zorba's wild and exuberant spirit, they had driven from San Francisco across the sierras straight to an all-night wedding chapel in Carson City, Nevada. Afterward, Mike, the confirmed bachelor, had refused to tell anybody. But now the secret was out, and now we had further cause to celebrate before we resumed our hike to the lovely Zen monastery at Tassajara, an oasis in the heart of the wilderness.

Our hike was emblematic of that reckless summer. We had started out on a rigorous journey unconditioned, poorly prepared, and ill equipped. Somehow we had gotten away with it, had had a wonderful time, and had learned a secret.

During the last week of August, at the time of the Democratic National Convention, millions of people saw television pictures of ferocious battles between antiwar demonstrators and Chicago police. Among the groups involved was the Youth International Party, better known as the Yippies. Yippie tacticians Jerry Rubin and Abbie Hoffman favored a sort of guerrilla street theater to attract attention to their cause. They planned to defy Mayor Richard J. Daley's refusal to grant permits for the protests, and to nominate a live, four-legged pig for president of the United States.

Mayor Daley was not amused. Every night he ordered the demonstrators cleared from their bivouacs in Lincoln Park. Police used clubs, tear gas, and armored vehicles. Fighting fanned out into surrounding streets. As the convention went on, the police became increasingly violent, assaulting television cameramen, news reporters, bystanders, and even convention delegates, clubbing their victims again and again, even when they were down. President Johnson called out the National Guard. Tanks rolled through the city. Troops with fixed bayonets took positions outside the Hilton Hotel, where many delegates were housed. Television switched back and forth between pictures within the convention hall and images of savagery in the streets outside. Newspapers ran pictures of U.S. Army bayonets side by side with photos of Soviet tanks in Czechoslovakia, which had been invaded by Warsaw Pact troops on August 20 in an effort to suppress liberalization — another dream destroyed.

While all this was going on, Paul Fusco and I were working on a cover story for *Look* to be called "The Man and Woman Thing." The story would compare traditional relations between the sexes with various experimental arrangements that were emerging in the late sixties — communal living, open marriages, group marriages, new ways of relating within monogamous marriages. On Tuesday morning, August 27, at the height of the Democratic convention, I was sitting alone in my office having coffee and thinking about the violent events of the past several days. Paul was at Esalen shooting a Schutz couples group. I had a speaking engagement on Wednesday and would join Paul on Thursday. There was a buzz on the intercom. It was an Arthur Free of the Diggers to see me. The Diggers, a radical group who set up soup kitchens in the panhandle of Golden Gate Park to feed hungry hippies, had helped inspire the Yippies. I asked him to come in.

The instant Arthur Free entered the room, I had a sense that something wasn't quite right. It wasn't his long, dark, wavy hair and prominent nose, cheekbones, and Adam's apple, or his threadbare tweed jacket, or the long scarf wrapped tightly around his neck. It had something to do with the way he walked straight up to me, jingling money in a cardboard box.

"Free change?" he said, holding the box in front of me. "Go ahead, take some. The Diggers are giving away money to the middle class."

I took a dime. Free said he was going to City Hall and give money away. He urged me to accompany him so I could see how he operated. Reluctantly, I acquiesced; the cultural revolution was in a sense my beat. City Hall is a large domed building in the style of the Capitol in Washington. Arthur Free took his stand in the center of the broad, impressive front steps and accosted everyone coming in or out of the building with a cry of "Free change!" Most of the people shied away, but now and then someone, smiling sheepishly, reached into the box and took a few coins. I kept rather far to the side, feeling embarrassed and annoyed. I could sense no charity in Free's actions. To the contrary, he seemed delighted by the embarrassment he was causing.

"We're going to see the mayor now," Free said. I followed him to the mayor's office, figuring he would be summarily rebuffed. He didn't get to see the mayor, but to my surprise he was ushered into the office of the chief administrative assistant, who listened courteously to his rambling discourse on the necessity of feeding the poor and educating the middle class. He insisted that the administrative assistant take a few coins before he left.

Free was beside himself with the triumph of having given money to the mayor's main man. As we walked back to the front entrance of City Hall, he explained his rationale.

"What I'm doing, see, is creating this funky street theater and then making the middle class walk through it. Yeah, making them walk through it."

The next day Price Cobbs and I were scheduled to present a panel on our black-white groups at the annual meeting of the American Association for Humanistic Psychology, which was being held at the Fairmont Hotel. The marriage between AAHP and the Fairmont, as it turned out, was not made in heaven. The AAHP had been founded by such psychologists as Abraham Maslow, Carl Rogers, and Rollo May as an academic association dedicated to third force psychology (the other two "forces" being behaviorism and psychoanalysis). In the effervescence of the mid-sixties, however, AAHP had turned increasingly from the academic to the experiental. The Fairmont meeting opened with a session in the grand ballroom during which about a thousand people wandered around in their stocking feet at the direction of AAHP president Jack Gibb, exchanging greetings, making close eye contact, dancing, improvising various exercises. Another session, entitled "Creative Risk-Taking," went even further. Participants massaged one another, formed circles that were to be broken into or out of, and gathered into groups to rock people and then lift them overhead. One thing led to another to create a carnival spirit that often spilled out into the Fairmont's elegant Victorian lobby. It was just the kind of disinhibition that Jane Howard had written about in *Life* magazine. Arriving businessmen and world travelers in their dark suits were bemused by the sight of middle-aged men and women in jeans and stocking feet massaging one another or playing patty-cake near the central bell station. The management, we heard, was already becoming nervous.

Fortunately, Price and I had nothing unconventional in mind. Our session was held in the hotel's Gold Room. When we arrived, dressed in conservative business suits, the five-hundred seats in the room were filled and the audience seemed expectant and subdued. A panel table with chairs and microphones was set up on the longer side of the rectangular room. Price and I took our seats in the chairs nearest the center of the table. There was no one to introduce us, so I did the introductions and Price began speaking.

In this setting Price was not the fierce, uncompromising group leader of our marathon sessions but the proper psychiatrist, judicious and engaging. I sat there totally at ease, warmed by admiration for my friend and colleague and comforted by the intent silence of the audience. After the storms of the past months, here at last was an interlude of peace and recognition.

Just then I noticed a movement at the back of the audience. There was Arthur Free, walking back and forth with the restlessness of a hungry timber wolf. I hardly had time to wonder what he was up to before he strode down the center aisle, mounted the platform, walked around the table, and took the seat to the left of me. Smiling wickedly, he leaned forward and spoke into the microphone in front of him.

"I'm joining the panel," he said.

Price paused and looked around me at Free. My mind spun for what seemed a long time before I could figure out what to do.

"Okay," I said to the audience, "let's have a show of hands. How many people want Arthur Free to join the panel?"

There was a scattering of raised hands.

"How many prefer that he not join the panel?"

There was an overwhelming show of hands.

"Sorry, Arthur," I said, reaching over to take his microphone.

Price went on with his presentation. But Free didn't leave the table. Very slowly, he unwrapped the scarf from his neck. He placed it on the table before him and started folding it with agonizing precision and care. I tried to ignore him, keeping my eyes on the audience and glancing at Price now and then. But from the corner of my eye I could see very well what Free was doing. As if in slow motion, he was removing his jacket and folding it on the table in front of him. I felt myself breaking out in a sweat. Then he started unbuttoning his shirt — very, very slowly, pausing after each button. There was no doubt that he was going to take off his shirt, and then his pants, and then every stitch he had on. He was going to create his funky street theater and make us walk through it right here in the Gold Room of the Fairmont Hotel.

I searched my mind for a way out. We could try to ignore him — but it would be impossible, even at an AAHP meeting, to ignore a nude man at the panel table. Or we could call for the authorities. But that would be just what he wanted. It would prove that we were part of the repressive Establishment, which had no recourse but to call out the pigs on the poor, oppressed Diggers. And it would diminish our meeting. I could come up with no other options. My rational mind, which had so often stood me in good stead, was helplessly spinning its wheels.

For Price, however, the solution was quite simple. He leaned around in front of me and spoke to Free in words he could understand.

"Hey, man, you jiving me? You probably think I'm one of those middle-class *Neegroes*." He turned to the audience and addressed a young black man who was sitting about four rows back. "Come on, Mike. Let's take him out of here."

Mike Brown had been a 210-pound All-America running back at Delaware, and had tried out with the Chicago Bears before going into graduate work in psychology. He rose from his seat without hesitation and headed for the platform. A young white man who was also one of Price's students got up from the front row to help out. Mike grabbed Free under the arms from the back and lifted him from his chair. The white student grabbed his legs. Price and I got on either side of Free to help carry him out of the Gold Room.

As soon as Mike Brown touched him, Free started struggling violently and screaming at the top of his lungs.

"You're hurting me! You're breaking my back!"

It was a long way to the door, and he writhed and screamed the whole way before the shocked eyes of the audience. Free's voice took on a preadolescent timbre. His shrieks were those of a twelve-year-old boy being tortured. No horror movie in my experience had ever managed to create such piteous and piercing sounds. Now and then he screamed, *"You're breaking my back!"* in that uncannily childish and tortured voice.

We emerged into the lobby at a particularly inopportune time. One of the workshops had finally gone over the edge: twenty or thirty people wearing blindfolds and earplugs were being led around the Fairmont lobby by their partners, using senses other than sight and hearing to experience their surroundings, touching the plush furnishing and marble columns, putting their total trust in their partners to keep them from bumping into things or otherwise hurting themselves. I couldn't imagine what the participants in this "trust walk" thought when they heard Arthur Free's tortured outcries (which no earplugs could shut out), but I did notice several of them shrinking back and tugging at their blindfolds.

We carried Free to the center of the lobby and dumped him on the floor amid several of the horrified trust walkers. He lay there writhing and screaming:

"Twelve psychiatrists have broken my legs!"

We started back for the Gold Room, and his piteous shrieks followed us:

"Twelve psychiatrists have broken my legs! Twelve psychiatrists have broken my legs!"

We re-entered the Gold Room and took our seats at the panel table, and I said we would now go on with our discussion. Then I noticed that the absolute hush in the room was one not of interest and attention but of outrage and hostility. Five hundred pairs of accusatory eyes were fixed on Price and me.

"Something very ugly has happened," a man in the front row said. "You can't just ignore it and go on." Several other people echoed these sentiments.

Suddenly I realized that the members of the audience didn't know that Free had been acting. As far as they were concerned, he might well have been seriously injured. Some of them probably didn't even realize he was starting to do a striptease. Here was a playful, essentially innocent person brutalized by the leaders of the panel. I tried to explain. I told the audience of my encounter with Free on the previous day. I explained Free's avowed purpose of making the middle class walk through his funky street theater. The tortured outcries, I said, were part of that theater. The screams had been carefully calculated. Gradually the hostility in the room melted, and we went on with our discussion of the interracial marathon session, followed by a lively question period.

I had nothing but admiration for the way Price had handled a situation that had left me paralyzed. His dispatch, his ability to cut through the limitations imposed by middle-class convention, delighted me.

The management of the Fairmont was less delighted. Their tolerance had already been stretched to the limit, and Arthur Free's screams exceeded it. They called in AAHP executive director John Levy and threatened to throw the whole conference out unless something drastic was done. Levy agreed to hire twelve Pinkerton guards to police the lobby and the meeting rooms. This had a chastening effect on the participants, and there were no more massages or trust walks in the Fairmont lobby.

We heard later that Arthur Free had left the hotel bent on revenge. He went to both major San Francisco newspapers (one version of the story had him on crutches) with his sad tale of having been attacked and injured by twelve AAHP psychiatrists. When the papers didn't buy it, he rushed from one radical organization to another, trying — unsuccessfully — to organize protesters who would picket the meeting.

The Diggers might be radical, but so, in its own way, was the AAHP. If a revolution was going on, it was a confused one, with an endless proliferation of radical organizations and splinter groups. St. Petersburg in 1910, historian Walter Truett Anderson pointed out, had no more varieties, no more wildly competing brands, of radical activism than did San Francisco in the summer of 1968.

I went home to my television set. Something was wrong with America. John Kennedy was dead. Martin Luther King was dead. Robert Kennedy was dead. The Republicans had nominated Richard Nixon. The Democrats had rejected Eugene McCarthy. There was no viable peace candidate. The nomination of Hubert Humphrey that night was accompanied by bloody scenes of protesters in Chicago chanting, again and again, "The whole world is watching."

31

The World Seemed
to Be Closing In

THE NATION WAS LOCKED in a war that seemed to exclude the possibility of victory. The word *patriotism* was losing its ancient gleam. Instead of the united home front of World War II, there was rhetoric and riots. Those who opposed the war were themselves slipping over the edge into violence, while those who opposed the opposition were seeking to disguise their repressive intentions in the robes of law and order. Was it true that FBI agents had infiltrated the student movement and were egging on its members to illegal actions so as to discredit them and crush all dissent? It was hard for me to believe that such a conspiracy existed, or that the assassinations of the Kennedy brothers and Martin Luther King were more than the crazed acts of unbalanced individuals. To believe otherwise without compelling evidence, it seemed to me, would affirm a paranoia that could disjoin the very structure of a free society.

And yet, in spite of all this, there was a wild and jubilant sense of hope in the air. "Breakdown is breakthrough," McLuhan had said, and maybe he was right. Something fresh and cleansing and also rather frightening was trying to break its way into the world. Something powerful and unimaginable was waiting to be born. I had felt that presence before, but now it was very near, presaging calamity or deliverance or perhaps both. In that summer of darkness and light, each moment was charged with dangers and possibilities. How could anyone who was alive and truly committed wish to be alive at any other time?

Six days after the nomination of Hubert Humphrey, the first of three lengthy installments of *Education and Ecstasy* appeared in *Look* magazine. The radical ideas that had been so long resisted now hit the public with the force of a news event. The first installment, titled "How School Stunts Your Child," was announced in full-page ads in the *New York*

Times and other major metropolitan dailies. The ads did nothing to bowdlerize the book's radical message. "STOP LEARNING!" they said in two-inch-high block letters. Then came a statement in boldface type describing "what the editors believe will be the most influential book on education in modern times. It shows how the average classroom of today is actually designed to *stop* a child's spectacular learning career . . . and how this situation can be changed." And then there were the radio and television talk shows, dozens of them.

In spite of all this, I was still a working journalist. All through the month of September, I continued to be more concerned with my current projects than with the book I had been dreaming of since January 10, 1963. But that was the way things had always been at *Look*. By the time a story came out, it was yesterday's business; I was always busy with something new. In any case, my notebooks of that period reveal nothing at all about *Education and Ecstasy* and a great deal about "The Man and Woman Thing" and "How to Have a Bloodless Riot," a picture story with Paul Fusco on a black-white encounter group.

"The Man and Woman Thing" was probably the most difficult and troubling story I had ever tackled. Through one long, intense interview after another, I listened carefully and filled yellow legal pads with notes. Couples from many walks of life revealed more of themselves than I could have ever expected. They told me of their unrealistic dreams, their shattered hopes, their sexual yearnings and misunderstandings; their mistakes made and repented of and made anew; their willingness to try and fail and try again. I listened and wrote as fast as I could, and they spoke for me as well as themselves; I sometimes thought I could write the whole story just from the experiences of my own marriage.

And how sad, how *unnecessary* all the problems seemed. It was an age when all the dreams of the ancient sorcerers were coming true. We had learned to fly, to see around the world, to transmute the elements, to turn matter into energy. We would soon travel to the moon. And yet we weren't even starting to devise a way for a man and a woman to live together for seven straight days with any assurance of harmony and personal growth. I was fascinated by the space program and followed every mission with the ardor of one who had once dedicated his life to the arcane rites of technology and flight. But why couldn't we dedicate just a fraction of that money and energy to the relationships between nation and nation, man and woman, black and white, person and person? Will Schutz's relentless encountering, his quest for astronauts of inner space, sometimes seemed corny, misguided, excessive. But perhaps he was the real pioneer of our age, the one from whose mistakes as well as successes we would all learn. While *Education and Ecstasy* was exploding on the public consciousness, I was writing my *Look* stories with the focused intensity of the afflicted. I delayed the moment when I would have to deal with the repercussions of the book. It was as if I knew how decisively they would change my life.

At first the response was not overwhelming. Then, while the second installment was still on the stands, the flood began. I would be out interviewing people, and would return to my office to find fifty to a hundred letters sent in a package from the New York office. I was both eager and reluctant to open them. They were from students, teachers, parents with children in school. They were charged with emotion, with despair for lost opportunities, with hope for something better. They cried out for change. They didn't ask for advice on how to get rich or win out over others, but simply for a chance to learn and keep learning, to fulfill more of their potential, to live more fully.

From a seventeen-year-old girl:

> Thank you very much for your article. It was beautiful. It made me want to cry at the inadequacies of my school, at what I could be but am not because of the system.
>
> I cry because I want to go to the 2001 school and I can't. I cry because I love to learn but find that trying to keep that spark alive in me is the hardest thing I must do. . . .
>
> I cry also for the teachers that want me to live. They too are bound by the system that limits what I can learn.
>
> Mr. Leonard, you are a beautiful man. I love you. May I go to your school?

When the book itself came out at the beginning of October, the stream of letters became a deluge. There were parents' urgent, often desperate requests for the names of alternative schools that subscribed to the principles set forth in the book. There were enthusiastic letters from young people who wanted to be teachers, asking me where they should go for teachers' training. There were letters from graduate students, asking me to be on their doctoral committees. There were invitations to speak or consult. And there were requests for help from ad hoc groups of parents, teachers, and ordinary citizens who wanted to band together and start schools based on *Education and Ecstasy*. As time passed, I got more and more letters demanding that I drop everything and start such a school myself.

I tried to answer every letter. I searched my records for the names of alternative schools; there were not many, and none could come close to matching the futuristic school I had dreamed up. I referred parents to the New Schools Exchange for information. John Holt, author of *Why Schools Fail*, gave me a list of recommended schools, and I sent copies to my correspondents. To recommend innovative teacher training institutes was even more difficult. I started doing research. I neglected my *Look* work. The letters I wrote elicited more letters. My secretary and I worked out stock answers, but they were often unsatisfactory. The receptionist helped with the typing, and sometimes the ad department's secretary pitched in. Still we fell behind. My editorial assistant started trying on her own to answer the increasingly demanding letter writers, especially those who, failing to get a quick answer, had gone on to write a second or third letter.

> Thank you for your letter to George Leonard. He has been trying to answer all the mail that has come in response to his book, in hopes that the volume would diminish so that he could catch up. However, this has not been the case. He has fallen several hundred letters behind, and has been hard pressed to keep up with his assignments for *Look*.
>
> Knowing that you deserve an answer, hoping that you will forgive him for being physically unable to send you one, he can only say that he is in this painful position because there is such a powerful hunger for educational change in America. Please do not be angry or give up your efforts to make the change because one man cannot handle all the mail that hunger brings him.

The reviews came in large batches from the publisher. My friend Leo Litwak had told me to brace myself for attacks, and I had received plenty of advance warning upon the publication of the 1966 California issue that my ideas were anathema to certain circles within the Establishment. So I was surprised by what happened. It seemed that almost every paper in the country, from the big city dailies to the country weeklies, ran a review, and most were positive. Reading the more extravagantly favorable reviews was a curiously intimate experience, both warming and poignant. "This book," said the *Christian Science Monitor,* "deals boldly, radically, imaginatively, tenderly, with a vital subject. Mr. Leonard is not hard-selling panaceas but diffidently offering modest suggestions for revolutionizing the world." And there was praise even in the *Washington Post:* "George Leonard has a deep reverence for the innate creativity of the human animal and has articulated with a poet's passion the mutilation and death of that creativity in the environment called school." And in the *Boston Globe:* "Highly literate, immensely readable. Anyone who thinks about education can never again think about it in the same way." And in the *San Francisco Examiner: "Education and Ecstasy* is perhaps the most important book on schools, their problems, and their potential written in this generation. It is as exciting a discovery as you are likely to make between book covers this year." Even the Jackson, Mississippi,

Clarion-Ledger ran a positive review. It was such a short time ago that I had considered Jackson the heart of enemy territory.

Could this really be? Were these words real? Was there going to be a new education, the beginning of a transformed society? Hope rose up inside me, and hope was painful. I tried to go on about my business. I didn't want to be swept away by praise. Still, there was often a thrilling and frightening vertigo in my solar plexus. When William F. Buckley's conservative magazine, the *National Review,* blasted me, I was almost relieved. It was a major review, two pages of spite and fury that were supposed to be merely sarcastic and clever. It was mean-spirited from title ("A New Gnostic Kook Book") to final paragraph: *"Education and Ecstasy is a kook performance from cover to cover, even down to phys-ical details. The fact that the book was designed by a man named Kamp, and that the jacket photo was taken by one John Poppy, only adds to the fun."*

And then came the anticipated attacks on the book from the central bastions of the Establishment. The *New York Review of Books* called it "sentimental." The review was by Edgar Z. Friedenburg, whom I had criticized mildly in the book. *Saturday Review* was "mixed" on the neg-ative side. And the *New York Times Book Review,* after waiting for quite a while, perhaps to see if the book would just go away, mounted its attack. At one point in his review, Joseph Featherstone reported that after reading my rather emotional description of the ending of the first black-white marathon, his heart "was as cold as stone." I didn't doubt that in the least. Nor had I expected anything else. The Establishment attacks only clarified the battle lines and confirmed that any truly fun-damental change in schooling would be fiercely resisted. For those who wrote in the *New York Times Book Review* and the *New York Review of Books,* the real stuff of education was the lecture. "Fundamental change" meant tampering with curriculum requirements in secondary school and college.

At *Look,* the cabal of senior editors was in an uproar. On my first New York visit after the book's publication, some of them simply turned away when they saw me coming. One finally brought himself around to approaching me, but cautiously, as if I might bite. "I must say I found your education book rather off-putting," he said after a significant pause. "I can understand that," I said. I had learned not to argue.

After work I went to the Barberry Room with *Look*'s Chicago editor, Jack Star, who was also in town on a visit. Star was an old-time news-hawk, an easygoing guy who was cynical-funny rather than cynical-mean. He was neither an enemy nor a supporter. After a couple of drinks, he grinned and told me that Joe Roddy had phoned him in Chicago and asked him to phone Pat Carbine and urge her to "do something about Leonard." Roddy had told Star that he had already used up all his credibility with Carbine.

"Do something?" I said. "Do what?"

"Come on, George," he said with a laugh. "You know."

From the very beginning, the book was sold out all around the country. For three full weeks before Christmas, it was completely out of stock. When a top aide in the White House asked for a copy, there were none to be had. I refused to send my very last copy; the others had all been donated to similar special requests from VIPs. Finally a high executive at Delacorte gave up her one remaining copy.

While in New York, I got a phone call from a Harvard sophomore who had read the book and "had to" see me. He and a friend skipped classes and flew down the next day. They appeared with shining faces and we chatted for a while. I had the feeling that I should say something memorable or else they would be disappointed. Actually, I figured they were bound to be disappointed in any case. I had worked on the book off and on for more than five years, had written and rewritten it, had poured the best of me into it. The flesh-and-blood version couldn't possibly match up.

Their visit furnished one interesting fact. From the day of its publication, the book had been almost impossible to get at the Harvard Coop, or at any other bookstore in the area. There was one copy in their dormitory, their "house," and the residents had agreed to use it as they would a library book. At first students were allowed to keep it three days, then the time was reduced to two days, and now borrowers had to read it overnight. Already there were more than thirty names in the flyleaf.

Back in San Francisco, I was summoned by Alan Cranston, the newly elected senator from California. I met the senator-elect in his suite in the Fairmont with two of his aides. He hadn't quite finished reading the book, but he knew there was a lot of talk about it, and he wanted to get my ideas firsthand. I tried to explain in terms a politician could appreciate. He asked specifically what could be done in the next six years. I referred him to the proposal in Chapter Twelve for the creation of six experimental early-education schools, three of them in ghetto areas. We discussed this for a while. Cranston wasn't given to smiles; I couldn't be sure what he was thinking. Then — suddenly, crisply — he turned to his aides and said, "Let's make this a top priority when we get to Washington." As I left, he assured me he would take early action on my proposals. I never heard from him again.

And then there were the Very Rich People, the putative financial angels. Rarely had I had much to do with people of great means, so I didn't know what to expect. They approached me through their secretaries or assistants, and from the very first contact there were delicious hints of some sort of monetary Aladdin's lamp, cautiously veiled references to huge sums that might go to the creation of my school of the year 2001. I didn't want to build and run the school myself, but offered my full co-operation. Ah, but first, the dinner party. My wife and I must come and join Mr. and Mrs. Very Rich Person for dinner. With a few friends, of course.

And there would indeed be dinner, but no discussion of the grant. Before saying goodnight, Mr. VRP would somehow manage to drop hints of wonders to come. Then another dinner with another set of guests, and then another. And there was always one catch: Dinner wasn't a good place to get down to business, and Mr. VRP was willing to meet only at dinner. I finally caught on. The Very Rich People were primarily inter-ested in displaying a specimen, someone whose work was in vogue, to their guests. If the work faded in popularity, the specimen would proba-bly be dropped in favor of a new one. I got the idea that if I was willing to play the game, I might eventually be able to get some kind of grant for an experimental school, but only after many, many dinners and cocktail parties and God knows what else, and even then perhaps only a small grant, a bit of seed money, some modest contribution to a start-up fund — certainly nothing at all to match the evanescent bonanza that had been flashed before my eyes.

I wasn't willing to play the game. Try as I might, I simply couldn't get as interested in money as I should have been. Roz Bernstein once told me that I must have flunked avarice in college. I knew it was a lack in me, a basic flaw. I knew that if I wasn't attracted to money, money wouldn't be attracted to me. But that couldn't be helped. There was a vision of a viable transformed society waiting to be unearthed. I wanted to get on with my work.

But getting on with my work was getting harder every day. At the beginning of January 1969, my family and I moved to Mill Valley, a lovely village at the foot of Mt. Tamalpais, just fourteen miles from downtown San Francisco. It was the first house we had ever owned — a large, unpretentious, shingled house on a hill with a view of the moun-tain, a place of many nooks and crannies, just the kind I would have liked to have lived in as a child. At eight and four, our daughters, Lillie and Emily, were now free to roam the neighborhood; we could get a dog. A main reason for the move was that the nearest public school was sup-posedly a happy place as well as a center of experimental education. Lillie later said that moving from the city to Mill Valley was like going from black-and-white to Technicolor.

The second week in our new house, the phone rang at one A.M. Was it some family emergency? My heart was beating fast when I got up to take the call. It was a young man's voice, very loud and very excited, with the sound of many other excited voices in the background. A group of people in a community south of the city, he told me, had just finished a very important meeting. They had decided to start a new school based on my book. They had all voted to get things started by putting on a benefit with me as the main speaker. They wanted to let me know as soon as possible.

I paused for a moment, collecting my thoughts. I told him I was glad they were going to start the school and I wished them well, but that I had a lot of work to do and was not going to make a speech for them. He seemed astonished. After all, it was my book that had inspired them. And they had voted unanimously that I would be the speaker. It was as if I were presuming to take something away from them that they already possessed. I tried to be courteous and encouraging. The young man became increasingly reproachful. When I finally got off the phone, I had a hard time getting back to sleep.

Less than a week later, the phone again rang after midnight. The call was from a different community but otherwise almost identical to the previous one. The next morning I asked to have my phone number unlisted, something I had never previously considered.

By late January the world seemed to be closing in. The letters were coming faster than ever, and the phone calls to the office, and the requests to speak and consult. Requests were also coming into the New York office, and Bill Arthur was urging me to make some public appearances; it would be good publicity for *Look*. I loved the success of the book and I took delight in my ever-increasing fame, but I didn't like the pressures and distractions that went along with it. Still, I could at least do my part for *Look* and for the book, and maybe still have some time for myself and my work.

But then one day I got a letter from a woman in Sacramento. She wrote that she and three of her friends, all teachers, had driven to Mill Valley and had spent the afternoon driving around the town looking for me. That gave me a start. What did they want of me? If they had found me, what would they have done with me? About the same time I began getting reports from downtown merchants that people indeed were hunting for me. I asked the merchants not to reveal my whereabouts. I found myself looking over my shoulder whenever I went walking in the village center.

I had dreamed of fame, but I didn't know it would be like this. Mine probably wouldn't last very long, and it was about one thousandth that of the Beatles, but I had at least a small insight into what it must be like for them. It was a ball. It was a nightmare.

Some of the hunters found their prey. I would generally stand with them on the porch and chat for a while, and that would be enough. But one sunny spring day in 1969, four college students from the Midwest appeared at the door, and I let them in. Mike Murphy had come over and we were in the midst of a long talk, but we interrupted it to give the young men our full attention. We inquired about their life. They wanted to talk only about *Education and Ecstasy.* One of them asked me a question about the book. Before I could respond, one of the others answered for me, and the four of them argued the point hotly among themselves. Finally I got another question, the answer to which did not please them. All four seemed curiously opinionated and even belligerent. They had come a long way to see me, and now I could hardly get a word in. I was later to learn that this phenomenon — inexplicable belligerence in the presence of a literary hero — is quite common. But on this day, as their arguments about my book raged while Mike and I sat speechless, I found myself becoming increasingly frustrated and angry. Then I had an idea.

"Let's go play a game of touch football," I said out of nowhere.

The four of them looked at each other. They could hardly refuse. I drove Mike, and they followed in their car.

"Let's play real dirty," I said. "Tripping, clipping, full body blocks. Wasn't that awful?"

"It was pretty bad." Mike laughed. "Are you serious about playing dirty?"

"Absolutely. Let's give them something to remember."

We staked out a truncated football field at a local park, and picked one of the four college students to play on our side. Mike and I had often thrown a football back and forth as we talked, and had worked out a few simple pass patterns. He was a superb passer. That was enough. We scored three quick touchdowns. The three students on the other side scored once, our team scored again, and the game was over. My visitors went back to their car grass-stained, disheveled, and bruised. Driving back to the house, Mike and I agreed that it was a childish way to handle the frustration and anger of the hunted, but we couldn't deny it was fun. I felt much better.

When all was said and done, getting late-night phone calls was only a nuisance, and one that could be dealt with rather easily. The thousands of letters would eventually be answered, even if some of the answers turned out to be six to eight months late. And people who hunted me down could be challenged to a touch football game. The real problem created by the publication of *Education and Ecstasy* had to do with a possible change of career.

As the weeks and months passed, I began getting viable propositions to join in starting a model school based on the book. Maybe this would be the most important thing I could do to further the realization of human potential. Maybe I could take a year's leave of absence from *Look* and act as an active consultant in the start-up of a new school. Maybe I would end up wanting to do it the rest of my life.

I was by no means the first or only person in the sixties to propose alternatives to conventional education. A number of "free schools" based on Summerhill School in England were already operating. And there were Montessori schools and Waldorf schools and others. I had done a *Look* story the previous year on the Fifteenth Street School in New York City — as free a school as could be. A number of contemporary writers, mostly disaffected teachers, were calling for radical school reform, among them John Holt, Herbert Kohl, James Herndon, and Jonathan Kozol.

But *Education and Ecstasy* was different. It offered a specific future vision that seemed to cry out for immediate change. It specified a "new domain" for schooling, involving sensory, kinesthetic, emotional, interpersonal, and volitional education as well as the usual cognitive and vocational training. It insisted upon the creation of highly ordered, highly interactive learning environments, including the use of modern computer technology. Though I had no formal training in pedagogy or in computer technology, I felt I could be useful in helping create a school that might constitute a model for other schools. My life's path had arrived at another fork. My mind told me I should take it. My heart insisted I pass it by. It was not just that I wanted to keep producing stories for *Look*. I was also beginning to imagine another book, this one about the transformation of society: something larger than *Education and Ecstasy*, with broader and deeper foundations.

One day I was sitting at my typewriter when my daughter Burr, a freshmen at Berkeley, walked swiftly into the room and stood before me, hands on hips.

"Daddy," she said sternly, "I've decided you *have* to drop everything you're doing and go out and start a model school."

Burr's opinion on this subject counted as much, maybe more, than anyone else's. She was a child of the sixties. She had a strong feeling for the reform of the culture. She was a fierce supporter of my work. At that moment, I realized I had already made a decision.

"Who's going to make me?" I laughed.

"If no one else, I am."

"How are you going to make me? Whips? A gun at my head?"

It was a path not taken. During the late sixties and early seventies, many people were to create schools they claimed were based on *Education and Ecstasy*. Some of them succeeded. Most did not. Most emphasized negative reform: Grades are bad, so take them out; final exams are bad, so take them out; required attendance is bad, so take it out. In the euphoria and haste of the times, these reformers didn't stop to think that such things as exams and grades, no matter how oppressive, inefficient, and antithetical to learning, do provide the bailing wire that holds the old structure together. To remove them, it's necessary to put something in their place. Any attempt to create an environment with no reinforcement system at all can only lead to the growth of a covert reinforcement system, which is dangerous because it is unacknowledged and unexamined.

The school I imagined was fluid and free but actually highly disciplined, highly structured. Educators would have to work hard to create an environment that would allow children to learn to read as easily and successfully as they learn to speak. One problem lay in the fact that the kind of computer technology I had imagined wasn't yet available. But there was a bigger problem than that, one I wouldn't really understand until years later: the human potential stands not only as a nearly limitless boon to any society but also as an enormous threat.

Now that twenty years have passed, now that the necessary computer technology is coming on line, now that model classrooms based essentially on the vision of *Education and Ecstasy* have been built under the auspices of such organizations as AT&T and GTE, there is a chance to discover not only whether the vision works but whether it works only too well. When *Education and Ecstasy* was published, the year 2001 seemed far in the future. Now it's just around the corner.

For my part, the vision of 1968 has been tempered by time but has never faded. What was urgent then is far more urgent today. "Technology and our human potential," John Naisbett wrote in his 1986 book *Megatrends,* "are the two great challenges and adventures facing humankind today." There's no question in my mind that learning can be joyful and that we have only begun to tap the human potential. It is a possibility that remains to be realized.

32

Almost as Bad as a Divorce

1 9 6 9

FROM CHRISTMAS EVE into the early morning hours of Christmas 1968, three American astronauts in the spacecraft Apollo 8 circled the moon ten times. There had already been color photographs of the earth from space, but the pictures the Apollo 8 astronauts brought back were even more breathtaking. One of them showed the planet on which we lived rising enormously from the barren horizon of the moon — our earth a triumphant shining globe of glistening blue and swirling white, with continents rich in greens and browns and deserts of a vivid golden orange.

Back in 1966, Stewart Brand had run a one-man campaign under the rubric "Why Haven't We Seen a Photograph of the Whole Earth Yet?" Wearing a sandwich board and bearing a box of buttons and posters, all asking that question, he visited media offices and major universities around the nation as well as NASA headquarters in Houston. When he came to see me in San Francisco, he explained that NASA already had had plenty of chances to photograph the earth from space. Instead, the cameras on the spacecraft had always been turned out to the moon and the stars, away from us. If NASA would only turn the cameras around and show us our own home floating in the vastness of space, it would have a profound effect on our consciousness. It would force us to realize our poignant aloneness, our total interdependence.

Brand's campaign, as quixotic as it might have seemed, did have an effect in getting the pictures taken and published in 1967, perhaps a few months earlier than otherwise would have been the case. The following year Brand published the first *Whole Earth Catalog,* subtitled "Access to Tools." The tools he referred to were books and pamphlets with instructions for the kind of simple, independent living that would not pollute or damage the earth, along with the actual items — tents, solar heating devices, and the like — that would make such living possible. "We are as gods," Brand proclaimed, "and might as well get good at it."

The first pictures of the whole earth (which Brand used on the cover of his catalogue) were infinitely more spectacular than I had expected. And the Apollo 8 photograph of the earth rising from the moon's horizon was even more so. I remembered the Hollywood version of the earth from space in such old science-fiction movies as *Destination Moon*. The best the animators had been able to come up with was something like a library globe bearing outlines of North and South America. But how could the animators have dared imagine anything as gorgeous as reality itself?

Brand was right. Consciousness did change. The year 1969 saw a huge growth in concern for the biosphere. Millions of people learned the meaning of ecology during that year, and the conservation movement, concerned primarily with preserving wild areas, became the environmental movement, concerned not only with that but also with the struggle against pollution and the rape of the earth wherever it might occur.

My own concern for the environment, dating from the 1962 California issue, was heightened. I saw the environmental movement and our work with human potential as traveling essentially in the same direction. The worship of aggression and exploitation that stifled the realization of human capabilities also threatened the survival of the planet. The mechanization of relationships, the deadening of the emotions, the general depersonalization of life, would ultimately make possible the ruin of the biosphere as well as the murder of human potential.

Those pictures from space clarified things. The final arbiter of our destiny would be not generals or industrialists or land developers but the earth itself. In the long run, the most grandiose plans of presidents, prime ministers, and general secretaries would run up against its carrying capacity. There would finally be only so much abuse it could take before it laid waste to the ambitions of the exploiters. That shining globe floating in the loneliness of space became an emblem of human unity. The pictures had one ultimate message, endlessly repeated: brotherhood and sisterhood or death.

Price Cobbs and I had an outrageous dream: The solution to the race problem contains within it the solution to almost everything else that is wrong with our society. Our fears of differences, of change, of crossing boundaries find expression at the deepest level in our feelings about race. Our most destructive mechanisms of denial, projection, and fantasy come together in stark black and white. Price and I agreed that if we here in America could lick our race problems, then what couldn't we do? The dream might have been an outrageous one, but in those dangerous times we felt we had no alternative but to try to make it come true. At the beginning of April 1969, a year after the death of Martin Luther King, Jr., neither of us could have possibly foreseen that a seemingly petty racial episode at Esalen Institute could change the course of our lives.

The black-white marathon encounters were continuing to bring about what seemed miracles in understanding between the races. The encounter that we had done for *Look* in October 1968 had been held at the Humanist House in San Francisco, independently of Esalen; since I was an Esalen officer, I still felt that I shouldn't do a story specifically on the institute for *Look*. I poured my emotions into the text that went along with Paul Fusco's emotional pictures. We called the piece "How to Have a Bloodless Riot." It seemed remarkable that *Look* would run it, and especially in an issue that led off with John Poppy's coolly reasoned essay "Violence: We Can End It," and my article "Beyond Campus Chaos." In that article I called for such measures as college admission by lottery, and urged college administrators to be even bolder than radical students in matters of educational reform. The cover showed a young man in academic cap and gown wearing a gas mask and making the V sign. I was filled with wonder at the courage of the board of editors, especially Bill Arthur and Pat Carbine. That issue would undoubtedly offend about half of the *Look* staff as well as millions of readers, but they believed it was right and they let the presses roll.

And that wasn't all. Price had been called to Atlanta by the Southern Christian Leadership Conference to be a consulting psychiatrist for its Executive Committee. On November 21 I flew to Atlanta with a speech scheduled for the next day. Late that night, five of us met in my room at the downtown Marriott: Martin Luther King's successor, Dr. Ralph Abernathy; his lieutenant, Dr. Andrew Young; Price Cobbs and his fellow consultant, Betty Brandon; and I. We worked out a proposal to invite the newly elected Richard Nixon to join with us in a series of black-white encounters at the White House. The invitation was published, boxed in heavy lines, at the end of "How to Have a Bloodless Riot." We took care to have the document delivered to President Nixon himself before the *Look* article came out.

AN INVITATION TO PRESIDENT NIXON

For too long, the nation's thinking on race has been cold and abstract. National leaders often make decisions that affect the minorities, the have-nots, without personal knowledge of these people's feelings. We invite you and your staff, Mr. President, to join in a series of interracial confrontations, in the sincere belief that all concerned will profit by the experience.

We, the Executive Committee of the Southern Christian Leadership Conference, offer to participate with you and your people, and with representatives of the poor, the disenfranchised, the forgotten. Your affirmative response will bring new hope to the nation.

RALPH D. ABERNATHY
ANDREW YOUNG
Southern Christian Leadership Conference

It wasn't just a ploy. We wanted to do the workshop. We felt quite sure that if Nixon participated sincerely, he would never again be quite the same on the matter of race. Thirty million *Look* readers had a chance to see the invitation, signed by the two top leaders of Martin Luther King's organization.

Richard Nixon never responded.

On Thursday, April 3, 1969, Price Cobbs called. His voice was grave. He said there had been a racial episode at the San Francisco Esalen office involving one of our black group leaders, Ron Brown, and the new assistant administrator, a man I had not met named Bill Smith.

During a phone call with Smith, Ron Brown had brought up the subject of money. The interracial marathons, he said, were well attended. They were physically and emotionally draining. He thought that the flat fee of $125 that each of the two leaders received was inadequate. Shortly after he said this, Bill Smith said, "Fuck you," and hung up. Brown got in his car and drove over to the Esalen office to confront Smith. Brown was short, round, and generally rather jolly. But he knew how to express his emotions. After all, that was the essence of the black-white groups that he had been leading so effectively for Esalen. There was a lot of angry shouting, and then Smith threatened to call the cops.

Both Ron Brown and Price Cobbs saw blatant bigotry in this episode, especially in the threat to call the police. Honest confrontation was encouraged at Esalen. People were always shouting at each other. But no one had ever threatened to call in the police. It was unlikely that such a threat would have been made if Ron Brown had been white. Brown wanted an apology. Smith coldly refused to give one. He had only recently come to work for Esalen. Nobody knew much about him. Now Price and I would have to figure out what to do.

The answer came to us at the same moment. As soon as possible, we would have a black-white encounter involving Bill Smith and other members of the San Francisco office staff, Ron Brown and other members of the interracial team, and, most important, Mike Murphy. The problem was, Mike had gone to New York on a fund-raising mission and wouldn't be back for a couple of weeks. I phoned him in New York, explained that the matter was urgent, and asked him to fly back immediately to attend the encounter. Both of us knew we were involved in something that went far beyond a simple conflict between two people. Mike agreed to drop everything and fly back the next day for a meeting on Saturday afternoon.

It was Good Friday. It was also the first anniversary of Martin Luther King's death. Price Cobbs and I met for lunch at a restaurant near his office. The interior light was dim. The electric candle flames along the walls seemed strangely radiant. I found myself near tears. People of later generations might find it hard to appreciate the intensity and fullness of emotion, the sense of being joined in a larger destiny, that attended such moments in the late sixties. Price and I began talking in hushed voices. We spoke of Dr. King and of his hopes and of our hopes. We reviewed the success of our interracial encounter program. Then Price began speaking of the many humiliations, both large and small, to which blacks are subjected almost every day: the slights that go unnoticed by whites, the eyes turned quickly away, the sudden pause in conversation upon the approach of a black person, the bigotry that the bigot would never, never admit as such, the subtle and not-so-subtle discrimination in jobs, in housing, even in seating arrangements at conferences and parties. And most of this ignored, treated as if it isn't really happening, as if it isn't real, creating a situation in which a black person must collude in denying reality and thus go slightly mad, or cling to reality at the cost of a persisting rage.

Now, Price continued, we had a case in point here at Esalen of all places, and we weren't going to collude in its denial. We wouldn't let it pass unnoticed. We wouldn't table it for further discussion. We had the best possible instrument for solving this problem and thus for creating a matrix for solving many other problems of overt and covert racism throughout our society. We wouldn't just skate around on the surface of things. We would plunge straight down to the heart of darkness. And the reconciliation that emerged from that deep plunge would be real and lasting.

"I really believe," Price said, "that if we can make this episode work out for everyone concerned, it will be a strong indication that the race problem in America can be solved."

His words seared my heart.

We gathered early Saturday afternoon in Price Cobbs's conference room and sat around in a circle on the floor. Ron Brown, Mike Brown, John Poppy, Price, and I represented the black-white group. Mike Murphy had come in from New York. Bill Smith was there with David Barr, the manager of the Esalen San Francisco office. Will Schutz and Ben Weaver, the current Esalen Big Sur manager, had driven up, uninvited, from Big Sur. Price and I argued that the Big Sur residents had no business at the meeting, but there was a consensus in the group to let them participate. I knew that Schutz was a strong supporter of the interracial program.

When I first saw Bill Smith, I was dismayed. He was wearing aviator-style dark glasses and was sitting rigidly against the wall. His jaw was tight. The encounter started off at full bore. Ron Brown shouted at Bill Smith and urged that he shout back, but Smith remained rigid and controlled. "I was only doing my job," he said between clenched teeth. Smith had talked with Mike Murphy before the meeting, had wept, and had told Mike that he had worked as a lobbyist for civil rights legislation. In the group, Mike lost his temper and tried to tell the blacks about Smith's civil rights work. But the blacks weren't having any of that. That was history. They wanted some sort of acknowledgment from Smith that he was *not* free of racism. But Smith was unyielding. "I was only doing my job" was practically the only thing he would say. After less than an hour, Smith walked out, supposedly to go to the bathroom. He didn't return.

The encounter continued, but it didn't seem quite right with the focal character of the drama missing. Still, we had to do something. For Price and me, the outcome of this particular group was going to be momentous. None of us, it turned out, really wanted Smith fired. We wanted him honestly illuminated on the matter of race, or at least put in a position where illumination would be possible. Finally we all agreed on a solution: We would ask him to go to Esalen at Big Sur for a period of contemplation before resuming his duties. It was a strange outcome for a meeting that had brought Mike Murphy all the way from New York. Getting a paid vacation at one of the most beautiful places in the world could hardly be considered a plunge to the heart of darkness. Still, we had done *something*. Smith wouldn't be at the San Francisco office for a while, and he would have a chance to reconsider his actions.

The meeting broke up and we all walked over to a nearby bar to celebrate. We drank toasts to the outcome of the encounter, to our solidarity, and to the future.

The next day the agreement came unraveled. What we hadn't known was that when Smith had left the meeting, he had gone straight to a phone and called Esalen cofounder Dick Price in Big Sur. Price was outraged by Smith's report. To him, the group meeting was a power play on the part of the interracial leaders, an attempt to dictate to Esalen. He phoned Mike Murphy and urged him not to give in to pressure. Dick Price's words had a strong effect. Through the years Mike had resisted every attempt by any group to achieve dominant power at Esalen. He had always sought reconciliation, had always wanted to make everybody happy. He knew that the issue meant a great deal to Price Cobbs and me, but despite the encounter, he didn't know how much.

It was around the middle of the day on Easter Sunday when I got Mike's phone call. His voice was flat. He told me of talking with Dick Price. He said that what he would like to do was to have breakfast with Bill Smith every morning for the foreseeable future, until Smith was clear on the matter of racism.

"Have breakfast every morning?" I said in disbelief. "But we have a firm agreement that he's going to Big Sur."

Mike went on in the same flat voice, obviously wanting to bring me around but with little hope of doing so. I made my points: that the issue of race was crucial to the whole nation, that we did have an agreement, that going down to Big Sur wasn't much to ask of Bill Smith. Mike said a little about Dick Price's feelings, but not much. He kept assuring me that he would see to it that there were no further racial incidents and that he would personally handle Bill Smith. Each word was like another blow. I could tell that Mike wasn't going to give an inch. I felt totally betrayed.

I asked Mike if he would mind holding the phone for five minutes. I had already made my decision, but I wanted to run it past someone. My twenty-year-old daughter Mimi, who was living in San Francisco, was staying in Mill Valley for the Easter weekend. She had spent a summer at Esalen. She had participated in the first interracial marathon. I had already told her what had happened in the previous day's encounter. Now I explained what Mike had said on the phone, and what I felt I had to do.

"I can't see that you have any alternative," she said.

Back at the phone, I told Mike that we would still be friends but that I was resigning as vice president of Esalen. Mike was so stunned that he could hardly speak; he had had no idea that I would resign. He asked me to reconsider, but didn't spend much time trying to talk me out of it. Both of us were too hurt, and too numb, to say anything else.

Price and the other members of the interracial team were also stunned by my action. The next day all of them resigned from Esalen. The encounters would still go on, but under the auspices of Price's organization, Pacific Management Systems. John Poppy and Earle Marsh and I, the other regular white leaders, would continue to participate. But it wouldn't be the same. Nothing would be the same. A friendship that had begun on February 2, 1965, was suddenly shattered. If something so deep and valuable could break so quickly, then what couldn't break?

*

Afterward Mike and I tried to be friends. We were civil and polite. We phoned each other when it was necessary to discuss something we had already set in motion. But days would go by without a call, then weeks. We rarely met. Mike kept trying to make things right. He had breakfast with Bill Smith for a while and found him more difficult than he had expected. Smith went on down to Esalen in Big Sur anyway, and presumably sat around reflecting on the matter of race, but that didn't make much difference. Finally Mike fired him. Maybe he had planned to do it all along, but not under pressure. Mike had already become friends with Ron Brown and Mike Brown, and now he began seeing them more often. It was ironic that the friendship between Mike and the two young black leaders of the interracial team continued and deepened while he and I remained estranged.

It was almost as bad as a divorce. I was well aware of Mike's quiet work toward reconciliation, but I couldn't shake the sense of betrayal. The hopes of Good Friday and the wounds of Easter Sunday were intricately joined with summers in Monroe, Georgia, with the illuminations of my childhood and the essential truth of my middle years. The pain of Easter Sunday was still sharp enough to prevent me from remedying the ache of separation.

33

Seven Ghettos in Seven Days

THE DECADE of the sixties was nearing its end. With Ronald Reagan in the California governor's mansion and Richard Nixon in the White House, the forces of repression grew bolder. As repression increased, protest movements became more and more revolutionary. There was no way, finally, to reject the rumors that FBI agents were infiltrating radical organizations, and in some cases providing weapons and materials to make bombs. But even where the FBI was not involved, reformist groups were beset by internal divisions. The intensity of the times encouraged unrealistic goals, hasty actions, and shattered relationships. If my breakup with Mike Murphy was unique, it was also representative.

In mid-July Martin Goldman came out for a staff visit. Goldman, a very serious, very passionate man, had been appointed managing editor of *Look,* and now it was his turn to be "California-ized," as *Look* staff members termed it. Lillie and I entertained him royally. There were overnight trips to Carmel, then along the precarious back road to the Zen center at Tassajara; a hike on Mt. Tamalpais, and dinner at the best restaurants in Marin County. We invited him for cocktails and a buffet supper with the leaders of the interracial team. I liked Martin very much and enjoyed his company. But for me there was a feeling of sadness, a sense of something missing. I knew that Martin had enjoyed Mike Murphy in New York. His absence now was always with us.

On May 15, a beautiful spring day, I arranged a brainstorming luncheon in San Francisco for Goldman and sixteen California futurists. After the meeting ended in midafternoon, he and John Poppy and my daughter Burr and I got into a rented convertible and headed across the Bay Bridge for Berkeley. Burr was going to be our guide on a tour of the university. As we approached the campus, we began to sense that something was amiss. There wasn't the usual amount of traffic, and up ahead we could see two helicopters circling at a low altitude. At the next stoplight I pulled up next to a van painted white with a crude red cross.

The long-haired young men in it were wearing white armbands.

"What's happening?" I asked.

"Man, they're shooting people up there. People's Park. We're taking care of the wounded."

Just then we began to smell tear gas. The authorities must have picked this day to clear out People's Park. About a month earlier, a group of young radicals had started to make a park of some unused university land. Thousands of students and local residents had joined in, laying sod, planting flowers, building benches and swings, playing music, cooking, and just hanging out. People's Park became a symbol of the youth movement's utopian impulse. But university officials announced they wouldn't tolerate this unauthorized use of their property. With Ronald Reagan's active support, they ordered the police to build a barbed wire fence around the park.

I turned the car radio on. There were live reports of a raging battle, with helicopters dropping tear gas not only on the People's Park area but on the whole city of Berkeley. The police were using shotguns on the students; many were wounded and one reportedly was dead. We didn't say a word. We just kept driving toward the campus. The main street was barricaded. We turned right, weaved around other barriers. There were more and more signs of battle: young men and women running with handkerchiefs tied over their noses, other limping along with blood on their faces.

Still not speaking, we parked the car and walked toward the campus. A series of explosions went off behind us. We started running, holding handkerchiefs over our noses. I didn't know exactly where I was going, but noticed we were getting closer to the campus. We ran across an empty lot, then slowed to a walk. A cloud of tear gas came rolling down the street to the left of us. We ran to the right. It all began to seem like a dream. Though we ran first one way, then the other, we kept getting closer to the campus. A curious thought went through my mind: We came here to show Martin Goldman the campus, and dammit, we're going to show him the campus.

We entered through Sather Gate. We started walking across Sproul Plaza, the scene of innumerable student protests. Now it was empty and blessedly clear of tear gas. Suddenly a police officer came running around the corner of a building. He startled us, but we must also have startled him. He dropped down into a crouch and aimed his revolver directly at us. We froze. For what seemed a long time — maybe it was three seconds — everything was balanced precariously between life and death. Then the policeman cursed and ran on.

We continued across Sproul Plaza and climbed the stairs to the Terrace, the place where some years earlier students had sat reading the "Explosive Generation" issue of *Look*. It too was deserted. The four of us had somehow made it to the center of the campus, to a vantage point from which we could see everything that might happen on the plaza.

There was a blast of trumpets and strings. Somebody had set up a powerful sound system on a store rooftop just outside the campus, and now, louder than several full orchestras, a joyful orchestral piece by Handel was sweeping over the scene of battle. Two policemen ran into the plaza from the right, their revolvers drawn. We ducked down beneath the waist-high wall of the Terrace. I peeked over the edge of the wall in time to see two tear gas canisters skittering across the concrete of the plaza. The whole scene was so surreal that I could note with a small surge of satisfaction that the canisters exploded in perfect rhythm with the triumphant music pouring from the rooftop. As the policemen retreated, three tall, long-haired young men, bare to the waist, ran into the plaza from the left and hurled large stones at them. The stones whistled through the air on an impressive trajectory and barely missed their targets. The wind carried the tear gas directly away from us. We were trapped, but we were safe.

For a while the battle raged back and forth across the plaza, and I was strangely detached, as if it were all a dream. Once an officer briefly aimed his revolver at us. We quickly ducked behind the wall, then peered up as the officers again retreated. I was not afraid. I was glad that if this had to happen, Martin Goldman was here to experience it. For years John and I had been writing about events that must have seemed improbable from the perspective of an office on Madison Avenue. And it was not just here in California. All over the nation, on sylvan campuses and in the ruined heart of the ghettos, human passions were being answered with tear gas and clubs and drawn guns, and a bloodless order was being purchased at the cost of broken skulls and bloody faces. Martin, along with the other top editors, had believed us and supported us in our proposals for a different kind of order, putting their own reputations on the line for our unconventional perception of things. Now we were at least in part validated, and more than that, so was he.

It was impossible to say how long we were trapped there on the Terrace, but the battles finally moved elsewhere and we were able to make our way back to the car. Martin thanked us for showing him the Berkeley campus. The experience, he told us, would change the way he thought. "There's something quite radicalizing," he said in his rather formal way, "about having a policeman aim his gun at you."

*

My break with Mike Murphy and Esalen was big news in the New York
Look office. On my next trip there, I noticed more than a few self-satis-
fied grins among the cabal. Joe Roddy was the leader of the opposition,
but at least he was open about it. He walked up to me in the research
department looking concerned, even sympathetic. Was it unfeigned? I
doubted that. He said he had heard about my breakup with Murphy, and
I must feel pretty bad.

"Yeah, I do," I said suspiciously, waiting for whatever was coming
next. Was there a little crack in his façade of brotherly-fatherly concern?
Did I spot a flicker of wicked glee?

He went on to say that perhaps he was not entirely misguided in ad-
ducing that this latest development might have somewhat altered my sentiments on the larger subject of Esalen.

He looked at me searchingly. I searched back, and to my astonishment
could find no hint of the incipient sly chuckle, the ironic twist of the lips
that I had become accustomed to. No, he seemed actually magnanimous.
My God, it seemed he might even reach out and *touch* me.

Suddenly I understood. He was offering to take me back into the fold.
With a word, a gesture, I could regain my membership in the club. And
how nice, how comfortable, how *restful* that would be. Actually, I had
no complaint whatever about what those who attacked me were producing for *Look;* it was the usual thoughtful, compassionate stuff. But I
hesitated only a moment. I told him that Mike Murphy and I had had a
conflict on an administrative matter having to do with the interracial
group, and that I had resigned as vice president in protest.

"But that doesn't change how I feel about Esalen," I said. "I think this
culture needs Esalen. If an Esalen didn't already exist, somebody would
have to invent one. I support it fully."

Roddy shrugged and walked off. He looked disappointed.

There was something bizarre about it from the beginning: fifteen
senior journalists from the nation's most influential media descending
from the sky in a luxurious jetliner and being swept away to the centers
of the nation's worst ghettos — seven ghettos in seven days. This junket
to the Third World culture within our own borders was cosponsored by
the National Urban League and Time-Life, with Boeing Aircraft Company providing the plane, a 737 fitted with easy chairs and couches and
two fully stocked bars. We would be given guided tours of the ghettos in
Cleveland, Detroit, Chicago, San Francisco-Oakland, Los Angeles, Watts,
and Atlanta. We would spend at least one night with ghetto residents.
We would end up in Washington for a meeting with Daniel Patrick Moynihan, President Nixon's adviser on urban affairs. The journalists on the

tour included Osborn Elliott, the editor of *Newsweek,* William F. Buckley, Jr., from the *National Review,* ABC's Joseph C. Harsch, the nationally syndicated columnist Joseph Kraft, and senior staffers from *Time, Life, Look, Atlantic Monthly,* NBC, the *Wall Street Journal,* the *Washington Post,* and the *New York Times.*

Despite the rather grotesque juxtapositions and the compressed time schedule, the tour might prove to be useful. It was the beginning of another long, hot summer; nobody knew whether the cities would again explode. Some of the journalists on the tour had done their own stories or edited those of others on "the situation in the cities" without ever having visited the ghettos. Maybe some perceptions would be changed. In any case, the journalists would write their own stories of the tour, and they wouldn't be able to complain that some armchair editor had distorted what they wrote. Bill Arthur asked me if I wanted to go. I had already spent a great deal of time in the ghettos and also had logged many hours in black-white encounter. Still, I might learn something new. Then too, I had a secret agenda: I wanted to see what I could learn about the media. My first lesson came on the very first day.

We took off before dawn. It was too early to get the morning *New York Times.* There were jokes on the flight about how hard it was to eat breakfast without reading the *Times.* It was still early when we landed at Cleveland, not at the municipal airport but at a small field at the edge of Lake Erie. Cars were waiting near the plane to sweep us into the heart of the ghetto. It was impossible to get a copy of the *Times.* We spent the whole morning touring the ghetto, and my colleagues still hadn't had their morning fix. Our schedule was tight; in the afternoon, we were hustled directly onto the plane for a quick flight to Detroit. Still no *Times.* Now the joking was getting a little edgy. Was I imagining things, or were some of my colleagues' eyes darting around? Were hands trembling a little more than usual? I had always suspected that the *Times* served as a mind-altering substance, a reality-fixative for the nation's media, but I hadn't previously witnessed what now appeared to be overt withdrawal symptoms.

At Detroit we again landed at a small airport. Most of the journalists were quickly out of their seats. As soon as the stairs went down, one of them ran to the small terminal building. As I descended the stairs, I saw him re-emerge at the door of the terminal, cup his hands around his mouth, and shout, "It's here! It's heeeeeeerrrre!" The others tried to keep from running. They stood in line, panting only slightly as they waited for their daily fix.

In Detroit I spent the night in the apartment of a Mrs. Hattie Frazier. The apartment was located in the center of a ghetto area, but it was clean and neat. Some residents had at the last minute refused to house white journalists, creating a scramble for substitute accommodations. But my stay was pleasant and uneventful, and Mrs. Frazier fixed me some wonderful grits and bacon for breakfast.

In Chicago we attended a church service led by the Reverend Jesse Jackson, the twenty-seven-year-old leader of SCLC's antihunger organization, Operation Breadbasket. Jackson gave new life to the word *charismatic*. He led his congregation in an antiphonal chant:

> (The preacher) I may be black —
> (The congregation) BUT I AM SOMEBODY!
> I may be poor —
> BUT I AM SOMEBODY!
> I may be on welfare —
> BUT I AM SOMEBODY!
> I may not have anything to eat in my pantry —
> BUT I AM SOMEBODY!

All of us were impressed by Jackson, enough to speculate that he might someday inherit the mantle of Martin Luther King. But I doubt if any of us would have predicted on that May morning in 1969 that in less than twenty years he would be a major figure in the race for president of the United States. And it would have been hard to imagine then how many big American cities would have black mayors in far less than twenty years. I would have been more than pleased — overjoyed would be a better word — to know that Martin Luther King's sidekick Andrew Young would be mayor of Atlanta.

It's true that when the miraculous happens it quickly begins to seem commonplace. Today we complain that the plight of black Americans is in some ways as bad as or even worse than it was in the sixties. But not to credit the enormous, breathtaking victories of the civil rights movement is to dishonor the sacrifices of those who made them possible and to discourage people who work to make further gains.

During the three short flights that had brought us to Chicago, I had spent most of my time sitting on the jump seat between the two company pilots Boeing had furnished for the flight. I had asked them scores of questions about the performance characteristics of the 737, about flight procedures, radio dialogue, and anything else I could think of. I had filled ten pages of my notebook with technical information. The two pilots seemed happy to have an interested observer; perhaps it alleviated the boredom.

When we took off from Chicago around lunchtime on Saturday, I stayed back in the cabin to sip a vodka-and-tonic and chat with columnist Joe

Kraft. Bill Buckley sat nearby at a table next to the cockpit door, typing away at his newspaper column. We rose smoothly through the hot, dirty air of Chicago to a brilliant blue upper atmosphere. As soon as we leveled off, the copilot came back into the cabin and walked up to me.

"If you haven't had anything to drink yet, maybe you'd like to come up front and get a little stick time."

"Oh no, nothing," I said quickly, and, "Yes, yes, I'd love to."

I followed him to the cockpit and strapped myself in the right seat. The pilot spent a few minutes briefing me on the control systems, then reached up to disengage the autopilot.

"It's all yours," he said.

I hadn't flown a plane for many years and had never flown a jet transport, but it all came back, a treasure still safely buried in neurons and nerve fibers and the memory of the musculature. There had been a time in my early twenties when I had loved flying more than anything else in life, and now I discovered that the love was still there, pulsing through my arms and legs, pervading my entire body, lifting my heart. I marveled at how well the swiftly moving plane responded to the controls as we sailed high over the rich green fields of Iowa. After the B-25s and A-20s I had flown in World War II, this was like going from a Model A Ford to a Cadillac. The pilot watched me closely from the left seat.

"Not bad," he said with a grin.

The pilot continued to handle the radio communications, but it wasn't long before I was handling everything else. There came a moment when he stepped out of the cockpit briefly, leaving the plane to me. He was gone only a few seconds, but during that period I heard a cry of alarm. I looked back and there was Bill Buckley, leaning around from his typewriter table to peer into the cockpit.

"My *God*, George, what are you *doing?*" he said. His normally ruddy face was ghostly white. Just then the pilot hurried back into the cockpit and took the left seat.

I continued to fly the plane for two hours, across the badlands of Nebraska, the deserts of Wyoming, the snow-capped Rockies. It was a day of vibrant blue and dazzling white and high vistas that recalled the photographs of the earth from space. I knew that those photographs in all their loveliness couldn't erase the ugliness we had seen in Cleveland, Detroit, Chicago. During all that time at the controls of the plane, however, I never once thought of anguished ghettos or cruel fences or lost friendships or wounded love. There was only the abstract purity of flight and high technology, the hypnosis of distance. It was probably not much different from the experience of young men thousands of miles away sitting at the controls of B-52 bombers over Vietnam, young abstractionists fascinated by objective problems of velocity and momentum and grid coordinates encoded in electronic inertial devices. But the bombs actuated by those devices, once released, would end their flight in a less abstract world of blood and suffering and death and individual accountability, from which even altitude offers no final sanctuary.

In San Francisco I played hooky and spent a night at home. My colleagues reported that they had been verbally abused most harshly at the downtown headquarters of the San Francisco State Black Students Union. But they had, as usual, maintained their composure and objectivity. In Los Angeles we were lectured by Black Congress leader Ron Karenga. In nearby Watts, we checked into the community's only motel. The rooms had no television sets or phones or hot water, but full-length mirrors were mounted on the ceiling above the beds. After checking in, we were driven to a community supper at the Watts Community Workshop. The meal was a happy occasion, with fried chicken, collard greens, black-eyed peas, and cornbread. But after supper, on a tour of the facilities, we white journalists again came under attack.

We were standing in a meeting room furnished with a large table, surrounded by blacks demanding to know why we didn't tell the truth about the situation in the black communities. As the attacks became increasingly abusive, I felt something swelling up inside me. I was sick of the attacks, but I was even sicker of our failure to respond. There was something almost shameful about the failure to answer expressions of frustration and rage. There was something pathetic not just about our *whiteness,* but about our flat, bloodless, colorless "objectivity." It was a feeling I had experienced many times during interracial encounters. Finally I could bear it no longer.

"Goddammit!" I shouted at the top of my voice, throwing the brochure I was holding down on the table. "I'm *sick* and *tired* of hearing this shit." The brochure slid across the table and knocked a drinking glass against the wall, shattering it with a most satisfying sound. "You haven't been reading my stories, dammit," I shouted. "For *years* I've been writing about what it's like in the ghetto. For *years.* Why the hell haven't you read my stories?"

The leader of the blacks paused a split second, then yelled back at me, and within seconds we were nose to nose, shouting at each other at the tops of our lungs, and the other blacks were joining in, and all our voices were rocking and rolling and resounding off the walls of the meeting room. It was a goddam, all-out black-white confrontation, and what made it wonderful was not the content of the words but the rhythm, the uninhibited, healing release of pent-up feelings. I noticed vaguely during the uproar that my white colleagues were absolutely still and pale. Later, several of them told me that they had been terrified. Here we were in the very middle of Watts, surrounded by militant blacks, and one of their group was acting like a madman.

The shouting lasted ten minutes or so. Then the black leader started trying to soothe me. "You shouldn't be getting yourself all frustrated," he said gently. "You know what we're talking about is our survival." I said I understood that. But still I wanted him to read the next issue of *Look,* which would carry the black-white encounter story and the open letter to President Nixon from Ralph Abernathy and Andy Young. I made him promise me that he would read it. Then I went around to each of the blacks who had been shouting at me, getting each one in turn to promise that he would read my story. This too was part of the essential rhythm of the encounter.

Shortly after that we were driven back to the motel. I tried to give my interpretation of what had happened to some of my colleagues. I said that my confrontation with the blacks hadn't been a case of verbal violence or aggression but only the acknowledgment of reality. I went ahead to propose that until we could acknowledge that reality, not just through objective analysis but through personal experience, the tension between the races could never be relieved. But I don't think I explained it clearly enough. In any case, I barely recognized myself in the descriptions of the episode later published by my colleagues. One article had me banging my fist on the table. In another, I threw my glass across the room. With all their objectivity, they didn't even get the opening salvo right.

Atlanta, my hometown: a new stadium, civic center, arts center; a new skyline that might be said to reveal the energy, the enthusiasm, and the values of this age and this people. Also a shadow self: slums. Our black guide seemed half out of his head. Words couldn't express his outrage. He opened his mouth, but nothing came out. The right half of his face contorted until an eye was almost closed. His head bobbed from side to side as if receiving invisible blows from right and left. There was, you see, this . . . *injustice.* He drove with dogged fury. He had a list of seventeen ghetto areas and would show us every one. Near the airport: unpainted shacks, sagging dirt roads, outhouses, no mail delivery. A freight train bumped heavily past; every car was loaded with three decks of shining new automobiles from the neighboring Ford plant. Our auto springs creaked as we porpoised over gulleys and shot out past the Carling Brewery toward the next ghetto. Six days of this kind of touring had exhausted us. The journalist who shared this guide and car with me wondered if we would have to see *all* seventeen. Our guide's head cocked to one side. He tried to answer, but nothing came out. He drove on fu-

riously. *(Injustice!)* Rutted roads, rotting wood. Two young blacks waiting to cross a street cursed our white faces. "What are you staring at? Go
on home." We glimpsed a headline, something about the flight of Apollo
10. It seemed that once again Americans would successfully circumnavi-
gate the moon. Our guide grunted. A front wheel had jammed in a deep
rut and the back wheel spun until the ugly, acrid smell of burning rubber
made us cough. At last we lurched out of our trap (during which interval
Apollo 10 had glided effortlessly a thousand or so miles through space)
and continued our tour. At the end, the odometer showed that we had
traveled more than a hundred miles, almost all of it within slums.

"Will there be riots?" I asked our guide.

"Not this summer maybe. People can't get together. But maybe . . ."
He smiled in, toward himself.

Our tour ended in Washington. We had breakfast with Whitney Young
of the Urban League, then went on to a meeting at the Executive Office
Building with urban affairs adviser Pat Moynihan, OEO director Donald
Rumsfeld, Agriculture Secretary Clifford Hardin, and other administration notables. We had elected *Newsweek* editor Oz Elliott to present our
"findings." In the middle of Elliott's summary, Bill Buckley was spirited
off for a tête-à-tête with President Nixon at the White House. The conservatives were in, no fooling.

The room was pleasant, high ceilinged, with pale yellow walls and
heavy draperies of red, green, and white. The hushed sound of the air
conditioning insulated us from the rest of the world. We all had on our
best suits and ties. Elliott spoke of the ghetto blacks' enormous distrust
of the Establishment. He told the administration officials how impressed
we all were with the quality of the black leadership. He spoke of an
urgent need for action. He said all of this in sincere, well-measured tones.
He was cool and reasonable.

Pay Moynihan appeared to be bored. I found myself fascinated by his
face, which at first glance seemed that of a genial Irish drunk, both ar-
rogant and foppish. My eyes were drawn to his wide bow tie of red and
gold, his luxuriant gray hair, his perpetually raised eyebrows, his moist,
mobile, always open mouth. What marvelous secrets lay beneath that
extraordinary exterior? What was he really up to? But we never talked
about things like that.

There were horrors out there in the ghettos. There was injustice. I felt
sure that Elliott wanted to do something about it. We all wanted to. But
why was he talking in such a matter-of-fact way, in such pleasant tones?
Why were all of us so calm, so well contained? I began to feel uncomfortable. Something was building up inside me. *(Injustice!)* I felt almost

as I had at Watts. I wanted to shout, to bang my fist on the table, to throw a glass across the room — anything to shatter this polite, proper, unfeeling recitation, anything to awaken these powerful, self-contained men not only to the tragedy of the ghetto culture but also to its richness and its joy.

It all came clear in the pleasant room with its cool, filtered air: We had settled for a Cartesian world, an objective world of extension and motion without feelings, color, taste, or smell. There were worse worlds. Unbridled emotion was by no means the answer; but neither was unbridled rationality uninformed by the wisdom of the heart and soul. Either one without the other would falsify human communication and action. I wanted to cry out, but this room was not a place of the heart and soul. Any attempt at the true expression of human feelings would be treated as an aberration. It would probably make things worse. Journalists, like the crews of B-52 bombers, were supposed to be objective.

In any case, whether out of wisdom or timidity, I kept quiet. And when my turn came to speak, I made my points about the need for empathy, for personal involvement, in measured, judicious words.

What could I do?

34

"I Read the News Today, Oh Boy . . ."

What could I do?

In the summer of 1969, the sixties revolution was still alive, but much of it had turned confrontational and violent. The civil rights movement, the inspiration for every liberation movement of the decade, had done its seemingly miraculous work in the South; legal segregation in America was dead. But the movement's stirring songs, its Gandhian self-sacrifice, had proven ineffective in the cities of the North and West. If violence, as H. Rap Brown claimed, was "as American as cherry pie," then black protest was becoming thoroughly Americanized. The year had begun with a series of student strikes and building seizures by militant blacks, who demanded black study programs, more black faculty members, and sometimes even open enrollment for all Third World people. The strikes gained some concessions, but also stiffened the resolve of conservative forces. Meanwhile, such Student Nonviolent Coordinating Committee leaders as Brown and Stokely Carmichael were flying around the country demanding revolution by almost any means, and the Black Panther party was calling for armed self-defense and a strategy of urban guerrilla warfare.

The New Left too was shifting from participatory democracy and consensus to inflammatory rhetoric, factionalism, and the call for violence. SDS had 304 chapters in 1969, an all-time high. But just at this moment of burgeoning local membership, the organization's national leadership burst apart. Out of the explosion emerged a revolutionary group called Weathermen. The name came from a Bob Dylan line, "You don't need a weatherman to know which way the wind blows," and the group planned attacks on the police and even bombings to end the Vietnam War and bring down the American government and its "racist empire."

There was still talk in the hippie culture of love and flower power, and of an overnight transformation of society through a radical change of consciousness. Communes still were springing up, in both rural and urban settings. The number of community-based underground newspapers had risen from 5 in 1967 to 150 in 1969. And in August of that year the Woodstock music festival gave the world an ecstatic vision of unselfish, nonmaterialistic community. But if the five hundred thousand people who lived in cow pastures near Woodstock, New York, for three summer days in near-perfect harmony thought that the next festival would attract a million people and be even more peaceful, they were wrong.

While some phases of the sixties revolution seemed to be peaking, others were just getting started. In June 1969, thousands of gays in New York City rioted, threw bricks, and set fire to police cars to protest police harassment of homosexuals; the previously unthinkable term "gay pride" burst upon the national consciousness. And it was also in that year that the women's liberation movement, which had smoldered throughout the decade, caught fire in the national media and the conscience of the nation — the belated recognition of a movement that was to change the shape of American life perhaps as much as all the others put together.

Still, in the summer of 1969 it was becoming increasingly clear that the transformation of America was not going to happen overnight. The Pentagon wasn't going to be levitated. We weren't going to wake up one day and find shoppers dancing in the aisles of the supermarkets. There wasn't going to be an interracial encounter session in the White House. The euphoria of 1966 was gone. During that year — it seemed a long time ago — I had been able to let my young daughters play on Haight Street with no thought for their safety. Now I made sure to check my own backside when I walked in that neighborhood. There were still flowers in the Haight-Ashbury, but there were also handguns. If the culture had turned hostile, so had the counterculture. One day I passed a white van parked near Haight Street with large block letters painted on the side: PEACE ON YOU. And still the Vietnam War went on.

My breakup with Mike Murphy and Esalen had sobered me. I began to realize that the transformation of a culture, even of an organization, was going to be a long, slow, laborious process. It wasn't going to proceed at an even tempo, but in fits and starts. Every significant change would create its own resistance to change; there were no straight lines in history. Social reform movements emerged, grew strong, did their work, and disappeared. Sometimes they disappeared because they had no effect on the culture. Sometimes they disappeared because they were absorbed and compromised by the culture. Sometimes they had such a powerful and pervasive effect that they were no longer needed or even recognized as different or separate from the culture.

What could I do? In an era of Nixon and Reagan and conservative backlash, I saw a transformation as more urgently needed than ever. Strident rhetoric and sporadic violence weren't the answer. To think that the U.S. government could be overthrown by homemade bombs and attacks on the police was arrant stupidity. And even if this sort of violence could prevail, I would hate to think about the kind of governance that would follow. A benign transformation might be possible in a democratic society if large numbers of people recognized that change was adaptive and necessary. This recognition would require the broad dissemination of accurate, relevant, understandable, and compelling information. It would further require the presentation of viable alternatives to our present way of life. That would be only a beginning; the whole system of values and rewards would eventually have to be revamped. But in a democracy, the flow of information ideally precedes and informs structural change; thus, the transformation of society requires the transformation of the media — television, radio, newspapers, and magazines.

It was in any case an exhilarating challenge. The human potential, a resource of unfathomable dimensions, still cried out for realization. Even the earth itself, as we were belatedly beginning to understand, demanded a fundamental change in our values and actions. When Neil Armstrong and Buzz Aldrin stepped onto the surface of the moon on July 20, they gave the inhabitants of this planet not just a giant step away from our home but a new platform from which to view it.

We had previously considered the lands and seas around us as infinitely exploitable. Now studies were coming out, one after the other, revealing the limits to growth. If we continued to go on increasing the human population and its production and consumption of energy, we would eventually make the earth uninhabitable, perhaps destroy it. Some of our most respected values, values that had served us well for centuries — aggressiveness, competitiveness, cool objectivity, conquest, fast economic growth, high fertility, power over others — now were leading us directly toward catastrophe. *Education and Ecstasy* had treated both the human potential and the need for a change in values. But there was a larger book to be written on the subject of individual and social transformation, one that would take more time than I could afford while working for *Look*.

I missed Mike Murphy. I missed his inexhaustible enthusiasm. I missed the endless dialogue, the brainstorming sessions, the quick conversion of ideas to action. With the firing of Bill Smith, the last real barrier to our reconciliation was removed. Our mutual friends tried gently to bring us back together. Even Ron Brown, the central figure in the racial incident, seemed to think it would be a good thing for us to resume our relationship. But I was reluctant. For Mike, the events leading up to the break had come like a series of unexpected shocks; it was only later that he really had known what was going on. For me, the break had been a statement — the most powerful statement I could make — of my absolute commitment to the interracial group, and through that group to the transformation of racial attitudes in America. I still felt unwilling to do anything that might diminish that statement.

The interracial encounters continued through Price Cobbs's organization, and they were as successful as ever. But it was becoming harder and harder to get blacks to participate. "Black Power" was the current watchword of the black community. And we had seen from the beginning that whites had more to learn from our group process than blacks did. Eventually, Price founded ethnotherapy and took his work on race to major corporations and other large organizations throughout the United States and overseas. Even as early as 1969, though, it was becoming clear that the lessons and the dynamics of the interracial marathon encounters would have to find different and larger applications.

As for Esalen, it continued to receive the flattery of imitation. In 1969 there were approximately two hundred Esalen-type "growth centers" in America, with names such as Kairos, Oasis, and Anthos. Some would survive, but many, from what I could tell, were built on sand. *Education and Ecstasy* was still selling strongly, and I was getting almost as many letters as before. An increasing number of them told of alternative schools based on the book, and a good proportion of these asked for assistance. Many of the schools seemed to be hastily conceived and organized, with inadequate funding and little thought given to such basic matters as administration or zoning and fire regulation. When I could, I referred the letter writers to documents and people who might help, but otherwise I didn't get involved.

There was one thing I could do: I had begun my voyage of the sixties with a special issue of *Look*. I could end it with another. I could do an issue on the seventies. The era of the big general magazines was clearly drawing to a close. *Collier's* was long gone, and the *Saturday Evening Post* had published its last issue in February 1969. *Life* and *Look* were all that was left, and both of them were on a plateau. *Look*'s advertising revenue, after years of growth, had peaked out in 1966 at $80 million, then had dropped down to just over $77 million for each of the next three years. Circulation had also hit a virtual plateau after 1966, the year of my second California issue and in many ways perhaps *Look*'s most glorious year. Specialty magazines were doing increasingly well, but the mass medium of the future was obviously television.

Even in its twilight years, *Look* had clout. It was widely accepted now as a thoughtful magazine, one that wasn't afraid to take on controversial issues. There was no longer any question about prestige and respectability. A whole new generation of readers had come along that didn't even know of *Look*'s rather sleazy, sensational early years. Somehow the magazine had managed to keep most of its older readers, but it was, perhaps more than any other mass medium, the voice of the new generation, of new ideas.

Which didn't sit at all well with the Nixon administration. Stanley Tretick, *Look*'s Washington photographer, told me of an encounter with Ron Ziegler, Nixon's press secretary. It had happened at a Washington cocktail party. Ziegler had approached Tretick and with no preface had said, "We have a shit list of magazines in the White House, and I want you to know that *Look* ranks above *Ramparts*."

Tretick said he was amazed. *Ramparts* was a thoroughly radical magazine. He asked Ziegler what he could possibly mean by this. He pointed out that *Look* ran stories on both sides of political issues, and had in fact run a rather favorable story on President Nixon.

"It's not your political stuff that we don't like," Ziegler had said, according to Tretick. "It's your lifestyle stuff." Then he had brusquely walked away.

This interchange gave me pause. "Lifestyle stuff" was a pretty good code term for the kinds of features and special issues that John Poppy and I had been doing over the years. Up until now, *Look* had been blessedly free from political or economic pressure. But I had a feeling that the people around Nixon would stop at nothing to stamp out the changes in living that threatened them — the new openness of discourse, the freeing of locked-in feelings, the emergence of diverse ways of living. How could they attack a medium as large and popular as *Look*? Maybe they would find a way.

Suddenly I was seized with a sense of urgency. A seventies issue might be the last chance I would have to express all that I had learned in the sixties, the last chance I or anyone else would have to offer 30 million readers a resplendent, four-color vision of a truly nonviolent, joyful revolution that might suggest not a utopia but a way of life that could serve both the human potential and the needs of the biosphere.

I invited John Poppy to lunch and laid out my hopes and dreams for an issue like no other that had ever been published. There would be no compromises in the issue — no food, fashion, or sports stories. From beginning to end it would be a document of advocacy and personal revelation — the polar opposite of most newsmagazines and newspapers. In my view, those journals that most fiercely proclaimed their lack of bias were generally most strongly biased toward depersonalization, subject-object dualism, and dependence on official sources. Their underlying, unacknowledged world view strongly shaped what they covered and how they covered it. The pretense of objective reporting was a continuing source of deception for unsuspecting readers. In the seventies issue, we would write in the first person. We would reveal our biases. We would serve as advocates, making absolutely no pretense of objectivity. Thus, our readers could be on guard and decide for themselves whether they agreed with us. I told John that I could foresee an issue that openly proclaimed its lack of neutrality. We wouldn't run a single neutral story, not one neutral picture, not one neutral word.

Nor would the issue be a forecast. A decade earlier I had seen what the sixties were going to be. I wasn't sure about the seventies. The backlash had already begun; I didn't know how far it would go. Anyway, the issue wouldn't be about what we thought the seventies *would* be but about what we thought the new decade *should* be.

John and I agreed to plan the issue together and to use a small core team of the people we trusted most to work on it with us. We started brainstorming right there at lunch. How about a page-long essay called "Why We Need a Woman President in 1976," by Gloria Steinem? Fine. Then how about "Why We Need a Black President in 1980"? Who could write it? Let's get completely crazy: how about William F. Buckley, Jr.? All through the ghetto tour he had tried to maintain his usual aloofness and control, but he had been touched. To have Bill Buckley calling for a black president would shatter some preconceptions, especially among his followers. Okay, how about a whole series of "Why We Need" essays? How about "Why We Need a New Schooling"? I could write that. No, we'll get John Holt. I'll write "Why We Need a New Sexuality." Then there's "Why We Need New Politicians," "New Businessmen," "a New Religion," "a Generation Gap," "a New Language." Yes, "Language" is Hedgepeth's. He'll probably create one right in his article. Maybe he'll need more than one page.

We walked back to the office and continued brainstorming. We planned lavish photo essays, designed to join ecology with technology with a new sense of human community. We looked for ways to dramatize the horrors of war, pollution, racism, and overpopulation in crowded, distorted black-and-white pictures. We came up with a name for the issue: "The Seventies: Mankind's Last, Best Chance." We had the entire plan done in two days, and sped it off to New York via teletype. Bill Arthur approved everything we sent in, but wanted one cautionary piece. I proposed a black-and-white picture story on a young police officer and his family in St. Joseph, Missouri, which was Lillie's hometown. We would call the story "The Troubling Taste of Change: A Young Man Makes the Case for Slowing Down."

Having granted this concession, we plunged into the production of the issue, pulling no punches. Throughout the late summer and fall of 1969, John and I worked day and night on the seventies issue. We organized one symposium on the seventies in San Francisco and another in New York. We made no bones about whom we invited to the symposia: young people, women, blacks, computer pioneer Doug Englebart, *Population Bomb* author Paul Ehrlich, futurist Herman Kahn, McLuhanite John Culkin, United Farm Worker leader Cesar Chávez. We weren't seeking balance.

When the time came to lay out the color photography, we took a suite in the Hotel Élysée so as to be totally separate from the rest of *Look* magazine. Our entire core team gathered there — art director Will Hopkins, photographers Fusco and Kane, Bill Hedgepeth, John Poppy, and I. We sealed the window shades with tape and projected slides against the wall. Hopkins did his layout sketches on the coffee table. From the beginning John Poppy and I had determined to have no illustrated text; there would be either pure picture essay or pure text. Hopkins went a step further; he wanted the entire magazine, insofar as was possible, to read as a single work of art; certain lines and key positionings would recur throughout the issue, but so subtly that the average reader wouldn't consciously notice it.

We worked all that October afternoon in the darkened suite, so deeply engrossed that we were almost entirely unaware of the passage of time. At one point I became vaguely aware of strange sounds filtering in through the tightly closed windows — church bells and sirens and shouts and the moan of a multitude of auto horns. But neither I nor any of the other people on our team thought of going over to look out. When we finally finished and walked out of the hotel into the autumnal darkness, the New York streets had been transformed. At first I thought there had been a heavy early snowstorm; the streets and sidewalks were completely white. It took a while for me to recover my equilibrium. We were probably the only people in the city who didn't know that the New York Mets, for the first time in their history and against all odds, had that afternoon won the National League pennant.

While I was working on the seventies issue, *Look* published an article purporting to link San Francisco mayor Joseph Alioto with the Mafia. The story came out in September, and Alioto immediately sued Cowles Communications, Inc., for $12.5 million. Among his initial charges was that *Look* had bypassed its West Coast editor in preparing the story. The article, it's true, was the brainchild of two California free-lance writers who had taken their proposal directly to *Look*'s New York office. But *Look* had always disregarded geography; I had covered the South and even the Iron Curtain from San Francisco, and it was not unusual for other people to produce California stories. Anyway, Martin Goldman had kept John Poppy and me fairly well informed about the Alioto story.

All I wanted was to get on with the seventies issue. At first the uproar over the Alioto story was only an annoying buzz on the edge of my consciousness. But the buzz wouldn't go away. Before the story went to press, I had voiced my concerns about it in a phone conversation with an attorney on Cowles's legal staff. He had responded with a blistering lecture about the evils of the Mafia and a ringing declaration that the story should by all means be published. Long experience had taught me to respect the accuracy of *Look*'s fact checkers and the rigor of its legal department, so I raised no more objections. Still, the whole project gave me an uneasy feeling. The unease was increased when I was called on to give a deposition. I feared that if my phone conversation with the lawyer somehow came out, it might seriously damage *Look*'s case. But I was questioned only briefly and, it seemed to me, rather gently, and nothing substantive was revealed. (As it turned out, the case remained unsettled for years. After three hung juries, Cowles agreed to a nonjury trial, and Alioto finally won a judgment of $350,000 in general damages.)

Compared to my feelings about the seventies issue, the Alioto affair was only an annoyance. But it cast a shadow. I was drawn to a vision. I wanted at the least to raise the possibility of new ways of relating in the future. It was clear, however, that I couldn't escape the dubious machinations of the present. Not long after the Alioto story came out, while I was still working night and day on the seventies issue, Cowles's attorneys decided it would be wise to have my house and John Poppy's house debugged; it seemed that Alioto's attorneys were somehow getting inside information on *Look*'s tactics. No bug was discovered at the Poppys'. No working bug was found in my house either, but there was an old, out-of-service listening device in a telephone line that ran in the crawlspace beneath the downstairs study. The previous owner of the house was a well-known radical lawyer.

The issue, a manifesto for the new decade, a valedictory for the sixties, was due to appear on the nation's newsstands on December 30, 1969. The San Francisco office, as usual, received an advance copy of the issue two weeks prior to publication date. When I finished flipping through it, I was overcome with a sensation of absolute completion. I felt at that moment that if I worked on magazines for another hundred years, I could never again do a special issue that so well presented an idea or so fully realized the potential of the magazine form as I saw it. What's more, I would never again need to.

With the sense of completion came an unexpected feeling of sadness. Something was ending. Some kind of weight was falling from my shoulders, a pressure leaving my chest. All the push over the past sixteen years to fulfill personal ambition, to make every story, every issue, better than the last one, to hurry straight from one assignment to another — all of that was falling away. I could keep on doing stories for *Look* or maybe for other magazines or media. But it would never be like this. This was the top of the mountain. I flipped through the pages again, reveling in my elation and sadness.

The issues began in a design scheme of horizontal and vertical lines like the bars of a prison, with stark black-and-white photographs squeezed into vertical strips, distorted like images in a funhouse mirror to make them even more crowded: starving children in Biafra, a black man dragged by his hair by a club-wielding deputy, a smokestack pouring black smoke behind a soot-stained American flag, an oil-drenched sea bird, soldiers dead and dying, a Klansman clenching a cigar in his teeth, a black child holding a cloth to his head with blood running down his face. And John Poppy's words pulling no punches. I scanned his prose again as if it were poetry:

"I READ THE NEWS TODAY, OH BOY . . ."

. . . it told about man avid to *control* everything he touches, carving his initials on the earth — and on his brothers. Hard, uptight man. For the national honor, you blew the guts out of a child this morning. I clubbed open the head of another for crying so loudly . . . black, you know. Together, we can poison whole species of animals, and it worries us a bit; DDT in mother's milk, now that comes too close. THE NEWS: Man has at last collected enough power of various sorts to affect his own evolution, or to destroy himself. Either way, for the first time the choice is his. So far, we have not behaved as if we care to survive. We help each other a little, yes, but the real game is, be the boss. We gnaw at our bleeding flesh bit by bit, only dully curious about why it hurts so much.

Turn the page past this horror and there is a boy of eleven and his nine-year-old sister exploring a mythical planet, taking a fantastical journey: running in a mountain field of rich golden rye above an endless sea of clouds; becoming acquainted with the planet's lavish gift of water in marsh, rocky beach, and shallow lake; walking along the sharp, sinuous ridge of a huge sand dune; peering into an enormous cave of ice; lying in an emerald forest of ferns. The mythical planet is our own earth, seen with new eyes in all its poignant loveliness and fragility. The children are Anthony and Marina Fusco, the scene not light years away but at easily accessible locations, the pictures (in my opinion) the most beautiful Paul had ever taken. And then four more pages of Paul's pictures on the beauties and dangers and humane possibilities of technology; and two more showing new modes of human community: the team of NASA controllers who monitored the moon landing, Anna Halprin's dancers creating new rituals, and a group of friends participating in a natural childbirth.

Then there was my essay on "The Future of Power," the one I might have written with McLuhan but chose to do alone, calling for an end to exploitative power-over-others and proposing a group presidency to replace the present single chief executive — an idea that might have sounded radical except that it was first proposed nearly two hundred years earlier by Benjamin Franklin, who feared that an individual president might prove "fond of war" or get sick while in office. Bill Hedgepeth's call for a new language was a verbal circus which began and ended with a wild outpouring of metalanguage simulating a performance by singer Janis Joplin, but it also made some cogent points about conventional language's tendency to limit our thought and action, calling attention, for example, to the fact that *Roget's Thesaurus* devotes 28 lines to *peace* and 162 lines to *warfare*.

"Why We Need a New Schooling," by John Holt, proposed leaving the responsibility for children's schooling entirely to teachers and parents, and the other "Why We Need" essays were just about as radical. Gloria Steinem held nothing back in calling for a woman president, perhaps a black woman president, in the seventies: "If all this seems mind-bending and impossible," she wrote, "think back to the beginning of the 60s. What seemed impossible to us then? Men on the moon? Assassinations? Tanks in our streets? Demonstrations the size of cities? Surely a woman in the White House is not an impossible feminist cause. It's only a small step in the humanist revolution."

Buckley's call for a black president was not quite so impassioned, but the very fact that he made it was news in itself. "A Vision of the Human Revolution" opened with a picture of a nude Betsy Ross sewing a star on the green flag of ecology, and unfolded in eight pages of surrealistic photographs by Art Kane with equally surreal words by Bill Hedgepeth. Even the following picture story on the police detective in Missouri had its place, its nostalgia vibrating almost psychedelically against the Kane-Hedgepeth vision of split-image nudes and people with television sets as heads.

In the concluding essay, I tried not only to sum up the issue but also to touch on the main points of the vision I had gained during my journey through the sixties. "The revolution already has begun," I wrote near the essay's end. "You'll not find the heart of it on the streets, nor does it readily lend itself to simple slogans. You may recognize it in private expectations, in new sensibilities, in yourself. It promises no end of dangers or agonies, but affirms that the seventies can be the start of mankind's *best* chance. And it offers no shortage of mighty tasks, any one of which could be bigger, bolder — and more joyful — than going to the moon." I listed some of these tasks, which had been treated in detail earlier in the issue — the creation of honest, caring politics; more pleasurable, less threatening sexuality; more humane business ethics; deeper religious concerns; the ending of poverty and pollution, the transformation of every city into a festival and the entire country into a garden; the radical reform of education; and the creation of the positive conditions of peace, starting with our own lives.

And if these goals seemed too sweeping and distant, I suggested, just as a beginning, two quite ordinary actions each reader could take to improve life in the seventies: first, insisting on doubling gas mileage per person, buying fuel-efficient cars, driving less, and taking other people along on necessary trips; second, beginning to build a sense of community in your own neighborhood by going to each neighbor within three houses of you and asking, "What can I do to make my being your neighbor more pleasant?"

The closing photograph showed Marina Fusco running away from the reader across tawny hills that looked for all the world like the back of some enormous animal. The picture took all of two pages and contained only one line of print: "We turn to the living earth for answers, and a vision." I sat looking at that picture, letting the curious mixture of happiness and sadness course through me, then turned back to the cover of gleaming metallic silver with an enormous blue "70's" printed on it. I knew the sheer visual impact of the cover and of the entire issue would draw readers into the magazine. But would they really care about what the words said? I wondered how these brave proposals would read in another twenty years. Would our hopes and dreams seem merely naive? Maybe. But that wasn't the important thing. At Selma, Martin Luther King had said, "Perhaps the worst sin in life is to know right and not do it." If that was true, maybe it was also true that the worst sin for a writer is to believe something deeply and not say it.

We had had our say. Now we would take the consequences.

35

The Great *Look* War

1970

IT BEGAN in a most unlikely manner. I was in Los Angeles in the first week of the new decade, just having finished the usual promotional chores for the seventies issue, when I received an excited phone call. It was a man with a French accent who introduced himself as Bert Castelli. He said he was the executive producer for *Hair*. I had not yet seen the phenomenally successful musical that currently was running in seventeen theaters throughout the world, but I knew it was pro-hippie and antiwar. Castelli said he had read the seventies issue and *had* to see me. I was just leaving for the airport to return to San Francisco. He said he would meet me near the ticket counter. "What I have to say will change your life."

We met in an airport bar. Castelli was an effusive French-Sicilian-American with dark, wavy hair and an aquiline nose. He said he had read the issue on the plane between New York and L.A., and it had made him higher than any LSD trip. He still hadn't come down. He wanted me to drop everything and come to work for *Hair*. But what would I do? He said I could have any job in the organization. Together we were going to change the world.

I shook my head and smiled, bemused but also charmed. To be specific, he went on, he and his organization had just obtained the rights for *Tarzan and the Apes,* and they were going to open a string of Tarzan Clubs, something like Club Med, all around the world, and maybe I would run that operation. I wondered how putting together a magazine issue had qualified me to manage a string of Tarzan Clubs. He said it didn't matter what I did. I could write my own ticket. I would become rich beyond my wildest dreams while helping realize the vision put forward in the seventies issue. I said I was very pleased to be working for *Look,* and I had a book in mind to write, and I had to go catch my plane. He insisted on seeing me on my next trip to New York. He had an antique late-thirties Cadillac with a liveried chauffeur, and he would have me picked up at the airport. He said I had already changed his life for the better.

The people in the New York *Look* office were not so pleased. Martin Goldman phoned and told me that the situation was worse than at the time of the 1966 California issue. Most of the staff had worked them-selves up into a state of outrage bordering on hysteria. Joe Roddy was beside himself; he wanted to talk with me personally. I also heard that Leo Rosten, the magazine's highly respected special editorial adviser, had gone to Mike Cowles and informed him that the seventies issue demon-strated conclusively that I was an ambulatory schizophrenic and would probably be hospitalized in a matter of months.

I could laugh at this kind of hysteria. What made matters more serious was a new development among the magazine's business and advertising executives. Previously there had been a rather firm line separating edito-rial content and business considerations. But now, with circulation and ad revenue on a plateau and expenses up, the Cowles organization was moving into financial trouble, and the jackals were beginning to circle the editorial conference room, growing bolder in making criticisms and demands.

Most of *Look*'s business executives were Nixon Republicans, and there was no question about where that administration stood regarding the media. Nixon's vice president, Spiro T. Agnew, was going around mak-ing tortuously worded speeches attacking "the nattering nabobs of neg-ativity" in the press. Strangely enough, he was joined in this kind of rhetoric by none other than *Look*'s publisher, Thomas R. Shepard, Jr. In his appearances before management and advertising groups, Shepard, who was married to Mike Cowles's niece, would launch a lively attack on the communications media for their liberalism and negativity, then amaze his audiences by citing just the kind of material that his own magazine was running. Bill Attwood told Cowles that this was hardly a help to ad sales. But if Cowles wasn't going to censor *Look*'s editors, he also wasn't going to censor its publisher. The seventies issue was just the kind of fuel that Shepard was looking for. While much of the editorial staff as well as almost all of the business staff were attacking me inside 488 Madison Avenue, Tom Shepard was going around making thinly veiled attacks on the outside.

The January 12 issue of *Advertising Age* gave headline treatment to a speech Shepard had given the week before at the New Jersey Advertising Club. According to the *Ad Age* article, which came out while the seven-ties issue was still on the newsstands, Shepard had said that there was no social or cultural revolution going on in the United States, just a lot of revolutionist propaganda — and it was time to stop it. The February 9 issue of *Ad Age* ran an even larger story, headlined "Shepard's Critics, Backers Point to Split Between His Views, *Look*'s." The story quoted at length from letters to *Ad Age* and also to Tom Shepard. "At the moment," *Ad Age* noted, "the editorial pages of *Look* appear to be one of the least likely places to find any adherence to Mr. Shepard's views, as several writers ventured to point out."

The Look Building was a battlefield. Every time *Look* president Vernon C. Myers got a particularly critical letter from a prominent advertiser, he shot a copy down to Bill Arthur, and Arthur invariably shot a copy of a favorable letter back upstairs in reply. Reader mail was particularly heavy; that one issue was to receive more mail than the next six combined. The letters, as in the case of the last California issue, were either highly enthusiastic or vehemently negative.

Almost five hundred of the letters came from people who identified themselves with two groups: the Community and the National Initiative Foundation, based in Palo Alto, just south of San Francisco. I knew these groups were made up of well-to-do, highly educated people who favored evolutionary changes in society toward social harmony and world peace. All the letters were favorable, and many of the letter writers entered new subscriptions to *Look*. Their efforts, however, had just the opposite effect from what was intended. *Look* business executives grasped the campaign to argue that most of the other favorable letters must have also come from California "kooks" and other suspect "liberals" who were not at all representative of the generality of Americans.

I later learned, in fact, that one of the top executives had gone to Anne Celli, the veteran manager of *Look*'s reader mail department, and pressured her to emphasize the unrepresentative quality of the favorable mail response. Celli was outraged. For many years she had been proud of her ability to analyze readers' responses intelligently and without bias. This was the first time, she told me, that anyone had ever suggested she falsify one of her monthly "Reader Mail Reports." In response, she took extra pains, using the knowledge and experience she had gained over the years, to analyze the mail in terms of geographical representation, sex, age group, education, and economic background. Her report turned out to be one of the most important documents in the battle over the seventies issue. At the end of January, Celli wrote, the letters on the issue as a whole were running better than three to one favorable, a ratio that, considering the radical nature of the issue, was stunning.

> Other than the almost 500 letters from the members of the two civic groups, no geographic pattern could be established as to the source of the pro or con mail. Letters came from all areas of the country; many letters lauding the issue came from places generally considered "conserva-

tive," and conversely, letters of condemnation came from "liberal" areas.

We received an almost equal number of letters written by women as by men, regardless of the nature of the letters.

No generalizations could be made on [age group, education, and economic background]. Many of the "establishment" people (including clergymen) praised the issue, while many who seemed to be in sophisticated positions condemned it. Many parents and grandparents told us they found the issue invaluable and would keep it for the young people in their families to read. On the other hand, we received a good number of letters from parents expressing the belief that the issue "was not fit for children to read."

The level of favorable and unfavorable remarks also transcended the expressed educational levels of the writers and, as much as could be determined, the economic levels.

The "Reader Mail Report" published numerous excerpts from the letters *Look* received:

Your January 13 issue is the most exciting, moving piece of popular literature I have ever enjoyed. You are a "family" magazine in the finest sense. A mixture of reality, beauty, dreams, love and hope, tenderness, education, concern. The format is delightful but also hard-hitting and pertinent. The articles are provoking, reassuring, compassionate, educational and just fun. I have also sent a letter to your Subscription Department ordering subscriptions for myself, various members of my family and friends. Congratulations. We all look forward to the issues to come.

I am tempted to write a lengthy letter stating my reaction to the January 13, 1970, issue of *Look* and the series "The 70's." Rather than do that I will simply say your view of the 70's is revolting. Your editors sound like they too have joined the sick. As a group you have displayed no responsibility and your views are offensive. Effective immediately, cancel my subscription.

As a mother, I am deeply concerned about the future my children will face on this planet. I feel your January 13 issue put forth clearly the issues mankind faces, and the alternatives available to him. Although I do not agree with all the views offered in your articles, I feel that you have been responsible in your presentation. I especially appreciate the positive emphasis on the challenge and opportunity man faces in this decisive age of the human revolution.

As an SDS activist . . . I salute your efforts to bring the best in radical change to *all* Americans in a most constructive way. Now *there* is an Establishment magazine our generation can read without laughing or retching. Please keep up your creative, courageous effort, even if it costs you subscriptions.

Anne Celli went on to total up, analyze, and give examples from letters that referred to specific articles within the issue. Again, I was astonished to learn that most of these letters were also favorable. Celli's report dealt a blow to the executives who were arguing that the issue would damage Look's reputation and financial future. In response, those executives simply stepped up their attacks, making much of the fact that one representative had attacked the issue on the floor of Congress and had sent a highly critical letter to Mike Cowles. Not long afterward, however, another representative commended the issue and read portions into the Congressional Record.

The battle continued, every shot calling forth an answering shot. Earlier, the U.S. Justice Department under Attorney General John Mitchell had returned an indictment against Cowles Communications, Inc., for the alleged illegal subscription practices of the Home Reader Service, a wholly owned Cowles subsidiary. A rumor began circulating around the editorial offices that the indictment was in fact a form of pressure against the editorial policy of Look, and that perhaps it would be dropped if Look changed its policy or its staff.

I didn't know what to think of this rumor, but I did know that strange things were happening. When I was next in New York, Bill Attwood said he had something to tell me. At a Cowles corporate party, he had been approached sometime after midnight by Look's president, Vern Myers. Myers asked Attwood if he would like to make a million dollars. Attwood said sure. Myers then said he would give him a million dollars if he would "get rid of Leonard." Attwood paused for a moment and then said, "I tell you what I'll do. You give me the million dollars. I'll give Leonard two hundred thousand, I'll keep eight hundred thousand, and we'll both leave." Myers said Attwood was making a joke of something he was serious about. Then he walked off angrily. I told Bill that I felt flattered.

I never considered the possibility that I would actually be fired. Surely Bill Attwood, Bill Arthur, Pat Carbine, and Martin Goldman would support me all the way. Perhaps it was a function of being an ambulatory schizophrenic to think that at least some of this group would resign in protest if I were forced out through business office pressure.

Anyway, I hadn't been just sitting around passively observing the battle from afar. Jim Martay, the latest in a long line of San Francisco advertising managers, wasn't like the others. He was much younger, only twenty-seven. He understood the seventies issue, and although he might not agree with all of it, he saw its great potential appeal to advertisers. For one thing, he realized that Will Hopkins's boldly innovative graphics would set a trend for advertising graphics for years into the future, on television as well as in the print media. So, with my encouragement, he set up luncheons on successive days for the top ad people in San Francisco and Los Angeles. The luncheons were well attended (extra tables had to be set up in Los Angeles) and I spoke for forty-five minutes at each city. Using slides of pages from the issue, I told how it was conceived, planned, and executed. Then I answered questions. I decided to be absolutely candid, to express feelings as well as thoughts, to pull no punches.

Letters to Jim Martay from the corporate and advertising executives started arriving the very next day. All were raves. They praised the luncheon presentation. They praised the issue. Some of them even took the occasion to attack Tom Shepard. One account executive, for example, wrote to "congratulate the articulate Mr. Leonard and his stimulating staff on producing a truly monumental masterpiece. Although it seems somewhat incredible to me that such a visionary work could be produced by a publication whose publisher spews forth such an abundance of antediluvian assertions, à la Spiro what's-his-name. I am referring, of course, to Mr. Shepard's January 6th speech in New Jersey."

As the praise continued pouring in from Tom Shepard's constituency, of all places, I didn't stop for a moment to congratulate myself, or to be coy or self-effacing; I simply put copies of the letters in a folder marked "Ammo." I knew I was in the midst of a battle against powerful forces, and I needed all the help I could get. I was fighting for a vision of a possible if not probable future. I was also involved in a struggle that could well determine the direction *Look* would take in the 1970s, and perhaps, in some minuscule way, the direction that the decade itself would take.

The supportive letters from the corporate world arrived none too soon. Two days after the West Coast ad luncheons, Bill Arthur summoned me to fly to New York the following week for a lunch in Mike Cowles's private dining room in the Look Building, where I would have a chance to confront my attackers. Bill Attwood, Bill Arthur, and Pat Carbine would be there from the editorial floor; Tom Shepard, Vern Myers, and executive vice president Gil Maurer, from the business side; plus corporate art director Allen Hurlburt, who would probably take a moderating position. Bill Arthur told me to bring all the ammunition I had and be prepared to defend the issue against all possible attacks.

I saw my position as a strong one, but reminded myself that Shepard and Myers were inside the fortress. They met with Mike Cowles every day. They were still trying to devalue the highly favorable reader mail. They would undoubtedly attempt to dismiss the enthusiasms of ad and corporate executives from far-out California.

Then two amazing and wonderful things happened. Jim Martay came in with a full-page ad from Bank of America, the result, he said, of the seventies issue. A couple of days later, out of the blue, I got a phone call from Fred Dickson, president of Coca-Cola USA. Speaking from Coke's Atlanta headquarters, Dickson congratulated me on the seventies issue and invited me to make a presentation at a Coke seminar in New York on "The Revolution in Values." The seminar, fortuitously, would be held the day after my scheduled lunch with Mike Cowles, and would involve sixteen of Coke's top marketing and advertising people. Dickson went on to say that I would probably be happy to know that the advertising people at Coke had been so impressed by the issue that they were shifting ten full pages of advertising from *Life* to *Look*.

Ten full pages! That would bring in around a half-million dollars just at the moment when *Look* desperately needed every dollar it could get its hands on. Surely that would end the attacks on the seventies issue among our own businesspeople. But no, the attacks only increased. It was an important lesson: To the ideologue, being right is even more important than surviving.

I arrived in New York on a Tuesday, and spent Wednesday meeting with members of the editorial board and fending off attacks from my colleagues on the editorial staff. Ammunition for the next day's confrontation with Shepard and Myers was still coming in from San Francisco by teletype. A California assemblyman had ordered 120 copies of the issue to give to each member of the state legislature. As I walked back and forth to the TWX machine, most of the senior editors I passed didn't bother to speak. Some of them had quit being polite.

But not Joe Roddy. He kept smiling, but only at the cost of ever-increasing infusions of irony. He wanted a head-to-head talk, so we had lunch that day. Despite the smiles, it was not a salutary meal. Roddy was predictably angry about the seventies issue. It had even gotten into his craw that my nine-year-old daughter Lillie had done another *Look* story. She had written the text and captions for a series of pictures of baby seals being clubbed to death for their fur. The story had run under the title "Why Must They Die?" in the November 4, 1969, issue and had received more mail than any other single article of that year. Roddy had written a memo to Pat Carbine, intended to be blindingly clever, in which he complained that "America's Family Magazine" was becoming "One Man's Family Magazine." *Look* was getting to be a place, he noted, "where the families of the staff do the writing while the obsolescents on the masthead stand around checking their retirement pay and the child labor laws."

At lunch Roddy didn't mention that note, but he appeared to be having trouble maintaining his ironic grin as our discussion heated up. He said he could never forgive me for having shouted "Plato is a fool" at a lunch some years earlier. What had upset him wasn't just that I had made such a statement, but that patrons at nearby tables had overheard it. Near the end of our lunch, I asked Roddy if he didn't consider it odd that on the Leonard Question, he and Tom Shepard were in the same camp. He said it was indeed strange.

Mike Cowles's private dining room was luxuriously fitted and so well soundproofed that even a smile seemed muffled. Cowles, a tall, slim, owlish man who knew how to play his cards close to his chest, shook my hand and thanked me for making the trip from the coast. Tom Shepard and Vern Myers were there next to him, and I also shook hands with them. A waiter asked for my drink order, then swiftly and silently brought me a Jack Daniels and water. I stood sipping my drink and making small talk with Shepard while waiting for the others to arrive.

Shepard could have been cast in any movie or play as the perfect corporate president. He was tall and erect and impeccably dressed. Not one hair was out of place, and the natural gray at his temples might have taken hours for a master of makeup to create. Both he and Vern Myers addressed whomever they were speaking to by his or her first name approximately every third sentence. Myers was as perfectly turned out as Shepard, but he wore glasses and wasn't entirely successful in concealing what appeared to be a deep inner anger. Shepard, however, was entirely genial and bland. It was impossible to detect even a hint of hostility within the man who was going around making angry, inflammatory attacks on his own magazine. He asked me unimportant questions about my life with what might be taken as genuine interest. There was only one indication that he might be hiding his true feelings: an unusual sort of blankness around his eyes.

Though I was sharply aware of how grotesque it was for the two of us, each of whom despised what the other stood for, to be standing there making polite small talk, I had no desire to shout my feelings or turn the event into an encounter group. I knew that this was war, and I understood the rules of engagement in this theater of operations. Under those rules, which reward disguised aggression, I moved slightly closer to Shepard each time I shifted my weight from one foot to the other, invading his personal space while continuing to respond genially to his genial questions. Finally he took a slight step backward. How ridiculous this whole thing was!

When everyone arrived, we sat in easy chairs and couches in one corner of the room with our drinks. Cowles began the proceedings in his dry, noncommittal voice, asking me to tell the group of the response I had been getting on the issue. I opened my file folder marked "Ammo" and began talking. I realized I was on trial. I talked for around twenty minutes, reading from some of the letters I had received, describing the West Coast ad luncheons, arguing that even the negative letters, precisely because of their vehemence, attested to our magazine's vitality. Cowles kept looking at me with his owl's eyes; I had no idea what he was thinking. When I started referring to the ten pages of new advertising from Coca-Cola, however, he looked slightly confused.

I had a sudden, wild thought: Maybe Shepard had never told Cowles that the Coke ads had come in as a result of the seventies issue. Coke president Fred Dickson had sent a letter to Tom Shepard that made the connection quite clear. And Dickson had sent me a blind carbon copy. Not knowing that I had a copy of the letter, Shepard wouldn't feel that he had to tell Cowles. Therefore, he wouldn't have shown Cowles the letter. *I was holding the trump card.* As I came to the end of my presentation, I handed Cowles my blind carbon copy and said in an offhand manner, "Of course Tom has shown you this letter from Fred Dickson."

Cowles glanced through the carbon, then looked at Shepard. The two men's eyes met, and it seemed to me that I detected, if only for a split second, a break in the protective blankness around Shepard's eyes.

The tournedos of beef were excellent, and the lunch conversation was pleasant, if restrained. Afterward, Bill Arthur, Pat Carbine, and I met in Bill's office. We were happy with the way the meeting had gone.

The next morning's Coca-Cola seminar at a nearby hotel meeting room was a total delight. I introduced the notion of psychological distance — that is, the perceived distance between the self and the self's experience of the world — as an instrument for understanding what was going on in the current youth culture. There was a lot to talk about: the almost total absence of psychological distance (I called it PD) in the primitive hunter and gatherer; the striking increase in PD between the *Iliad* and the *Odyssey*; the Victorian period as a high point of PD; the explosive, painful shattering of PD in the novels of E. M. Forster and Ford Maddox Ford; the artificial reconstruction of PD through irony in John Fowles's new book, *The French Lieutenant's Woman.* I proposed that the twentieth century had rather consistently narrowed psychological distance — as seen in sex, human relations, management, religion, architecture, the arts, movies, photography, even advertising. The vanguard of the younger generation, moreover, was probably seen as humorless primarily because of the way it experienced reality. No less than its ideology, the fact that its mode of political discourse had moved from irony to invective was what had alienated the old-time liberal. The important thing for any individual in any generation was to avoid getting stuck at any one psychological distance.

I spoke for almost an hour, then invited members of the group to reveal how they distanced themselves from their own experiences. After a brief hesitation, the executives jumped into a discussion that became a series of revelations of feelings about their work and personal lives. Soon the discussion was rolling along with hardly any help from me — the ideal situation for a seminar leader or a teacher. The executives were so excited that they let the meeting run a half hour overtime.

Emboldened by the success of the Coca-Cola seminar, I went back to the office and dashed off a very brash memo to Mike Cowles. The memo started by praising the intelligence and intensity of the Coke executives and contrasting their enthusiasm with "the weary, negative expression of recent weeks," then launched into a radical plan to save the magazine.

> Meanwhile, I can't resist a few words on our favorite subject, the future of *Look*. With realistic awareness of the current advertising difficulty, I still hold the highest hopes for our prospects. I am personally committed to those prospects and this magazine. Explosive growth of the educated, articulate, concerned portion of our population is creating a logical place for a mass *quality* magazine. We have the editorial resources to go for that market. As it is now, newspapers, newsmagazines, television and radio glut us with news and news analysis. But there is no powerful, boldly-proclaimed national voice of advocacy and personal revelation. We already are moving into that potentially profitable area. My recent experiences with advertisers (as you'll read in my detailed report) indicate a ready acceptance of this concept. Once the ad community becomes fully aware that we are moving firmly towards this mass quality market, they will respond.

I went on to suggest that we do an evolutionary weeding-out of readers by raising our newsstand and subscription price in two stages, thus arriving at a more realistic, more manageable total circulation, which I saw as about five million. At this point I couldn't resist taking a crack at Shepard and Myers. it would be very hard, I wrote, for someone who didn't understand and like *Look* to sell *Look* ads. Perhaps we should seek out a new breed of ad salespeople who were young and enthusiastic, "who truly and deeply like our magazine, who are conversant (as are those Coke executives) with the major currents of hope among the young in years and heart, and who believe in the diversity and potential of the American Experiment."

The next day was Saturday and I had a noon flight. Bert Castelli had insisted on giving me a ride to the airport in his limousine. He told me that the *Hair* organization was considering buying or renting old churches and putting on a musical, as yet unwritten, to be called *Bread*. Maybe I would like to manage the *Bread* organization. I told him I had written two original musical comedies for the air force and that I had much rather write *Bread* than manage it. He said fine. I said he should see my agent.

Castelli had a notebook in his lap, and I soon realized he was taking notes on what I said. There was only one problem: Whenever I made a lame, poorly phrased statement or repeated a cliché, he eagerly wrote it down. On the few occasions I said something I thought fairly original, he merely looked out of the window.

The war over the seventies issue makes the kind of story that deserves a happy ending, or a Götterdämmerung. I felt there was no doubt that our side had won the battle of the Cowles luncheon. But that was just the beginning of a larger war.

For the next two months I got very little work done. I was mostly occupied instead with collecting ever more ammunition, writing ever longer memos to Bill Arthur (with copies to Mike Cowles), writing a major speech for Bill Arthur on the subject of the new decade, and talking on the phone with Arthur or Carbine. I flew to New York to address the Art Directors Club. I even did another round of radio and TV appearances in support of the ideas in the seventies issue. More and more members of the advertising community joined in the battle with their own letters to Cowles and other *Look* executives — a clear majority of them, it seemed to me, on our side. I made another file folder, naming it "The Great War." I stayed in the conflict, not because I wanted to be some sort of power at a revamped *Look* magazine; in fact, I made it clear to Bill Arthur that I wouldn't move to New York for any reason. I kept fighting for the portrait of the future that had appeared in the seventies issue because I cared about that future. And I believed with all my heart that the majority of Americans were closer to the vision of peace, ecological harmony, personal independence, and unselfish community than to the dog-eat-dog competitiveness, macho aggressiveness, and cowboy economics that emerged in the vision of some of those who called themselves realists. The broad-based favorable response from readers of *Look*, truly a mass magazine, lent support to my belief, as did the results of opinion polls by the Louis Harris Organization.

We kept winning battles, and still the war went on. Mike Cowles responded courteously but noncommittally to my plan of a change in *Look*. He had always supported the editorial department's independence, but he was under extraordinary pressures. Tom Shepard's speeches were now attacking *Look* by name. Fred Dickson wrote a strong letter to Mike Cowles praising my performance at his seminar, which he called "the best kind of selling for *Look*." With every victory for our side, the opposition struck back with greater force. Finally the business executives did the previously unthinkable: they demanded that a story already planned for publication be killed.

The story, "Is Freedom Dying in America?," was written by the distinguished historian Henry Steele Commager, and would almost certainly offend the Nixon administration. Members of the editorial board vowed no retreat, no compromise on this question. Bill Attwood took a copy of the essay to retired Supreme Court Chief Justice Earl Warren, and Warren wrote to Mike Cowles that the piece was appropriate and important. I was in New York at the time of the crisis. Bill Attwood, Pat Carbine, and I agreed that we would resign in protest if the Commager piece wasn't run, and we wouldn't do it quietly. We would call a press conference and reveal the whole situation involving Shepard and Myers. I went around lobbying for other editorial staffers who might resign with us. We figured we could count on (at the least) editor Bill Arthur, managing editor Martin Goldman, assistant managing editor Jack Shepherd, art director Will Hopkins, and senior editors John Poppy, Dave Maxey, Chris Wren, and Ernie Dunbar. And — who knows? — maybe Joe Roddy as well. Before leaving town, I wrote my letter of resignation and gave it to Pat Carbine to use immediately if the decision went against us and Commager's piece was killed.

"Is Freedom Dying in America?" ran as a six-page lead piece in the July 14, 1970, issue. It was handsomely laid out and headlined on the cover. Again our side had won an important battle. And the war went on. I finally realized that it was going to be like Vietnam. There would be no conclusive victory, no happy ending. The other senior editors and I would go on researching and writing our pieces and getting them in the magazine. Shepard would go on attacking his own magazine and trying to stop us. Cowles would make some moves; already he had started a planned cutback in circulation to 6.5 million, which would be concentrated in sixty major population centers. But he didn't have the energy or the money to initiate a bold, decisive, widely advertised shift in editorial style and emphasis. The previous October he had suffered a loss of $15 million when he folded the *Suffolk Sun,* a three-year-long attempt to compete with the highly successful *Newsday* on Long Island. And that loss was followed by a nationwide economic recession that made it even harder to sell ads. With his capital reserves depleted, Cowles would have to sell his successful *San Juan Star* for $11 million.

Look would survive for a while, but the excitement was gone. With the seventies issue, I had already reached my personal mountaintop in the world of magazines. Another book was soon to be published, this one a collection of my *Look* essays under the title *The Man & Woman Thing and Other Provocations.* And there was the book I was planning on the transformation of society. Maybe it was time, after seventeen years, to say goodbye to magazines and go on to other things.

I wasn't at all sure what was going to happen in the seventies, but I didn't expect calm and sunny weather. The war at *Look*, the ferocity and persistence of the attacks on social and individual change at 488 Madison Avenue, reflected what was happening and what was going to happen for quite a while in the society at large. Since June 1966 I had spent much of my time in outlaw country but somehow had managed to retain a foothold in the Establishment. Lacking that, life might be desolate and insecure. But I really didn't have a choice. My heart was on the frontier, out there on the edge of the world with the explorers, the men and women who "dream of things that never were and say why not?"

By April 1970, when it was certain that the Henry Steele Commager essay would run in *Look*, I made my final decision to leave the magazine. But only after one more trip — a happy one, I hoped — not only to do a *Look* assignment but also to put the seal on my reconciliation with Michael Murphy, the man who was to be my closest fellow explorer through the seventies, and beyond.

36

A Search for
Deeper Foundations

THE BREAKUP HAD HAPPENED all at once, an unexpected fall from a high place. The reconciliation was a long, slow climb back. All through the summer and fall of 1969, when I was working on the seventies issue, into the winter of 1970, when I was defending it, Mike Murphy and I were gradually putting our friendship together again. We met sometimes at parties; occasionally Mike visited me in Mill Valley to bring news. In June 1969 he signed a separation agreement with Pat Murphy, moved into a small but elegant bachelor apartment on Telegraph Hill with a view of the bay, and set about trying to create a way of living that would include a modicum of peace and privacy.

The eight-hour-a-day meditator had become the nexus of a widespread network, a man whom hundreds of people wanted to meet, confer with, have lunch with, or just talk to on the phone. The first time I visited Mike at his Telegraph Hill apartment, he showed me a phone jack he had just installed that made it possible for him to unplug the phone.

"I bet it's ringing right now," I said.

I suggested he plug it in. I was right. Whenever I visited Mike after that, I glanced at the jack in the wall, that tiny connection with the outside world, and imagined it silently pulsing with electricity, begging for a response. Mike had an extraordinary talent for bringing people and ideas together, a gift for inspiring individuals and groups to surpass themselves. Just by being himself, he created a powerful gravitational field that attracted more human energy than any one person could handle. Teachers from all over the world wanted to offer their wares at Esalen. Managers of other centers sought advice and collaboration. Esalen itself was recurrently beset with management and financial crises. The media blitz continued unabated; rarely was there a time when some reporter, television producer, or book writer wasn't beating on the door. Mike had wanted to make an impact on the world, but not quite this way. He later said that the events of the late sixties reminded him that Lyndon Johnson had once compared progress to whiskey. A little of it is a good thing. Too much, and it starts to come up on you.

But even Mike's attempts to slow down couldn't impede Esalen's forward motion. At the end of 1969 the institute was planning two large-scale public events: a benefit featuring a score of Esalen leaders in New York City in April, and a similar event in London in May. Clearly, I had initiated the break with Esalen, but still I felt a little left out, a little hurt, when I wasn't asked to the New York event. The slow, steady process of reconciliation continued anyway, and at the last moment, just before the promotional mailer for the London event went to press, Mike most diffidently asked if I would like to be a part of it. I hesitated only because I wanted to figure a way to combine the trip with a *Look* assignment.

During my seventeen years at *Look*, I had generally hurried back from foreign assignments to New York with my stories. In my haste to get home, I had overflown England several times. I had visited Scotland, but had never once been in London. It was my turn, and maybe my last chance, to use the magazine as a vehicle for a full month in London. I thought up two stories: an interview with Mick Jagger and a picture portfolio tracing the lives of the Pilgrims before they boarded the *Mayflower,* to commemorate the three-hundred-fiftieth anniversary of the landing at Plymouth Rock. I could do those stories easily while participating in the Esalen event and enjoying London with Mike Murphy and the other Esalen leaders.

For decades, for centuries, our culture had taught us to keep much that was important to our lives locked away. The stuff that we never mentioned had ruled us: the secret desires, the shameful familial crimes; the evil and the ecstatic, the destructive and the redeeming. And now, in a period of only a few years, we had ripped away the covering and let much of that stuff out, in the belief that only by getting it in the open could we deal with it. The release had been euphoric, and I had little doubt that the potential of individuals and groups could be more easily realized without the constant drag of that hidden baggage. But the repressed material was out there now, a new force in the culture, and it would take a while to deal with it. The fact that the release occurred in the midst of an ugly and questionable war exacerbated the situation.

And indeed the decade ended with a series of startling and confusing events that bore harsh witness to Machiavelli's dictum that nothing is more perilous to conduct or uncertain in its success than the introduction of a new order of things. The trial of the eight radicals indicted for conspiracy to incite a riot at the Democratic National Convention began in late September 1969 and went on for five months. The Chicago conspiracy trial, as it was called, became a long-running entertainment piece, part guerrilla theater, part modern morality play. The trial revealed conservative judge Julius Hoffman as a buffoon and made Jerry Rubin, Abbie Hoffman, Tom Hayden, and Bobby Seale mythic figures in the eyes of many young people. Like so much else that was happening at the time, it settled nothing; the defendants were convicted, but the convictions were overturned because of Judge Hoffman's numerous judicial errors and his show of open hostility.

In November some five thousand antiwar demonstrators besieged the U.S. Justice Department; Attorney General John Mitchell described the scene as looking like the Russian revolution. A few days later U.S. Army Lieutenant William Calley was charged with covering up a massacre of civilians by his troops in Vietnam. In December a Rolling Stones concert at Altamont, California, which was supposed to be another Woodstock, became a nightmare instead when Hell's Angels "security guards" beat spectators with sawed-off pool cues and stabbed a black man to death. In that same month, Charles Manson and his fellow commune members were indicted for murdering movie actress Sharon Tate and four other people for no apparent reason. The violence continued to escalate; an estimated 174 bombings took place on college campuses between the fall of 1969 and the spring of 1970. On May 4, 1970, just two weeks before I left for London, National Guardsmen shot and killed four white students at Kent State University in Ohio, and ten days later two black students were killed in Jackson, Mississippi. Liberation was turning into a dangerous business. FBI agents who had infiltrated activist organizations took advantage of the situation by sowing distrust and fomenting paranoia within the ranks. For the most militant of the sixties protest groups, the decade was coming to a close in a climate of suspicion, dissension, and doubt.

Somewhere within each of us, according to Jung, is a shadow self, deeper than consciousness, comprising all the material that has been suppressed by society. This material has tremendous energy, which we lose when we completely disown it. But there is the other side of this equation: When we simply express this material without thought or discipline — and this is one of the most significant lessons of the sixties — we not only become destructive to others but also risk unhinging our own egos. By the end of the decade, some of us who proposed a transformation of self and society were beginning to understand that there are ways to honor the shadow without indulging it, and thus to tap some of its hidden energy.

I arrived at Heathrow Airport around midnight and got to the Inn on the Park in time for the tail end of a huge cocktail party that a wealthy Englishman named Leslie Elliot had put on for Esalen. About thirty of the five hundred or so guests were still holding forth at a long table in the cocktail lounge. When I came in, Mike Murphy leaped to his feet and rushed up to embrace me. He started trying to tell me all that had happened before my arrival and simultaneously to introduce me to his new English friends. I couldn't keep up with the introductions, but it didn't matter. I was drawn into the party like a shipwrecked sailor pulled aboard a luxury yacht. Will Schutz and Alan Watts and other Esalen leaders were there, and the radical London psychiatrist R. D. Laing and his friends, and people from Tavistock Clinic, and a goodly contingent of London theater and film people, and several members of Parliament, and a few lords and ladies, and writers and artists, and just plain café society people. And there was novelist Edna O'Brien looking at Mike with adoring eyes, and Mike flirting back when he wasn't busy keeping the party going.

Sometime later the room closed, and Mike asked me if I would like to go out and see London. The moon was full, and the night was clear and utterly still. We took a taxi straight to Buckingham Palace and got out and leaned against the tall iron bars of the fence and gazed in on the empty moonlit courtyard where the palace guards walk. We rode to Westminster Bridge, where Mike asked the driver to let us out and follow closely. We walked across the bridge, talking unrestrainedly while the taxi ticked along at our heels like a faithful dog. The streets were silent, the city asleep, and it was as if all of London were congealed in moonlight for our benefit alone.

Mike was exultant. At the Houses of Parliament, he walked up boldly to the guard at the side door and asked him to let us go in. The guard said that would be quite impossible.

"We'll just take one quick glimpse," Mike said, "then we'll leave."

The guard was a young man. It was after three A.M. He started looking around for help, but no other guard was in sight.

"Be on your way," he said with an attempt at sternness.

Mike kept insisting, but I pulled him gently back and we continued our tour of London. By the time we returned to the hotel, the moon had descended nearly to the western horizon and the first traces of the early English dawn could be seen in the east.

*

The next four weeks were kaleidoscopic. During that brief period, everyone in the Esalen contingent was a celebrity. London's party-givers vied to entertain the whole group or some part of it. The BBC showed an hour-long documentary on Esalen shot in California, after which Mike and I did a half-hour commentary. We were surprised when our TV hosts served chilled champagne; it was truly Merrie England. The daily press was for the most part so irresponsible that it didn't really matter what it wrote. One day Mike came in waving a headline at us and laughing hilariously: "STRANGE CULT VISITS ENGLAND." Another tabloid interviewed Mike, then totally changed his words to give him the cadence of an American gangster: "I got this mountain, see? On this mountain I got Huxley. I got Bateson. I got Toynbee. . . ."

Every station of London's marvelous underground transit system had a poster announcing the upcoming public event at the Inn on the Park and listing all of our names. The poster was black with large white type, and it began with an excerpt from an English writer's romantic, somewhat melodramatic article about the people of Esalen: *"they have a special way of walking . . ."* Whenever I saw the poster, I found myself trying to walk some special way, then breaking up. Maybe it was special to see a tall American chuckling to himself as he walked through the station, but probably not in such a gala city.

To set up the pictures for *Look* that would be shot later by photographer Phillip Harrington, I took brief trips to the country towns of Scrooby and Boston, to Plymouth, and to Amsterdam and Rotterdam. I found that Mick Jagger didn't want to have a *Look* story done. I made friends with the people in his office and included them in some Esalen events. They arranged for a talk between Jagger and me. The powerful aura of androgyny that he projected in his performances seemed even more pronounced as we sat in easy chairs in his office. We talked for an hour, but he wouldn't budge. In all my years at *Look*, Jagger was the first person to refuse coverage. Earlier I would have been chagrined. Now I was relieved; I would have more time for the ongoing Esalen fête.

But parties and laughter were not the only items on my London agenda. During the months preceding the trip, I had become preoccupied with foundations. Upon moving into my new house in Mill Valley, I had discovered several flaws in its underpinnings. A contracter corrected the major flaws, but then I went a step further, strengthening the posts that held up the center of the structure and adding new ones. I would lie on my back underneath the house in the dark crawl space lit by a single bulb, sweating profusely as I jacked up one of the supporting girders so that I could replace a faulty post and concrete pier. I would hold my breath as the big old house creaked and moaned with each turn of the jack, but after I had finished my work at this deep level I would feel more comfortable and relaxed. The San Andreas Fault, that awesome rift between tectonic plates, was only six miles away, and an earthquake could occur at any moment.

The sixties had shown us other kinds of earthquakes, and if any one factor had caused failures in the attempts to build new cultural structures during that decade of upheavals, it was a lack of firm underpinnings. The civil rights movement had succeeded because, for one thing, it was firmly grounded. It had grown from years of pioneering work by the NAACP and other groups. It was based on the nonviolent civil disobedience theory and practice of Thoreau and Gandhi, and on the deep faith of southern black Christians. And perhaps most important, it enlisted people of all ages. When black protest moved off of these firm underpinnings in the late sixties, eschewing nonviolence and the wisdom of its elders, it quickly collapsed.

The same lack of grounding was reflected in the debris of the hippie movement, comprised almost entirely of young people who expected instant transformation. "All you've got to do is change your head," they cried. Heads had been truly changed, and that change was still reverberating in the culture at large. But many bodies had crashed. Throughout the decade, a number of other bright and attractive edifices had been raised on flimsy underpinnings, and they now were tottering. If the liberating and transforming impulses of the sixties were to have a lasting influence in the culture, it was time for some foundation work.

Early in the euphoric year of 1966, at my first Esalen seminar, I had made a statement that now haunted me. The tape of my talk at the session was played occasionally on the local public radio station, and I would cringe as I waited for the inevitable moment when I would cry out, "Fuck history," and my audience would explode with approving laughter. If that cry was taken as simply a warning against inertia in the face of precedent, it might have had some merit. But to the extent that it would be taken as permission to ignore the lessons of the past, it had to rank among the dumbest things I had ever said.

Now I had a book to write about cultural transformation and I needed solid foundations. I needed to know everything I could about how cultures had changed in the past, about the resistance to change, about the failures as well as successes of new social forms. I needed to know everything possible about "human nature," about mental breakdown under social pressure, about the effects of technological change on social values and the individual psyche. History would be my teacher in building a deep foundation. Anthropology would take me even deeper.

Seeking guidance, I went to anthropologist Alan Dundes at the Univer-

sity of California at Berkeley and asked him to recommend a young anthropologist who might be available to do an ambitious research project.
Without hesitation he named Richard Cowan, a brilliant doctoral candidate who was sympathetic to countercultural ideas. Before I left for
London, Cowan and I signed a letter of agreement: He would save me
great chunks of time by guiding me directly to the material I would need
in writing my book, and he would write a research report. The guidance
was to prove even more useful than I had expected, and the report — to
me it was close to being a publishable manuscript in its own right — was
to total well over four hundred pages.

Before I went to London, I had already started on my studies, and
London was a feast for one obsessed with foundations. I visited the city's
incomparable museums and galleries and historic sites. I went back again
and again to the British Museum, filling page after page in my notebook.
One morning Mike Murphy, Will Schutz, and I bemused other museum-
goers by attempting to mimic the precise poses of the classic figures in
the Elgin Marbles in order to understand the consciousness of the ancient
Greek culture better.

It was one of those intervals of grace when everything I saw seemed to
trigger an idea. I wrote down one after another, as fast as I could, under-
lining with bold slashes of my pen:

5/25 — British Museum

Earlier Civ. periods: A major goal has been the mastery of solid matter.
Already we're departing from that. New hi-rises reveal *lack of interest* in
arrangements of solid matter. Jet is attempt to *slip through* molecules of
gaseous matter. Electronic networks. Disposables. Gone so far as to create,
really, a *disregard* of matter to the extent of threatening the planet.

We are not materialists!

Bishop John Robinson, the dean of Trinity College, a man who had
led Esalen seminars, invited us to spend a day with him. Mike Murphy,
Alan Watts, and I took a train to Cambridge. We had lunch in Robinson's quarters, which he told us were supposed to occupy the site of Sir
Isaac Newton's laboratory. When he said that, all the hair on the back
of my neck stood up. I had become fascinated with Newton, not just the
Newton of universal gravitation and the nature of white light, of the
calculus and the apple, but also the Newton that the eighteenth century
had tried to hide: the alchemist, the tireless investigator of the occult.
The West had chosen to reinforce the Newton of the *Principia,* then had
remade itself in his image. The world of alchemy embraced metamorpho-
sis and ambiguity, and would bring to an end the reign of stable matter
and perhaps of death itself. The world of the *Principia* was one of fixed

measurements, objective space, and linear time, a world of isolated cases within an all-encompassing System, a world without angels or smells. All of this — both Newtons — was material for my new book.

It was a beautiful day in England and sun was streaming through shutters into John Robinson's study where we were having lunch. I imagined Newton as a young Cambridge don at this same spot, capturing that happy sunlight in his prism, splaying it out in all its secret splendor against the opposite wall. After lunch we walked to the Trinity chapel to see the statue of Newton, as Wordsworth had during his Cambridge days:

> . . . I could behold
> The antechapel where the statue stood
> Of Newton with his prism and silent face,
> The marble index of a mind for ever
> Voyaging through strange seas of Thought, alone.

We had dinner with the Trinity Fellows at high table. Mike sat near the head of the table, which was occupied that night by the president of Cambridge University. At Mike's side was the heard tutor of Trinity. I was seated next to the philosopher C. D. Broad. There, as King Henry VIII, an early Trinity Fellow, gazed sternly down at us from his portrait, I tried to answer the great philosopher's questions about Esalen.

Back in London, I visited St. Paul's Cathedral for the third time, drawn not by its beauty but its sheer size and weight, the audacity of its design. Again I explored every nook and cranny, climbed up to the little platforms outside its dome, second in size only to St. Peter's in the Vatican. How did Christopher Wren have the courage or the arrogance to have it built back at the end of the sixteenth century? What was holding it up? I imagined foundations both ponderous and deep. That day, in a dim antechamber near the main sanctuary, I came across a man with a clipboard and a powerful flashlight. He was aiming a beam up at the corners of the ceiling. I introduced myself and asked what he was doing. He was an engineer who was checking for cracks that would indicate subsidence of the foundations. He showed me a series of diagrams; by charting the cracks, he could rather precisely determine the subsidence. I inquired about the foundations. He said they were relatively quite slight, never more than eight feet deep.

"It's amazing what they thought they could get away with in those days," he said. But now so much water was being taken out of the water table beneath London that the foundations were gradually sinking. "We can keep track of it, but there's not much we can do about it, you know."

We talked for a while, then I drifted back to the hotel, only vaguely aware of the bustling city traffic. If what the engineer said was true, here was one more symbol of the essential spirit of the West. It was always *up* and *out* — the huge dome on slight foundations, the Gothic steeple thrusting skyward, and then the skyscraper, pointing always toward a destination up there, out there, somewhere *away* from the roots of life. "And at last it stands on its launching pad," I wrote in my notebook, "the ultimate symbol of frustrated escape: an immense Gothic spire denuded of its bristling ornamentation and gargoyles, made aerodynamically clean, ready to launch clean-profiled young men *out there*, to a high orbit from which they can try to comfort us with spiritless readings from the Bible or mechanical mouthings of party slogans." The space program could be seen as a triumph of Newtonian physics, but its leaders had failed to understand the psychological laws of motion. Any decisive outward movement of human consciousness requires an equal and opposite movement to greater depths. Much that had happened in the sixties was liberating and perhaps inevitable, but all of it — the leap into space, the expansion of consciousness, the creation of new social and educational forms — would falter to the extent that it failed to explore its own roots: the legacy of the past, the cavernous spaces of individual and communal consciousness, the profound rhythms of existence embodied in the natural world. The work of transformation would go on, but it would require deep foundations. Deeper than St. Paul's.

It was my last day in London, Wednesday, June 10, 1970. The public event of the previous weekend had been a greater success than we had expected. Around a thousand people had come to the grand ballroom of the Inn on the Park and had participated wholeheartedly in the simple exercises we offered. We succeeded not by being particularly skillful but simply by positioning ourselves in a vacuum in Western culture. We did nothing more than offer the participants a chance to experience their bodies as more than machines, their emotions as more than threats to the imperial mind, and their instinct for the infinite as more than superstition. It was strange that they had to pay money and travel to a hotel ballroom to do so.

Before I left for the airport for an early afternoon flight, I met Mike at the top-floor restaurant at the Hilton. He was leaving the next day for Florence, where he and some other Esalen people would visit Roberto Assagioli, the founder of a philosophical-therapeutic system called psychosynthesis. It was a sunny, hazy day and we could see out of the window that the grass in Hyde Park was beginning to turn yellow; not a drop of rain had fallen during our stay in London. We had coffee and Danish pastry but didn't pay much attention to our food. It was good just to be there, to be secure in a friendship that was stronger than ever for having mended after a break, that now embodied a deeper resonance than before, a poignant awareness of Jung's shadow. We knew now that our work was only beginning, that it wasn't going to be as easy as we once had assumed, and that whatever happened, we would be friends and colleagues for as long as we lived.

The Atlantic was covered with a single cloud, as level and shiny as ice. The 747 slid across its surface like a giant snail, and time and space lost their customary power over my consciousness. Newton, the great magician, had built this craft and had started the space program on its uncertain journey to the stars. He and his scientific progeny had also made it possible to destroy everything that could support such a journey. But no need to fight science and technology. Just regard it as magic, and (since it could be black as well as white) make sure to find reliable magicians.

I looked out of the window and imagined the world. Back to the east, running down the middle of the Eurasian continent, the Fence still stood, the watchtowers, the plowed death strip, the machine guns. To the west, in the richest country in the world, legal segregation was dead, but injustice still walked the streets, north and south. Children still sat squirming in schoolrooms cannily designed to squash their awesome learning ability and rob them of brain tissue. Men and women still lived together, engaged in the most intimate physical acts, had children, and finally went to the grave without ever having revealed their hearts. And everywhere, all over the world, men, women, and children of every ethnic background, every culture, every economic status, were still being routinely cheated and choked of their potentiality, while the very idea of a society organized around the full development of the human capacity to learn, to love, to feel deeply, and to create was still considered impractical, if not a bit eccentric.

And yet in spite of all this, I knew that most people did want to develop their potential. After seventeen years on what was truly a mass magazine, I felt absolutely sure that millions of Americans were ready and eager for better ways to learn, to love, to feel deeply, and to create. And on those occasions when it was possible to penetrate — by way of such an instrument as the seventies issue, for example — down through the layers of cultural conditioning and hypnosis, their responses showed that they wanted those things more than they wanted bigger cars or fancy job titles or endless rises in purchasing power. But despite individual desire, despite the across-the-board benefits that would flow from the development of human resources, almost every established institution in the culture still fiercely resisted any reform that might threaten not just its survival but its style.

I had published the book on fundamental reform that I had envisioned in 1963, and with Mike Murphy had helped fire a shot heard — if vaguely, incompletely — around much of the world. And still this was the way it was. I lay back against my seat and considered one last time how easy and comfortable it would be to retreat into cynicism, to rejoin the Establishment that I had been drummed out of in the mid-sixties. I knew that pessimism could be liberating. Why not just raise the white flag on the subject of human potential, and spend the rest of my life taking potshots at those fools who insisted on marching forward against the odds?

But it was too late for that. I had already said it in *Education and Ecstasy:* "A certain naiveté is prerequisite to all learning. A certain optimism is prerequisite to all action. When a nation's best minds desert all hope and decry all enthusiasm, they leave the nation susceptible to nihilism and anarchy. When they refuse to be committed, they leave commitment to those who would destroy, not build, those who would go back, not forward. Existential despair is the ultimate cop-out. I'll have no more of it."

The day had passed and I had hardly noticed its passing. The sheet of cloud was finally behind us. Late afternoon sunlight sparkled up off the sea. And there it was at last: the distant eastern edge of the great laboratory of human change, bursting with energy and potential, most of it yet to be used and realized. The flight had taken me outside of ordinary time, and now, as I returned, I felt the surge of a new excitement. I leaned forward and watched the distant shore, willing it to come closer. What challenges, what adventures were waiting there! The sixties had ended, but my quest was only beginning. What would happen to all the idealism and hope of those vivid years just past, the craziness and the joy, the color and the darkness? How would the future view the time of our awakening?

37

The Invitation

1988

MICHAEL MURPHY likes to take down fences, cross boundaries. The higher the fence, the more it calls him. He doesn't have to think twice; he can see possible alliances where others see irreconcilable differences — between mind and body, black and white, physics and mysticism, the Occident and the Orient, Western sports and Eastern yoga, the United States and the USSR. More than anyone I know, Murphy embodies the force of Eros as Freud defined it, "whose purpose is to combine single human individuals, and after that families, then races, peoples and nations, into one great unity, the unity of mankind." Some people have said that he is intent on giving a party for the whole world. Even those who disapprove secretly yearn to attend.

Beneath the charm, the dazzling and unassailable enthusiasm, there is in Murphy a consistent talent for viewing the deep structure of existence. His mind moves easily in that realm where discreet objects and occasions give way to pure relationship, where Eros has already triumphed and the world is one. At the same time, he reveals a child's fascination with the surface of things, the intricate interweavings of a Hegelian argument or the play of firelight on his friends' faces. He loves spy novels and sports, especially football. In the spy novels he sees that ineluctable human impulse to know the secret heart of those we would call "the enemy," but more than that, to know the web of the world, to know *everything*. In sports he has discovered a gateway to the mysteries, the mysteries of the body and the blood, of those subtle psychic learnings and secret exultations that never appear on the sports pages.

For all the geniality of his personality and the sweep of his thought, Murphy is possessed of a certain fastidiousness. Walking the grounds at Esalen, he will always go out of his way to pick up a piece of trash. Once, halfway through viewing Fellini's *Satyricon*, a movie noted for its celebration of the freakish and grotesque, Murphy leaned over to me and said, "This makes me feel like going home and cleaning my apartment."

Esalen in the early 1970s wasn't Fellini's *Satyricon*, but it was a tough place for anyone who cared about neatness and reserve. The San Francisco office overflowed as one new program crowded in after another. Teachers, therapists, and gurus from all over the world converged on Big Sur and tried to use it for their own purposes. Seekers swarmed onto the grounds, offering their bodies and souls, asking in return only some kind of enlightenment over one long weekend. Mountain men and outlaws from up and down the coast slipped onto the property to get handouts from the kitchen. Managers came and went, each leaving his particular trail of red ink.

Physically and philosophically, it was the frontier, no place for refinement and quietude. "Truth is often found in dirty wells," Mike would say to justify the messiness of pioneering, but his heart was sometimes heavy; he knew Esalen missed being exactly the artwork he had wanted to create. There were some things he could control; he could make sure that the institute was never captured by any one school of thought, any single dogma. But he couldn't control the inevitable gravity that draws the fringe elements to the edge of social change or the need among the avidly converted to reduce a large and complex vision to a few misleading slogans ("Lose your mind and come to your senses"; "Get out of your head and into your body"; "If it feels good, do it"). How could he guard the vision with so many people liking it too much, too soon?

He still had his apartment in San Francisco, but he was spending more and more time not far from my house in Mill Valley with Dulce Cottle, the woman he would marry. I had introduced the two of them; Dulce's daughter was a friend of my daughter Lillie's. I had left *Look* and was working on *The Transformation*. He was working on *Golf in the Kingdom*. We saw each other often, talked on the phone every day. It was a time of prodigious learning. I was swept along on a flood of ideas, which I invariably shared with Mike, phoning him at all hours of the day and night.

One October morning in 1970 he sounded even more enthusiastic than usual as he began describing a martial art called aikido. It was, he said, just the balanced, long-term practice we had been looking for. It joined body, mind, and spirit. It was not only an effective means of self-defense but also a philosophy of life. It promised extraordinary, perhaps paranormal, powers of mental concentration and physical control.

He paused, then went on to say that he had discovered a remarkable aikido teacher in a suburb south of San Francisco, a man who had studied in Japan with the founder of the art, and had arranged for him to come up and give twice-a-week classes for the Esalen San Francisco office staff. He was going to join the class, and he asked if I would also like to join. I knew nothing about the martial arts and had never heard of aikido. I had imagined many things in my life but had never pictured myself as a martial artist. I paused only a moment before saying yes.

Robert Nadeau looked more a fifties leather-jacket type than a martial arts master, and he spoke in a way that was both unschooled and eloquent. With him was a slim young woman with luminous eyes and long, straight dark hair. He asked her to attack him and she rushed in to strike the top of his head. He moved swiftly and easily in a way that was totally unfamiliar to me. It was not exactly that he had momentarily disappeared, but rather that he had ended up in a position none of us could have anticipated, a position in which he had total control of his attacker. He asked that I stiffen my arm and resist his attempt to bend it at the elbow. After a struggle, I had to give in. Then he had me imagine my arm as part of a laserlike beam of pure, smooth, unbendable energy that would go right through the wall, across the horizon, to the ends of the universe. Everything seemed to change: My arm felt quite relaxed yet resisted all attempts to bend it.

It was November 11, 1970. Nadeau had us come to the windows and look out at the full moon rising over the hills of San Francisco. He had us focus our attention on a point in our abdomens about an inch below our navels. He asked that we retain awareness of this center of power and stability while viewing the moon. He suggested that we silently repeat, "I'm here, not there." He told us that distant scenes of great beauty and future visions of great promise could easily unbalance us, sap our power, unless we retained awareness of our present position in time and space. The moon would be even more beautiful, the future even more promising, if viewed from a firm and stable center.

Nadeau's words penetrated me. What of my own strivings, my dreams of a transformed culture? How many times had I lost my balance in reaching out for a vision of the future? An unfamiliar feeling of anticipation and power radiated out from my center and filled my body. Though I had no idea what it would mean to my life, I knew at that moment that I had found a new path. Still, it would never have occurred to me — it was simply not in the realm of the possible then — that I would someday hold a third-degree black belt in aikido and be the co-owner of a respected martial arts school, or that I would someday develop a training system based on aikido that would be presented to tens of thousands of people all over the country and overseas.

The fourteen of us in the special Esalen class entered our training with a sort of crazed enthusiasm, boring our friends with tales of the remarkable Nadeau, paining them with demonstrations of wrist locks. Then we began working on the strenuous and scary falls and rolls required of every student of the art, and the less physically fit began dropping out. Eventually everyone quit, even Michael Murphy (who later became a world-class competitive senior runner), and I joined Nadeau's public class. At first I was dismayed by the attrition rate, but I later learned that thirteen out of fourteen defections is just about normal. Aikido, I finally realized, was not for everyone. But it fully represented the kind of long-term, disciplined practice that was missing in the wild and euphoric early days of Esalen and that is still largely lacking in the American culture. Nearly eighteen years later, I am still approaching the art as a beginner, realizing that the more I know, the more there is to know, and that in the realm where the physical body meets the infinite, aikido is endlessly mysterious and wonderful.

For as long as I could remember, I had wanted to be possessed by some fascinating and significant work, something that would allow me the incomparable privilege of abandoning caution and totally spending myself. In the early seventies I had not one but two possessing angels: my book and aikido. Every day from nine to one I sat in my study in Blithedale Canyon in Mill Valley overlooking wooded ridges that rose like great green ocean swells, writing sentences and paragraphs as if the words were fire. In the afternoon I worked with my researcher, Richard Cowan, or with Mike Murphy or Leo Litwak, or practiced aikido. Almost every morning before starting to write, I phoned Mike and read him what I had written the previous day. I vowed that this book, quite apart from my own existence, would be completed. When I reached the halfway point, I got Mike to promise that he would finish it if one of the planes that took me to my speaking engagements should go down.

I wrote of the hunters and gatherers of prehistoric times, of the two great transformations of society and consciousness that already had occurred, of the birth of civilization, the development of the neuroses, the abstraction and categorization that finally murders living things, the deadly celebration of aggression and competition and heedless material growth. It couldn't possibly go on forever, not within the confines of this planet; sooner or later, the vibrant beauty that I beheld all around me would grow dim and fade away, or else meet some swifter, more violent end. If human society and the natural world were not to be degraded or de-

BREAKDOWN IS BREAKTHROUGH 379

stroyed, there would have to be some significant change in basic values and behavior, some transformation. Just when it would come no one could say. Maybe it had begun with the Industrial Age or even earlier, with Newton and the realization that through modern science all the dreams of the sorcerers and alchemists would eventually come true, that human intelligence would eventually gain the power to destroy itself or else discover a transformed way of living that would prevent that destruction. If logic and history were to be believed, a thoroughgoing transformation would most likely require a catastrophe. But if in a darkened room there was only a thin shaft of light through a crack in a door, wouldn't it be worth almost anything to follow that light?

Look published its last issue on October 5, 1971, and *Life* folded fifteen months later, both of them the victims of television, high postal rates, and their own overexpansion. Readers still wanted those magazines; at the time of *Look*'s death, response to subscription and renewal offers was as good as or better than at any time in its history.

I had left a year earlier, at about the same time as Pat Carbine, who became editorial director of *McCall's* and then editor-in-chief and publisher of *Ms.*, and Bill Attwood, who replaced Bill Moyers as publisher of *Newsday*. As *Look*'s executive editor, Pat had been perhaps the key person on the staff. But Mike Cowles had let her know that he would never be able to bring himself to have a woman at the top of the masthead. Pat and I had had lunch at Brussels, a restaurant not far from *Look*, and had discussed what we should do. There had been more than a few tears when we had agreed we would both leave.

When *Look* went under, I figured that something would come along to take its place — some innovative national newspaper or alternative television network or information medium entirely unforeseen. But I was wrong. *Look* left a void that has never been filled. *Life* was part of a viable empire that continued to celebrate that magazine's history, to exhibit its photographs, and finally, in 1978, to start a new monthly of the same name but with little of its predecessor's majesty and zest. *Look,* in contrast, brought down its parent company with it, and simply disappeared.

Now millions of young people have grown to adulthood with no memories of a national medium of communication that for a few golden years dominated its field, not by being an arbiter of style or power, not by hiding behind a shield of cynicism, but simply by feeling deeply for the people in its stories, by fighting injustice wherever it appeared, and by daring to dream things that never were. "For more than three decades," the *New York Times* wrote in its editorial requiem, "*Look* sought to appeal to thoughtful Americans concerned with understanding and help-ing to solve the country's problems. . . . It will be remembered as a civilized magazine, faithful to the conviction that an alert and informed public is the best insurance for a sound America — a magazine neither complacent nor despairing, but never given to easy tolerance of the in-tolerable." *Look* senior editor Leonard Gross provided another epitaph in *Mirror*, a novel based on the magazine's life and death: *Look* "was unashamedly evangelical, a goad to this country's conscience, and for this reason, those of us who worked there exulted in what we did. We were not the best-paid journalists, but we may have been the proudest. We were never coerced, never ashamed."

I let my eyes sweep over my old copies of *Look*, not so much with nostalgia as with a recurrent sense of wonder — at its unpretentious boldness, its unflagging concern for social issues. George Sand has called indignation at what is wrong in humanity one of the most passionate forms of love. If this is so, hope for something better may be love of a more enduring sort. The note of indignation and hope that this one mag-azine sounded so clearly all across our nation is gone. It has never been replaced. A generation has come of age in that silence.

On the shores of time, there is no beginning and no end, no culminating wave. The sixties left us with questions we are still dealing with. The nightmarish denouement of the Vietnam War dismayed all Americans, whatever their politics. Our treatment of the returning veterans shamed us all. Watergate and the Iran-contra scandal brought to light the irony of ironies: Those very national administrations that had promised to turn back the excesses of the sixties and restore law and order were far too often themselves unlawful and disorderly. Then there was the tragic and humiliating taking of U.S. hostages, and the needless death of 241 Ma-rines in Beirut, and the gradual sapping of U.S. economic independence, and the turn to materialism and greed among some of the young people who had once proclaimed selfless idealism. A bad time for social reform and individual transformation, it would seem.

And yet most of the initiatives that surfaced in the sixties have contin-ued to advance. The struggle for women's rights has gained most of its now unstoppable momentum in the years since 1970. The environmental movement, which didn't even exist as such in the mid-sixties, now boasts some six million active supporters in the United States alone, and current opinion polls show overwhelming support for environmentalist posi-tions, far more than twenty years ago. "Antiwar" has become "pro-peace," and considerably stronger for the change in emphasis. If all this has es-caped our attention, it might be simply because of a switch in styles. The extreme conservatives and the religious right have become noisy and flamboyant while those who hold the reformist values of the sixties have been going quietly about their business.

And how about the ideas associated with Esalen and human potential? By the mid-seventies, university extension divisions, community colleges, YMCAs, church groups, self-help groups, and individual practitioners were offering the kinds of programs that five or ten years earlier could be found only at places like Esalen. And not just on the East and West coasts; my workshop sessions in Minnesota, Iowa, Nebraska, Missouri, Texas, and indeed throughout the South and Midwest were as well attended as those on the coasts. It was also clear that such things as gestalt, encounter, meditation, and body work were having a significant affect on psychotherapy, health care, fitness practices, and management throughout the country.

Of all the ideas proposed by people associated with the term "human potential," perhaps none has been more central or more influential than a re-evaluation of the physical, not as something apart from the mental, emotional, and spiritual but as a fully integrated and coequal aspect of human existence. The sheer power and magnitude of the participatory sports boom and the movement toward good health in America surprised even those of us who started in the sixties to raise the issue of mind-body unity, of sports as having intrinsic value rather than being a means to some end. The issue is still central in our work, as reflected in a continuing outpouring of books, articles, symposia, workshops, and special magazine sections on these subjects.

By the early eighties, human potential practices had moved decisively into corporate training and development programs. Old friends from the sixties such as Price Cobbs and Will Schutz now spend most of their time flying around the world consulting with giant corporations. People I've certified in Leonard Energy Training (LET) now take that work to organizations such as AT&T, Apple computers, and the U.S. Army.

So why is it that today you'd be hard-pressed to find a good old-fashioned encounter group? Simply because you just have to switch on your television to see and hear the kind of material that in the mid-sixties was largely limited to Esalen-type group sessions. And if you want to talk about a previously taboo subject, there are telephone hotlines available on almost anything you might imagine, and there are weekend training groups in hotel ballrooms, and if you don't want that, there are your own friends and colleagues, who are probably far more willing to talk openly about intimate subjects than they would have been before the sixties. The truth of the matter is that the boundary of admissible expression, especially in the sexual area, has radically shifted. A play or movie originally set in 1960 would most likely have to be rewritten from beginning to end before it could be set in 1980. The convulsions of the sixties, in fact, probably did more to change the essential stuff of daily American life — the feel, look, and sound of it — than either of the world war decades did.

The ground has shifted, no question about it, and some people say that Esalen, once the far outpost of human potential thought and practice, is now quite a bit nearer the center of the culture. Some even accuse it of respectability. It's true that the red ink has turned to black and that the programs have been upgraded and that intellectual weight has been added — with numerous invitational conferences on such subjects as appropriate governance, psychoneuroimmunology, new directions in physics, and the psychology of Soviet-American relations — to balance the one-time overemphasis on the body and the feelings. An Esalen program of dialogues in philosophy joins thinkers from all over the world in a quest for modern relevance. Esalen's twenty-fifth birthday, in 1987, was celebrated in an outpouring of magazine and newspaper articles. Surprisingly (after the press sniping of the seventies), all the articles were favorable, if not laudatory.

This new attitude toward Esalen is due in part to the success of Mike Murphy's initiative in crossing one of the most ominous boundaries of all: the six-thousand-mile-long fence that Paul Fusco and I traced back in 1961, the fence that still stands between West and East. In 1979 Murphy and Esalen associate Jim Hickman went to Moscow and uncovered a small and idiosyncratic Soviet human potential movement. ("Hidden human reserves" is what the Russians call it.) Murphy kept going back, with Dulce or Hickman or Jim Garrison, Hickman's successor as director of the Esalen Soviet-American Exchange Program. He kept meeting people, gradually moving to higher and higher circles within the Soviet hierarchy. He stayed in shape by running on the streets of Moscow, Leningrad, Tbilisi. Once he and Dulce spent two winter months in a Moscow apartment, living in accord with the Soviet economy. Eventually, ambassadors, senators, and other high U.S. officials began asking the Murphys' advice and using Esalen contacts to meet Soviet citizens who were otherwise unapproachable. Soviet officials came to Esalen for meetings, visited the Murphys in Mill Valley, ran with them, meditated with them, visited our aikido school.

By no means pro-Soviet (hot arguments with Soviet guests about Afghanistan and other thorny subjects have raged at the Murphy dinner table), Michael Murphy has simply aimed to cross boundaries and to seek understanding that others might have missed. "It would gladden the heart of the world," he said, "if the two superpowers joined to unlock the human potential in many fields." Esalen arranged the first astronaut-cosmonaut meetings, established the first "Space Bridges" (two-way rock concerts and conferences via satellite), signed the first nongovernmental agreement with the Soviet Writers Union, held joint book fairs, established a health promotion project under the leadership of Dulce Murphy, and started a similar exchange program with China. More than that, the institute has guided the way for other private U.S. groups and has set the pattern for the recent floodtide of citizens' diplomacy. Joseph Montville of the State Department credits Esalen with the current wave of what he calls track-two diplomacy. It is one of the more hopeful recent developments in international relations.

I stand on the cliff above the Pacific at sunset, as I have so many times during the past twenty-three years. I know this land now as well as my own back yard — the lush gardens, the springy lawns, the canyon with its waterfall, the beach far below, the jagged rocks, the surging waves. How many times have I watched the sun burn its way down into the sea, turning gold, then burnished copper, then fiery red? I recall one early October morning when on the way to meditation I saw a preternatural full moon, dusky and almost as red as the sun, follow the same path.

The place is peaceful now. The outlaws are for the most part gone; the staff members are concerned with their health insurance and pension plans. And if on certain fog-shrouded evenings (as some maintain) the ghost of Fritz Perls walks the property, it's a gentler entity than the formidable presence from which it descends. But despite this twilight grace, there is still a sense here of tantalizing possibilities, of unexpected things waiting to happen. Esalen still stands on the continent's edge; the winter storms still eat away at the cliff; the edge crumbles; boulders and trees crash into the ocean. In a dangerous world, respectability is not enough. The journey is unending. There are resting places, but as long as blood and breath can last, there is no permanent place of rest.

The sun is gone. The magic line between sky and sea grows indistinct. I feel peace but not triumph. I know the work of transformation that began long before the sixties will never be finished. History itself is a record of change, a reminder that to survive, a culture must make new adaptations to new challenges, sometimes renouncing those very values it once held most dear. Our passion for unbridled rationality, rigid categorization, hot competition, high aggressiveness, rampant individualism, and heedless material growth has come under question but still prevails, and might yet destroy us. The difficult and painful process of shifting our values is only just beginning.

My thoughts go back to the tragic racial heritage that started me on this journey. How sad it is to realize that the situation facing young American blacks in housing and employment has in some ways deteriorated since the mid-seventies. The emergence of an urban black underclass, along with sporadic outbreaks of racism in the 1980s, has led some to say that things are worse now than they've been since slavery. This line of argument dissolves with one simple question: Would you like to go back to the years before 1960? The civil rights movement wrought a miracle, the dimensions of which only a southerner, black or white, can fully understand. A thousand years from now, if human society moves toward more balanced, more humane ways (and since nature bats last, I think it eventually must), Martin Luther King and the movement he symbolizes will still be praised.

But we've taken only the first few timid steps across the barriers of racial and cultural differences. Nothing is more urgent, especially in America, where what we call the ethnic population is moving toward overall majority status. Again California will provide a test case. By the year 2000, Hispanics, Asians, and blacks might make up nearly half the work force in the state and account for well over half the public school population. Even without disruptions similar to those of the civil rights period in the South, no state or nation will be able to field a winning team with significant disparities among population groups — as the civic leaders of Birmingham, New Orleans, and Little Rock in the sixties would be glad to tell you.

In July 1987 Price Cobbs and I celebrated the twentieth anniversary of the first interracial marathon encounter at an Esalen seminar. The kitchen staff made a large birthday cake with candles, and the group was warm and appreciative. But it was not a large group, and in any case it will take more than a few seminars to remedy this situation. At that meeting I once again proposed that the nation cancel all school and college classes and other nonessential activities for a week of workshops, teach-ins, television and radio specials, and public meetings devoted to the way we deal with human diversity. The focus of these events would be not the tolerance but the celebration of ethnic differences, and the richness, variety, and power these differences can bring our neighborhoods and our nation. If this plan should seem unreasonable and impractical, I suggested, we might consider where reasonable men with practical plans have taken us.

Though the sun is down, the mountains of the Los Padres wilderness on the other side of the coast road are still alive in its light. I'll wait a while on this cliff, for there is one more thing to consider before walking on. In the matter of educational reform — and what could be more important? — the promise of the sixties has not yet been fulfilled. Most of the educational experiments of that decade have been swept away by the winds of the seventies, partially because so many of them were built on flimsy foundations. But there is something else I've come to understand more and more clearly over the years: Nothing is more threatening to a school system, or a culture, than the free development of the human potential. We must accept the fact that every viable self-regulating system — a bacterium, a frog, a human individual, a family, an organization, a whole culture — has a built-in resistance to any significant change, whether that change is for what we would term the bad or the good.

This homeostatic tendency, mediated by countless feedback loops, deserves our praise before our blame, since it makes for stability and survival. But there are times when, in response to new challenges, systems need to change. At those times, it's essential that we at least understand that the built-in resistance is proportionate to the scope and speed of the change, not necessarily to whether it's ultimately adaptive or maladaptive.

In a radically changing world, our basic structure of schooling — separate classrooms presided over by teachers who present the same material at the same rate to around thirty students — has resisted any significant change for hundreds of years. This structure is primarily an administrative scheme, a way of dealing with mass education. One of the ways in which it does this is by damping down the full expression of human potentiality. Even with the rudimentary programmed instruction of the sixties, some students, freed from the rigidity of the conventional classroom, could enjoy prodigious learning in amazingly short periods of time. But there was a problem: When a student has finished a semester's work in solid geometry over one long weekend, what next? And what do you do when numerous students of differing backgrounds, abilities, and learning styles start moving at different rates, often making the teacher's worst nightmare come true by outrunning his or her prepared material? If you don't think there would be resistance to such a development, consider the confusion and dismay created by a child who enters first grade already knowing how to read.

So the conventional school devises a thousand ways, overt and covert, to reduce the torrent of human potential to a trickle and to train that trickle along narrow, well-marked channels. And school becomes by and large a dreary, boring place, in which a child's highest realistic goal is to become brilliantly less than he or she could be. In Einstein's words, "It is in fact nothing short of a miracle that the modern methods of instruction have not yet entirely strangled the holy curiosity of inquiry."

Eventually we must ask if we really want to reform our schools so that they will elicit significantly more of our largely untapped human resources. If so, we can now use computers along with such proven methods as individual contracts, mastery learning, and peer tutoring to break the lockstep of the conventional classroom and provide individualized, self-paced instruction for everyone. This will also make it possible to get on with learning in the nonacademic subjects that contextualize and integrate the academics — the arts and the bodily arts, creativity, problem solving, interpersonal relations, service to others. Computer experts who have worked on educational environments with such corporations as AT&T, IBM, and GTE have repeatedly told me that given the will, we could now create schools comparable to those presented in *Education and Ecstasy* and in my later articles and speeches. Some promising innovations are in fact moving forward, but have not yet made it to the center of the national stage.

Instead, we have had since 1983 a highly publicized "school reform" movement that is actually a monument to homeostasis. The April 1983 report of the National Commission on Excellence in Education, under the title *A Nation at Risk: The Imperative for Educational Reform*, set the style for numerous other reports. It called for more homework, a longer school day, and a longer school year. It demanded more academic subjects in high school, higher admission standards for college entrance, more rigorous grading, nationwide achievement tests, and higher standards and pay for teachers.

To the extent that these reports focused more attention on public schooling, they did a useful service. But to claim, as the national commission report did, that they were proposing *fundamental* reform was to insult the intelligence of the American public. Even if everything proposed was put into effect, the resulting school would be pretty much the same as the school of a hundred years ago. That most of the reports deal almost entirely with high school should alert the public that the authors are less than serious about real school reform. High school is very late in the day; far more change for far less money could be accomplished at the earliest grades.

And still the press goes on giving headlines to every "new" plan that comes along, which is probably preoccupied with curriculum requirements at high school level (three rather than two years of science, for example, as if that would create any substantial change) without a word about breaking down the present classroom structure and reforming the present mode of instruction so as to open the treasurehouse of knowledge that is already available, even at our inner-city schools. There are the kingdoms, phyla, classes, orders, families, genera, and species of living things. And there are the canons of geology and astronomy and physics; and the chronicles of human history; and the hard-won codes of governance and law; and the body of Western literature with its lyrics and epics, its tragedy, comedy, and history; and libraries carefully ordered in the Dewey decimal classification system. And at the heart of our schools (and of our civilization) there is also the majestic system of abstract relationships that we know as mathematics, and the structure of language itself, perhaps a voiceprint of the underlying structure of the human brain. All this order and beauty is there for the taking — and largely unused. Let's be clear. It's not that our students' minds have been closed; it's that, owing to our present pedagogy, the overwhelming majority of those minds have never had a chance to open.

The so-called school reform movement of the eighties is clearly an attempt to bolster an outmoded system for a few more years. Neither the needs of our economy nor the potential of the human individual will be served until that "movement" is seen for the hoax it is, and until educators, parents, and national leaders join to begin the difficult and exhilarating journey toward true educational reform.

As dusk falls over the earth and the sea, the heavens become even more luminous. Air pollution from the north and the south hasn't yet reached Big Sur. The stars will be bright tonight, the sky dark and deep. In this clarity I am content for a while to accept the past for what it is and to give the future the benefit of the doubt. To have walked a long time on this planet is both useful and reassuring, for the rhythms of the years have taught me that just as the excesses of the sixties have passed, so will the reaction of the seventies and eighties. My faith is strong that eventually the human potential will break through even the most powerful barriers that prevent the journey to destinations beyond our present imagining. That journey, I know, will often be difficult and sometimes dangerous, and will rarely if ever proceed at a steady rate. Again and again it will meet the resistance of established authority, and when it overcomes that resistance, it will frequently disrupt the ordered flow of society and bring new problems along with its gifts.

The human potential of which I speak and toward which I will always direct my best efforts is diverse and unpredictable, and no less divine for being human. It is about solving mathematical problems, but not just about that. It is about feeling deeply for others, but not just about that. It is about loving and dancing and entering unfamiliar states of consciousness and imagining things that never were, and it is also about social justice, without which individual potential is invariably cheated and choked. More than anything, it is about discovering new form and order in the stuff of existence, and being reformed by that discovery. Ultimately, the potential within each of us is as deep as gravity and as wide as space and time. Unless we succeed in destroying ourselves, it will finally overcome any force that tries to stop it.

In essence, the human potential is an invitation, not for the few but for the many, to learn and never stop learning, to view with increasing clarity the ever-emerging, intricate, inevitable pattern of existence, and to realize again and again — on the stroke of every hour, every minute, every passing moment — that it is beautiful.